Bibliography of

New Religious Movements
in Primal Societies

Volume 6

The Caribbean

Other Volumes

Bibliography of

New Religious Movements

in Primal Societies

Volume 6

The Caribbean

Harold W. Turner

G.K. Hall & CO.
An Imprint of Macmillan Publishing Company
NEW YORK

Maxwell Macmillan Canada
TORONTO

Maxwell Macmillan International
NEW YORK   OXFORD   SINGAPORE   SYDNEY

G.K. Hall & Co.
An Imprint of Macmillan
  Publishing Company
866 Third Avenue
New York, NY 10022

Maxwell Macmillan Canada, Inc.
1200 Eglinton Avenue East
Suite 200
Don Mills, Ontario M3C 3N1

Macmillan Publishing Company is part of the Maxwell Communication Group of Companies.

Library of Congress Catalog Card Number: 77-4732

Printed in the United States of America

Printing number
1 2 3 4 5 6 7 8 9 10

Library of Congress Cataloging-in-Publication Data
(Revised for vol. 6)

Turner, Harold W.
    Bibliography of new religious movements in primal societies.

    (v. 1: Bibliographies and guides in African studies)
    Includes indexes.
    Contents: v. 1. Black Africa – v. 2. North America – [etc.] – v. 6. The Caribbean.
    1. Religion – Bibliography. 2. Religion, Primitive – Bibliography. I. Series: Bibliographies and guides in African studies. II. Title
    Z7835.C86T87 1977 [BP603]   016.291'046 77-4732
    ISBN 0-8161-9089-5 (v. 6)

The paper used in this pubication meets the minimum requirements of American National Standard for Information Sciences – Permanence of Paper for Printed Library Materials.
ANSI Z39.48-1984

*To the Centre for New Religious Movements,
Selley Oak Colleges, Birmingham, England.
And the staff, past and present,
who have participated more than they know
in the production of these last four volumes.*

Contents

Contents

Preface

This is the sixth and final volume of a bibliographic series that began with the two volumes on Black Africa and North America in 1977 and 1978, when completion was expected with two further volumes. The subsequent expansion of the series to a total of six volumes reflects the literary and research activity within this field during the interval that elapsed before publication resumed with volume 3, *Oceania*, in 1990.

It should be remembered that this series represents what has become a new field in the study of religions, and that for the fullest understanding of the phenomena involved the local, regional, and world perspectives are all important. Despite the wide variety of religious forms there remains a certain coherence across this spectrum and it is my hope that these volumes will bring this into view.

Something like two-thirds of the items included will be found in the documentation of the Centre for New Religious Movements at the Selly Oak Colleges in Birmingham, England. Most of these materials, and especially the journal articles, have been placed on more than twelve hundred microfiches that cover all continents. Inquiries concerning duplicate microfiche sets should be addressed to the Centre.

It is appropriate to express or renew thanks at this concluding point to all those who assisted in the manifold chores underlying this series: to Jocelyn Murray for the first two volumes; to Harold and Ruth Lehman and Douglas Beck for volume 3 especially, but the later volumes also; to James Glick and Ralph Woodhall for special help with the Latin languages of volume 5; to Jeanette Kraybill, who helped with the Francophone areas of volumes 3-6 and worked against time to place these volumes on computer disk before I left Britain in April 1989; and to my daughter Carolyn, who continued the task of editing and indexing on the disks in New Zealand – entering bibliographical material is a most exacting task and the proofreading stage indicated how well they had done it.

While library staffs in many countries have been helpful, those in the interlibrary loan offices at the libraries of the universities of Aberdeen and

Birmingham (and especially the then librarian of the latter) have played a crucial part. The intermittent assistance of the library at the Selly Oak Colleges in Birmingham goes back to the 1960s when bibliographic work began so tentatively. Since 1981 the Centre for New Religious Movements has taken shape at Selly Oak, and this library has provided the main base for the bibliographic task, and may be regarded as possessing a stake in this series.

Although all stages of preparing bibliographies demand careful attention to detail, I have been most fortunate in the highly skilled and meticulously careful editing provided by the staff of the publisher, G. K. Hall. Ara Salibian was my patient immediate correspondent; behind him were others equally assiduous in seeking high standards of completeness and of accuracy. Where there are imperfections in these dimensions – and any realistic bibliographer had better confess to them in advance – they remain my own responsibility; one trusts that readers will surmount any obstacles between them and the writers to whom they seek to refer.

Two successive directors of the Centre for New Religious Movements, Jack Thompson and Stan Nussbaum, together with Phyllis Thompson as secretary, offered the overall support during the Selly Oak years from 1981 to 1989 that helped maintain the sagging morale of a bibliographer who finds he has taken on all the world's continents.

Behind this large contingent of those who have been involved in many different ways there stand two without whom there would have been no start on this project, much less the conclusion that has now been reached. Professor Andrew Walls has been my professional colleague at three universities in three countries since 1957, and in Aberdeen in the 1970s made possible the systematic development of this work and contributed the example of his own vast documentation and bibliographic work in neighboring areas. His inspiration, erudition, and warm personal support have played an essential part in the project for a quarter of a centnury.

There is no way of describing the most basic contribution of all, from someone who makes no claims to be an academic. It was a quiet parish future in New Zealand that seemed to lie ahead for Maude when we married in 1939. In the event, she has risen to the travail of homemaking on four continents and of traveling in all except South America. Travel has seldom been free of the bibliographical concern: the tiring fieldwork; the dull routines of library checking; precision typing or copying; the careful filing and refiling of those three-by-five cards; the evenings photocopying the latest batch of interlibrary loan materials in Atlanta, Georgia; and then those winter nights by the fireside in Aberdeen when we bound the seemingly endless documentation of the nascent center for these religious movements. Without such labors, so cheerfully and loyally undertaken, and prolonged into our retirement years, this bibliographic series would never have emerged. Under different publishing conventions, Maude's name would appear on the title page along with that of the compiler; let it be placed here, and with fullest gratitude.

The bibliographer cannot stop the flow of events in his field, or impose a moratorium on further publications. But it will be the task of others to correct these volumes and to cope with the ongoing literary flood. May they enjoy the kind of help I have so freely received as these volumes retire into the history of the subject and are supplemented or replaced by those that display its further development.

Introduction

The Geographical-Cultural Area and Its Main Divisions

As explained in the introduction to the Latin America volume in this series, the Caribbean is only in part "Latin," both culturally and historically, as in Cuba, the Dominican Republic, Puerto Rico, and Venezuela, which were all formerly related to Spain, and in Haiti and the small island territories, which were historically related to France. Otherwise it is of both African and northern European (i.e., British, Dutch, and Danish) ancestry, with more recent United States influences. It now possesses its own identity as a geographical-cultural area. This includes the island world of the West Indies together with those littoral South and Central American countries with which it is associated through a colonial history and through a culture that includes indigenous Amerindian, European, and African contributions. Thus, French Guiana, Surinam, Guyana, at least the Venezuela littoral, Belize, and the peoples of the Caribbean coasts of Panama, Costa Rica, Nicaragua, and Honduras may all be regarded as "Caribbean."

Since we have dealt with the above Central American countries in the Latin America volume as a separate group (except for the Black Caribs of Belize), the countries in our Caribbean category consist of the islands of the West Indies and the four neighboring countries of northeast South America. The small islands forming the eastern boundary of the area are so numerous and possess such varying political status that it is not possible to deal with each as a separate "country" and so they are grouped together as the "Lesser Antilles," which is extended to include the "Netherlands Antilles." A small remaining group is designated "Other Territories."

The original Amerindian population (Caribs and Arawaks, etc.) has virtually vanished from the islands and remains as a minority in the mainland countries. African peoples imported in the era of slavery dominate the area, except in Cuba and Puerto Rico, which are predominantly white. Although much acculturation has occurred through contact with European peoples, the

African tradition continues in sufficient strength for us to regard the new religious movements here as akin to those related to primal religions in Africa and elsewhere.

At the same time, the concept of a specific "new movement" is treated less strictly and much of the material concerns long-standing and more gradual religious developments of a mixed or syncretistic nature, that were not specifically "new" at any point. For a similar reason, it is difficult to separate developments in the Caribbean from those of the black population of the United States, and some items trace Caribbean religious forms into North America.

Likewise some religious developments at the folk or popular religious level in Cuba, Puerto Rico, and Venezuela have been included when there was a phenomenological similarity, an African influence (as in Cuba), or an Amerindian reference (as in Venezuela). Other materials relevant to the Caribbean will be found under "Afro-American" in the Latin America volume.

The two movements chosen for seaparate bibliographies in the last section, "Particular Movements," are the Black Caribs (which otherwise would be scattered over several areas) and the Rastafari. The latter has produced a large literature specifically on this movement, but of course it also appears in a wider context in other items and especially in Jamaican materials.

Bibliography of

New Religious Movements
in Primal Societies

Volume 6

The Caribbean

Theory

This small section is hard to distinguish from much in the next section of general materials, which must also be examined for theoretical discussions. See B. Chevannes (entry 2) for African aspects of the common worldview, and also K. Ramchand (entry 14) and M. G. Smith (entries 19 and 20), who take account of slavery.

H. P. Van Dusen (entry 25) discusses Pentecostalism as the "third force" in Christendom; see also F. E. Manning (entry 13) on Pentecostalism as a bridging force between African and Western worldviews, and L. Margolies (entry 13a). A. W. Singham (entry 18) suggests millenarianism marks the terminal stages of the colonial era; for a different view see M. Craton (entry 37, in the General section).

1   Bisnauth, Dale A. "Religious pluralism and development in the Caribbean." *Caribbean Journal of Religious Studies* 4, no. 2 (September 1982): 17-33.

      Pp. 22-25 and 30-33 are more relevant to Afro-Caribbean religions and their place in the future.

2   Chevannes, Barry. Review of *Religious cults of the Caribbean*, by G. E. Simpson (entry 85, 1970 ed.). *Social and Economic Studies* 24, no. 1 (1975): 162-63.

3   Chevannes, Barry. "Some notes on African religious survivals in the Caribbean." *Caribbean Journal of Religious Studies* (Kingston) 5, no. 2 (1983): 18-28.

      Mainly on the common worldview pervading all religious forms and allegiances, including Obeah and folk medicine – as remnants of African religions.

4   City of Birmingham Education Department. "The plural society of the Caribbean: African retentions." *Living Together Supplement* (Birmingham, U. K.), 1982, pp. 50-51.

5   Collier, H. C. "Obeah–The witchcraft of the West Indies." *Canada West Indies Magazine* 30, no. 8 (1941): 24-25.

6   Glazier, Stephen D[avey]. "Bibliografía del medium espiritista y la posesión." Parts 1, 2. *Boletin del Museo del Hombre Dominicano*, no. 8 (1977), pp. 125-29; no. 9 (1978), pp. 137-59.

7   Glazier, Stephen D[avey]. "Caribbean pilgrimages: A typology." *Journal for the Scientific Study of Religion* 22, no. 4 (1983): 316-25.
      The differences between "fixed" pilgrimages (with specific destinations) and "flexible" pilgrimages (without fixed destinations) reflect attitudes to the land, mobility of the gods, and national sentiments. The former reflect V. W. Turner's model of pilgrimage behavior.

8   Glazier, Stephen D[avey]. "Religion and social justice: Caribbean perspectives." *Phylon* 46, no. 4 (Winter 1985): 283-85.
      Surveys papers at a symposium in honor of G. E. Simpson in 1983 in Knoxville: Simpson on Rastafari, E. Bourguignon on Vodou, and M. Singer with overall conclusions. Suggests the protest and prophetic roles are being affected by upward mobility and a relation with the establishment that modifies social and moral concerns.

9   Hope, Corrie S. "The social psychological determinants of minority uprising: A comparison of the Nat Turner slave rebellion (1831), and the Newark riot (1967)." Ph.D. dissertation (sociology), University of Massachusetts, 1975, 204 pp.
      The relation of other factors to relative deprivation in determining whether or not violent agression occurs.

10   Lex, Barbara W. "Hallucination, healing, and trance: Review of Goodman, Henney, and Pressel. *Trance, healing, and hallucination*" (entry 51). *Reviews in Anthropology* 2, no. 4 (1975): 473-78.

11   Lowenthal, David. *West Indian societies*. London: Oxford University Press, 1972, 385 pp.
      Pp. 114-17, religious faith; pp. 280-92, negritude and black power (Garvey and the Rastafari).

12   Manning, Frank E. "Cup match and carnival: Secular rites of revitalization in decolonizing, tourist-oriented societies." In *Secular*

ritual, edited by S. F. Moore and B. G. Meyerhoff. Assen: Van Gorcum, 1978, pp. 265-81.

13   Manning, Frank E. "Pentecostalism: The emergence of Christian reputation." In *Perspectives on Pentecostalism*, edited by S. D. Glazier. Washington, D.C.: University Press of America, 1980, pp. 6-10.
Surveys the interpretations of Pentecostalism in the essays in this symposium; concludes that it is Protestant Christian in theology, Western in worldview and therefore modernizing, but able to identify with and revitalize indigenous forms.

13a   Margolies, Luise. "The paradoxical growth of Pentecostalism." In *Perspectives on Pentecostalism*, edited by S. D. Glazier. Washington, D.C.: University Press of America, 1980, pp. 1-5.
On the volume and variety of interpretations of this new phenomenon in relation to social change and modernization.

14   Ramchand, Kenneth. "Obeah and the supernatural in West Indian literature." *Jamaica Journal* 3, no. 2 (1969): 52-54.

15   Simey, T. S. *Welfare and planning in the West Indies*. Oxford: Clarendon Press, 1946. Reprint. 1947, 267 pp.
Pp. 36-42, origins of Caribbean religion in Africa.

16   Simpson, George Eaton. "Afro-American religions and religious behaviour." *Caribbean Studies* (Río Piedras, University of Puerto Rico) 12, no. 2 (1972): 5-30, bib.
A survey of the cultural, sociological, and psychological approaches; the political influence, especially of clergy, in black nationalist movements in the 1960s. An important methodological essay on the many facets of such movements.

17   Singer, Merrill. "The concept of justice in the religions of the Caribbean." *Phylon* 46, no. 4 (1985): 296-99.
An overview of papers by G. E. Simpson on Rastafari and E. Bourguignon on Haiti at a symposium on this theme in 1983.

18   Singham, A[rchie] W. *The hero and the crowd in a colonial policy*. Caribbean Series, 12. New Haven, Conn.: Yale University Press, 1968, 389 pp.
Pp. 309-15, on charisma as an aspect of social relationships rather than of an individual personality; pp. 315-17, the terminal colonial stage as a fourth type of situation in which millenarian movements arise, to add to P. M. Worsley's three types.

19   Smith, M[ichael] G[arfield]. "The African heritage in the Caribbean."
      In *Caribbean studies: A symposium*, edited by V. Rubin. Kingston,
      Jamaica: Institute of Social and Economic Research, University of
      the West Indies, 1957, pp. 34-46. 2d ed. Seattle: University of
      Washington Press, 1960.

20   Smith, M[ichael] G[arfield]. *The plural society in the British West
      Indies*. Berkeley: University of California Press, 1965, 359 pp.
          Pp. 164-65, revivalism; pp. 32-35, acculturation factors,
      especially slavery.

21   Tax, Sol, ed. *Acculturation in the Americas: Proceedings and selected
      papers of the XXIXth International Congress of Americanists*. Chicago:
      University of Chicago Press, 1952, 339 pp. Reprint. New York:
      Cooper Square Publications, 1967.
          See essays by W. R. Bascom (entry 111), R. Métraux (entry
      727), and G. E. Simpson (entry 858).

22   Toch, Hans. *The social psychology of social movements*. Indianapolis:
      Bobbs-Merrill Co., 1965.
          Chap. 2 (pp. 28-44), "Illusions and solutions" – referring to
      Rastafari (pp. 30-33, 43); Alfred C. Sam's back-to-Africa movement
      (pp. 33-38, 43); millenarianism and Melanesian cargo cults (pp. 38-
      42).

23   Turner, H[arold] W[alter]. Reviews of *Soul-force: African heritage in
      Afro-American religion* (entry 29) and *The sun and the drum* (entry
      950), by L. E. Barrett. *Journal of Religion in Africa* 10, no. 1 (1979):
      72-75.

24   University of the West Indies. *The roots of witchcraft in the
      Caribbean*. A culturo-historical overview ... radio broadcast,
      Government Broadcasting Unit, 2 and 16 November 1969. St.
      Augustine, Trinidad: University of the West Indies, 1969, 13 pp.

25   Van Dusen, Henry P. "Caribbean holiday." *Christian-Century*
      (Chicago), 17 August 1955, pp. 946-48.
          The "third force" in Christendom is Pentecostalism.

26   Ward, Colleen, and Beaubrun, Michael [H.]. "Trance induction and
      hallucination in Spiritual Baptist mourning." *Journal of Psychological
      Anthropology* 2 (1979): 479-88.

27   Wittkower, Eric D. "Transcultural psychiatry in the Caribbean: Past,
      present, and future." *American Journal of Psychiatry* 127, no. 2 (1970):
      162-66.

General

As elsewhere, this category includes both Caribbean-wide discussions and items that span more than one country in the region, as in A. Pollak-Eltz (entry 76) on Trinidad and Grenada. There are many general surveys: A. Pollak-Eltz (entry 77) is a simple overview, including also Brazil; others include H. W. Turner (entry 92), and the various surveys by the doyen of this field in the Caribbean, G. E. Simpson (entries 83-85) and especially his encyclopedia article (entry 82).

On the African influence and survivals, and on Obeah, see B. Chevannes (entry 3) and K. Ramchand (entry 14) in Theory. Refer to E. G. Parrinder (entry 74) on the African worldview and to R. T. Smith (entry 86), D. V. Trotman (entry 91), and J. S. Udal (entry 93) for the older colonial and legal viewpoint. M. J. Herskovits (entry 53) provides a seminal article on African transpositions into Western Christian forms.

On possession and Pentecostalism see S. D. Glazier's symposium (entry 50) and the articles therefrom distributed in the relevant sections; see also J. H. Henney (entry 52). On revivals, see J. E. Orr (entry 72), covering the Mosquito coast (Nicaragua), Suriname, and the 1860s Jamaican revival (and for the latter, see more fully in the Jamaica section). On the changing scene, especially on the relations of these movements to society and politics, see S. D. Glazier (entry 48).

28   Barrett, Leonard [Emmanuel]. "African religion in the Americas: The 'islands in between.'" In *The black experience in religion*, edited by C. E. Lincoln. Garden City, N.Y.: Doubleday, Anchor, 1974, pp. 310-40. Reprinted in *African religions: A symposium*, edited by N. S. Booth, Jr. New York: Nok Publishers, 1977, pp. 183-215.

Pp. 192-93, Myallism and Kumina; pp. 195-98, "Cumina-Pukkumina" in Jamaica; pp. 198-206, Vodou in Haiti; pp. 206-8, Shango in Trinidad.

29 Barrett, Leonard E[mmanuel]. *Soul-force: African heritage in Afro-American religion*. C. Eric Lincoln Series on Black Religion. Garden City, N.Y.: Doubleday, Anchor, 1974, 251 pp.

Summary accounts of West African religions and both British and "Latin" slave systems; the spiritual resistance to slavery seen in Obeah and Myallism and later in millennial movements for the anglophone areas, and in syncretistic cults with public rites in Latin areas; pp. 87-90, Jamaican balmyards (Mammy Forbes as case study); pp. 95-111, Haitian Vodou; pp. 111-27, George Liele, the Great Revival, Pukumina, Revivalism, and the Bedwardites in Jamaica; pp. 153-202, good, full account of the Rastafari; pp. 207-12, unsatisfactory account of African independency.

30 Barrett, Lindsay. *Song for Mumu: A novel*. London: Longmans, 1967, 154 pp.

Fiction, on the "Black Soul" theme.

31 Bascom, William R[ussell]. "Shango in the New World." In *Actas y Memorias XXXIX Congreso Internacional de Americanistas, Lima, 1970*. Vol. 6. Lima: Instituto de Estudios Peruanos, 1972, pp. 37-46, bib. (pp. 280-92).

A useful survey, starting with the Shango cult in Nigeria, and with references to the literature on the cult in Cuba, Brazil, Trinidad, Grenada, and Haiti.

32 Bascom, William R[ussell]. *Shango in the New World*. Occasional Publication 4. Austin: University of Texas Press, for African and Afro-American Research Institute, 1972, 23 pp., illus., bib. (pp. 21-23).

33 Beauvois, Eu[gène]. "La fontaine de jouvence et le Jourdain dans la tradition des Antilles et de la Floride." *Le Muséon* (Louvain) 3 (1884): 404-29.

Especially among the aboriginal Taino; corresponds to the Tupinamba, Guarani, etc., search for paradise in South American traditional millennialism.

34 Bourguignon, Erika [Eichhorn]. "Ritual dissociation and possession belief in Caribbean Negro religion." In *Afro-American anthropology: Contemporary perspectives*, edited by N. E. Whitten and J. F. Szwed. New York: Free Press, 1970, pp. 87-101, bib.

The Spiritual Baptists or Shakers of St. Vincent (as representing independent fundamentalist Protestant churches) compared with Vodou in Haiti (as representing spirit cults) – the two polar forms of lower-class Negro religion.

35   Cassecanarie, Myal Djumbo. *Obeah simplified: The true Wanga! What it really is and how it is done*. Port of Spain: Mirror Office, 1895.

A professional Obeah man defines his craft as magic – "the true Wanga" being white (i.e., good) magic.

36   Coleman, Stanley Jackson. "Treasury of folklore: Myth and mystery in curious Caribbean cults." Douglas, Isle of Man: Folklore Academy, 1960, 14 pp. Mimeo.

A folklorist visitor's account of Vodou, Obeah, Shango, Spiritual Baptists (music of two songs, symbolic colors, career of F. A. M. Mayhew, etc.), Rada (its founder, hair-washing rite, songs, etc.), Myallism, Revivalism, Pocomania. Copy in Institute of Jamaica.

37   Craton, Michael. "Proto-peasant revolts? The late slave rebellions in the British West Indies, 1816-1832." *Past and Present*, no. 85 (November 1979), pp. 99-125.

Surveys revolts in Barbados (1816), Demerara (1823), and Jamaica (1831-32); emphasizes the role of rebel leadership and notes the role of black religion in the latter two incidents; pp. 115-16, rejects the simple millenarian explanation.

38   Cross, Malcolm. *Urbanisation and urban growth in the Caribbean*. Urbanization in Developing Countries. Cambridge: Cambridge University Press, 1979, 175 pp.

Pp. 93-101, religious organizations – including Rastafarians.

39   Dahlin, Terry, and Nelson, Reed. *Caribbean religion: A survey, and bibliography*. 24th SALALM Seminar Working Paper. Los Angeles: University of California at Los Angeles, 1979.

40   Debien, Gabriel. "La christianization des esclaves des Antilles Françaises aux XVIIe et XVIIIe siècles." *Revue d'Histoire de l'Amérique Française* (Montreal) 20, no. 4 (1967): 525-55; 21, no. 1 (1967): 99-111.

Slave religion in the French-speaking Caribbean, including also Haiti and the Dominican Republic.

41   Dias, H. de los. "The fetishism of the British West Indies." In *Negro Anthology made by Nancy Cunard, 1931-1933*. London: Nancy Cunard at Wishart & Co., 1934, pp. 452-54.

42   Dix, Jabey. "Adolphe – One of the most terrible of Obeah-men." *Canada-West Indies Magazine* 22, no. 2 (1933): 53-55.

43 Fichte, Hubert. *Xango, Bahia, Haiti, Trinidad*. Die Afroamerikanischen Religionen, 2. Textband. Frankfurt am Main: S. Fischer, 1976, 353 pp., map.

44 Fichte, Hubert (text), and Mau, Leonore (photos). *Petersilie: Santo Domingo, Venezuela, Miami, Grenada*. Die Afroamerikanischen Religionen, 4. Frankfurt am Main: S. Fischer, 1980, 403 pp., many color plates, with notes.

   Pp. 7-64, Santo Domingo; pp. 65-150, Venezuela; pp. 151-252, Miami; pp. 253-355, Grenada; pp. 359-402, Appendix, including "new science of man," remarks on A. Haley's *Roots*, Afro-Cuban religion in Miami, and Vodou. "Petersilie" ("parsley") in Spanish is pronounced "perelil" in Dominican Republic by Haiti immigrants, who were thus identified in Trujillo's mass murder in 1937.

45 Footner, Hubert. *The Obeah murders*. New York: Harper & Brothers, 1937.

   A mystery story.

46 Froude, James Anthony. *The English in the West Indies, or The bow of Ulysses*. London: Longmans Green & Co.; New York: Charles Scribner's Sons, 1888, 373 pp., illus.

   Pp. 256-62, in defense of Governor Eyre during the Morant Bay "revolt"; p. 344, local popular religion as "West African superstitions . . . serpent worship . . . child sacrifice and cannibalism."

47 Glazier, Stephen [Davey]. "Afrocaribbean religion." In *Harper's dictionary of religion*. In preparation, 1990.

48 Glazier, Stephen D[avey]. "Prophecy and ecstasy: Religion and politics in the Caribbean." In *Prophetic religion and politics*, edited by J. K. Hadden and A. D. Shupe. New York: Paragon House, 1986, pp. 430-47.

   Religion and politics, with emphasis on church-state relations, in Rastafari, Vodou, and the Spiritual Baptists – the first as showing much accommodation to society, the second as legitimating the ruling family, the third in an ambiguous position. The situations are complex and changing.

49 Glazier, Stephen D[avey]. "Religion and contemporary religious movements in the Caribbean: A report." *Sociological Analysis* 41, no. 2 (1980): 181-83.

   Report of panel at 4th annual meeting, Caribbean Studies Association, in Fort-de-France, Martinique, May 1979.

50   Glazier, Stephen D[avey], ed. *Perspectives on Pentecostalism: Case studies from the Caribbean and Latin America*. Washington, D.C.: University Press of America, 1980, 197 pp.

    See items by F. J. Conway (Haiti, entry 418); A. L. La Ruffa (Puerto Rico, entry 1272); F. E. Manning (Theory, entry 13); L. Margolies (Theory, entry 13a); W. Wedenoja (Jamaica, entry 1158); and in vol. 5 of this series, *Latin America*, D. Birdwell-Pheasant under Central America: Belize, and G. N. Howe under Particular Movements: Umbanda.

51   Goodman, Felicitas D.; Henney, Jeanette H[illman]; and Pressel, Esther. *Trance, healing, and hallucination: Three field studies in religious experience*. Contemporary Religious Movements. New York and London: John Wiley & Sons, 1974, 388 pp., tables.

    See also J. H. Henney (entry 1226) and in vol. 5 of this series, *Latin America*, F. D. Goodman under Central America: Mexico and E. Pressel under Particular Movements: Umbanda.

52   Henney, Jeannette H[illman]. "Comparison of the Shakers and similar groups in the Caribbean." In *Trance, healing, and hallucination: Three field studies in religious experience*, by F. Goodman, J. H. Henney, and E. Pressel. Contemporary Religious Movements. New York and London: John Wiley & Sons, 1974, pp. 80-95.

    Fundamentalists in St. Vincent, Umbanda in Brazil, and an Apostolic Church in the Yucatan.

53   Herskovits, M[elville] J[ean]. "African gods and Catholic saints in New World Negro belief." *American Anthropologist*, n.s. 39, no. 4 (1937): 635-43. Reprinted in *Reader in comparative religion*, edited by W. A. Lessa and E. Vogt. New York: Harper & Row, 1958, pp. 492-98. Reprinted in *The New World Negro*, by M. J. Herskovits. Bloomington: Indiana University Press, 1966, pp. 321-29. Portuguese translation. "Deuses africanos e santos catolicos nas crenças do Negro do Novo Mundo." In *O Negro no Brasil*, compiled by E. Carneiro and A. do C. Ferraz. Rio de Janeiro, Civilização Brasileira, 1940, pp. 19-29.

53a   Hickerton, J[ames] P[hilip]. *Caribbean Kallaloo*. London: Carey Kingsgate Press, 1958, 99 pp., illus.

54   Horowitz, Michael M., ed. *Peoples and cultures of the Caribbean: An anthropological reader*. Garden City, N.Y.: Natural History Press, 1971, 606 pp.

    Includes "Section H: Religion and folklore" – see items by S. Cook (Puerto Rico, entry 1246), A. de Waal Malefijt (Suriname, entry 1401); S. Kitzinger (Jamaica, entry 1748), and N. L. Gonzalez (Black Caribs, entry 1563).

55   Hurbon, Laënnec. *Cultures et pouvoirs dans la Caraïbe: Langue créole, vaudou, sectes religieuses en Guadeloupe et en Haïti.* Paris: Harmattan, 1975.

56   Hurbon, Laënnec. "New religious movements in the Caribbean." In *New religious movements and rapid social change,* edited by J. A. Beckford. Beverly Hills: Sage Publications; UNESCO, 1986, pp. 146-76.
         "Imported movements"–Jehovah's Witnesses, Seventh Day Adventists, Mahikari, Apostles of Infinite Love; "native movements"–Rastafarians, Mita (Puerto Rico), La Palma Sola (Dominican Republic); Vodou also discussed; theoretical reflections.

57   Hurbon, Laënnec. "Los nuevos movimentos religiosos en el Caribe." *Los Nuevos Movimientos Religiosos: Revue Cristianismo y Sociedad* (Mexico), no. 93 [25, no. 3] (1987): 37-63.

58   Hutton, Joseph Edmund. *A history of Moravian missions.* London: Moravian Publication Office, [ca. 1922], 550 pp., bib., maps.
         Pp. 334-39, the revival, 1881-96, among Miskitos of Nicaragua; pp. 220-22, Obeah and Myallism; pp. 224-27, Great Revival, 1858-60, Jamaica; pp. 121-25, Bush Negroes of Surinam; pp. 78-116, North American Indian missions (background).

59   Johnston, Harry H[amilton]. *The Negro in the New World.* London: Methuen, 1910, xxix + 489 pp., illus. Reprint. New York and London: Johnson Reprint Co., 1969, xi + xxix + 499 pp., illus. (with a new introduction by G. Shepperson).
         Pp. 193-94, Vodou in Haiti; pp. 64-66, in Cuba.

60   Kuna, Ralph R. "Hoodoo: Médecine et psychiatrie indigène du Noir Américain." *Ethno-Psychologie: Revue de Psychologie des Peuples* (Le Havre) 32, no. 4 (1977): 323-41, bib.
         The hoodoo healer compared with Vodou (W. African and Haitian), Obeah (Jamaica), and Umbanda (Brazil), etc., in peaceful coexistence with modern medicine.

61   Lekis, Lisa. "The dance as an expression of Caribbean folklore." In *The Caribbean: Its culture,* edited by A. C. Wilgus. Gainesville: University of Florida Press, 1955, pp. 43-73.
         Pp. 62-70–Shango, the Shouters, Calypso, Nago, Vodou (pp. 66-70), Rada, etc., as connected with dance forms.

62 Lepkowski, Tadeusz. "Katolicyzm i proteskntyzm a procesy marodotwórcze na Antylach" [Catholicism, Protestantism, and the formation of nations in the Antilles]. *Etnografia Polska* (Warsaw) 16, no. 2 (1972): 51-66; English summary (p. 67.)
    Includes Haiti, Cuba, French Antilles, and Jamaica.

63 Lewis, Gordon K[enneth]. *The growth of the modern West Indies*. London: MacGibbon & Kee; New York: Monthly Review Press, 1968, 506 pp.
    Pp. 29-30, 194-96, mention of various groups.

64 Makin, William J[ames]. *Caribbean nights*. London: Robert Hale, 1939, 287 pp., illus.

65 Mau, Leonore (photos), and Fichte, Hubert (text). *Petersilie: Santo Domingo, Venezuela, Miami, Grenada*. Die Afroamerikanischen Religionen, 3. Frankfurt am Main: S. Fischer, 1980, 199 pp. + 79 color and 32 black-and-white photos.
    See H. Fichte, accompanying volume 4, and note explaining "Petersilie." Pp. 8-165, photos with introductory "poem" to each area; pp. 167-93, text by H. Fichte; pp. 195-99, captions to photos.

66 Mau, Leonore. *Xango, Bahia, Haiti, Trinidad*. Die Afroamerikanischen Religionen, 1. Bildband. Frankfurt am Main: S. Fischer, 1976, 172 pp., 103 photos.
    A magnificent photo essay; see also accompanying volume 2 by H. Fichte.

67 Melton, J[ohn] Gordon. *The encyclopaedia of American religions*. 2 vols. A Consortium Book. Wilmington, N.C.: McGrath Publishing Co., 1978, 608 + 595 pp.
    Vol. 1, pp. 74-75, African Orthodox Church; vol. 2, p. 269, Yoruba religion–Oyotunji Village in South Carolina, 1973-; pp. 268-69, African witchcraft (Haitian Vodou); p. 270, Afro-American Vodou (of Madam Arboo in Harlem).

68 Mintz, Sidney W[ilfred], and Price, Richard. *An anthropological approach to the Afro-American past: A Caribbean perspective*. ISHR Occasional Papers in Social Change, 2. Philadelphia: Institute for the Study of Human Relations, 1976, 64 pp., bib.
    Pp. 29-30, 31, the Rada cult in Trinidad; pp. 30-31, Afro-Cuban religion.

69 Mischel, Frances [Osterman]. "Faith, healing, and medical practice in the southern Caribbean." *Southwestern Journal of Anthropology* 15, no. 4 (1959): 407-17.

Shango in Trinidad and Grenada.

70   Nettleford, Rex M. "Foreword." *Caribbean Quarterly* (Mona, Jamaica) 24, nos. 3-4 (1978): v-vi.
      Introducing the special theme of this issue – religion.

71   Olawaiye, James Adeyinka. "Yoruba religious and social traditions in Ekiti, Nigeria and three Caribbean countries: Trinidad-Tobago, Guyana, and Belize." Ph.D. dissertation (education), University of Missouri (Kansas City), 1980, 502 pp.
      On Yoruba elements in Caribbean religions: (1) worship of the gods – Ogun in Nigeria and Shango in Trinidad, and Nigerian Aladura-type churches in Trinidad and Guyana; (2) cult of ancestors – parallels in Ekiti and Belize among Black Caribs.

72   Orr, J[ames] Edwin. *Evangelical awakenings in Latin America*. Minneapolis: Bethany Fellowship, 1978, 216 pp. + notes, bib., and index.
      Pp. 22-31 and "Notes on ch. 4" (no pagination), Caribbean awakening 1860 – on the Jamaica revival and similar movements elsewhere (e.g., in Surinam and on the Mosquito coast of Nicaragua).

73   Ottenberg, Simon, ed. *African religious groups and beliefs*. Papers in Honour of William R. Bascom. Meerut, India: Archana Publications, for the Folklore Institute (Berkeley, Calif.), 1982, 355 pp.
      See essays by J. G. Moore (Jamaica, entry 1082) and E. Bourguignon (Haiti, entry 368).

74   Parrinder, [Edward] Geoffrey [Simons]. "The African spiritual universe." In *Afro-Caribbean religions*, edited by B. E. Gates. London: Ward Lock Educational, 1980, pp. 16-25.
      Pp. 23-24, briefly on African forms "preserved" after "migration into the New World, with some mixture with Christianity."

75   Pitt, F. E[dward] A. "Acculturative and synthetic aspects of religion and life in the island of St. Vincent and other predominantly Protestant islands and areas of the West Indies and the Caribbean." *Actes du IVe Congrès International des Sciences Anthropologiques et Ethnologiques, Vienne . . . 1952*. Vol. 2. Vienna: Verlag A. Holzhausens, 1955, pp. 385-90.
      Especially on Shakerism on St. Vincent; some reference to other forms of "spiritism"; by a Methodist missionary.

76   Pollak-Eltz, Angelina. *Afro-Amerikaanse godsdienstein en . . . culten*. Roemond, Netherlands: J. J. Romen, 1970, 221 pp., illus. Spanish translation, rev. and enl. *Cultos afroamericanos*. Caracas: Instituto de

Investigaciones Historicas, Universidad Catolica Andrés Bello, 1972, 268 pp., bib.

A survey of cults in Brazil, the Antilles (Trinidad, Grenada, Jamaica, Haiti, Cuba), Venezuela, and Suriname.

77 Pollak-Eltz, Angelina. "The Yoruba religion and its decline in the Americas." *Verhandlungen des XXXVIII Internationalen Amerikanistenkongresses, Stuttgart-München, 1968.* Vol. 3, pp. 423-27.

A comprehensive overview of Afro-American religious movements, including Brazil.

78 Proudfoot, Mary. *Britain and the United States in the Caribbean.* A Comparative Study in Methods of Development. London: Faber & Faber, 1954, xix + 434 pp.

Pp. 272-80, religion.

79 Raboteau, Albert J. *Slave religion: The "invisible" institution in the antebellum South.* New York: Oxford University Press, 1978, 382 pp., illus.

Pp. 16-42 (pp. 330-35, notes), survey of cults in the Caribbean and Brazil; pp. 44-92, "death of the gods" – on the survival of African religion in the Caribbean and Brazil being much greater than in the U. S. and the reasons for this; pp. 139-41, 267-68, the first black independent church (Silver Bluff, South Carolina) and George Liele's establishment of Baptist work in Jamaica.

80 Schuler, Monica [Elaine]. "Ethnic slave rebellions in the Caribbean and the Guyanas." *Journal of Social History* (Berkeley) 3, no. 4 (Summer 1970): 374-85.

Pp. 382-84, leaders' sanctions included religion – Vodou, Obeah, and traditional.

81 Sherlock, Philip. *West Indies.* London: Thames & Hudson, 1966, 215 pp.

Pp. 124-28, religious groups, including Rastafarians, Shango, etc.

82 Simpson, George Eaton. "Afro-Caribbean religions." In *The encyclopedia of religion*, edited by M. Eliade. Vol. 3. New York: Macmillan, 1987, pp. 90-98.

Includes Vodou, Santeria, Shango, Kumina, Kele, Black Caribs, Revival Zion, Spiritual Baptists, Shakers, and Rastafarians.

83 Simpson, George Eaton. *Caribbean papers.* Sondeos, 70. Cuernavaca, Mexico: Centro Intercultural de Documentación, 1970 (grouped pagination).

A second collection, of which only two ("The Vodun cult in Haiti" and "Folk medicine in Trinidad") occur also in the University of Puerto Rico collection of 1970.

84   Simpson, George Eaton. "Religions of the Caribbean." In *The African diaspora: Interpretative essays*, edited by M. L. Kilson and R. I. Rotberg. Cambridge, Mass., and London: Harvard University Press, 1976, pp. 280-311.
      Includes historical perspective and a typology of cults.

85   Simpson, George Eaton. *Religious cults of the Caribbean: Trinidad, Jamaica, and Haiti*. Caribbean Monograph Series, 7. Río Piedras: Institute of Caribbean Studies, University of Puerto Rico, 1965. Rev. enl. ed. 1970. 2d rev. ed. 1977.
      A collection of eleven journal articles (entries 856, 860, 867, 869, 1459, 1460) and *The Shango cult in Trinidad* (entry 1461).

86   Smith, Raymond T[homas]. "Religion in the formation of West Indian society: Guyana and Jamaica." In *The African diaspora: Interpretative essays*, edited by M. L. Kilson and R. I. Rotberg. Cambridge, Mass., and London: Harvard University Press, 1976, pp. 312-41.
      Especially pp. 328-32, African dances, syncretism, and Obeah in Guyana; pp. 332-34, 337-41, the same forms in Jamaica.

87   Smith, Ronald Richard. "The Society of Los Congos of Panama: An ethnomusicological study of the music and dance-theatre of an Afro-Panamanian group." Ph.D. dissertation (folklore), Indiana University, 1976, 342 pp.

88   Sobel, Mechal. *Trabelin' on: The slave journey to an Afro-Baptist faith*. Contributions in Afro-American and African Studies, 36. Westport, Conn.: Greenwood Press, 1979, 454 pp., illus.
      By an Israeli historian, with extensive documentation by extracts and abundant bibliographic information in the notes; pp. 159-68, on Nat Turner and religion; pp. 48-57, and notes 38-41 on pp. 378-79, "Voodoo" from Haiti in Louisiana; pp. 140-49, Sea Islands religion (Atlantic coast, southern U.S.) and "shouts" in Negro religion – the Sea Islands being less acculturated than mainland U.S. blacks. All useful for comparative purposes.

89   Szulc, Tad, ed. *The United States and the Caribbean*. Englewood Cliffs, N.J.: Prentice-Hall, 1971, 212 pp.
      Pp. 9-10, general mention of religions (by G. K. Lewis); pp. 146-56, Black Power, and relevance of *Abeng*, a radical newspaper; pp. 153-54 – largely based on Garvey (by F. McDonald).

90   Thomas-Hope, Elizabeth. "The pattern of Caribbean religions." In *Afro-Caribbean religions*, edited by B. E. Gates. London: Ward Lock Educational, 1980, pp. 4-15.
      Pp. 11-15, various movements and influence; pp. 11, 13, Vodou; p. 14, Bedward and Rastafari.

91   Trotman, David V. "The Yoruba and Orisha worship in Trinidad and British Guiana, 1838-1870." *African Studies Review* 19, no. 2 (1976): 1-17.

92   Turner, Harold W[alter]. "New religious movements in the Caribbean." In *Afro-Caribbean religions*, edited by B. E. Gates. London: Ward Lock Educational, 1980, pp. 49-57, table.
      Shouters and Shakers (pp. 50-51); Pocomania (pp. 51-52); Shango and Santería (pp. 52-53); Rastafari (pp. 53-54); Hallelujah religion and Pidima (pp. 54-56); Maldevidan (p. 56).

93   Udal, J. S. "Obeah in the West Indies." *Folklore* (London) 26, no. 3 (1915): 255-95.
      Pp. 256-61, Vodou in Haiti, based on Spencer St. John (entry 843); pp. 261-68, Obeah, based on H. Johnston (entry 59) and his own experiences in the Leeward Islands and on other court cases; pp. 284-86, text of a letter by "Our Lord Jesus Christ" – much on human sacrifice and ritual murders as seen from the colonial and legal angle.

94   Underwood, Frances W. "The Vodun complex in the West Indies." Ph.D. dissertation (anthropology), Yale University, 1947, [about 122 pp.]

95   Waite, Arthur Edward. *The book of black magic and of pacts*. Edited by L. W. de Laurence. Chicago: The de Laurence Co., 1910.
      An occult book, akin to *The sixth and seventh books of Moses* in its influence, especially on Obeah.

96   Walendowska[-Zapendowska], Barbara. "Wspóine elementy w religiach synkretycznch Antyli" [Common elements in the syncretic religions of the Antilles]. *Etnografia Polska* (Warsaw) 16, no. 2 (1972): 117-32; English summary.
      Santería in Cuba, Vodou in Haiti, and Shango in Trinidad as representing a conjunction of the African and the Catholic religious traditions rather than a synthesis; Catholic elements predominate in rites, and African elements in beliefs, although the latter influence is the stronger overall.

97   Willeford, Mary Jo. "Negro New World religions and witchcraft." *Bim* (St. Michael, Barbados) 48 [12] (January-June 1969): 216-22.

The origin and location of Vodou, Shango, and Obeah – the latter treated in detail as sorcery and not as a religion.

98   Williams, Joseph J[ohn]. *Voodoos and obeahs: Phases of West Indian witchcraft*. New York: L. Macreagh, Dial Press, 1932, xix + 257 pp. Reprint. London: George Allen & Unwin, 1933, xix + 257 pp., bib. Reprint. New York: AMS Press, 1970.

A Jesuit scholar, on religion as much as witchcraft or magic; ch. 4, origins of Obeah – pp. 108-118, valuable reprints of long sections on Obeah in Jamaica, Barbados, Antigua, Grenada, and St. Christopher from the *Report of the Lords of the Committee of the Council appointed for the consideration of all matters related to trade and foreign plantation*, Part 3, "Treatment of slaves in the West Indies" (London, 1789, over 1200 unnumbered pages); pp. 119-41 on the origin of Obeah in Ashanti, Ghana. See further under Haiti and Jamaica.

99   Wilson, Bryan R[onald]. *Magic and the millennium: A sociological study of religious movements of protest among tribal and third-world peoples*. London: Heinemann Educational Books; New York: Harper & Row, 1973, 547 pp. Reprint. Frogmore, St. Albans: Granada Publishing Co., Paladin Books, 1975.

Pp. 123-25, syncretism and the thaumaturgical demand.

Bahama Islands

Despite a population of over two hundred thousand, of whom well over 80% are black or mulatto, no very obviously African-related movements have been reported; it is said these would be despised (D. J. Crowley, entry 101).

On the other hand, the black Baptist churches (the largest denomination) derive from the missionary work of Amos, an ex-slave Negro Baptist from the U.S. from 1783, about the same time and in the same circumstances as George Liele in Jamaica. The item "Bahama Islands" from the *Baptist Magazine* (entry 100) reports a revival in 1815, and E. B. Underhill (entry 104) describes these churches in the mid-nineteenth century. The parallels with Jamaica are sustained.

Crowley also describes African features such as the spirit possession and ancestor practices of the Baptists and of the Church of God, originating from Cleveland, Tennessee, but locally known as "The Jumpers," who were also described thirty years earlier by A. D. Defries (entry 102). C. S. and K. F. Otterbein (entry 103) also describe, indirectly, survivals of African worldviews in a village in 1968, and the widespread practice of Obeah is included in Crowley's survey.

A number of small black indigenous churches exist, without available accounts; likewise the Rastafari, who have arrived from Jamaica.

100   "Bahama Islands." *Baptist Magazine* (London) 7 (May 1815): 212-13.
       A letter to Dr. Rippon from the Baptist Church at New Providence, which originated in the work of Amos (an ex-slave Negro Baptist missionary from the U.S., in the Bahamas from 1783), reporting a revival in 1814-15.

101   Crowley, Daniel J[ohn]. "L'héritage africain dans les Bahamas." *Présence Africaine*, n.s. 23 (December 1958-January 1959): 41-58.
       Pp. 44-47, "Les Africanismes dans la vie religieuse." Mostly Baptists, Anglicans, Roman Catholics, and Adventists; no totally African cults, which are despised; but Baptists and a Church of God

called "The Jumpers" exhibit African traits–spirit possession, "Obeahmen" using magic (drawing on de Laurence literature from Chicago) and ancestral practices, but not as ancestral cults.

102   Defries, Amelia [Dorothy]. *The fortunate islands: Being adventures with the Negro in the Bahamas*. London: Cecil Palmer, 1929, 160 pp., illus., map.

        Pp. 72-75, describes a casual visit to the "Holy Jumpers."

103   Otterbein, Charlotte Swanson, and Otterbein, Keith F. "Believers and beaters: A case study of supernatural beliefs and child rearing in the Bahama Islands." *American Anthropologist* 75, no. 5 (1973): 1670-81, bib.

        The beliefs in the supernatural of twenty mothers and grandmothers in Congo Town, Long Bay Cays, Andros Island.

104   Underhill, Edward Bean. *The West Indies: Their social and religious condition*. London: Jackson, Walford, & Hodder, 1862, 493 pp. Reprint. Westport, Conn.: Negro Universities Press, 1970.

        Pp. 427-75, missionary report on Independent Baptist congregations.

Bermuda

104a   Manning, Frank E. "Myth, memory, and radicalism: History and ideology in Bermuda." Paper presented at the Annual Meeting of the American Society of Ethnohistory, Athens, Ga., 14-16 October 1971.

Cuba

Since there are now no Amerindians (Taino or Ciboney) in Cuba, we are concerned with the minority population of about 12% black and about 15% mulatto in a population of some ten million, of whom over 70% are white, predominantly Spanish and Catholic. The influence of an African ancestry derived through the 27% black/mulatto sector is, however, far greater than the figures suggest. In the mid-nineteenth century the African population was actually larger than the white, and since intermarriage has been common, Cuban culture is substantially "mestizo." Hence the term "Afro-Cuban" has wide application and applies to many forms of religion, and there is much overlap between these forms and folk Catholicism.

One sign of the African influence is found in the popularity of music and dance that have an African background and are often related to the new forms of religion. See J. Dumoulin (entry 141), M. A. Marks (entry 175), R. Nodal-Consuega (entry 187), and the scholar who made these studies respectable, F. Ortiz (entry 199).

For general surveys see R. Bastide (entry 112), W. MacGaffey and C. R. Barnett (entry 174), J.-P. Tardieu (entry 215), H. Thomas (entry 216), U.S. Government, Department of the Army (entry 218), and especially F. Ortiz (entry 196). More especially on the African influence and syncretism, see W. R. Bascom (entry 110), and A. Léon (entry 171).

The most widespread form is Santería, or Regla de Ocha (Religion of the Orishas), which includes groups mixing Spanish with Lucumí (i.e., Yoruba language) and Arara, or Fon language (Dahomey) – see L. Cabrera (entries 119, 120, 129). See J. M. Murphy (entry 183) for a recent survey; C. A. Echánove (entry 142); L. González Huguet (entry 151), especially for Santería house-shrines and general significance; R. Nodal and M. Andre (entry 186); G. E. Simpson (entry 214); and M. González-Wippler(entry 153). For the more magical Mayombe, see L. Cabrera (entry 126). For the spread of Santería to the U.S., etc., see J. M. Murphy (entry 185), M. C. Sandoval (entry 213) (Florida), and C. V. Wetli and R. Martinez (entry 219).

The men's secret society, Abakuá, or Naniguismo, is confined to Cuba but includes blacks and whites and was "discovered" by the black folklorist L. Cabrera in the 1950s; see especially entries 127 and 128. See also H. Courlander (entry 135), G. E. Simpson (entry 214) (also on Santería), United States Government, Department of the Army (entry 218), and especially F. Ortiz (entry 192).

On Spiritualism, see A. A. Bermúdez (entry 114). On Vodou from Haiti, see A. Pedro (entry 203).

On what might be seen as independent churches, such as independent Pentecostal and evangelical churches, the American-related African Methodist Episcopal Church, and especially the African Orthodox Church connected with Marcus Garvey, there seem to be no studies available for inclusion.

105   "Los Abakuá misteriosa herencia africana." *Revista Mensual de Cuba*, no. 41 [4] (September 1965).

106   Alen, Olavo. "Die Tumba-Francesa-gesellschaften in Kuba." *Ethnographisch-Archaologische Zeitschrift* 22, no. 1 (1981): 71-75.

107   Alvarez, Ana Gloria. "La santería y la educación en Cuba." Dissertation, Universidad de Oriente.

108   Angarica, Nicolas. *El 'Lucumí' al alcance de todas*. Havana, n.d.
       On Santería.

109   Barreal Fernández, Isaac. "Tendencias sincréticas de los cultos populares en Cuba." *Etnología y Folklore* (Havana), no. 1 (1966), pp. 17-24.
       Afro-Catholic popular religion, Lucumí, Santería, Abakuá, and Spiritualist cults.

110   Bascom, William R[ussell]. "The focus of Cuban *Santería*." *Southwest Journal of Anthropology* 6, no. 1 (1950): 64-68.
       Combines Christian veneer and symbols for traditional values with African elements, but claims to be Roman Catholic; reports on stones, blood, and herbs in a Yoruba-background cult in Jovellanos, Matanzas province.

111   Bascom, William R[ussell]. "Two forms of Afro-Cuban divination." In *Acculturation in the Americas*, edited by S. Tax. 29th International Congress of Americanists, 1952. New York: Cooper Square Publications, 1952. Reprint. 1967, pp. 169-79.
       The *'dilogun* and *Ifa* systems in Santería as closest to Yoruba forms in West Africa.

111a   Bascom, William R[ussell]. "Yoruba acculturation in Cuba." In *Les Afros-Américains*. Mémoires de l'Institut Français de l'Afrique Noire, no. 27. Dakar: IFAN, 1952 (1953 on cover), pp. 163-67.

On the retention of Yoruba religion and language in Cuba – mainly on the latter.

112   Bastide, Roger. *Les Amériques noires*. Paris: Payot, 1967. English translation. *African civilizations in the New World*. London: C. Hurst, 1971, 232 pp.

Pp. 111-15 (English translation), Cuban religions.

113   Bermúdez, Armando Andrés. "La expansión del 'espiritismo de cordón.'" *Etnología y Folklore* (Havana), no. 5 (1968), pp. 5-32.

One of the popular forms of spiritualism, with songs and dances, syncretized with Catholicism.

114   Bermúdez, Armando Andrés. "Notas para la historia del espiritismo en Cuba." *Etnología y Folklore* (Havana), no. 4 (1967), pp. 5-22.

A survey of the four forms of popular spiritualism and their history, with extensive notes.

115   Bermúdez, Armando Andrés. "Tres cruces del espiritista Juan González." *Etnología y Folklore* (Havana), no. 1 (1966), pp. 85-99, illus.

Forms of the cross found in "Espiritismo de cordón," with detailed study of three forms of the "cruz papal" found in three cult centers of Juan González.

116   Brandon, George Edward. "The dead sell memories: An anthropological study of Santería in New York City (Afro-Cuban)." Ph.D. dissertation (anthropology), Rutgers University, 1983, 593 pp.

Based on New York and Oyotunji Village, South Carolina; shows Santería in Cuba combined Yoruba ritual and cosmology, Catholic cults of saints, and Kardecist spiritual traits in ritual and cosmology, emerging between 1790 and 1850; includes transcriptions of religious songs and a compendium of herbs used in healing and ritual.

117   Bustamente, José Angel. "Importance of cultural patterns in psychotherapy." *American Journal of Psychotherapy* 11, no. 4 (1957): 803-12.

Pp. 809-11, Afro-Cuban cult practices in the context of treatment of Cuban patients.

118 Cabrera, Lydia. *Anagó: Vocabulaire lucumi (el yoruba que se habla en Cuba)*. Colección del Chicherekú en el Exilio. Havana: Ediciones C. R., 1957, 326 pp. Reprint. Miami: Ediciones C. R., 1970. 2d ed. 1986.
Yoruba vocabulary surviving as a ritual language.

119 Cabrera, Lydia. "El dueño de Ewe (Oluwa-Ewe)." In *Les Afro-Américains*. Mémoires de l'Institut Français de l'Afrique Noire, no. 27. Dakar: IFAN, 1952 [1953 on cover], pp. 169-80.
The ideas of the Lucumí cult adherents in Cuba concerning their main divinity.

120 Cabrera, Lydia. *Koeko igawó, aprende novicia: Pegueño tratado de regla Lucumi*. Miami: Ultra Graphics, 1980, 231 pp.

121 Cabrera, Lydia. *La laguna sagrada de San Joachín*. Photographs by Josefina Tarafa. Madrid: AIP Publications, 1973, 105 pp.
Amphibious divinities of the Lucumí pantheon worshipped at rivers, lagoons, and small streams; with magnificent photographs.

122 Cabrera, Lydia. *El monte*. Igbo-finda; Ewe orisha: Vititi Nfinda. Notas sobre las religiones . . . y el folklore de los Negros criollos. Havana: Ediciones C. R., 1954, 573 pp.; Miami: Mnemosyne Publishing, 1954. Reprint. Miami: Rema Press, 1968. 2d ed. 1971. 4th ed. Miami: Ediciones Universal, 1975, 588 pp., illus.
On Yoruba and Congolese religious beliefs as modified in Cuba. "El monte" refers to the forest, or wooded hill, that is the home of the ancestors, spirits, and other "powers."

123 Cabrera, Lydia. *Música de los cultos africanos en Cuba*. Havana: Burgay y Cia, 1958.
Recorded music.

124 Cabrera, Lydia. *Otan Iyebiye, las piedras preciosas*. Colección del Chicherekú en el Exilio. Miami: Ediciones C. R., 1970. Reprint. 1986.

125 Cabrera, Lydia. *La regla Kimbasa del Santo Cristo del Buen Viaje*. Colección del Chicherekú en el Exilio. Miami: Peninsular Printing, 1977. 2d ed. 1986, 98 pp.

126 Cabrera, Lydia. *Reglas de Congo: Palo Monte Mayombé*. Colección del Chicherekú en el Exilio. Miami: Peninsular printing, 1979. Reprint. 1986, 225 pp.
Beliefs, rites, and chants of Congolese slaves in Cuba in the nineteenth century, and their interaction with the Lucumí, Mandingas, Araras, and Carabalis.

127   Cabrera, Lydia. "Ritual y símbolos de la iniciación en la sociedad secreta Abakuá." *Journal de la Société des Américanistes* (Paris) 58 (1969): 139-71. Reprinted, with three extra sections and illustrations, as *Anaforuana: Ritual y símbolos de la iniciación en la sociedad secreta Abakuá*. Madrid: Ediciones C. R., 1975.
       Detailed study of Abakuá rites and communion meal, also of preparations of the altar and sacred objects.

128   Cabrera, Lydia. *La sociedad secreta Abakuá: Narrada por viejos adeptos*. Colección del Chicherekú en el Exilio. Havana: Ediciones C. R., 1958, 296 pp., illus. Reprint. Miami: Ediciones C. R., 1970.
       A study of an Afro-Cuban cultic society.

129   Cabrera, Lydia. *Yemayá y ochún: Kariocha, iyalorichas y olorichas*. Colección del Chicherekú en el Exilio. Madrid: Editiones C. R., 1980, 370 pp.
       On the Yoruba-derived Lucumí cult, and its popular festivals of the patron saints of Havana and Cuba. Pp. 362-70, bibliographical notes on her books.

130   Canet, Carlos. "La historia de chango." *Réplica: Revista de la Semana* (Miami) 2, no. 62 (1971): 60-63, illus.
       A Lucumí cult member on the Yoruba background to the cult.

131   Canet, Carlos. *Lucumí: Religion de los Yorubas en Cuba*. Miami: Talleres Air Publications Center, 1973, 187 pp., illus., bib.
       A detailed study by a Cuban member of the cult who visited Nigeria to explore the origins, and seeks to correct outsiders' false views. Sections on the gods, rituals, music, possession, and problems of language.

132   Castellanos, Israel. *La brujería y el ñañiguismo en Cuba desde el punto de vista médico-legal*. Lema: Kulturkampf; Havana: Impr. de Lloredo y Cía, 1916, 11 pp.
       On Santería.

133   Castellanos, Israel. *Instrumentos musicales de los afrocubanos*. Havana, 1927.

134   Conde, Nicholas. *The religion*. London: Hutchinson, 1982. Reprinted as *The believers*. London: Hutchinson, 1984, 427 pp.
       A novel on Santería. Set in New York and including white adherents.

135   Courlander, Harold. "Abakwa meeting in Guanabacoa." *Journal of Negro History* 29, no. 4 (1944): 461-70.

136   Courlander, Harold. *Cult music of Cuba*. New York: Ethnic Folkways Library, 1951.
Recorded music.

137   D'Anna, Andrea. *La religioni afroamericane*. Bologna: Editrice Nigrizia, 1972.
Pp. 65-76, Santería, Mayombe, Naniguismo, and Spiritism.

138   Deschamps Chappeaux, Pedro. "El lenguaje Abakuá." *Etnología y Folklore* (Havana) 4 (July-December 1967).

139   Díaz Fabelo, Teodoro. *Lengua de Santeros, Guiné Góngorí*. Havana: Adelante, 1956, 232 pp.
Vocabulary of an Afro-Cuban nature, including religious terms and proverbs.

140   Díaz Fabelo, Teodoro. *Olórun*. Havana: Departamento de Folklore del Teatro Nacional de Cuba, 1960, 118 pp., map, bib.
African forms in Cuba. Pp. 11-18, introduction; pp. 19-30, Olórun; then other divinities.

140a   Duany, Jorge. "Stones, trees, and blood: An analysis of a Cuban Santero." *Cuban Studies/Estudios Cubanos* (Pittsburgh) 12, no. 2 (July 1982): 37-53.
A ceremony analyzed as a syncretic response to the situation of a plantation.

141   Dumoulin, John. "The participative art of the Afro-Cuban religions." *Abhandlungen und Berichte des Staatlichen Museums für Völkerkunde* (Dresden) 21 (1962): 63-78.
Religion, dance, and drama in folk religions: Palo Monte (Western Bantu), Santería (Yoruba), and Abakuá (Calabar?).

142   Echánove T[rujillo], Carlos A. "La santería cubana." *Actas del Folklore* (Havana) 1, no. 1 (1961): 21-27. Reprinted from *Revista Bimestre Cubana* 72, no. 1 (1957) and from *Revista Universidad de la Habana*, nos. 136-41 [22-23] (1957): 83-100.
Santería treated as a spontaneous syncretism of African, Spanish Catholic, and spiritualist elements; its beliefs, priesthood, divinities, and relation to Vodou and Candomble.

143   Efunde, Agun. *Los secretos de la santería*. Miami: Edition Cubamerica, 1978, 119 pp., illus.

144   Fall, Ndeye Anna. *La santeria dans la société cubaine*. Dakar: University of Dakar, 1981.

145   Fichte, Hubert. "Uber die afrokubanischen Religionen in Miami." *Ethnomedizin* 6, nos. 1-4 (1980): 61-91; English summary.

146   Franco, José L[uciano]. *Olorun*. Havana, 1960.
      Santería or Yoruba cults.

147   Garcia Cortéz, Julio. *El santo (la ocha): Secretos de la religión lucumí*. Miami, 1971, 582 pp., illus.
      On Santería.

148   Garcia Herrera, Rosana. "Observaciones etnológicas de las sectas religiosas afrocubanas en una comunidad lajera, La Guinea." *Islas* (Santa Clara, Universidad Central de la Villas), no. 43 (September-December 1972), pp. 143-81.
      Two Afro-Cuban sects (Union Lajera and Sociedad Africana Casino San Antonio) in the largely black population of the Guinea area descended from the plantation slaves; Africanisms and acculturation are surveyed.

149   George, Victoria. "Santeria cult and its healers: Beliefs and traditions preserved in Los Angeles." M.A. thesis, University of California at Los Angeles, 1980.

150   Gleason, Judith [Illsley]. *Santeria*. Bronx, N.Y.: Atheneum, 1975, xiv + 223 pp., illus.
      Fiction: An African museum exhibit draws Raymond into a mystical religion based on Yoruba beliefs.

151   González Huguet, Lydia. "La casa-templo en la regla de ocha." *Etnología y Folklore* (Havana), no. 5 (1968), pp. 33-57, illus.
      The house-shrines of a Santería cult derived from Yoruba *orisha* cults: detailed descriptions and their common features, together with their religious and social significance.

152   González-Wippler, Migene. *Rituals and spells of Santería*. New York: Original Publications, 1984.
      Source materials.

153   González-Wippler, Migene. *Santería: African magic in Latin America*. New York: Julian Press, 1973, 181 pp.
      The first longer work in English on Santería, dependent on Spanish sources.

154   González-Wippler, Migene. *The Santería experience*. Englewood Cliffs, N.J.: Prentice Hall, 1982, 228 pp.
      A detailed first-hand account of Santería in New York.

155 Gregory, Steven. "Santeria in New York City: A study in cultural resistance." Ph.D. dissertation (cultural anthropology), New School for Social Research, New York, 1986, 179 pp.

Among the post-1959 migrants from Cuba, whose religious groups have helped preserve identity and resist acculturation; with critique of acculturation theory in this area.

156 Guerra, G[eraldine] T[orres]. "Un elemento ritual: El 'Osun.'" *Etnología y Folklore* (Havana), no. 3 (1967), pp. 65-80, illus.

157 Harrison, Tony. "Shango the shaky fairy." *London Magazine*, n.s. 10, no. 1 (1970): 5-27.

Literary account of the Cuban search for a mythology for the revolution in its African inheritance, with oblique references to Shango cults, Santería, Abakuá, etc.; pp. 26-27, on similar cults in Brazil. Not much factual information and a rather strained style.

157a Hesse, Axel. "La génesis de las transmisiones espiritistas cubanas y la dialéctica transculturativa en el semi-proletariado politécnico urbano." *Revista Venezolana de Folklore* (Caracas) 6 (October 1975): 67-91, bib.

Spiritism in Cuban history in the period before 1959, studied through twelve songs (with music) used in spiritist sessions.

157b Hewitt, Julia Cuervo. "Ifá: Oráculo Yoruba y Lucumí." *Cuban Studies/Estudios Cubanos* (Pittsburgh) 13, no. 1 (Winter 1983): 24-40.

158 Institut Français de l'Afrique Noire. *Les Afro-Américains*. Mémoires de l'Institut Français de l'Afrique Noire, no. 27. Dakar: IFAN, 1952 [1953 on cover], 268 pp.

Essays organized by P. Verger: see W. R. Bascom (entry 111a), L. Cabrera (entry 119), and R. Lachatañeré (entry 164).

159 Jahn, Janheinz. *Muntu: Umrisse der neoafrikanischen Kultur.* Dusseldorf: E. Diederichs, 1958, 262 pp. English translation. *Muntu: An outline of neo-African culture*. London: Faber & Faber, 1961, 267 pp., illus. French translation. *Muntu: L'homme africain et la culture néo-africaine*. Paris: Éditions du Seuil, 1961, 293 pp., map. Spanish translation. *Muntu: Las culturas neo-africanas*. Mexico, D.F.: Fondo do Cultura Económica, 1963, 348 pp., illus.

Pp. 62-68 (English translation), Santería; pp. 69-78, Naniguismo as a secret society; pp. 78-95, Rumba.

160 Jahn, Janheinz. *Rumba Macumba: Afrocubanische Lyrik*. Munich: C. Hauser, [ca. 1957], 79 pp.

161 Johnston, Harry H[amilton]. *The Negro in the New World.* London: Methuen, 1910, xxix + 489 pp. Reprint. New York and London: Johnson Reprint Co., 1969, xi + xxix + 499 pp., illus. (with a new introduction by G. Shepperson).

Pp. 64-67, an impressionist account of Negro religion in Cuba, by a visitor in 1908.

162 Lachatañeré, Rómulo. *Manual de santería: El sistema de cultos "lucumis."* Estudios Afrocubanos. Havana: Editorial Caribe, 1942, 88 pp.

163 Lachatañeré, Rómulo. *¡Oh! ¡mío yemayá!* Havana, 1938. Manganillo: Editorial El Arte, 1948, 214 pp.

164 Lachatañeré, Rómulo. "Rasgos Bantu en la santería." In *Les Afro-Américains.* Mémoires de l'Institut Français de l'Afrique Noire, no. 27. Dakar: IFAN, 1952 [1953 on cover], pp. 181-84.

On some ten saints held in common in the Mayombe, Lucumí, and Catholic traditions in Cuba, with Bantu elements in the cults distinguished from west African elements – Ibo, Yoruba, and Ewe.

165 Lachatañaré [*sic*, Lachatañeré], Rómulo. "Las religiones negras y el folklore cubano." *Revista Hispanica Moderna* 9 (January-April 1943): 138-43.

166 Lachatañeré, Rómulo. "La santería." *Bulletin du Bureau d'Ethnologie* (Port-au-Prince), no. 2 (1943), pp. 28-30.

167 Lachatañeré, Rómulo. "El sistema religioso de los lucumís y otras influencias africanas en Cuba." Parts 1-3. *Estudios Afrocubanos* 3 (1939): 28-84; 4 (1940): 27-38; 5 (1945-46): 191-216. Last part reprinted in *Actas del Folklore* (Havana) 1, no. 7 (1961): 9-20.

168 Lachatañeré, Rómulo. "Tipos étnicos que concurrieron en la amalgama cubana." *Estudios Afrocubanos* 3, nos. 1-4 (1939). Reprinted in *Actas del Folklore* (Havana) 1, no. 3 (1961): 5-12.

On Santería.

169 Léon, Argeliers. "Un caso de tradición oral escrita." *Islas* (Santa Clara, Universidad Central de la Villas), nos. 39-40 (May-December 1971), pp. 139-51.

The written records (which brought status and wealth to their guardians) of religious beliefs and practices that commenced this century in syncretist religions such as Santería and Regla de Ocha (both regarded as Yoruba-Catholic).

170   Léon, Argeliers. "*Elebwa*: Una divinidad de la santería cubana."
       Abhandlungen und Berichte des Staatlichen Museums für Völkerkunde
       (Dresden) 21 (1962): 57-62 + 2 plates.
       Elebwa as comparable to the *loa* in Vodou.

171   Léon, Argeliers. "Presencia del africano en la cultura cubana." *Islas:*
       Revista de la Universidad Central de las Villas (Santa Clara, Cuba),
       no. 41 (January-April 1972): 155-69.
       Includes the Africanisms in Santería.

172   Léon, Argeliers. "Símbolos gráficos de la sociedad secreta Abakuá."
       Abhandlungen und Berichte des Staatlichen Museums für Völkerkunde
       (Dresden) 34 (1975): 339-54, illus., bib.

173   López Valdéz, Rafael. "El complejo mitológico de los jimaguas en la
       religión de ascendiente Yoruba de Cuba." *Abhandlungen und*
       Berichte des Staatlichen Museums für Völkerkunde (Dresden) 38
       (1980): 46-58.
       The mythological complex concerning the "divine twins" in the
       Yoruba ancestor cult.

174   MacGaffey, Wyatt, and Barnett, Clifford R. *Cuba: Its people, its*
       society, its culture. New Haven, Conn.: HRAF Press, 1962, 392 pp.
       Pp. 205-10, Afro-Cuban religions: Santería, Abakuá, minor
       cults.

175   Marks, Morton A. "Uncovering ritual structures in Afro-American
       music." In *Religious movements in contemporary America*, edited by I.
       I. Zaretsky and M. P. Leone. Princeton: Princeton University Press,
       1974, pp. 60-116; appendix (pp. 117-34, words and music of five
       songs).
       Pp. 75-87, Santería in Cuba, its development, music, and
       migration to New York; passim, Afro-American music's ritual
       structures conveying information.

176   Martin, Juan Luis. *Ecué, changó y yemayá*. Ensayos Sobre la Sub-
       religion de los Afro-cubanos. Havana: Cultural, 1930, 164 pp.
       Essays on Vodou and Cuban religion.

177   Martinez, R. "Afro-Cuban Santería among the Cuban-Americans in
       Dade County, Florida." M.A. thesis (anthropology), University of
       Florida, 1979.

177a   Matas, Julio. "Revolución, literatura y religión afro-cubana." *Cuban*
       Studies/Estudios Cubanos (Pittsburgh) 13, no. 1 (Winter 1983): 17-
       23.

The persistence of Afro-Cuban religions and their problem for the Cuban revolution, as interpreted in the fiction of Antonio Benítez Rojo.

178 Montejo, Esteban (as told to M. Barnet). *Biografía de un cimarrón*. Havana: Academia de Ciencias de Cuba, Instituto de Etnología y Folklore, 1966, 228 pp. Reprint. Barcelona: Editiones Ariel, 1968, 200 pp.; Mexico: Siglo Veintiuno Editores, 1968, 205 pp.; Buenos Aires: Editorial Galerna, 1968, 219 pp. English translation. *The autobiography of a runaway slave*. London: Bodley Head, 1966, 223 pp. French translation. *Esclave à Cuba: Biographie d'une "Cimarron" du colonialisme à l'indépendence*. Paris: Gallimard, 1967, 205 pp. Italian translation. *Autobiograia di uno schiavo*. Turin: Einaudi, 1968, 183 pp.

A former slave, a centenarian, on African-related religions; as related to Miguel Barnet. See also J.-P. Tardieu (entry 215).

179 Montero Bascom, Berta. "Seven Afrocuban myths." In *Actes du 42è Congrès International des Américanistes*, Paris, 1976. Vol. 6. Paris: Société des Américanistes, Musée de l'Homme, 1979, pp. 605-13.

180 Montoto, Roberto. *El manuel de la ocho: Secretos de la religión lucumi*. Los Angeles, 1975.

181 Murphy, Joseph M. "Afro-American religion and oracles: *Santeria* in Cuba." *Journal of the Interdenominational Theological Center* (Atlanta) 8, no. 1 (1980): 83-88.

Santería as an oracular system of communication between gods and men, and as including divination.

182 Murphy, Joseph M. "Ritual systems in Cuban Santeria." Ph.D. dissertation (religion), Temple University, 1981, 398 pp. Digest in *Newsletter of the Afro-American Religious History Group* (Worcester, Mass.) 5, no. 2 (Spring 1981).

Yoruba slaves preserved their identity by combining transplanted Yoruba and Catholic elements in a syncretism that is due to these religious forms as much as to Cuban social forces.

183 Murphy, Joseph M. "Santería." In *The Encyclopedia of religion*, edited by M. Eliade. Vol. 13. New York: Macmillan, 1987, pp. 66-67.

184 Murphy, Joseph M. *Santería: An African religion in America*. Boston: Beacon Press, 1988.

185 Murphy, Joseph M. "Traces of African religiosity came to the U.S. as Santería." *Liturgy* 24, no. 6 (1979): 10-12, illus.

186   Nodal, Roberto, and Andre, Maud. "Dynamique de la santeria afro-cubaine." *Présence Africaine* (Paris), nos. 105-6 (1st and 2d quarters, 1978), pp. 109-22.

187   Nodal-Consuega, Roberto. "A note on Afro-Cuban music." *Ethnos* 34 (1969): 130-40, illus.

188   Novoa, M. Eduardo. "La situación religiosa en Cuba." *Mensaje* (Santiago de Chile), no. 167 (March-April 1968), pp. 104-97.

189   Olmstead, David L. "Comparative notes on Yoruba and Lucumí." *Language* 29, no. 2 (1953): 157-64.
       Tests and supports Bascom's view of Lucumí, the Santería cult language, as genetically related to Yoruba.

190   Ortiz [Fernández], Fernando. *La Africanía de la música folklórica de Cuba*. Havana: Ministerio de Educación, Dirección de Cultura, 1950, 477 pp.
       Pp. 450-56, a nineteenth-century form of spiritualism known as *cordoneros de Orilé* (the Orile ropemakers).

191   Ortiz [Fernández], Fernando. *La antigua fiesta afrocubana del "Dia de Reyes."* Havana: Ministerio de Relaciones Exteriores, Departamento de Asuntos Culturales, 1960, 43 pp., illus.
       The Sixth of January festival among Cuban Negro slaves, and its African origins.

192   Ortiz [Fernández], Fernando. *Los bailes y teatro de los Negros en el folklore de Cuba*. Publicaciones del Ministerio de Educación. Havana: Editions Cardenas, 1951, xvi + 466 pp.
       Includes Abakuá (i.e., Naniguismo) and Santería.

193   Ortiz [Fernández], Fernando. "Brujos o santeros." [*Revista de*] *Estudios Afrocubanos* 3 (1939): 85-90.

194   Ortiz [Fernández], Fernando. "La cocina afro-cubana." *Casa de las Americas*, nos. 36-37 [6] (1966): 63-69.

195   Ortiz [Fernández], Fernando. *Las fases de la evolución religiosa*. Havana: Tipografía Moderna, 1919.

196   Ortiz [Fernández], Fernando. *Hampa afro-cubana: Los Negros brujos*. Apuntes Para el Estudio de Etnología Criminal. Madrid: Libería de Fernando Fé, 1906, xvi + 432 pp., illus.; Miami: New House Publishers, 1906. Reprint. Madrid: Editorial-América,

[1917?], 406 pp., illus. Reprint. Miami: Ediciónes Universal, 1973, 259 pp.

Still the basic study of Yoruba cults in Cuba, by the most comprehensive student of Afro-Cuban culture. The Cubanization of African rituals and beliefs.

197   Ortiz [Fernández], Fernando. "El kinfuiti: Un tambor para 'jalar' muertos." *Bohemia* (Havana), no. 35 [42] (27 August 1950): 20-21, 131, 140.
On a friction drum used in the Afro-Cuban Congo cult.

198   Ortiz [Fernández], Fernando. "La música religiosa de los Yorubas entre los Negros cubanos." [*Revista de*] *Estudios Afrocubanos* 5 (1945-46), pp. 19-60.

199   Ortiz [Fernández], Fernando. "La música sagrada de los Negros yorubá en Cuba." [*Revista de*] *Estudios Afrocubanos* 2, no. 1 (1938): 132.

200   Ortiz [Fernández], Fernando. "La religión en la poesía mulata." [*Revista de*] *Estudios Afrocubanos* 1, no. 1 (1937): 15-62.

201   Ortiz [Fernández], Fernando. "La 'tragedia' de los ñañigos." *Cuadernos Americanos* 4 (July-August 1950): 79-101.

202   Otero, Lisandro. "Fernando Ortiz, 'the father of Caribbean studies.'" *UNESCO Courier* 34, no. 12 (1981): 31.
His contributions to Cuban identity, including especially the Afro-Cuban dimension and the symbiosis of cultures. See entries 190-201.

203   Pedro, Alberto. "Guanamaca, una comunidad haitiana." *Etnología y Folklore* (Havana), no. 1 (1966), pp. 25-29, illus.
On Haitian migrants taking Vodou to Cuba.

204   Pedro, Alberto. "La Semanu Santa haïtian-cubana." *Etnología y Folklore* (Havana) 4 (July-December 1967), pp. 49-78, illus.
Describes the Holy Week festival among Haitians in Cuba – mainly the rituals in Guanamaca (Camagüey province).

205   Piron, Hippolyte. *L'île de Cuba: Santiago – Puerto Principe – Matanzas et la Havane*. Paris: E. Plon, 1876. Reprint. 1889, 325 pp., illus.
Includes Vodou in Cuba.

206   Pollak-Eltz, Angelina. "La santeria cubana." In *Cultos afroamericanos*. Caracas: Instituto de Investigaciones Historicas, Universidad Católica Andrés Bello, 1972, chap. 4, sec. 9, pp. 178-90.
      Spanish translation of *Afro-Americaanse godsdiensten . . . en culten* (see entry 76). Based on L. Cabrera (entries 122 and 127) and F. Ortiz (entry 196).

207   Ramos, Arthur. *As culturas negras no Novo Mundo*. Bibliotheca de Divulgaçao Scientifica, 12. Rio de Janeiro: Civilizaçao Brasileira, 1937, 399 pp., illus., maps. 2d ed. São Paulo, 1946, 373 pp. Spanish translation. *Las culturas negras en el Nuevo Mundo*. Mexico, D.F.: Fondo de Cultura Económica, 1943. German translation. *Die Negerkulturen in der Neuen Welt*. Erlangen and Zurich, 1947.
      Pp. 111-39 (Spanish translation), on Santería.

208   Rochon, Lise. "La sociedad agropecuaria 'Jesus Feliu': Un caso de cambio en el medio rural bajo un régimen socialista de transición." *Etnología y Folklore* (Havana) 4 (July-December 1967): 23-37.

209   Sánchez, Julio C. *El ñañiguismo: Un tema de sociología cubana*. Havana, 1951.

210   Sánchez, Julio C. *La religión de los orichas*. Hato Rey, Puerto Rico: Ramallo Bros. Print, 1978, 149 pp., bib.
      An anthropologist's survey.

211   Sandoval, Mercedes Cros. *La religión afrocubana*. Colección Libre. Madrid: Playor, 1975, 287 pp., illus.
      An anthropological study.

212   Sandoval, Mercedes C[ros]. "Santeria: Afrocuban concepts of disease and its treatment in Miami." *Journal of Operational Psychiatry* 8, no. 2 (1977): 52-63.

213   Sandoval, Mercedes C[ros]. "*Santeria* as a mental health care system: An historical overview." *Social Science and Medicine* (Oxford) 13B, no. 2 (1979): 137-51.
      Outline of religious aspects; historical overview of development in Cuba; Santería as developed in Miami and Dade County, with the changes found in this flexible system in a new context.

214   Simpson, George Eaton. *Black religions in the New World*. New York: Columbia University Press, 1978, 415 pp.
      Pp. 86-95 (plus notes, pp. 333-35), Santería and Abakuá in Cuba.

215 Tardieu, Jean-Pierre. "Religions et croyances populaires dans *Biografía de un cimarrón* de M. Barnet: De refus à tolérance." *Cahiers du Monde Hispanique et Luso-Brésilien* (Université de Toulouse), no. 43 (1984), pp. 43-67.

About the account of African-related religions by the Cuban, Miguel Barnet, based on information from a former slave, Esteban Montejo, a centenarian.

216 Thomas, Hugh. *Cuba, or The pursuit of freedom*. London: Eyre & Spottiswoode, 1971, 1696 pp, illus., map.

P. 39, Afro-Christian syncretism; pp. 517-22, 1124-26, Afro-Cuban religions, especially Santería (p. 520) and Abakuá (pp. 521-22).

217 Tyson, Ruell W., Jr. "Journalism and religion." In *The encyclopedia of religion*, edited by M. Eliade. Vol. 8. New York: Macmillan, 1987, pp. 120-27.

Pp. 124b-125b, the reporting of Santería in New York.

218 United States Government, Department of the Army. *Area handbook for Cuba*. Prepared by Foreign Area Studies, American University, Washington, D.C. Edited by H. I. Blutstein, et al. DA PAM 550-152. Washington, D.C.: U.S. Government Printing Office, 1971, 503 pp., map, illus.

Chap. 11 (pp. 177-97), religion; pp. 192-97, Afro-Cuban cults and magic–Santería (pp. 192-94), Abakuá or Naniguismo (pp. 194-95). Good surveys.

218a Valdéz-Cruz, Rosa. "The black man's contribution to Cuban culture." *Americas* (Washington, D.C.) 34, no. 2 (October 1977): 244-51.

Includes religion.

219 Wetli, C. V., and Martinez, R. "Forensic sciences aspects of Santeria, a religious cult of African origin." *Journal of Forensic Sciences* 26, no. 3 (1981): 506-14.

As observed in Florida, Dade County Medical Examiner's office–the anatomical, cultural, and legal aspects of Santería in relation to human skeletal parts.

220 Wright, Irene [Aloha]. *Cuba*. Chicago, 1907. Reprint. New York: Macmillan, 1910, 1912. Havana: H. E. Swann, 1910, xiv + 512 pp., illus.

P. 149, a traveler's description of a Yoruba-related *cabildo* of St. Joseph in Havana; extract in H. Thomas (entry 216), pp. 517-18.

221 Yai, Olabiyi Babalola. "Influence yoruba dans la poésie cubaine: Nicolas Guillen et la tradition poétique yoruba." In *Actes du 42è Congrès International des Américanistes*, Paris, 1976. Vol. 6. Paris: Société des Américanistes, Musée de l'Homme, 1979, pp. 641-58.

Dominican Republic

Over 80% of the approximately six million inhabitants of the Dominican Republic are black or mulatto, and their religion is predominantly Catholic and mostly of a "folk" form. Since the large island once known as Hispaniola is shared with Haiti and many Haitians find work in this republic, Vodou is widespread. Since Vodou is not centralized or organized, it takes many local forms, but available information is scant; however, see A. Jiménez Lambertus (entry 232), and C. E. Deivé (entry 229), who also examines the differences from Haitian Vodou. There is also little information available on the many small indigenous spiritist movements or independent and often Pentecostal churches. A. Pollak-Eltz (entry 238) provides case studies of two women mediums in the Vodou/spiritist tradition. Rastafari from Jamaica are also known to be present.

The most accessible surveys including the churches in general are in the two distinct editions of the United States Government, Department of the Army handbooks (entries 245-246); they refer to one of the indigenous cults, Liborista, with a pilgrimage shrine in Palma Sola village, San Juan province, as well as to Vodou from Haiti, and the Brotherhood of the Congo.

Otherwise our materials refer to an atypical small black Christian community derived from freed American Negro slaves who were sent as settlers in 1824-25. Those who became farmers at the old town of Samaná, because of its remoteness on a peninsula in the northeast, preserved their American Methodist faith and culture into the present century, with help from British Methodists; experienced a secession to set up an African Methodist Episcopal Church; and were eventually absorbed into the Iglesia Evangélica de Santo Domingo in 1931. M. E. Davis has written on these "Americanos" of Samaná, especially on their music (entries 224-226), and H. Hoetinck (entry 231) offers a detailed history of the earlier period, and of their later acculturation.

222   Aimard, Gustave. *Les vaudoux*. Paris: Amyot, 1867, 404 pp. 3d ed. Paris: E. Dentu, 1885, 404 pp.

Historical fiction. An adventure story inspired by the lurid accounts of S. B. St. John (entry 843); set in Santo Domingo in 1863-64, during the brief reannexation by Spain.

222a Bonetti, Mario. "Die soziale Bedeutung der 'religiosidad popular' in Dominicana." *Zeitschrift für Lateinamerika* (Vienna) 20 (1981): 55-72, photos.
    Includes the varieties of syncretist religion.

223 Davis, Martha Ellen. "Afro-Dominican religious brotherhoods: Structure, ritual, and music." Ph.D. dissertation (anthropology), University of Illinois (Urbana), 1976, 453 pp., illus., maps.
    Studies the African contribution denied by many elitist Dominican scholars, especially the long drums and the African music that gave identity to Afro-Dominican cofradías; these differ from pilgrimage brotherhoods and from fraternities related to fiestas for saints of personal devotion.

223a Davis, Martha Ellen. "Cantos de esclavos y libertos: Cancionero de 'Anthems' de Samaná." *Boletín del Museo del Hombre Dominicano* 18 (1983) 239-56.

224 Davis, Martha Ellen. "Himnos y anthems ('coros') de los 'Americanos' de Samaná: Contextos y estilos." *Boletín del Museo del Hombre Dominicano* (Santo Domingo), no. 16 [10] (1981), pp. 85-107.

225 Davis, Martha Ellen. "La cultura musical religiosa de los 'Americanos' de Samaná." *Boletín del Museo del Hombre Dominicano* (Santo Domingo), no. 14 [9] (1980), pp. 165-96.

226 Davis, Martha Ellen. "That old-time religion: Tradición y cambio en el enclave 'Americano' de Samaná." *Boletín del Museo del Hombre Dominicano* (Santo Domingo), no. 14 [9] (1980): 165-96.

227 Davis, Martha Ellen. *Voces del purgatorio: Estudio de la salve dominicana*. Santo Domingo: Museo del Hombre Dominicano, 1981.
    On Dominican Vodou as an authentic part of Dominican culture.

228 Deivé, Carlos Esteban. "Cromolitografias y correspondencias entre los loa santos católicos en el vodú dominicano." *Boletín del Museo del Hombre Dominicano* (Santo Domingo), no. 4 (1974).

229 Deivé, Carlos Esteban. *Vodú y magia en Santo Domingo*. Serie Investigaciones Antropológicas, 2. Santo Domingo: Museo del

Hombre Dominicano, Taller, 1975. 2d ed. 1979, 427 pp., illus., maps, bib. (pp. 403-15).

A comprehensive study of folk religion and its differences from Haitian Vodou; its socioeconomic setting; Vodou and magic in Dominican literature.

230   Herrera, Julio González. *La gloria llamó dos veces*. Santo Domingo: Cuidad Trujillo, 1944.

A novel set in the mid-nineteenth century with a background of Vodou.

231   Hoetinck, H. "Americans in Samaná." *Caribbean Studies* (Río Piedras, University of Puerto Rico) 2, no. 1 (1962): 3-22, bib. Spanish translation. "Los Americanos en Samaná." *Revista Eme-Eme* 2, no. 10 (1974): 3-36.

History of free Negroes from the U.S. who settled in the 1820s in Spanish Santo Domingo; they preserved their Wesleyan Methodism in their own churches, assisted from 1837 by British Methodists, until they joined the Iglesia Evangélica de Santo Domingo in 1931; pp. 14-15 (1962), a secession, connected with the African Methodist Church of U.S.A., in the early twentieth century – still existing, but acculturated.

232   Jiménez Lambertus, Abelardo. "Aspectos históricos y psicológicos del culto a los luases en República Dominicana." *Boletin del Museo del Hombre Dominicano* (Santo Domingo), no. 15 [9] (1980): 171-82.

Historical and psychological aspects of Vodou, including selection of *caballos*.

233   Martinez, L. "Un estudio preliminar acerca del movimiento de Palma Sola como movimiento mesiánico y social campesino." *Revista Dominicana de Antropologia e Historia*, nos. 19-20 [10] (1981): 83-209.

Rebirth of Liborio Mateo's movement (1910-22) in the early 1960s on the Haitian border.

233a   Ortiz, Dagoberto Tejeda, comp. *Cultura y folklore de Samaná*. Santo Domingo: Lotería Nacional, Depto. de Bienestar Social, 1984, 279 pp.

Eight articles, etc., on the black "Americans" of Samaná – republished from sources difficult to locate.

234   Parsons, Elsie Clews. "Spirituals from the 'American' colony at Samaná Bay, Santo Domingo." *Journal of American Folklore* 41 (1928): 525-28.

Based on one Sunday's visit in 1927 to the congregation at Villa Clara.

235   Patín, Enrique. "El luasismo en sus diferentes aspectos." *Le Manss*, 4, 7, 25, 29 November 1946.
        On Vodou.

236   Patín, Enrique. "El vodú y sus misterios." *Tabú* (Santo Domingo), no. 4 (1973-74).

237   Peguero, Rafael Bello. *Cofradía de Nuestra Señora del Carmen y Jesús Nazareno (1592-1872)*. Santo Domingo, 1974.

238   Pollak-Eltz, Angelina. "Ritos africanos en Santo Domingo." In *Cultos afroamericanos*. Caracas: Instituto de Investigaciones Historicas, Universidad Católica Andrés Bello, 1972, pp. 173-78.
        Spanish translation of Dutch original, rev. and enl. (see entry 76). Based on limited information, mainly from a middle-aged woman operating as an independent medium who had been initiated into Vodou and who also attends Catholic mass, etc., regularly, and more briefly from another lower-class medium.

239   Puig Ortiz, José Augusto. *Emigración de libertos norteamericanos a Puerto Plata en la primera mitad del siglo XIX: La Iglesia Metodista Wesleyana*. Santo Domingo: Editorial "Alfa y Omega," 1978.
        On what became a virtually independent church.

240   Rodriguez, Manuel Tomás. *Papá Legbá: La crónica del voudú o pacto con el diablo*. Cuidad Trujillo: Imprimerie Arte y Cine, 1945, 190 pp. 2d ed. Santo Domingo: A. Morales, 1962, 195 pp.

240a   Rosenberg, June C. *El Gagá: Religión y sociedad de un culto dominicano, un estudion comparativo*. Publicaciones de la Universidad, 272. Colección Histórica y Sociedad, 37. Santo Domingo: Universidad Autónoma de Santo Domingo, 1979, 233 pp., bib., illus.
        Detailed account of a syncretist religion, Gagá, its nineteenth-century origins and relation to Haitian and Dominican Vodou and to other cults in the Caribbean.

241   Rosenberg, June [C.]. "Influencias africanas en prácticas religiosas en República Dominicana." *Renovación* (Santo Domingo), nos. 234-35 (1973).

242   Stephens, Jean. "La emigración de Negros libertos norteamericanos à Haiti en 1824-25." *Revista Eme-Eme* 3, no. 14 (1974): 40-71.

The Wesleyan Methodists at Samaná Bay.

243 Tejada, Valentin. *Vodú*. Mexico, D.F.: Editorial "Proa," 1944, 205 pp.
   A novel treating Vodou as rural paganism; not factually reliable.

244 Tejada Ortiz, Juan Dagoberto. *Mana, monografía de un movimiento mesiánico abortado*. Santo Domingo: Editoria "Alfa y Omega," 1978 179 pp., illus., bib.
   Mana de Haina cult and Bibiana de la Rosa.

245 United States Government, Department of the Army. *Area handbook for the Dominican Republic*. Prepared by American University, Foreign Area Studies Division. Edited by T. D. Roberts, et al. DA PAM 550-54. Washington, D.C.: U.S. Government Printing Office, 1966, 446 pp, illus., map.
   Pp. 143-61, religion: pp. 154-56, popular Catholicism; pp. 160-61, Vodou among Haitian Negroes or their descendants, mostly practiced secretly, with an outline of Haitian Vodou; p. 160, rural cults – Liborista (centered on Palma Sola village, San Juan province) and Brotherhood of the Congo [Hermandad del Congo].

246 United States Government, Department of the Army. *Area handbook for the Dominican Republic*. Prepared by American University, Foreign Area Studies Division. Edited by T. E. Weil, et al. DA PAM 550-54. Washington, D.C.: U.S. Government Printing Office, 1973, 261 pp.
   P. 71, Liborista cult and Brotherhood of the Congo; pp. 71-72, Vodou; pp. 72-73, popular Catholicism.

French Guiana

In a population of about 70,000, over 50% are mulatto and about 8% are black, known also as Bush Negroes or Maroons, in three main groups–the Djuka, the Saramaka, and the Boni. The first two groups have been studied mainly where they are chiefly located, in neighboring Suriname, and items under French Guiana concern the Boni, the last tribe to form from the rebel and escaped African slaves, and numbering about a thousand.

The French geographer, J. Hurault, has provided several studies of the Boni (see entries 247-248). The High God, Masa Gadu, has no cult and is equated with the Christian God. Possession cults differ from those in Brazil and Haiti in not revealing direct African ancestry. Ancestral cults also flourish; on these and on the messianic signs also present, see P. Massajoli and M. Mattioni (entry 249). The only survey is in English, that of G. E. Simpson (entry 250).

247   Hurault, Jean. *Africains de Guyane: La vie matérielle et l'art des noirs réfugiés de Guyane*. The Hague: Mouton, 1970, 224 pp., drawings, photos, maps.
       Pp. 33-37, beliefs and agricultural rites; Supreme God (Nana), lesser divinity (Odoun), ancestor and possession cults; pp. 45-46, photo of a possessed woman.

248   Hurault, Jean. *Les noirs réfugiés bonis de la Guyane Française*. Dakar: IFAN, 1961, 362 pp., illus.
       Chap. 7 (pp. 191-265): beliefs–the Supreme God (Nana, or Masa Gadu) and lesser divinities, possession cults (their organization and rituals), ancestral cults, divination, dreams, magic, agricultural rites, relations with other communities, and future prospects. By a geographer.

249   Massajoli, Pierleone, and Mattioni, Mario. "I Palikur della Guyana Francese." Part 2. *L'Universo* (Florence), 1976, pp. 785-806, illus.

Pp. 791-98, 800-804, traditional ancestral cults underlying a superficial Christianity to produce messianic and nativistic developments among the Palikur.

250   Simpson, George Eaton. *Black religions in the New World*. New York: Columbia University Press, 1978, 415 pp.

Pp. 208-11, religion of the Boni or Bush Negroes, descendants of eighteenth-century rebellious slaves; based largely on J. Hurault.

Guyana

Of less than a million people, some 50% are of Asian Indian origin, 30% are mulatto, 11% are black, and under 5% are Amerindian.

For movements among the Amerindians, who are mainly in the interior, see A. Posern-Zielinski (entry 287) for an overview and E. Schaden (entry 290) for two early Carib millennial movements in the 1840s. The chief movement, known as the Hallelujah religion, has existed in varying strength among the Akawaio Indians in the area of Mt. Roraima for over a century. A good popular account is that of C. Henfrey (entry 281); for more anthropological accounts, see the works of A. J. Butt (entry 261), or A. Butt Colson, her married name (entry 265). Various Christian missions have made contact and reported. For the Pilgrim Holiness Mission (Unevangelized Fields Mission), see C. Bennett (entry 257); C. Cary-Elwes (entry 270) showed early understanding as a Jesuit visitor; the British Anglican society, United Society for the Propagation of the Gospel (U.S.P.G.), has had the closest and most sympathetic relations – see D. Arden and P. Rosheuvel (entry 254) for the history of relations, and J. Dorman (entry 275) for the forms of cooperation between the two faiths.

The chief movement among the coastal population, embracing blacks, mulattos, and some Indians, is the Jordonite (or Jordanite) Church, also known as the "White-Robed Army," which derives from an earlier body formed in the 1890s by a Grenadian and known as the West Evangelist Millennial Pilgrims. It syncretizes Judaic, Christian, Asian Indian, and folk Guyanese elements. J. Roback (entry 288) covers both stages of its history; only the contents outline of R. P. Mattai's dissertation of 1974 (entry 284) can be given here. See also J. Carew (entry 269), a first-hand account, and N. E. Cameron (entry 267).

Some black movements have entered from the U.S., such as the House of Israel – see G. Esper (entry 276). The People's Temple included some blacks when it arrived in 1974 to establish Jonestown, which ended in the mass suicide of 1978; the extensive literature on this movement belongs elsewhere. There are also some Rastafari from Jamaica, but these are presented at the end of the book under Particular Movements.

Movements of religious innovation or change in the Hindu segment of the population occur, and there are also many other unreported movements in all segments of the coastal population, such as the Triune Mystical Order of St. Michael, the "Spiritual University," the Institute of Yoga, and other Vodou, spiritist, and "spiritual science" movements.

251 Abrams, Ovid S. *Guyana Mete'Gee*. Georgetown, Guyana: The Author, 1970.
Includes description of religion among Afro-Americans, by a Guyanese.

252 Appun, Carl Ferdinand. *Unter den Tropen: Wanderungen durch Venezuela, am Orinico, durch British Guyana, und am Amazonenstrome, 1849-1868*. 2 vols. Jena, 1871.
Vol. 2, pp. 257-64, a "new religion," ca. 1846, near Mt. Roraima.

253 Appun, Carl Ferdinand. "Der Zauberer von Beckeranta." *Familienjournal*, 1869.
A "new religion," ca. 1846, near Mt. Roraima.

254 Arden, Donald, and Rosheuvel, Patrick. In "The Warden's letter." *Friends of USPG Newsletter* (London), Spring 1982, pp. 1-7.
Pp. 3-5, history and nature of and present relations with the Hallelujah religion – plans for training Hallelujah leaders.

255 African Society for Cultural Relations with Independent Africa. *The teachings of the Cultural Revolution*. Georgetown, Guyana: ASCRIA, 1968.
P. 2, a favorable account of the Jordonite movement, by a nationalist organization to which Elder Klein was a chaplain.

256 Beatty, Paul B., Jr. *A history of the Lutheran Church in Guyana*. South Pasadena, Calif.: William Carey Library (and by the author in Guyana), 1970, 135 pp., illus., maps.
Pp. 81-82, Obeah; pp. 105-6, Hallelujah religion (passing reference); p. 115, Black Muslims from the U.S.

257 Bennett, Chuck. "A nativistic movement in west central Guyana." N.p.: Missionary Aviation Fellowship, 19 December 1968, 5 pp. Mimeo.
A member of the Missionary Aviation Fellowship interviewing J. Sayers, a member of the Pilgrim Holiness Mission, on the Hallelujah religion.

258   Burnham, Forbes. "A crime no longer." *Daily Nation* (Georgetown), 3 November 1973.

News report of the Prime Minister's plan to legalize Obeah as a means of promoting Guyanese culture.

259   [Butt] Colson, Audrey [J.]. "The Akawaio shaman." In *Carib-speaking Indians: Culture, society, and language*, edited by E. B. Basso. Anthropological Papers, University of Arizona, 28. Tucson: University of Arizona Press, 1977, pp. 43-65, illus.

A revision of her article, "Réalité et idéal dans la pratique chamanique," *L'Homme* 2, no. 3 (1962): 5-52. P. 45, Hallelujah religion as currently compatible with shamanism. Includes appendix with notes on individual shamans working in 1951-52 and 1957.

260   Butt [Colson], Audrey J. "The birth of a religion." *Journal of the Royal Anthropological Institute* 90, no. 1 (1960): 66-106. Reprinted in *Gods and rituals*, edited by J. Middleton. Garden City, N.Y.: American Museum of Natural History, 1967, pp. 377-435. French translation in *Anthropologie religieuse: Les dieux et les rites, textes fondamentaux*, edited by J. Middleton. Paris: Larousse – Universités, pp. 181ff.

The Hallelujah religion among the Akawaio.

261   Butt [Colson], Audrey J. "The birth of a religion (the origins of 'Hallelujah,' the semi-Christian religion of the Carib-speaking peoples of the borderlands of British Guiana, Venezuela, and Brazil)." *Timehri* (Demerara, Royal Agricultural and Commercial Society of British Guiana), 4th ser., no. 38 (September 1959): 37-48; no. 39 (September 1960): 27-48.

262   Butt [Colson], Audrey J. "'The burning fountain, whence it came' (a system of beliefs of the Carib-speaking Akawaio of British Guyana)." *Social and Economic Studies* 2, no. 1 (1953): 102-16, bib. Reprinted in *Timehri* (Demerara, Royal Agricultural and Commercial Society of British Guiana), 4th ser., no. 33 [1] (October 1954): 27-40.

Pp. 105-16, Hallelujah religion; pp. 106-16, pre-Hallelujah beliefs. No rituals, worship, or required behavior revealing earlier religion, therefore were dependent on their own reports regarding their beliefs. The quotation is from P. B. Shelley, "Adonais."

263   [Butt] Colson, Audrey [J.]. "Comparative studies of the social structure of Guiana Indians and the problem of acculturation." In *The ongoing evolution of Latin American populations*, edited by F. M. Salzano. Springfield, Ill.: C. C. Thomas, 1971, pp. 61-126, maps, bib.

A comprehensive survey, especially useful on the problems of acculturation and on mission policies; pp. 87-98, millennial movements (including Waiyana sky-boat cult of 1963).

264   [Butt] Colson, Audrey [J.]. "Guyana." *Survival International*, no. 28 [4, no. 4] (Winter 1979): 30-31.
       Report of her address to a World Bank seminar in August 1979 on the threat to the Akawaio and their holy village from the Upper Mazaruni hydroelectric scheme.

265   [Butt] Colson, Audrey [J.]. "Hallelujah among the Patamona Indians." *Antropologica* (Caracas) 28 (1971): 25-58, folding map, bib.; English and Spanish summaries.
       How the Hallelujah religion was introduced to the Patamona, based on unpublished and other sources: (1) MSS of Jesuit missionary C. Cary-Elwes reporting visits between 1917 and 1921 (entry 270); (2) C. Henfrey (entry 281); (3) pp. 31-48, transcription of a tape recording made by Henfrey in 1962, in Creole English, by an Akawaio member of Hallelujah giving his own account from Bichiwung's "visit to England" to recent prophets; pp. 48-55, comment on syncretist processes leading to "Christian Shamans."

266   [Butt] Colson, Audrey [J.]. "Update on the Upper Mazaruni Project (Guyana): A report to Survival International by Professor George Primov." *Survival International Reviews* (London) 5, no. 1 (1980): 30-31.
       On the Akawaio and the hydroelectric project with several references to Makusi and the Hallelujah religion as evidence of Akawaio adaptability to change and contact.

267   Cameron, Norman E. "An interview with a Lord Elder." In *Thoughts on life and literature*. Georgetown, British Guiana: The Author, 1950.
       Pp. 135-41, contains account of E. N. Jordon's 1917 vision and the Jordonite movement, etc. By a Guyanese whose account comes from Jordon.

268   Carew, Jan. *Black Midas*. London: Longman's Green & Co., 1969.
       A novel by a Guyanese. Pp. 34-36, fictional description of West Evangelical Millennial Pilgrim Church. Written in 1959; later the author took this Jordonite movement more seriously; it contains "mistaken impressions" and "glowing fallacies" (J. Roback, entry 288, p. 254).

269   Carew, Jan. "The fusion of African and Amerindian folk myths." *Caribbean Quarterly* (Mona, Jamaica) 23, no. 1 (1977): 7-21.

Pp. 7-8, 20, 21, Prophets Wills and Jordan (*sic*, for Jordon) as perceived by the author as a child in Agricola village.

270 Cary-Elwes, Cuthbert. "Journal of the Rupunumi mission 1909-23." Edited by John Bridge, S.J. Jesuit Province Archives, London. Typescript.
A Jesuit missionary visits the Hallelujah people. Appendix by the editor (as a response to Audrey Butt). Copy in the Centre, Selly Oak Colleges.

271 Cole, Richard L. "Alleluia." *Network* (London, United Society for the Propagation of the Gospel), n.s. 8 (January 1973): 6.
Letter from an Anglican missionary, supporting the presence of a Christian element in the Hallelujah religion of the Akawaio in Guyana.

272 "Controversy arises over Voodoo legalization issue." *Jet* (Chicago) 45, no. 25 (1974): 46.
Guyana's prime minister considering legalization of Obeah. See entry 258.

273 Cott, Betty [Buhler]. *Jewels from green hell: Stories of the Davis Indians of British Guiana*. Washington, D.C.: Review and Herald Publishing Association, 1969, 256 pp., illus., map.
Includes an unexpected meeting by Seventh Day Adventist missionaries with an independent Christian-seeming movement, resembling, or part of, the Hallelujah religion.

274 Despres, Leo A. "Ethnicity and ethnic group relations in Guyana." In *The new ethnicity: Perspectives from ethnology. 1973 Proceedings, American Ethnological Society*. St. Paul, N.Y.: West Publishing Co., 1975, pp. 127-47.
Pp. 134-35, ASCRIA [African Society for Cultural Relations with Independent Africa] as a religiocultural revitalization movement.

275 Dorman, John. "Four people." *Network* (London, United Society for the Propagation of the Gospel), n.s. 5 (October 1972): 4, map, photo (see also p. 5).
On two missionaries and two Akawaio Indians encouraging extensive cooperation between the Hallelujah religion and the Anglican church.

276 Esper, George. "Focus turns now to the 'House of Israel.'" *Daily Nation* (Georgetown), 3 December 1978.

David Hill (Omari Oba; [Rabbi] Edward Emmanuel Washington) and his House of Israel (1975-), a Hebraist movement founded by this American black who had an earlier church in Cleveland.

277 Fiedler, Arkady. *Spotkalem szezésliwych Indian* [I have met happy Indians]. Warsaw, 1968.
Pp. 94-97, a Polish traveler in Guyana incorporates Appun's account of the pre-Hallelujah movement.

278 Guyana Government. *Report by the Amerindian Lands Commission, August 1969*. Georgetown: Government Printers, 1970, 236 pp.
Pp. 131, 135, 137, Hallelujah religion as existing in three Akawaio villages, and the missions involved.

279 Guyana Information Services. "The Jordanites." Georgetown: Guyana Information Services, 1968. Mimeo.

280 "Guyana's Alleluia Church 'official' ... joins Council." *USPG Network* (London), n.s., no. 5 (Spring 1977), p. 10.
Report of the Hallelujah religion affiliating to the Guyana Council of Churches, and of cooperation with the local Anglican USPG mission.

281 Henfrey, Colin. *Through Indian eyes*. New York: Holt, Rinehart & Winston, 1960, 285 pp. As *The gentle people: A journey among the Indian tribes of Guiana*. London: Hutchinson, 1964, 286 pp., illus., map.
Pp. 72-95, 108-20, 126-35, Hallelujah religion; pp. 270-75, sources and original versions of Hallelujah songs and prayer; pp. 272-75, millennial cults similar to Hallelujah.

282 Kirke, Henry. *Twenty-five years in British Guyana*. London: Sampson Low, Marston & Co., 1898. Reprint. Westport, Conn.: Negro Universities Press, 1970, 364 pp., map, illus.
Pp. 281-84, Obeah, and Christianity regarded as a higher form of Obeah.

283 [Klein, (Elder)]. *Peace! Peace! Peace! The evangelistic echo of the West Evangelical Millennial Pilgrim Church*. Georgetown, British Guiana: The Author, [1940s?].
The commonest account from 1882 among its members of the history of the Jordonite movement.

284 Mattai, Rudolph Parmanand. "The Jordonite Movement of the Republic of Guyana." B.A. dissertation in Church history (theology),

United Theological College of the West Indies/University of the West Indies (Kingston, Jamaica), 1974, 111 pp. Typescript.

A comprehensive study by a Guyanese of this Hebraist-type movement originating in the late nineteenth century.

285 Menezes, Mary Noel. *British policy towards the Amerindians in British Guiana, 1803-1873.* Oxford: Clarendon Press, 1977, 326 pp., maps.

Pp. 37-38, Hallelujah religion among the "Akawoi" [*sic*]; pp. 222-23, 234-37, 246-53, et passim, missions among the Akawaio, and in general.

286 Métraux, Alfred. *Religions et magies indiennes d'Amérique du Sud.* Édition posthume . . . par Simone Dreyfus. Bibliothèque des Sciences Humaines. Paris: Gallimard, 1967, 290 pp., illus., map, bib.

Plates 2-7 on the Hallelujah religion among the Akawaio: showing dances and prayers both indoors and out, and the fourth and fifth prophets or leaders (Kwiabong and Aibilibing) since Abel, who refounded the movement.

287 Posern-Zielinski, Aleksander. "Religious ferment among the Indians of British Guyana at the turn of the nineteenth century." *Estudios Latino-americanos* (Warsaw, Polska Akademia Nauk, Instytut Historii) 4 (1978): 97-125.

Origins of the Hallelujah religion in the mid-nineteenth century, in escapist movements seeking to transform interethnic relations and in mass movements for speedy Christianization.

288 Roback, Judith. "The White-Robed Army: An Afro-Guyanese religious movement." *Antropologica*, n.s. 16, no. 2 (1974): 233-68, bib.

A general account of the Jordonite movement from 1882 – history, personnel, beliefs and practices, organization, and ethnic relations (based on her Ph.D. dissertation, McGill University, 1973). It is viewed as a distinctive syncretism since it combines Judaic, Christian, African (as mediated by Guyanese folk culture), and East Indian (Hindu and Muslim) elements.

289 Roback, Judith. "The White-Robed Army: Cultural nationalism and a Guyanese religious movement in Guyana." Ph.D. dissertation (anthropology), McGill University, 1973, 312 pp.

290 Schaden, Egon. "La région des Guyanes." In *Histoire des religions*, edited by H. C. Puech. Encyclopédie de la Pléiade, vol. 3. Paris: Gallimard, 1976, pp. 1079-80.

Two Carib Indian millennial movements in 1845-46.

291   Skinner, Elliot Percival. "Ethnic interaction in a British Guiana rural community: A study in secondary acculturation and group dynamics." Ph.D. dissertation (anthropology), Columbia University, 1955, 303 pp.
         P. 234, call experience, preaching, and the death of E. N. Jordon, leader of the Jordonites; secondary acculturation is the passing on of European culture by Africans to more recent East Indian, Chinese, etc., immigrants.

292   Smith, Raymond T[homas]. *British Guiana.* London: Oxford University Press, 1962, 218 pp., map.
         P. 119, "Coptic" Church of Mar Lukos (back-to-Africa movement); pp. 119-20, brief outline of the Hallelujah religion, based on A. J. Butt; pp. 124-27, Obeah.

293   Survival International. "Appeal for help by the Akawaio of Guyana." *News from Survival International* (London), no. 12 (October 1975), pp. 16-17.
         The threat from the Upper Mazaruni hydroelectric project, which would submerge Amakokopai, the Akawaio sacred village and pilgrimage center of some 10,000 Indians.

294   Survival International. "The protest of the Akawaio of Guyana against the Upper Mazaruni hydro-electric project." *Survival International Review* (London) 1, no. 15 (1976): 13-14, illus.
         English translation from a tape recording of two Akawaio Indians appealing against the scheme, and basing their relation to their land on the Hallelujah religion.

295   Swan, Michael [Lancelot]. *British Guiana: The land of six peoples.* The Corona Library. London: H. M. Stationary Office, 1959, xv + 235 pp., illus., maps.
         Pp. 102-7, Obeah, and its resemblance to Myallism; a wake described.

296   Turner, Harold [Walter]. "Further comments on *Survival's* philosophy." *News From Survival International* (London), no. 8 (October 1974), p. 9.
         On pessimistic or optimistic interpretations of new religious movements, especially Hallelujah in Guyana and the Peyote cult.

297   United States Government, Department of the Army. *Area handbook for Guyana.* Foreign Area Studies Division, American University. Edited by G. B. Mitchell, et al., of Johnson Research Associates. DA Pam 550-82. Washington, D.C.: Government Printing Office, 1969, 378 pp.

Pp. 125, Jordonites, and Coptic Church; pp. 128-29, Obeah, and African values.

Haiti

Haiti (called St. Domingo during the French period) occupies the western side of the island known as Hispaniola by the Spanish. In a population of over five million, about 95% are black and 4% mulatto, and about four million would be regarded as Catholics, although most of these are also involved in the "national religion," a local religious system largely of African origin with Christian overlays, here called "Vodou" (the official spelling), as against other forms: Voodoo, Vodoun, Vodun, Vaudou, or Hoodoo. The term "Vodou" should be confined to the religion of Haiti and its specific dispersion. The literature is extensive and of varied quality, the more sensational being represented here by H. Austin (entry 317), J. H. Craige (entry 431), M. A. Owen (entry 761), and S. B. St. John (entry 843); D. Bellegarde (entry 342) offers a Haitian refutation.

There are many general surveys. See L. E. Barrett (entry 325), R. Bastide (entry 327), R. Bastien (entry 338), D. Bellegarde (entry 343), K. M. Brown (entry 387), H. B. Cave (a sympathetic missionary, entry 400), M. J. Herskovits (entries 543-544, rural only), S. Larose (entry 625), E. H. Loughlin (entry 645, popular), H. Marks (entry 669), A. Métraux (entry 725, English translation, the fullest survey in English on urban Vodou), C. Planson (entry 791, vivid), G. E. Simpson (entry 857), and E. P. Thoby-Marcelin (entry 898).

The Amerindians were virtually eliminated within the first century of Spanish occupation, but H. B. Alexander (entry 302) discusses their contribution. For Vodou's early history and its relation to the revolution of 1791 and independence in 1804 see R. E. Hood (entry 552), C. L. R. James (entry 572), M. S. Laguerre (entry 607), O. Mennesson-Rigaud (entry 694), and J. Price-Mars (entry 797).

For the African heritage see A. Aristide (entry 309), L. Denis (entry 445), L. G. Desmangles (entry 467), W. Harris (entry 539), O. Mennesson-Rigaud (entry 695), and A. Métraux (entry 704).

For the relation to Christianity see F. Bing (entry 351, on A. Métraux), L. G. Desmangles, A. E. Isaac (entry 569, on Protestantism), A. Métraux (entries 717 and 723, and especially the material in entry 725), C. Pressoir (entry 795, a negative view), and C. P. Romain (entry 828).

On the relation to Catholicism see J. Breda (entry 379), J. L. Comhaire (entry 409, schism from Rome), L. E. Elie (entry 501), F. Gayot (entry 526, pastoral relations), L. Hurbon (entry 555), M. S. Laguerre (entry 609), B. Mathews (entry 685, could be incorporated into Catholicism), V. Y. Mudimbe (entry 746, a review of L. Hurbon, entry 555), D. Nicholls (entries 753, pp. 224-28, and 756, pp. 412-13), and P. Robert (entry 822, a bishop's negative view).

For relation to politics see D. Bebel-Gisler, et al. (entry 340), S. Bonsal (entry 357), H. Courlander and R. Bastien (entry 430, the best account), L. Hurbon (entries 554 and 557), D. Nicholls (entries 754 and 756, detailed), and R. I. Rotberg (entry 835).

For professional psychological and psychiatric studies see J. C. Dorsainvil (entry 482), E. Douyon (entry 487), T. W. Dow (entry 490), F. Huxley (entry 561), A. Kiev (entries 591, as obstacle to progress, and 595, therapeutic value), and L. Mars, the son of J. Price-Mars (entry 680).

For relation to Pentecostalism, regarded as an alternative possession cult, see F. J. Conway (entry 418) and L. P. Gerlach (entry 527). For possession as such see E. Bourguignon (entry 369), M. K. Bowers (entry 374), and L. Mars (especially entries 672, 677, and 679).

On the relation of intellectuals to Vodou see R. Bastide (entries 328 and 330, on J. Price-Mars), R. Bastien (entry 336), E. Bourguignon (entry 363), and D. Nicholls (entry 753, good on individuals, grouped in "schools" – Pan-African, ethnological, literary, Negritude, and antisuperstition).

For the diffusion abroad see R. Bastide, et al. (entry 332, France) and M. Sobel (entry 877, Louisiana).

Healing and medicine: A. Métraux (entry 714). See also the psychological and psychiatric studies.

Art and symbols: K. M. Brown (entry 382), M. S. Laguerre (entry 618, see appendix), S. Rodman (entries 825-826), S. Williams (entry 929), and especially U. Stebich (entry 885) and R. F. Thompson (entry 904).

Dance: E. Bourguignon (entry 371), H. Courlander (entry 421), Y. Daniel (entry 435), M. Deren (entry 455, by a black American who became a "serviteur"), and P. de Félice (entry 505, in world context).

Music: H. Courlander (entries 422 and 427), C. Dumervé (entries 493-494), V. Juste-Constant (entry 581), F. Laguerre (entry 601), and M. S. Laguerre (entries (?) and 614).

The gods: E. P. Thoby-Marcelin (entry 898, a major study).

Reincarnation: R. Bastide (entry 331).

Zombies: E. Douyon (entry 484).

Houngans: R. Bastien (entry 337).

Development, relation to: C. Souffrant (entries 880, 882, and 884).

298 Acquaviva, Marcus Cláudio. *Vodu: Religão e magia negra no Haiti.* São Paulo: Ed. Nosso Brazil, 1976, 31 pp. 2d ed. 1977, 90 pp., illus.

299 Addin Hon, Torias. *Contes et proverbes créoles.* Port-au-Prince: Imprimerie du Collège Vertières, 1945, 50 pp.

300 Agosto [de Muñoz], Nélida. *El fenómeno de la posesión en la religión vudú.* Caribbean Monograph Series, 14. Río Piedras: Institute of Caribbean Studies, University of Puerto Rico, 1975, 119 pp.
　　　Spanish version of a Bachelor's thesis in English.

301 Alaux, Gustave d'. *L'Empereur Soulouque et son empire.* Paris: Michel Lévy, 1858.
　　　Vodou and its role in the politics of the Empire.

302 Alexander, H[artley] B[urr]. "Some elements of Arawakan, Carib, and other Indian cultures in Haitian Voudoun." In *Divine horsemen,* by M. Deren (entry 455) as Appendix B, pp. 271-86.
　　　Derived from *Mythology of all races,* edited by H. B. Alexander, vol. 11 (Marshall Jones Co., 1920). Reprint. New York: Cooper Square Publishers, 1964.

303 No entry.

304 Alexis, Jacques Stéphen. *Les arbres musiciens; roman.* Paris: Gallimard, 1957, 392 pp.
　　　A novel, showing the peasantry supported by Vodou, in the context of the Catholic "anti-superstition" campaign.

305 Alexis, Jacques Stéphen. *Compère Général Soleil.* Paris: Gallimard, 1955, 350 pp.
　　　A Marxist novelist showing the peasants' reliance on Vodou during crises.

306 Antoine, Jean Baptiste Delille. *Le catéchiste face au vaudou haïtien.* Port-au-Prince: La Phalange, 1969.

307 Argent, Jacques d'. *Voodoo.* For the Millions Series, FM4. Los Angeles: Sherbourne Press, 1970, 160 pp.

308 Aristide, Achille. "Les croyances des masses haïtiennes." *Optique* (Port-au-Prince), no. 32 (October 1956), pp. 59-64.

309 Aristide, Achille. *Problèmes haïtiens.* Port-au-Prince: Imprimerie de l'État, 1958, 123 pp., illus.

Pp. 11-42, "Introduction à l'étude comparée de l'ontologie bantoue et du paysan haïtien."

310 Ascensio, Michaelle. "Le langage du vaudou: Introduction à la linguistique vaudou." Thèse de Licence (ethnologie), Université d'État d'Haïti, 1975.

311 Aubourg, Michel. "La divination dans le vodou." *Bulletin du Bureau d'Ethnologie* (Port-au-Prince), 2d ser., no. 12 (1955), pp. 36-46.

312 Aubourg, Michel. "Survivances dahoméennes dans le folklore haïtien." *Bulletin du Bureau d'Ethnologie* (Port-au-Prince), 4th ser., no. 29 (November 1963), pp. 30-36.

313 Aubourg, Michel, and Viaud, Léonce. *Folklore ceremony of Petro rite (Voodoo cult)*, or *Voodoo cult: Ceremony of Petro rite*. Translated by E. Arthur. Port-au-Prince: Imprimerie du Commerce, 1945. Reprint. 1954, 8 pp.
   Description of Christmas Eve 1944 ceremony in Port-au-Prince, including sacrifice of a black pig to Pétro, "God of war."

314 Augustin, Joseph. "Tamboula ou le tambour conique au service du Dieu." *Le Précurseur* 9 (1965): 400-402.

315 Augustin, Joseph. "Le tambour entre à l'église." *Revue Orient* 81 [1960s]: 31.

316 Augustin, Rémy. *Cantiques pour la campagne anti-superstitieuse*. Port-au-Prince: Chéraquit, 1942.
   As part of the Catholic campaign against Vodou.

317 Austin, Henry. "Worship of the snake: Voodooism in Haiti today." *New England Magazine* (Boston) 47 (June 1912): 170-82.
   A sensational account of Vodou, as including human sacrifice. By an American traveler.

318 Bach, Marcus. *Strange altars*. Indianapolis: Bobbs-Merrill Co., 1952, 245 pp. Rev. ed. *Inside Voodoo*. New York: New American Library, Signet Books, 1973, 176 pp. French translation. *Vaudou: Religion, sorcellerie, magie*. Paris: Hachette, 1955, 264 pp.

319 Bach, Marcus. "Water and fire in Voodoo rituals." *Tomorrow* (New York) 1, no. 2 (1953): 97-103.

320 Bachmann, Kurt, et al. *Popular paintings from Haiti*. Exhibition Catalogue. London: Arts Council, 1968, illus.

321   Bajeux, Jean-Claude. *Pastoral consideration on Haitian Voodoo cults*. Colección Sondeos, 2. Cuernavaca: CIDOC (Morelos, Mexico), 1967.

321a   B[alandier], G[eorges]. Reviews of "Les grands dieux du vodou haïtien" (entry 898), by Philippe Thoby-Marcelin and *Mythologie vodou (rite arada)* (entry 665), by Milo Marcelin. *Haïti. Poètes noirs. Présence Africaine* 12 (1951): 237-38.

322   Baptiste, J.-B. "Cultural values. . . ." *Cultures* 5, no. 3 (1978).
       Pp. 103-4, 107-8, a brief, sympathetic Caribbean survey, with special reference to Vodou.

323   Barnes, J. "Voodoo terror." *Newsweek* (New York) 61 (13 May 1963): 54.

324   Barosy, Gisèle. "Un culte de famille au Belair: La Cour Blain, sa danse notable, ses chants, et ses coutumes." Thèse de License (ethnologie), Université d'État d'Haïti, 1964.

325   Barrett, Leonard E[mmanuel]. *Soul-force: African heritage in Afro-American religion*. C. Eric Lincoln Series on Black Religion. Garden City, N.Y.: Doubleday, Anchor, 1974, 251 pp.
       Pp. 99-111, Vodou in Haiti.

325a   Barron, Bernard. "Dateline Caribbean." *World Vision-Heartline* 10, no. 2 (1973): 21.

326   Bastide, Roger. "Adaptations des Haïtiens en pays étrangers: Le cas des Haïtiens en France." In *Culture et développement en Haïti*. Ottawa: Leméat, 1972, 203 pp.

327   Bastide, Roger. *Les Amériques noires*. Paris: Payot, 1967. English translation. *African civilizations in the New World*. London: C. Hurst, 1971, 232 pp.
       Pp. 110-11, 130-33, 138-51, 218-19, Vodou.

328   Bastide, Roger. "Le Dr. Price-Mars et le vodou." In *Témoignages sur la vie et l'oeuvre du Dr. Jean Price-Mars*, edited by E. C. Paul and J. Fouchard. Port-au-Prince: Imprimerie de l'État, 1956, pp. 196-202.

329   Bastide, Roger. "Introduction à l'étude de quelques complexes afro-brésiliens." *Bulletin du Bureau d'Ethnologie* (Port-au-Prince) 2 (July 1948): 41 pp.
       On Joachim Pedro – Negro messiah, saving the world by sacrificing an infant on Easter Day.

330   Bastide, Roger. "Price-Mars et le vaudou haïtien." *Présence Africaine*, no. 71 (3d quarter, 1969): 19-23.
    The scientific contribution of Price-Mars (died 1969) to the study of religion and folklore.

331   Bastide, Roger. "La théorie de la réincarnation chez les Afro-Américains." In *Réincarnation et vie mystique en Afrique noire*, edited by D. Zahan. Paris: Presses Universitaires de France, 1965, pp. 9-29.

332   Bastide, Roger; Morin, Françoise; and Raveau, François. *Les Haïtiens en France*. Paris: Mouton, 1974, 229 pp.
    Studies mostly students and middle-class Haitians in France, from a psychosociological viewpoint, using the questionnaire method. Includes dreams and religious attitudes and practices, both Catholic and Vodou, showing how Vodou has been transported to France.

333   Bastien, Rémy. "Anthologie de folklore haïtien." *Acta Anthropologica* (Mexico City) 1, no. 4 (1946).

334   Bastien, Rémy. *La familia rural haitiana: Valle de Marbial*. Mexico: Libra, 1959, 184 pp.
    The decadence of Marbial family life and the economy in 1948. Vodou, almost eradicated seven years before, had not recovered. Protestants as an active and economically progressive minority.

335   Bastien, Rémy. "Haití: Ayer y hoy." *Cuadernos Americanos* (Mexico City) 10, no. 3 (1951): 153-63, illus.
    Pp. 158-59, Vodou and the revolt of 1791; otherwise useful as background.

336   Bastien, Rémy. "The role of the intellectual in Haitian plural society." *Annals of the New York Academy of Sciences* 83 (1959): 843-49.
    Includes attitudes toward Vodou, changing during the twentieth century.

337   Bastien, Rémy. "Vodoun and politics in Haiti." In *Religion and politics in Haiti*, edited by H. Courlander and R. Bastien. Washington, D.C.: Institute for Cross-Cultural Research, 1966, pp. 39-68. Pp. 41-48, 56-68 reprinted in *Black society in the New World*, edited by R. Frucht. New York: Random House, 1971, pp. 290-307.
    A good summary on the *houngan* figure in Vodou.

338   Bastien, Rémy. "El vodu en Haiti." *Cuadernos Americanos* (Mexico City) 11, no. 1 (1952): 147-64. Reprinted separately, 1952, 24 pp.
    A sober survey of Vodou as a popular religion, with comment on the dysfunctional aspects of magic.

339   Beach, Harlan P. *A geography and atlas of Protestant missions*. Vol. 1, *Geography*. New York: Student Volunteer Movement, 1901, 571 pp.
P. 94, the common Protestant view of Vodou.

339a Beauvoir, Max. *The Vodun tradition in Haiti*. 1981.

340   Bebel-Gisler, Dany, and Hurbon, Laënnec. *Cultures et pouvoir dans la Caraïbe: Langue créole, vaudou, sectes religieuses en Guadeloupe et en Haïti*. Paris: IDOC-France, Librairie Éditions l'Harmattan, 1975, 145 pp.
Pp. 109-17, Vodou in Haiti – as folklore, as political resistance, and in relation to development; by a Guadeloupian and a Haitian Catholic priest.

341   Begot, Danielle. "Le vaudou dans la peinture." *Espace Créole* (Fort-de-France, Martinique) 4 (1979): 99-108.

342   Bellegarde, Dantès. *Haïti et ses problèmes*. Montreal: Édition Bernard Valiquette, 1941, 299 pp.
Pp. 81-100, "Vaudou et civilisation chrétienne."

343   Bellegarde, Dantès. *Haïti et son peuple*. Paris: Nouvelles Éditions Latines, 1953, 121 pp., illus.
Pp. 88-99, a general account of Vodou.

344   Bellegarde, Dantès. *Histoire du peuple haïtien (1492-1952)*. Collection du Cent-cinquantenaire de l'Indépendance d'Haïti. Port-au-Prince, 1953; Lausanne: Imprimerie Held, 1953, 365 pp.
"The best 'official' history in French, by a Haitian," but unsympathetic to the African heritage (e.g., see p. 59).

345   Bellegarde, Dantès. *La nation haïtienne*. Paris: J. de Gigord, 1938, 351 pp.
Chap. 24 (pp. 308-14), on religion. A "mulatto reaction" to the "negritude school" – see D. Nicholls (entry 753), pp. 177-78.

346   Benoit, Max. "Simbi, loa des eaux." *Bulletin du Bureau d'Ethnologie* (Port-au-Prince), 3d ser., nos. 20-22 (June-December 1959), pp. 12-22.

347   Bernard, Régnor C. "Hommage à Marie-Noël." *Bulletin du Bureau d'Ethnologie* (Port-au-Prince) 2 (March 1947): 27-29.

348   Betsch, Johnetta. "The possession pattern in traditional West African and New World Negro cultures." M.A. thesis, Northwestern University, [pre-1974].

349   Béyle, Rodrigo. "Razon de ser vudu haitiano." *Nueva Democracia*
       (New York) 42 (1962): 54-57.
          The raison d'être of Haitian Vodou.

350   Bijou, Legrand. "Aspects psychiatriques du vodou haïtien." In
       Psychiatrie simplifiée: Les maladies mentales et leur traitement. 2d ed.
       Port-au-Prince: Imprimerie de l'État, 1965. Selection reprinted in
       Études sur le vodou, edited by R. G. Montilus. Sondeos, 2.
       Cuernavaca, Mexico: Centro Inter-Cultural de Documentación, 1966,
       pp. 62-68. Reprinted from *Rond-Point* (Port-au-Prince), no. 8 (June-
       July 1963).

351   Bing, Fernande. "Entretiens avec Alfred Métraux." *L'Homme* (Paris)
       4, no. 2 (1964): 20-32.
          Includes comments on Vodou (e.g., pp. 28-32, that it is
       practiced by 90% of the population and is not opposed to
       Christianity).

352   Bissainthe, Gérard. "Catholicisme et indigénisme." *Des prêtres noirs
       s'interrogent*. 2d ed. Paris: Présence Africaine, 1957, pp. 111-36.

353   Bissainthe, Max, ed. *Dictionnaire de bibliographie haïtienne*.
       Washington, D.C.: Scarecrow, 1951, 1052 pp. *Supplement*. Vol. 1
       (covers 1950-70), with Appendix to the main work. Metuchen, N.J.:
       Scarecrow Press, 1973.
          The fullest bibliography of Haitian works.

354   Bitter, Maurice. *Haiti*. Collections Microcosme: Petite Planète, 41.
       Paris: Éditions du Seuil, 1970, 190 pp., illus.
          Pp. 131-32, 139-67, "Le vaudou"; pp. 164-66, Vodou songs in
       French and Creole.

355   Bitter, Maurice. "J'ai participé aux cérémonies secrètes du vaudou."
       Sciences et Voyages (Paris), 7 August 1956, pp. 7-9.

356   Bonneau, Aléxandre. *Haïti: Ses progrès et son avenir*. Paris, 1862.
       Extract in *The Haitian people*, by J. G. Leyburn. New Haven, Conn.:
       Yale University Press, 1966, p. 141.
          Pp. 24-26, a careful criticism of Vodou.

357   Bonsal, Stephen. *The American Mediterranean*. New York: Moffat,
       Yard & Co., 1912. Reprint. London: Hurst & Blackett, 1913, 488 pp.,
       illus., map.
          Pp. 58-60, role of Vodou priests in state affairs; chaps. 5-6 (pp.
       87-120), the "Truth about Voodoo." By an American diplomat.

358   Boucard, Arnoux. "Signification symbolique de la cérémonie du bouler zinc dans le culte vodou." Thèse de Licence (ethnologie), Université d'État d'Haïti, 1969.

359   Boucard, Violette. *Le vodou et ses antécédents*. Port-au-Prince: Les Éditions Fardin, 1979.
        A Catholic girl's pilgrimage through Adventism, Protestantism, and Rosicrucianism to become a Vodou priestess; her somewhat occult theology.

359a   Boulton, Laura. "Le culte vaudou." In *Encyclopédies des musiques sacrées*. Vol. 1. Paris: Éditions Labergerie, 1968, pp. 111-16.

360   Bourguignon, Erika [Eichhorn]. "Class structure and acculturation in Haiti." *Ohio Journal of Science* 52, no. 6 (1952): 317-20.

361   Bourguignon, Erika [Eichhorn]. "Dreams and dream interpretation in Haiti." *American Anthropologist* 56, no. 2:1 (1954): 262-68.
        On the role of dreams in Vodou.

362   Bourguignon, Erika [Eichhorn]. "George E. Simpson's ideas about ultimate reality and meaning in Haitian vodun." *Ultimate Reality and Meaning* (Toronto) 3 (1980): 233-38.

363   Bourguignon, Erika [Eichhorn]. "Haïti et l'ambivalence socialisée: Une reconsidération." *Journal de la Société des Américanistes* (Paris) 58 (1969): 173-205, bib.
        Vodou and spirit worship, African elements, affect the worldview of the elite as well as of the lower classes.

364   Bourguignon, Erika [Eichhorn]. "Illness and possession: Elements for a comparative study." *Newsletter Review* (Montreal, R. M. Bucke Memorial Society) 7, nos. 1-2 (1974): 37-47, bib.
        With special reference to Vodou and Zar in Ethiopia.

365   Bourguignon, Erika [Eichhorn]. "The persistence of folk belief: Notes on cannibalism and zombis in Haiti." *Journal of American Folklore*, no. 283 [72] (1959): 36-46.

366   Bourguignon, Erika [Eichhorn]. *Possession*. San Francisco: Chandler & Sharp Publishers, 1976, 78 pp.
        See chapter on Haiti.

367   Bourguignon, Erika [Eichhorn]. "Religion and justice in Haitian Vodoun." *Phylon* 46, no. 4 (1985): 292-95.

Justice amounts to maintenance of a harsh social order through adherence to the hierarchical and reciprocal relationships between humans, and between humans and the spirits, whose supernatural sanctions are expressed through rewards and punishments.

368 Bourguignon, Erika [Eichhorn]. "Ritual and myth in Haitian *Vodoun*." In *African religious groups and beliefs*. Meerut, India: Archana Publications, for the Folklore Institute (Berkeley, Calif.), 1982, pp. 290-304.

369 Bourguignon, Erika [Eichhorn]. "The self, the behavioral environment, and the theory of spirit possession." In *Context and meaning in cultural anthropology*, edited by M. E. Spiro. New York: Free Press; London: Collier-Macmillan, 1965, pp. 39-60, bib. Reprinted in *Transcultural Psychiatric Research Review* (Montreal) 3 (1966): 43-45.
    "Dissociation as institutionalized in the Vodou cult with its attendant theory of spirit possession, from the perspective of the self and its behavioral environment"; pp. 45-55 especially on Vodou.

370 Bourguignon, Erika [Eichhorn]. "Syncretism and ambivalence in Haiti: An ethnohistoric study." Ph.D. dissertation, Northwestern University, 1951. See *Summaries of doctoral dissertations ... of Northwestern University* 19 (January 1952): 209-12.
    Five processes of acculturation distinguished, with reinterpretation and syncretism dominant in Vodou religion, which reveals great similarity to its African origins.

371 Bourguignon, Erika [Eichhorn]. "Trance dance." *Dance Perspectives* (New York), no. 35 (Autumn 1968).
    Pp. 27-37, dance in Vodou; pp. 37-41, the Caribbean and Brazil; pp. 46-51, southeast Asia.

371a Bourguignon, Erika [Eichorn]. "Voodoo." In *Colliers encyclopedia*, edited by W. D. Halsey. New York: Macmillan, 1979, pp. 200-201.

372 Bourguignon, Erika [Eichhorn]. "Voodoo." In *The encyclopedia Americana*. Vol. 28. New York: Americana, 1975, pp. 233-34, illus.
    A good outline.

373 Bourguignon, Erika [Eichhorn], and Pettay, Louanna. "Spirit possession, trance, and cross-cultural research." In *Proceedings, American Ethnological Society, annual spring meeting, 1964: Symposium on community studies in anthropology*. Seattle, 1964, pp. 38-49.
    Haiti and other Caribbean evidence.

374   Bowers, Margaretta K. "Hypnotic aspects of Haitian Voodoo." *International Journal of Clinical and Experimental Hypnosis* (Baltimore, Md.) 9, no. 4 (1961): 269-82.

On possession and trance states, as understood in terms of hypnosis and hypnotically induced secondary personalities; greater understanding here could help in retaining the valuable aspects and reducing the harmful aspects.

375   Bowman, Laura, and Leroy, Antoine. *The voice of Haiti: Original ceremonial songs, Voodoo chants, drum beats*. New York: Clarence Williams Music Publishing Co., 1938, 41 pp.

376   Brand, Roger. "Dynamisme des symboles dans les cultes vodun." Thèse de 3e cycle, Université René Descartes (Paris), 1972, 475 pp.

377   Brand, Roger. "Initiation et consécration de deux vodun dans les cultes vodu." *Journal de la Société des Africanistes* (Paris) 44, no. 1 (1974): 71-90, bib.

378   Brand, Willem. *Impressions of Haiti*. Institute of Social Studies: Series Minor, vol. 8. The Hague: Mouton, 1965, 77 pp., maps.

379   Breda, Jeremie [pseud.]. "Life in Haiti: Voodoo and the Church." *Commonweal* (New York) 78 (24 May 1963): 241-44.

The recent expulsions of Catholic clergy set in the context of the involvement of both Catholicism and Vodou in Haitian life, and of the interdependence of these two religions: an illuminating article.

380   Brewster, Paul G. "Hantu and loa: Some similarities between Malay popular religion and Haitian Vodun." *Archivo per l'Antropologia e la Etnologia* 87 (1957): 95-108.

381   Brouard, Carl. "Paganisme et vaudou." *Les Griots* (Port-au-Prince), January-March 1940, pp. 617-19.

A Haitian poet and intellectual who rejected Christianity and embraced Vodou.

382   Brown, Karen McCarthy. "The center and the edges: God and person in Haitian society." *Journal of the Interdenominational Theological Center* (Atlanta) 7 (Fall 1979): 22-39.

383   Brown, Karen McCarthy. "Olina and Erzulie: A woman and a goddess in Haitian Vodou." *Anima* (Chambersburg, Pa.) 5 (Spring 1979): 110-16, illus.

Olina, a "marginal townswoman," and her relations to the two contrasting goddesses – Maitresse Erzulie (sensuous lover of all) and Erzulie Dantor (protector of the chosen few).

384 Brown, Karen McCarthy. "'Plenty confidence in myself': The initiation of a white woman scholar into Haitian Vodou." *Journal of Feminist Studies in Religion* 3, no. 1 (1987): 67-76.

Reports from personal experience of the resources of spirituality for Western women outside the Western tradition.

385 Brown, Karen McCarthy. "Structure and visual imagery: A preliminary analysis of the *Vever* of Haitian Vodun." *Synergos* 1 (Fall 1972): 9-16.

386 Brown, Karen McCarthy. "The *'veve'* of Haitian Vodou: A structural analysis of visual imagery." Ph.D. dissertation (religion), Temple University, 1975, 427 pp., illus. (pp. 390-418).

"Vèvè" are Vodou symbolic drawings.

387 Brown, Karen McCarthy. "Voodoo." In *The encyclopedia of religion*, edited by M. Eliade. Vol. 15. New York: Macmillan, 1987, pp. 296-301.

388 Brown, Oral Carl, Jr. "Haitian Vodou in relation to negritude and Christianity: A study in acculturation and applied anthropology." Ph.D. dissertation (anthropology), Indiana University, 1972, 366 pp.

Vodou in the modern nativist movement for a Haitian identity, supported by the "new generation" of intellectuals since F. Duvalier, represents a throwback to tribalism and absorption of Catholicism by Vodou rather than vice versa. The Christian mission leads to internationalism and rationality.

389 Buch, Hans Christoph. *Die Hochzeit von Port-au-Prince*. Frankfurt am Main: Suhrkamp Verlag, 1984.

A novel. Pp. 235-42, account of a Mormon missionary's attempt to convert Vodou members at one of their annual festivals in 1930.

390 Butler, John F. *Christianity in Asia and America after A.D. 1500*. Iconography of Religions, 24:13. Leiden: E. J. Brill, 1979, 45 pp. + 48 plates.

Pp. 26-27, briefly on Vodou; plate 53:2, a Vodou painting.

391 Cabon, Adolphe. *Histoire d'Haïti*. 4 vols. Port-au-Prince: Édition de la Petite Revue, 192?.

By a French priest; lectures at the Petit Séminaire Collège Saint-Martial.

391a   Cabon, Adolphe. *Notes sur la histoire religieux d'Haiti: De la révolution au Concordat (1789-1860)*. Port-au-Prince: Petit Séminaire Collège Saint-Martial, 1933.

392   *Campagne antisuperstitieuse*. Le Cap: Imprimerie du Progrès Almonacy, 1941.
      Documentation at the time of the major Catholic offensive against Vodou, ca. 1939-42.

393   Campbell, Michael D. "Spirit possession: Dimensions for a typology and an example from Haiti." M.A. thesis (anthropology), University of Washington, 1968.

393a   Cannon, W. B. "Voodoo death." *Psychosomatic Medicine* (Washington, D.C.) 19 (1957): 182-90.

394   Caplain, Jules. *La France en Haïti: Catholicisme, vaudoux, maçonnerie*. Paris: Imprimerie de F. Leve, 1903. Reprint. 1905, 81 pp.

394a   Capo, José María. "En las Antillas: Haiti: La vida social de los espiritus." *Alma Latina* (San Juan, P.R.) 1, no. 325 (1961): 16-17.

395   Carpentier, Alejo. *El reino de este mundo*. Mexico, D.F.: IberoAmericano de Distribuciones, 1949, 198 pp. Many further printings in different countries. English translation. *The kingdom of this world*. New York: A. A. Knopf, 1957, 150 pp. Reprint. London: V. Gollancz, 1967. Reprint. Hammondsworth: Penguin Books, 1975, 113 pp. Italian translation. *Il regno di questa terra: Romanzo*. Milan: Longanesi, 1969, 150 pp.
      A distinguished novel on slavery in Haiti under the French, and of oppression under the black rule of King Henri Christophe and the mulatto rule of J. P. Boyer. The Vodou religious background is not detailed.

396   Casséus, Maurice A. *Mambo*. Port-au-Prince: Imprimerie de Séminaire Adventiste, 1949, 120 pp.
      Stories for school children.

397   Cassidy, Jack, and Wakin, Edward. "Saturday night Voodoo: Sunday morning Mass." *United States Catholic Historical Magazine* (New York) 43, no. 7 (1978): 35-38.
      Among Haitian immigrants in the U.S.

398   Cave, Hugh B[arnett]. *Black sun*. Garden City, N.Y.: Doubleday, 1960. Reprint. London: A. Redman, 1961, 355 pp.
      A novel.

399   Cave, Hugh B[arnett]. *The cross and the drum*. Garden City, N.Y.: Doubleday, 1959. Reprint. London: T. Werner Lawrie, 1960, 383 pp. Reprint. London: Foursquare Books, 1961, 256 pp.

Fiction, in a "composite Caribbean setting": a sympathetic account of Vodou, with a liberal Episcopalian missionary who seeks to establish a positive relationship with its *houngan* or priest.

400   Cave, Hugh B[arnett]. *Haiti: Highroad to adventure*. New York: Henry Holt & Co., 1952, 306 pp., illus.

Written after long residence in Haiti; includes a very readable study of Vodou.

401   "Un centenaire: Jean Price-Mars, 1876-1976." *Conjonction* (Port-au-Prince), no. 132 (December 1976-January 1977), pp. 4-40, bib., illus.

On a noted scholar–a partial bibliography, excerpts, and tributes.

402   Chevannes, Barry. Review of *Voodoo heritage*, by M. S. Laguerre (entry 618). *Caribbean Quarterly* (Mona, Jamaica) 27, no. 4 (1981): 49-50.

403   Chezi, Gert. *Voodoo-Afrikas, geheime macht*. Wörgl, Austria: Perlinger Verlag, 1979. English translation. *Voodoo: Africa's secret power*. Cape Town: C. Struik Publishers, 1979, 275 pp., illus. (black-and-white and in color).

Pp. 213-24, 229-32 (English translation), descriptions of ceremonies and superb photographs; claims that forms of Caribbean Vodou have influenced the primal religions of West Africa.

404   Cinéas, Jean-Baptiste. *Le drame de la terre*. Bibliothèque Haïtienne–Collection Capoise. Cap-Haïtien: Imprimerie de Séminaire Adventiste, 1933, 171 pp.

A novel of Haitian life.

404a   Clark, Vèvè A. "Fieldhands to stagehands in Haiti: The measure of tradition in Haitian popular theatre." Ph.D. dissertation (Latin American literature), University of California, Berkeley, 585 pp.

Discovers natural links between popular theatre and Vodou, as one of three components of folk theatre–besides work and carnival.

405   Clerisme, Enel. "Le symbolisme des couleurs dans le culte vaudou et son emprunt au catholicisme." In *Cahier de folklore et des traditions orales d'Haïti*, edited by M. Benoit. Port-au-Prince: Imprimerie des Antilles, 1980, pp. 115-27.

A student research paper of 1969.

406   Coachy, Lucien Georges. *Culto vodu y brujeria en Haiti*. Mexico: Ed. Diana, 1982, 143 pp.

406a   Coen, Edwig. *Science, religion et superstition*. Port-au-Prince: Typographie Alexis, 1967.

407   Cohen, David. *Voodoo, devils, and the new invisible world*. New York: Dodd Mead, 1972, xii + 204 pp., illus.
       Includes "Voodooism" along with witchcraft and demonology.

408   Coll Gilabert, Jordi. "El vudú: Religión del pueblo Haitiano." *Misiones Etranjers* 90 (1985): 455-60.
       History, evolution, and religious significance.

409   Comhaire, Jean L. "The Haitian schism: 1804-1860." *Anthropological Quarterly* 29, no. 1 (1956): 1-10.
       On the schism with the Roman Catholic Church, and Protestant missions during the period; useful background.

410   Comhaire, Jean L. "Religious trends in African and Afro-American urban societies." *Anthropological Quarterly* (Washington, D.C.), n.s. 1, no. 4 (1953): 95-108.
       Pp. 104-8, on Vodou in Haiti as of African origin.

410a   Comhaire-Sylvain, Suzanne. "À propos du vocabulaire des croyances paysans." *La voix des femmes* (Port-au-Prince), February-March 1938, pp. 6-7; June 1938, pp. 8-9.
       Also published separately. Port-au-Prince: 1938, 13 pp.

411   Comhaire-Sylvain, Suzanne. "La chanson haïtienne." *Haïti, poètes noirs*. *Présence Africaine* (Paris) 12 (1951): 61-87.
       Pp. 61-70, songs and musical instruments used in Vodou.

412   Comhaire-Sylvain, Suzanne. "Voodoo." *New Catholic encyclopedia*. Vol. 14. New York: McGraw Hill Co., 1966, pp. 752-53.

413   Comhaire-Sylvain, Suzanne, and Comhaire-Sylvain, Jean [L.]. "Survivances africaines dans le vocabulaire religieux d'Haïti" [African survivals in the religious vocabulary of Haiti]. *Études Dahoméennes* (Porto Novo, Dahomey) 14 (1955): 5-20.
       A list of terms, with their meanings in Haiti and their African tribal linguistic origins.

414   Comhaire-Sylvain, S[uzanne], and Comhaire-Sylvain, J[ean L.]. "Urban stratification in Haiti." *Social and Economic Studies* 8, no. 2 (1959): 179-89, map.

P. 183, the numbers of Vodou shrines in four districts of Port-au-Prince – total, 110.

415 Conus, Georges. "Le créole, une langue pour l'Église en Haïti." *Neue Zeitschrift für Missionswissenschaft* 43, no. 2 (1987): 98-106.

416 Conus, Georges. Review of *Dieu dans le vodou haïtien*, by Laënnec Hurbon (entry 555). *Neue Zeitschrift für Missionswissenschaft* 32, no. 3 (1976): 229-30.

417 Conway, Frederick J[ames]. "Pentecostalism, as a competitive form of spirit possession in Haiti." In *Anthropology 3250. Regional studies: The Caribbean*, edited by F. Manning. St. John's, Newfoundland: Division of University Relations and Development, Memorial University of Newfoundland, 1978, pp. 87-93.

418 Conway, Frederick J[ames]. "Pentecostalism in Haiti: Healing and hierarchy." In *Perspectives on Pentecostalism: Case studies from the Caribbean and Latin America*, edited by S. D. Glazier. Washington, D.C.: University Press of America, 1980, pp. 7-26.

419 Conway, Frederick J[ames]. "Pentecostalism in the context of Haitian religion and health practice." Ph.D. dissertation (cultural anthropology), American University, 1978, 292 pp.
      Pentecostalism is distinct from Vodou (whereas Catholicism merges with it), is adopted by conversion, often when ill, yet emphasizes similar forms – trance, possession, and healing.

420 Cordon, Wolfgang. *Tod auf Haiti*. Düsseldorf and Cologne, 1961.
      Includes Vodou (e.g., pp. 79ff. on the *houngan's* ceremonies).

421 Courlander, Harold. "Dance and dance-drama in Haiti." In *The function of the dance in human society*. New York: Boas School, 1944, pp. 41-53.

422 Courlander, Harold. *The drum and the hoe: Life and lore of the Haitian people*. Berkeley, Calif.: University of California Press, 1960, 371 pp., illus. Reprint. California Library Reprint Series, 31. 1973 and 1981.
      An expansion of *Haiti singing* (entry 425).

423 Courlander, Harold. "Gods of Haiti." *Tomorrow* (New York) 3, no. 1 (1954): 53-60.
      A compact survey.

424   Courlander, Harold. "Gods of the Haitian mountains." *Journal of Negro History* 29, no. 3 (1944): 339-72.
       A general survey; pp. 351-72, annotated list of names of gods.

425   Courlander, Harold. *Haiti singing.* Chapel Hill: University of North Carolina Press, 1939, 273 pp., illus. Reprint. New York: Cooper Square Publications, 1973.
       See *The drum and the hoe.* ... (entry 422) for expanded discussion.

426   Courlander, Harold. "The loa of Haiti: New World African deities." *Miscelanea de Estudios Dedicados a Fernando Ortiz ... por sus discipulos, colegas y amigos.* Vol. 1. Havana, 1955, pp. 421-43.
       A very comprehensive list of the Vodou pantheon; syncretism between *loa*s and Christian saints.

427   Courlander, Harold. "Musical instruments of Haiti." *Musical Quarterly* (New York) 37, no. 3 (1941): 371-83.
       As used in Vodou.

428   Courlander, Harold. *Uncle Bouqui of Haiti.* New York: William Morrow & Co., 1942.

429   Courlander, Harold, ed. *Creole songs of Haiti.* New York: Ethnic Folkways Library.
       Recorded music: 13 examples of drumming, and the playing of other instruments.

430   Courlander, Harold, and Bastien, Rémy. *Religion and politics in Haiti.* ICR studies, 1. Washington, D.C.: Institute for Cross-Cultural Research, 1966. Reprint. 1970, xvi + 81 pp., illus., maps, bib.
       Essay 1 (pp. 1-26), Vodou in Haitian culture, by Courlander; essay 2 (pp. 39-68), Vodou and politics in Haiti, by Bastien; pp. 41-48, 56-68 reprinted in *Black society in the New World,* edited by R. Frucht (New York: Random House, 1971), pp. 290-307.

431   Craige, John Houston. *Black Baghdad: The Arabian nights. Adventures of a Marine captain in Hayti.* London: Stanley Paul & Co., 1931. 2d ed. New York: Minton, Balch & Co., 1933, 276 pp.
       By an officer of the U.S. Marines during their occupation of Haiti, who naively accepted horror stories about Vodou.

432   *La Croix.*
       Journal founded by Mgr. Kersuzan in 1896, which served for a period in his opposition to Vodou. See entry 588.

433   Dalencour, François. *Précis méthodique d'histoire d'Haïti*. Port-au-Prince, 1935.
       A mulatto who criticizes Vodou strongly; see p. 51.

434   Daniel, Christophe-Jocelyn. "La médecine traditionelle en Haïti." Ph.D. dissertation, University of Bordeaux, 1977.
       Includes the relation of Vodou to healing.

435   Daniel, Yvonne. "The potency of dance: A Haitian examination." *Black Scholar* (Sausalito, Calif., Black World Foundation) 11, no. 8 (1980): 61-73, illus., bib.
       The place of dance in Haitian society, especially the Vodou Pétro dance.

436   Danneskjold-Samsoe, Axel. "Der Schlangenkult in Oberguinea and Haiti." Inaugural dissertation, University of Leipzig, 1907.

436a   D'Argent, Jacques. *Voodoo*. For the Millions Series, FM 41. Los Angeles: Sherbourne Press, 1970, 160 pp.

436b   Davis, E. Wade. "The ethnobiology of the Haitian zombi." *Journal of Ethnopharmacology* (Lausanne) 9, no. 1 (November 1983): 85-104, bib. illus.
       Suggests a pharmacological basis in tetrodotoxins derived from puffer fish, and describes the place of zombies in Vodou.

436c   Davis, E. Wade. "The ethnobiology of the Haitian zombie: On the pharmacology of black magic." *Caribbean Review* (Miami) 12, no. 3 (Summer 1983): 18-21, 47.
       Zombie poisons in various parts of the world, in relation to Vodou theology.

437   Davis, [E.] Wade. *Passage of darkness: The ethnobiology of the Haitian zombie*. Chapel Hill: University of North Carolina Press, 1988, 344 pp.
       Includes scientific information about the possibility of "zombies," based on the drug tetrodotoxin.

438   Davis, [E.] Wade. *The serpent and the rainbow: A Harvard scientist's astonishing journey into the secret society of Haitian voodoo, zombies, and magic*. New York: Simon & Schuster, 1985. Reprint. London: Collins, 1986, 299 pp.

439   Davis, Harold Palmer. "Sunlight on Voodoo mysteries." *Travel* (Floral Park, N.Y.) 73 (May 1939): 34-37.

440   Dean, David McEwan. *Defender of the race: James Theodore Holly, black nationalist bishop.* New Centre, Mass.: Lambeth Press, 1978, 150 pp., map, bib..

Founder of the Église Orthodoxe Apostolique Haïtienne, an independent Anglican church, in 1864, after leading a black colonizing group to Haiti from the U.S. Pp. 83, 84, 92, references to Spencer St. John's and Holly's attitudes to Vodou.

440a De Carlo, Louis Joseph. "Ignorance, poverty, and Vodun: The life of the Haitian peasant presented in various selected novels." M.A. thesis, University of Miami, 1959, 73 pp.

441   Delbeau, Jean-Claude. "La médecine populaire en Haïti." Ph.D. dissertation, University of Bordeaux, 1969.

Includes the relation of Vodou to healing.

442   Denis, Lorimer. "Baptême de feu dans le culte vodouesque." *Bulletin du Bureau d'Ethnologie* (Port-au-Prince) 2 (March 1947): 1-4.

443   Denis, Lorimer. "La cimitière." *Bulletin du Bureau d'Ethnologie* (Port-au-Prince), 2d ser., no. 13 (1956), pp. 1-16.

On the cult of the dead.

444   Denis, Lorimer. "Mariage mystique dans le vodou suivant les notes inédites de L. Denis." *Bulletin du Bureau d'Ethnologie* (Port-au-Prince), 3d. ser., no. 14 (1958), pp. 19-26.

445   Denis, Lorimer. "Origine des loas." In *Les Afro-Américains.* Mémoires de l'Institut Français de l'Afrique Noire, no. 27. Dakar: IFAN, 1952 [1953 on cover], pp. 195-99.

A Vodou leader's verbatim account of the migration of Haitian divinities from Africa, given by Ogoun Badagris (god of fire) through priestess Gracieuse Joachim.

446   Denis, Lorimer. "La religion populaire." *Bulletin du Bureau d'Ethnologie* (Port-au-Prince) 1 (December 1946): 16-30.

447   Denis, Lorimer. "Rituel observé en vue de la protection du nouveau-né contre les maléfices des sorciers, le mauvais oiel ou maldiocre, les mauvais-airs ou loups-garous." *Bulletin du Bureau d'Ethnologie* (Port-au-Prince), 2d ser., no. 2 (March 1947), pp. 5-6.

448   Denis, Lorimer, and Duvalier, François. "Une cérémonie d'initiation: Le 'laver-tête' dans le culte vodouesque." *Les Griots* (Port-au-Prince) 2-3, nos. 2-3 (October-December 1939, January-March 1940): 657-69.

By a "mystic" intellectual, collaborating with F. Duvalier (later president, "Papa Doc") as his mentor and assistant director of the new Bureau of Ethnology, jointly fostering the "negritude" movement and sympathetically studying Vodou. *Les Griots* (a Guinean word meaning "poets," with five issues between 1938 and 1940) served this movement. For the essence of its position, see an extract in B. Diederich and A. Burt (entry 474), p. 53, note 2.

449   Denis, Lorimer, and Duvalier, François. "Une cérémonie du culte Pétro." *Les Griots* (Port-au-Prince) 2, no. 2 (October-December 1938): 156-59.
      "Pétro" refers locally to Vodou blood-sacrifice ceremonies, tracing perhaps to one Pedro, late eighteenth century.

450   Denis, Lorimer, and Duvalier, François. "Une cérémonie en l'honneur de Damballah." *Les Griots* (Port-au-Prince) 3, no. 3 (January-March 1939), pp. 316-19.

451   Denis, Lorimer, and Duvalier, François. "La culture populaire de la poésie, du chant, et des danses dans l'esthétique vodouesque." *Bulletin du Bureau d'Ethnologie* (Port-au-Prince) 2, no. 12 (1955): 1-29.
      As cited by N. A. de Muñoz (entry 749).

452   Denis, Lorimer, and Duvalier, François. "L'evolution stadiale du vodou." *Bulletin du Bureau d'Ethnologie* (Port-au-Prince), no. 3 (February 1944), pp. 9-32. Reprinted in *Oeuvres essentielles*, by F. Duvalier. Vol. 1. 2d ed. Port-au-Prince: Presses Nationales d'Haiti, 1968.
      Text of a lecture delivered at the City Hall of Port-au-Prince by Denis: that the independence of Haiti was the fruit of Vodou – the hostility of Toussaint L'Ouverture and Dessalines to the cult is ignored.

453   Denis, Lorimer, and Duvalier, François. "Psychologie ethnique et historique." *Les Griots* (Port-au-Prince), 1939. Reprinted in *Oeuvres essentielles*, by F. Duvalier. Vol. 1. Port-au-Prince: Presses Nationales d'Haiti, 1966, p. 161.
      As cited by D. Nicholls (entry 756), p. 404.

454   Denis, Lorimer, and Paul, Emmanuel[-Casséus]. *Essai d'organigraphie haïtienne*. Port-au-Prince: Bureau d'Ethnologie de la République d'Haïti, n.d.
      Includes musical instruments used in Vodou.

455 Deren, Maya. *Divine horsemen: The living gods of Haiti*. London and New York: Thames & Hudson, 1953, 350 pp., illus., bib. Reprint. New York: Chelsea House Publications, 1970, 350 pp. Reprint. New York: Dell, 1972, 350 pp. Reprinted as *The Voodoo gods*. Frogmore, St. Albans: Paladin, 1975, 318 pp., illus. Reprint. New Paltz, N.Y., 1983.

After World War II, there were a large number of apologists for Vodou. This book, by an American black woman who became a *serviteur*, while good on music and dancing, deals in pseudoscientific fashion with the meaning of Vodou.

456 Deren, Maya. "Religion and magic." *Tomorrow* (New York) 3, no. 1 (1954): 21-51.

With a "cyclic view of history," Vodou's collective morality serves both the individual and society.

457 Deren, Maya. "Religion and magic in Haiti." In *Beyond the five senses*, edited by E. J. Garrett. Philadelphia: J. B. Lippincott Co., 1957, pp. 238-67.

458 Dérose, Radolphe. *Caractère, culture, vodou: Formation et interprétation de l'individualité haïtienne*. Port-au-Prince: Bibliothèque Haïtienne, 1956, 240 pp.

458a Descardes, Jean Rosier. "La vengeance des loas." In *Cahier de Folklore et des Traditions Orales d'Haiti*. Edited by M. Benoit. Port-au-Prince: Imprimerie des Antilles, 1980, pp. 129-49.

A student research essay, 1978.

459 Descos, L. [Aubin, Eugène, pseud.]. *En Haïti: Planteurs d'autrefois, Nègres d'aujourd'hui*. Paris: Armand Colin, 1910.

By a French ambassador in Haiti who traveled widely and was friendly with *houngans*; extract in W. B. Seabrook (entry 852), pp. 302-3.

460 Descourtilz, Michel-Etienne. *Voyage d'un naturaliste ... à Saint Dominique ... (1799-1803)*. 3 vols. Paris: Defart, 1809. Abridged ed. *Voyage d'un naturaliste en Haïti, 1799-1803*. Librairie Plon. Paris: Jacques Boulenger, 1935, 232 pp.

Vol. 3, pp. 28, 181, 186, 383-84, religion; pp. 116-18 (1935 ed.), observations on Vodou, especially its occult aspects.

460a Désil, Hérold Clothers. "Une esquisse ethno-sociologique de la communauté de Ville-Bonheur considérée dans ses rapports avec certains phenomènes d'ordre religieux." Mémoire de License (ethnology), Université d'État d'Haiti, 1967.

461   Desmangles, Leslie Gérald. "African interpretations of the Christian cross in Vodun." *Sociological Analysis* 38, no. 1 (1977): 13-24, bib.

Vodou interprets the cross in the context of Dahomean mythology.

462   Desmangles, Leslie Gérald. "God in Haitian Vodun: A case in cultural symbiosis." Ph.D. dissertation (religion), Temple University, 1975, 434 pp.

463   No entry.

464   Desmangles, Leslie G[érald]. "The Maroon republics and religious diversity in colonial Haiti." *Anthropos* 85, nos. 4-6 (1990): 475-82.

African religious traditions were transformed by mixed ethnicity, new social situations, and incorporation of Catholic beliefs and practices.

465   Desmangles, Leslie G[érald]. "Rites baptismaux: Symbiose du vaudou et du catholicisme à Haïti." *Concilium*, no. 122 (Winter 1977), pp. 65-76. English version. "Baptismal rites: Religious symbiosis of Vodun and Catholicism in Haiti." *Science of Religion Bulletin*, no. 122 [2, no. 3] (Winter 1977): 51-61. Reprinted in *Journal of the Interdenominational Theological Center* (Atlanta) 8, no. 1 (1980): 73-82.

Vodou baptisms are basically African, with Catholic elements in symbiosis.

466   Desmangles, Leslie Gérald. "Roman Catholicism or Vodun in Haiti: What of the future?" *Freeing the Spirit* (Washington, D.C.) 4, no. 2 (1978): 29-35, illus.

467   Desmangles, Leslie Gérald. "The Vodun way of death: Cultural symbiosis of Roman Catholicism and Vodun in Haiti." *Journal of Religious Thought* 36, no. 10 (1979): 5-20.

468   Desquiron, Lilas. *Évolution historique d'une religion africaine: Le vaudou*. Brussels: Université Libre de Bruxelles, Mémoire de Maitrisse, 1968.

469   Desrosiers, Toussaint. "Haitian Voodoo." *Americas* (Washington, D.C., Pan American Union) 22, no. 2 (1970): 35-38.

A general description; regarded as a compensation for frustrated peasants but wasteful of money and energy, and therefore to be opposed.

470   Devillers, Carole. "Haiti's Voodoo pilgrimages: Of spirits and saints." *National Geographic Magazine* 167, no. 3 (1985): 394-408, illus.

Pilgrim festivals equally celebrating African ancestors and Catholic saints.

471   Devlin, Eileen Bonnie. "'Vwa Guine': An original performance piece derived from the 'Vodou coucher tambour' ceremony: The sacred and the aesthetic in ritual and performance." Ph.D. thesis, New York University, 1986, 530 pp.

472   Dewisme, C. H. "Une séance d'initiation au vaudou haïtien." *Sciences et Voyages* (Paris) 115 (1955): 11-12.

473   Dewisme, C. H. *Les zombis; ou le secret des morts-vivants.* Paris: Grasset, 1957, 159 pp.

473a   Diederich, Bernard. "On the nature of zombie existence: The reality of a vodou ritual." *Caribbean Review* (Miami) 12, no. 3 (Summer 1983): 14-17, 43-46.

Haiti's main "zombiologist" and his work on three zombies who had recently appeared.

474   Diederich, Bernard, and Burt, Al. *Papa Doc: Haiti and its dictator.* New York: McGraw Hill, 1969. Reprint. London: Bodley Head, 1970. Reprint. Hammondworth: Penguin Books, 1972, 424 pp. French translation. *Papa Doc et les tontons macoutes.* Paris: Albin Michel, 1971.

Pp. 345-57, "Voudou is his arm"–on President Duvalier's political use of Vodou; see index for his intellectual interest in it in the context of negritude.

474a   Dohrman, Richard. *The cross of Baron Samedi.* Boston: Houghton Mifflin, 1958, 502 pp.

Historical fiction set in the period of the American occupation, 1915-34.

475   Dominik, Maks. "Vodou ak litérati Ayisyin." *Sel. Jounal Ayisyin Alétrangé* (New York) 6, no. 41 (1978): 26-31.

In Creole. Vodou and Haitian literature.

476   Dominique, Jean Léopold. "Une quête d'haïtianité: Collier maldioc et transistor." *Conjonction* (Port-au-Prince), no. 129 (May 1976), pp. 107-78.

Pp. 115-20, Vodou and syncretism; pp. 145-47, Vodou in society; pp. 162-65, Vodou in relation to progress. Subtitle means "amulets and portable radios."

477 Dorcély, Roland. "Les cérémonies de mort en Haïti." *Les Lettres Nouvelles* (Paris), no. 64 [6] (October 1958): 418-23.

By a young Haitian painter-poet.

478 Dorsainvil, Justin Chrysostome. *Essais de vulgarisation scientifique et questions haïtiennes*. Port-au-Prince: Imprimerie Théodore, 1952, 166 pp.

Fourteen of his essays, posthumously collected: see the fourth essay, on possession in Vodou.

479 Dorsainvil, Justin Chrysostome. *Une explication philologique du vòdú*. Port-au-Prince: V. Pierre-Noël, 1924, 40 pp.

A reputable Haitian physician's address to the Société d'Histoire et de Géographie d'Haïti; extract in W. B. Seabrook (entry 852), pp. 276-79.

480 Dorsainvil, Justin Chrysostome. *Manuel d'histoire d'Haïti*. Port-au-Prince: Procure des Frères de l'Instruction Chrétienne, 1934, 408 pp.

Includes Vodou, passim (e.g., pp. 76-79, the Jamaican, Boukman, the Vodou priest who led the rising in 1791).

481 Dorsainvil, Justin Chrysostome. *Psychologie haïtienne: Vodou et magie*. Port-au-Prince: Imprimerie Nemours Télhomme, 1937, 47 pp.

482 Dorsainvil, Justin Chrysostome. "Vôdou et névrose." *Haïti Médicale* (Port-au-Prince). A series of articles, 1912-13, reprinted as *Vodou et névrose: Étude médico-sociologique*. Port-au-Prince: La Presse, 1931, 177 pp. Reprint. Éditions Fardin, 1975, 175 pp.

A mulatto Haitian physician's view of Vodou as "a racial psycho-nervous disorder, of a religious character bordering on paranoia," and wholly explicable by psychobiological factors. The first professional study, by a sympathetic Haitian. See D. Nicholls (entry 753) for an evaluation of Dorsainvil.

483 Douyon, Emerson. "Alcoolisme et toxicomanie en Haïti." *Toxicomanies* (Quebec) 2, no. 1 (1969): 31-38, bib. Reprinted in *Les Cahiers du Chiss* 5 (1970): 21-29.

Vodou experience in possession as an escape from reality, and also as addictive, thus being similar to drugs and alcohol in these respects, and replacing them.

484 Douyon, Emerson. "Crimes rituels et mort apparenté en Haïti: Vers une synthèse critique." *Caraïbes: Anthropologie et Sociétés* (Montreal) 8, no. 2 (1984): 87-120; 218-19; French and English summaries. English version. "Ritual crimes and deathlike comas in Haiti:

Towards a critical synthesis." *Anthropology and Societies* (Montreal) 8, no. 2 (1984): 87-120, 218-19.

On the Vodou phenomenon of "zombiism."

485   Douyon, Emerson. "La crise de possession dans le vaudou haïtien." Ph.D. dissertation (psychology), University of Montreal, 1965, 303 pp. Abstracted as "Trance in Haitian Voodoo." *Transcultural Psychiatric Research* 2 (October 1965): 155-59.

486   Douyon, Emerson. "L'examen au Rorschach des vaudouisants haïtiens." In *Trance and possession states*, edited by R. Prince. Montreal: R. M. Bucke Memorial Society, 1968, pp. 97-119, tables, bib.

Based on examination of illiterate Catholic peasant women; there was no single "possession personality" type, but depressive tendencies were common.

487   Douyon, Emerson. "Research model on trance and possession states in the Haitian Voodoo." In *Papers, Conference on Research and Resources of Haiti*. New York: Research Institute for the Study of Man, 1969, pp. 415-27. Reprinted as "A research model on trance and possession states in Haitian Vodun." In *The Haitian potential: Research and resources of Haiti*, edited by V. Rubin and R. P. Schaedel. New York and London: Teachers College Press, 1975, pp. 167-72.

Through an understanding of Vodou (regarded as pathological) trance, possession, and mythology, the Haitian personality and value system is revealed.

488   Douyon, Emerson. "La transe vaudouesque: Un syndrome de déviance psycho-culturelle." *Acta Criminologica* (North Cohocton, N.Y.) 2 (January 1969): 11-70, bib.; English, Spanish, German, and Russian summaries.

Discusses the literature on trance and reports on trance among some women Vodou members; their psychological profile combines depression and anger or aggression. Low Haitian crime and suicide rates are partly due to Vodou.

489   Douyon, Lamarck. "Phénoménologie de la crise de possession." *Revue de la Faculté d'Ethnologie* (Port-au-Prince) 12 (1967): 28-40.

490   Dow, Thomas W. "Primitive medicine in Haiti." *Bulletin of the History of Medicine* (Baltimore, Md.) 39, no. 1 (1965): 34-52.

A modern psychiatric evaluation of Vodou concepts of disease and methods of diagnosis and treatment.

491   Drot, Jean-Marie. *Journal de voyage chez les peintres de la fête et du vaudou en Haïti*. Paris: Skira; Geneva: Éditions d'Art, 1974, 89 pp., color illus.

492   Dubuisson, Wilfrid. "Le vodou dans le carnaval gonaivien." Thèse de Licence (ethnology), Université d'État d'Haïti, 1970.

493   Dumervé, Constantin. "Musique et danse vaudouesque." *Les Griots* (Port-au-Prince) 3 (1939): 411-14.

494   Dumervé, Constantin. "Musique vaudouesque." *Les Griots* (Port-au-Prince) 4 (1939): 559-64.

495   Dunham, Katherine. "Las danzas de Haiti." *Acta Anthropologica* (Mexico City) 2, no. 4 (1947), with English version. French version. *Les danses d'Haïti*. Paris: Fasquelle, 1950.

495a Dunham, Katherine. *Island possessed*. Garden City, N.Y.: Doubleday, 1969, 280 pp.
      By an anthropologist who was initiated into Vodou.

496   Durant, Frank. *Cent ans de Concordat: Bilan de faillite, 1860-1960*. Port-au-Prince: Imprimerie de la Presse, 1960.
      Includes the Catholic church's "anti-superstition" campaigns of 1860, 1896, 1913, 1931, and 1941.

497   Duvalier, François. *Oeuvres essentielles*. 2 vols. Port-au-Prince: Presses Nationales d'Haiti, 1966. 2d ed. 1968.
      See L. Denis and F. Duvalier (entries 452 and 453).

498   Duvalier, François, and Denis, Lorimer. "Les civilisations de l'Afrique noire et le problème haïtien." *Revue de la Société Haïtienne d'Histoire et de Géographie* (Port-au-Prince), no. 23 [7] (1936): 1-29.
      Duvalier later became president and was interested in Vodou for academic and political reasons.

499   Eddah. "Le vaudoux." *Le Nouvelliste* (Port-au-Prince), 28 September, 16 October, 9 November 1905.

500   Ekis, X. "Le vodou." *Jeunes Églises* 26 (1966): 1-7; 27 (1966): 14-16.

501   Elie, Louis E[mile]. *Histoire d'Haïti*. Vol. 2. Port-au-Prince, 1945, 305 pp.
      Chap. 4 (pp. 113-29), Vodou and African dances; Vodou and the Catholic clergy in the late eighteenth century.

502   Ellis, A[lfred] B[urton]. "On Vodu-worship." *Popular Science Monthly*
       38 (1891): 651-63.
          An exponent of Ghanaian religions tracing Vodou to the Ewe
       peoples of "Whydah and Allada."

503   Escoffier. "Le culte de vaudoux en Haïti." *France-Amérique Magazine*
       (Paris), May 1924, pp. 97-99.

504   Fabins, Theodore. "Le vaudou dans la lutte de libération haïtienne."
       Mémoire pour le diplôme d'études supérieures (sciences politiques),
       Université de Paris I, 1976, 170 pp.

505   Félice, Philippe de. *L'enchantement des danses et la magie du verbe:*
       Essai sur quelques formes inférieures de la mystique. Paris: Éditions
       Albin Michel, 1957, 416 pp.
          Pp. 67-75, Vodou; part of a general study of religious dance.

506   Férère, Gérard Alphonse. "Haitian Voodoo: Its true face." *Caribbean*
       Quarterly (Mona, Jamaica) 24, nos. 3-4 (1978): 37-47.
          Description of rites and divinities; Vodou is a positive help to
       Haitians under difficult circumstances.

507   Férère, Gérard Alphonse. *What is Haitian Voodoo?* Philadelphia:
       Saint Joseph's College Press, 1979, 21 pp.
          A sympathetic account.

508   Ferguson, James. *Papa Doc, Baby Doc: Haiti and the Duvaliers.*
       Oxford: B. Blackwell, 1987, 216 pp., illus.
          Pp. 3-5, et passim (see index), Vodou (e.g., p. 148, post-
       Duvalier influx of anti-Vodou American sects).

509   Findlay, G. G., and Holdsworth, W. W. *The history of the Wesleyan*
       Methodist Missionary Society. Vol. 2. London: Epworth Press, 1921,
       534 pp.
          Pp. 260-61, Vodou as "developed obeah" in Haiti.

510   Florival, Pierre Joseph. "Oratoire et vodou." Thèse de Licence
       (ethnologie), Université d'État d'Haïti, July 1973.

511   Foisset, Joseph. "Quelques considérations générales sur la campagne
       anti-superstitieuse." *La Phalange* (Port-au-Prince), 25 February 1942,
       p. 1.
          A priest, in the Catholic daily newspaper; also, other articles in
       the same paper.

512   Forbes, Rosita. *Women called wild*. London: Grayson & Grayson, 1935, 317 pp., illus.

Chap. titled "Priestess of the impossible" (pp. 150-67), a personal account of Vodou worship, and of an apparent human sacrifice outside Vodou, told in a rather lurid fashion.

513   Forbin, Victor. "Les mystères du vaudou." *La Nature* (Paris), January 1947, pp. 27-30, illus.

514   No entry.

515   Fouchard, Jean. *La méringue: Danse national d'Haïti*. Montreal: Leméac, 1973, 198 pp., illus., music.

516   Fouché, Franck. *Vodou et théâtre: Pour un nouveau théâtre populaire*. Collection Pratiques Culturelles. Montreal: Les Éditions Nouvelles Optiques, 1976, 123 pp., bib.

Vodou as "living theatre of Haitian history" with a popular role in defining identity and resisting neocolonialism.

516a Fowler, Carolyn. "Poésie et religion dans la rossée." *Conjonction* (Port-au-Prince) 148 (July 1980): 103-12.

On Jacques Roumain's novel, *Gouverneurs de la rosée* (entry 838).

517   Franck, Harry A[lverson]. *Roaming through the West Indies*. New York: Century Co., 1920. Reprint. 1923, xiv + 486 pp, illus., map.

Pp. 163-66, a traveler's second-hand account of Vodou.

518   Franco, José Luciano. "Idioma y sincretismo religioso en Haití." *Casa de las Américas* (Havana), no. 100 [16] (1977): 176-78.

519   Franco, Victor. "À Haïti, en quête du vaudou." *Connaissance du Mode* (Paris), n.s., no. 83 (October 1965), pp. 74-83.

520   Frank, Henry. "A survey of Haitian Vodun ritual dance." *Caribe* 7, nos. 1-2 (1983): 39-40, illus.

521   Freeman, H. Lawrence. *Voodoo: A grand opera in three acts*. Negro Opera Company, 1926.

Libretto and music, both by Freeman.

522   Gallegos, Gerardo. *Los ritos magicos el vudu*. Madrid: Fomento Editorial, 1973.

523 Garbel, Louis. "Le vaudou: Sa signification socio-culturelle." *Maintenant* (Montreal) 96 (May 1970): 158-59, illus.

524 Gates, Henry Louis, Jr. *Figures in black: Words, signs, and the racial self*. New York: Oxford University Press, 1987, 350 pp., illus.
    Studies in the context of Vodou.

525 Gayot, François. *Approches de la culture religieuse haïtienne*. Port-au-Prince, 1973, 17 pp.
    "Stage de formation missionnaire."

526 Gayot, François. "Vodou et action pastorale." In *Pastorales et Vodu: Église en Marche* (Port-au-Prince), no. 2 (December 1963), pp. 3-14. Reprinted in *Études sur le vodou*, edited by R. G. Montilus, et al. Cuernavaca, Mexico: Centro Inter-Cultural de Documentación, 1966, pp. 84-95.

527 Gerlach, Luther P. "Pentecostalism: Revolution or counter-revolution?" In *Religious movements in contemporary America*, edited by I. I. Zaretsky and M. P. Leone. Princeton, N.J.: Princeton University Press, 1974, pp. 669-99.
    Pp. 686-96, Haitian Pentecostalism and Vodou. Pentecostalism generates individual and social change; the similarities and differences between Pentecostalism and Vodou, and the attack of the former on the latter.

528 No entry.

529 Gilfond, Henry. *Voodoo: Its origins and practices*. London: Franklin Watts, 1976, 114 pp., bib, illus., map.
    Covers Haiti and Santo Domingo, and relation to the Catholic Church.

530 Goldberg, Alan Bruce. "Commercial folklore and Voodoo in Haiti: International tourism and the sale of culture." Ph.D. dissertation, Indiana University, 1981, 318 pp.
    Tourist entertainment does not alienate Vodou performers for there have long been tensions between commercial pressures and conservative kinship-based ritual; while tourist stereotypes are reinforced, performers find satisfaction in their performances.

531 Goldberg, Richard S. "Vodou and mythology: The culture/personality question revisited." *Ethnos* (Stockholm) 49, nos. 1-2 (1984): 80-97.
    Similar mythic patterns in the collective and individual experiences of the Kanzo initiation rite, with theoretical reflections.

532   Gover, Robert. *Voodoo contra.* York Beach, Maine: Weiser, 1985, 160 pp.

533   Gräbener, Jürgen. "Vodou und Gesellschaft in Haiti." *Religionen im sozialen Wandel – Internationales Jahrbuch für Religionssoziologie* 6 (1970): 158-76; English summary (pp. 175-76).
       Vodou as a stabilizing influence, yet accepting various alternative values; the move toward "European" culture.

534   Greene, Graham. *The comedians.* London: Bodley Head, 1966, 313 pp. French translation. *Les comédiens.* Paris: Laffont, n.d.
       A novel, set in Haiti, and conveying the political situation; pp. 194-98, a Vodou ceremony invoking the god of warriors on behalf of would-be insurgents.

534a   Grohs-Paul, W. "Notes sur les chants vodouesques de Werner A. Jaegerhuber." *Bulletin du Bureau National d'Ethnologie d'Haiti* 2 (1985): 73-101; English summary.

535   Haïti, Bureau d'Ethnologie. *Bulletin du Bureau d'Ethnologie* (Port-au-Prince), 3d ser. (1958), 51 pp., 2 parts.
       A pamphlet containing: "Mariage mystique dans le vodou suivant les notes inédites de L[orimer] Denis"; "Étude comparée du syncretisme religieux à Haïti et à la Jamaïque par George Eaton Simpson."

536   "Haiti's search for a social order." *Times* (London), 1 May 1963.
       Duvalier's appeal to Vodou to increase his influence with the masses.

537   Hall, Robert Burnett. "The Société Congo of the Île de la Gonave." *American Anthropologist* 31 (1929): 685-700, illus., map.
       The isolated Haitian island of Gonave is more purely African, with many small agricultural cooperative societies, called in general Sociétés de Congo, and with some religious functions in a Vodou form attached to them; the religious aspect is not developed in this article.

538   Hanna, S[tewart] W[illiam]. *Notes of a visit to some parts of Haiti: Jan. Feb. 1835.* London: R. B. Seeley & W. Burnside, and L. & G. Seeley, 1836, lxii + 153 pp.
       By a clergyman.

539   Harris, Wilson. "History, fable, and myth in the Caribbean and Guianas." *Caribbean Quarterly* (Mona, Jamaica) 16, no. 2 (1970): 1-32. Reprinted as Edgar Mitselholzer Memorial Lecture, 3d series.

Georgetown, Guyana: National History and Arts Council, Ministry of Information and Culture, 1970, 32 pp.

Pp. 12-17, Vodou as "creative fulfillment of African Vodou," with further cultural potential.

540   Hayden, J. Carleton. "James Theodore Holly (1829-1911), first Afro-American Episcopal bishop: His legacy to us today." *Journal of Religious Thought* 33, no. 1 (1976): 50-62. Reprinted in *Black apostles: Afro-American clergy confront the twentieth century*, edited by R. K. Burkett and R. Newman. Boston: G. K. Hall & Co., 1978, pp. 129-40.

541   Heinl, Robert Debs, Jr., and Heinl, Nancy Gordon. *Written in blood: The story of the Haitian people, 1492-1971*. Boston: Houghton Mifflin Co., 1978, 785 pp., illus.

Pp. 669-90 (and notes, pp. 761-62), "Voodoo."

542   Herivel, Jean-William. "Haïti au point de vue religieux." Doctoral dissertation, University of Paris, 1887.

543   Herskovits, Melville Jean. *Life in a Haitian valley*. New York and London: Alfred A. Knopf, 1937, xvi + 350 pp., illus. Reprint. Garden City, N.Y.: Doubleday, 1971, 371 pp.

Chap. 3 (1971 reprint, pp. 139-250), Haitian religion; pp. 270-95, Catholicism and Vodou; Appendix 1 (pp. 313-30), the gods of the Vodou pantheon. Chap. 8 abridged as entry 544.

544   Herskovits, Melville Jean. "What is Voodoo?" *Tomorrow* (New York) 3, no. 1 (1954): 11-20. Reprinted in *The New World Negro*. Bloomington: Indiana University Press, 1966, pp. 354-61.

Treats Vodou as organized worship and not as disorderly hysteria or "Black magic." An abridgement of chap. 8 of entry 543.

545   Heusch, Luc de. "Cultes de possession et religions initiatiques de salut en Afrique." In *Religions de salut*, edited by A. Abel. Annales du Centre d'Étude des Religions, 2. Brussels: Institut de Solvay, Université Libre de Bruxelles, 1962, pp. 127-67.

General considerations and African examples; pp. 140-67, Vodou and its relations to Dahomean (Benin) phenomena.

545a   Heusch, Luc de. "Kongo in Haiti: A new approach to religious syncretism." *Man*, n.s. 24, no. 2 (1989): 290-303.

546   Heusch, Luc de. "Le vodou haïtien." In *Encyclopaedia universalis: Le grand atlas des religions*. Paris: Encyclopaedia universalis France, 1988, p. 132, illus.

Vodou as the religion of the illiterate peasantry, essentially opposed to Christianity despite Christian veneers and influences, and with two categories of divinities – *rada* originating among the Fon of Dahomey, and *pétro*, of Creole origin. Associated magical practices and secret societies.

547   Hill, Adelaide C. "Revolution in Haiti, 1791 to 1820." *Présence Africaine*, no. 20 (1958), pp. 5-24.

A detailed history of the revolution – nothing on the religious background, but useful for reference.

548   Holder, Geoffrey, and Harshman, Tom. *Black gods, green islands*. Garden City, N.Y.: Doubleday, 1959, 235 pp., illus. Reprint. New York: Negro Universities Press, 1969.

Fictional tales against a background of Afro-Caribbean witchcraft, Obeah, and religion: two are set in the context of Haiti and Vodou – "Revolt" (pp. 48-138), concerns the sea-god Agwe and a slave rebellion, and "A goddess" (pp. 204-35), on "Mistress Erzulie Freda Dahomey" as goddess of love.

549   Holly, Arthur C. *Les daimons du culte vaudou*. Port-au-Prince: Edmond Chenet, 1918. Reprint. 1937, 523 pp.

By a Haitian supporter of Vodou – a moral and philosophic defense of Vodou as a vehicle for the contribution of Africa to human progress. Extract in W. B. Seabrook (entry 852), pp. 299-302.

550   [Holly, Arthur C.] HER-RA-ME-EL (pseud.). *Dra-Po: Étude ésoterique de Egregore africain, traditionel, social, et national d'Haïti*. Port-au-Prince, 1928.

By one of the founders of the "ethnological movement" supporting "noirisme."

551   No entry.

552   Hood, Robert E. "The role of black religion in political change: The Haitian revolution and Voodoo [1791-1803]." *Journal of the Interdenominational Theological Center* (Atlanta) 9 (Fall 1981): 41-69.

Vodou, based on African gods, as a source of solidarity for the various tribes in Haiti and in the Haitian revolution; does the Western view of spirits and demons have to be accepted in Haiti, or in the black diaspora in general?

553   Horay, Pierre. *Vaudou, rituels et possessions*. Paris: Imprimerie Pierre Horay, 1975, 78 pp.

554 Hurbon, Laënnec. *Cultures et dictature en Haïti: L'imaginaire sous contrôle*. Paris: Harmattan, for CNRS, 1979.

555 Hurbon, Laënnec. *Dieu dans le vaudou haïtien*. Bibliothèque Scientifique. Paris: Payot, 1972, 269 pp., bib. (pp. 259-68). Spanish translation. *Dios en el vudú haitiano*. Buenos Aires: Casteñada, 1978.

    By a Haitian Catholic priest; a systematic analysis and interpretation, not in terms of African survivals, magic, etc., but as a coherent new religious system enabling men to survive within the peculiar situations of Haitian history. This is a new departure in Vodou studies, using phenomenological, anthropological, and theological methods, and critical of Catholicism.

556 Hurbon, Laënnec. "Incidences culturelles et politiques du christianisme dans les masses haïtiennes." *Présence Africaine*, n.s. 74 (2d quarter, 1970): 98-110.

557 Hurbon, Laënnec. "Sorcellerie et pouvoir en Haïti." *Archives de Sciences Sociales des Religions* 48, no. 1 (1979): 43-52.

558 Hurbon, L[aënnec]. "Vaudou." In *Encyclopaedia universalis*. Vol. 16. Paris: Encyclopaedia Universalis France, 1973, pp. 638-39, illus.

559 Hurston, Zora [Neale]. *Tell my horse*. New York: J. B. Lippincott & Co., 1938, 290 pp., illus., maps. Reprinted as *Voodoo gods: An enquiry into native myths and magic in Jamaica and Haiti*. London: J. M. Dent & Sons, 1939, 290 pp., illus., maps.

    Pt. 3, "Voodoo in Haiti," including pp. 126-32, Erzulie; pp. 133-35, Papa Lespa; pp. 202-9, Sect Rouge; pp. 253-69, Vodou songs, with music. A. Métraux calls her "very superstitious"; other comments – "journalistic and often pretentious."

560 Huxley, Francis. "Anthropology and ESP." In *Silence and ESP*, edited by J. R. Smythies. London: Routledge & Kegan Paul; New York: Humanities Press, 1967, pp. 281-302.

    His own experiences of Vodou in Haiti, which had little need of explanation in terms of ESP.

561 Huxley, Francis. *The invisibles: Voodoo gods in Haiti*. London: Rupert Hart-Davis, 1966. Reprint. New York: McGraw Hill, 1969, 247 pp., illus., glossaries of Vodou terms and Haitian plants.

    A detailed description of his experiences of Vodou, spirit possession, initiation, and healing during a nine-month study of how these are related to mental illness and personal problems. More concerned with individual practitioners and their clients than with the cultic aspect.

562   Huxley, Francis. "The ritual of Voodoo and the symbolism of the body." *Transactions of the Royal Philosophical Society* B251, 1966, pp. 423-27.

562a   Huxley, Francis. "Voodoo." In *Man, myth, and magic*. Edited by R. Cavendish. Reference edition, vol. 11. New York and London: Cavendish Marshall, pp. 2967-76, illus.

562b   Huxley, Francis. "Zombies." In *Man, myth, and magic*. Edited by R. Cavendish. Reference edition, vol. 11. New York and London: Cavendish Marshall, pp. 3095-96, illus.

563   Hyppolite, Michelson-Paul. *Une étude sur le folklore haïtien*. Collection du Cent-cinquantenaire de l'Indépendence d'Haïti. Port-au-Prince: Imprimerie de l'État, 1954, 53 pp. English translation. *A study of Haitian folklore*. Port-au-Prince: Imprimerie de l'État, 1954, 51 pp.
        A lecture in Jamaica, introducing Vodou and its place in Haitian life.

564   Hyppolite, Michelson-Paul. *La mentalité haïtienne et le domaine de rêve: Psychanalyse de quatres rêves prémonitoires ou prophétiques. . . .* Port-au-Prince: Imprimerie de l'État, 1965, 88 pp.

565   Ibon, Laenek [Hurbon, Laënnec]. "Vodou ak lit sosial an Ayiti." *Sel. Jounal Ayisyin Alétrangé* (New York) 6, no. 41 (1978): 14-19.
        In Creole. Vodou and the struggle for liberation.

566   [Illustrations of farmer-god, Zaka, Vodou dancing and rites, and vèvè symbols.] *Unesco Courier* 34, no. 12 (1981): 17, 19, 21.

567   Innocent, Antoine. *Mimola, ou l'histoire d'une cassette*. 1st ed. Port-au-Prince: Imprimerie E. Malvál, 1906, 175 pp., petit tableau de moeurs locales. Reprint. New York: Kraus, 1969-70. 2d ed. Port-au-Prince: V. Valcin, 1935, 169 pp. + xxvii + 18 pp.; Port-au-Prince: Éditions Fardin, 1981, 169 pp.
        A Haitian novel, with description of rituals, and showing Vodou at its best.

568   Institut Français d'Afrique Noire. *Les Afro-Américains*. Mémoires de l'Institut Français de l'Afrique Noire, no. 27. Dakar: IFAN, 1952 [1953 on cover], 268 pp., illus.
        Essays organized by P. Verger: see L. Denis (entry 445), M. Leiris (entry 635), L. Mars (entry 677), O. Mennesson-Rigaud (entry 695), A. Métraux (entry 704), Y. Oddon (entry 758), J. Price-Mars (entry 809).

569 Isaac, Acelius E. "The influence of Voodoo on the lives of the Haitian people." *Jamaican Journal* (Kingston) 9, no. 4 (1975): 2-4, 6-7, 9-11.

Vodou as the way of life in Haiti, and its relations to African, Catholic, and Protestant religion, and to family, agriculture, commerce, etc. By a Haitian Protestant.

570 Jaegerhuber, Werner A. "Contribution à la musique vaudouesque." *Conjonction* (Port-au-Prince) 10-11 (August-October 1947): 63-64.

571 Jahn, Janheinz. *Muntu: Umrisse der neoafrikanischen Kultur.* Dusseldorf: E. Diederichs, 1958, 262 pp., illus. English translation. *Muntu: An outline of neo-African culture.* London: Faber & Faber, 1961, 267 pp., illus. French translation. *Muntu: L'homme africain et la culture néo-africaine.* Paris: Éditions de Seuil, 1961, 293 pp., illus. Spanish translation. *Muntu: Las culturas neo-africanas.* Mexico, D.F.: Fondo de Cultura Económica, 1963, 348 pp., illus.

Chap. 2: "Voodoo" – The earliest accounts, the Arada rite ceremonies, the gods or *loa*s and their embodiments, religion and politics.

572 James, C[yril] L[ionel] R[obert]. *The black Jacobins: Toussaint l'Ouverture and the San Domingo revolution.* New York: Vintage, 1938. 2d rev. ed. New York: Random House, 1963, 426 pp.

Pp. 86-87, "Voodoo" under Boukman as "High Priest" or *Papaloi*, in the 1791 rising. See also Hyacinthe's claim to divine inspiration (p. 108).

573 Jan, Jean-Marie. *Campagne anti-superstitieuse: Documentation.* Cap Haïtien: Imprimerie de Progrès, 1941, 112 pp.

By a Catholic priest.

574 Jan, Jean-Marie. *Port-au-Prince: Documents pour l'histoire religieuse.* Port-au-Prince: Henri Deschamps, 1956, 527 pp.

575 Janzen, John M. *Lemba, 1650-1930: A drum of affliction in Africa and the New World.* New York: Garland, 1982, 383 pp., illus.

Pp. 273-92, Congo parallels with the Dom Pedre/Pétro cult, pp. 277-92 being specifically on Haiti.

576 Johnson, F. D. "Voodoo is common belief in Haiti: What looked like a PR drawback turned into an opportunity." *Marketing* (Toronto) 80 (September 1975): 20.

576a   Johnson, James Weldon. "Throbbing Voodoo drums, villa hotels heighten Haiti's spellbinding allure." *Travel* (Floral Park, N.Y.) 109 (1958): 37-40.

577   Johnston, Harry H[amilton]. *The Negro in the New World*. London: Methuen, 1910, xxix + 489 pp., illus. Reprint. New York and London: Johnson Reprint Co., 1969, xi + xxix + 499 pp., illus. (with a new introduction by G. Shepperson).

     Pp. 193-95, a colonial officer's "period piece" account of Vodou.

578   Jones, Ernest. *Nightmare, witches, and devils*. International Psycho-Analytic Library, no. 20. New York: W. W. Norton, 1931, 374 pp. As *On the nightmare*. International Psycho-Analytic Library, no. 20. London: Hogarth Press, 1931, 374 pp.

579   Joseph, Rony. "La naturaleza de la conversion en Haiti." In *La evangelización entre las religiones tradicionales en América Latina y el Caribe*. Document de Pattaya '80. London: Lausanne Committee Strategy Working Group, [1981?], pp. 10-13.

580   *Journal of Caribbean Studies* (Coral Gables, Fla.)
     Special theme – late 1970s, early 1980s?

581   Juste-Constant, Voegeli. "Approche ethnomusicologique du vovou [*sic*] haïtien." *Folklore Americano* (Mexico City) 21 (June 1976): 95-140, bib., illus.

     Based on the chapter on Haitian Vodou ceremonial music in his Caracas thesis of 1974, with ten long musical examples of songs designed to induce possession states, and including Christian references as well as African components.

582   Kerboull, Jean. "Une enquête sur le vodou domestique en Haïti." Thèse de doctorat de 3e cycle (lettres), Université de Nice, Faculté des Lettres et Sciences Humaines, 1972, 419 pp.

583   Kerboull, Jean. *Vaudou et pratiques magiques*. Paris: Éditions Pierre Belfond, 1973. Reprint. 1977. English translation. *Voodoo and magic practices*. London: Barrie & Jenkins, 1978, 192 pp.

     A complementary work to his 1973 item (entry 584). Religion in Vodou is of African inspiration, but its magical practices derive from France.

584   Kerboull, Jean. *Le vaudou: Magie ou religion?* Les Énigmes de l'Univers. Paris: R. Laffont, 1973, 349 pp., map, illus., bib.

     Pt. 1, a comprehensive study of beliefs, priests, rites, sects, etc.; pt. 2 emphasizes domestic or family Vodou as basis of the cults. Pp.

315-42, French translations of statements in Creole gathered from Vodou members, as evidence for Kerboull's stress on the domestic cult and its features.

585   Kergoz, Jean. *L'expulsion des vaudoux*. Librairie Générale Catholique. Paris: A. Savaete, 1921.

586   Kersuzan, François-Marie. *Allocution synodale de Monseigneur K . . . prononcée le 13 février 1898 sur la nécessité sociale d'observer les commandements de Dieu, et allocution à la réunion contre le vaudoux le même jour*. Cap-Haïtien: Imprimerie de Progrès, 1898, 21 pp.
       By a Catholic priest who organized an unsuccessful "League against Voodoo" in 1896.

587   Kersuzan, François-Marie. *Conférence populaire sur le vaudoux donnée par Monseigneur l'Évêque du Cap-Haïtien le 2 août 1896*. Port-au-Prince: Imprimerie H. Amblard, 1896, 27 pp.

588   Kersuzan, François-Marie. [Extracts of articles opposing Vodou in various local journals, including *La Croix*]. In *Catholicisme et vaudou*. Collection Sondeos, 82. Cuernavaca, Mexico: Editions du CIDOC, 1971, pp. 4/50-4/54.

589   Kiev, Ari. "Danse rituelle dans le vodou haïtien." *Bulletin du Bureau d'Ethnologie* (Port-au-Prince) 3, no. 28 (1962): 36-42.

590   Kiev, Ari. "Folk psychiatry in Haiti." *Journal of Nervous and Mental Disease,* no. 940 [132, no. 3] (1961): 260-65.
       Vodou treatment of the mentally ill resembles Western psychiatry and is a reasonable and successful method.

590a Kiev, Ari. "Folklore de la psychiatrie en Haiti." *Bulletin du Bureau d'Ethnologie* (Port-au-Prince) 4th ser., no. 29 (1963), pp. 40-48.

591   Kiev, Ari. "Obstacles to medical progress in Haiti." *Human Organization* 25, no. 1 (1966): 10-15.
       Vodou hinders the introduction of Western medicine; its priests and native medical practice might be integrated with Western practice.

591a Kiev, Ari. "Psychotherapy in Haitian Voodoo." *American Journal of Psychotherapy* 16 (1962): 469-76.

592   Kiev, Ari. "Ritual goat sacrifice in Haiti." *American Imago* (Boston) 19, no. 4 (1962): 349-59.

593 Kiev, Ari. "Spirit possession in Haiti." *American Journal of Psychiatry* 118, no. 2 (1961): 133-38.

Vodou possession is useful both socially and for the individual when controlled in the cultic context, but otherwise is seen as a form of madness.

594 Kiev, Ari. "The study of folk psychiatry." In *Magic, faith, and healing: Studies in primitive psychiatry today*. New York: Free Press of Glencoe, 1964, 475 pp.

595 Kiev, Ari. "The therapeutic value of spirit-possession in Haiti." In *Trance and possession states*, edited by R. Prince. Montreal: R. M. Bucke Memorial Society, 1968, pp. 143-48.

Possession allows an outlet for suppressed feelings and thoughts, and helps support belief in the Vodou system and the socialization of individuals in this context.

596 Kloppenburg, Boaventura. "Ainda o exemplo de Haiti na reação contra a umbanda." *Revista Eclesiástica Brasileira* (Petrópolis) 16, no. 1 (1956): 122-25.

By a Catholic priest with extensive study of Umbanda in Brazil.

597 Kloppenburg, Boaventura. "Reação contra a umbanda e o exemplo de Haiti." *Revista Eclesiástica Brasileira* (Petrópolis) 15, no. 4 (1955): 968-73.

The Haitian situation as analogous to that of Brazil.

598 Krauss, William A. "Voodoo village." *Holiday* (Philadelphia) 10 (November 1951): 62-63, 148-50, 152-53, illus.

Pp. 63, 150, 152-53, Vodou described.

599 Lacovia, R. M. *Caribbean aesthetics: A prolegomenon. Black Images* 2, no. 2 (n.d.).

Pp. 21-24 (and notes, p. 46), Vodou.

600 Lagarde, Lebeaubrun. "Vaudoux." *Haiti Littéraire et Sociale*, March 1907.

601 Laguerre, Férère. "De la musique folkorique [*sic*] en Haïti." *Conjonction* (Port-au-Prince), no. 126 (June 1975), pp. 9-31, illus.

602 Laguerre, Michel [Saturnin]. *American Odyssey: Haitians in New York City*. The Anthropology of Contemporary Issues Series. Ithaca, N.Y.: Cornell University Press, 1984, 198 pp., maps.

By a Haitian scholar and Jesuit priest. Pp. 28-29, 59-61, 117-19, 130-31 (healers), Vodou among Haitian emigrants.

603   Laguerre, Michel [Saturnin]. "Belair, Port-au-Prince: From slave and Maroon settlement to contemporary black ghetto." In *Afro-American ethno-history in Latin America and the Caribbean*, edited by N. Whitten. Washington, D.C.: American Anthropological Association, Latin American Group, 1976.

604   Laguerre, Michel [Saturnin]. "Bizango: A Voodoo secret society in Haiti." In *Secrecy: A cross-cultural perspective*. New York: Human Sciences Press, 1980, pp. 147-60, bib.
      Traces the roots of Bizango to preindependence Maroon communities, which continued in secret; describes recruitment, initiation, monthly meetings, signs, and symbols.

605   Laguerre, Michel Saturnin. "The black ghetto as an internal colony: Socio-economic adaptation of a Haitian urban community." Ph.D. dissertation (anthropology), University of Illinois (Urbana-Champaign), 1976, 302 pp., maps.
      Vodou as a means of adapting to oppression, with its symbolic inversion of status in relation to powerful elites. Based on Belair, a black ghetto in downtown Port-au-Prince. Describes temples, religious brotherhood houses, the Vodou priest and cult group as political intermediaries, and spirit possession as a ritual of resistance and protest.

606   Laguerre, Michel [Saturnin]. *The complete Haitiana: A bibliographical guide to the scholarly literature, 1900-1980*. 2 vols. New York: Kraus International, 1982, 1562 pp.

607   Laguerre, Michel [Saturnin]. "An ecological approach to Voodoo." *Freeing the Spirit* (Washington, D.C.) 3, no. 1 (1974): 3-12. Reprinted in *Journal of the Interdenominational Theological Center* (Atlanta) 5 (Fall 1977): 47-60.
      The African ancestry and development of Vodou during the slave period.

608   Laguerre, Michel [Saturnin]. *Études sur le vodou haïtien: Bibliographie analytique*. Montreal: Centre de Recherches Caraïbes, Université de Montréal, 1979, 50 pp.

609   Laguerre, Michel [Saturnin]. "The failure of Christianity among the slaves of Haiti." *Freeing the Spirit* (Washington, D.C.) 2, no. 4 (1973): 10-24.

610   Laguerre, Michel [Saturnin]. "The festival of gods: Spirit possession in Haitian Voodoo." *Freeing the Spirit* (Washington, D.C.) 4, no. 4 (1977): 23-35.

611   Laguerre, Michel [Saturnin]. "Haitian Americans." In *Ethnicity and medical care*, edited by A. Harwood. Cambridge, Mass.: Harvard University Press, 1981, 523 pp.

611a   Laguerre, Michel [Saturnin]. "Haitian pilgrimage to O.L. of Saut d'Eau: A sociological analysis." *Social Compass* (The Hague) 33, no. 1 (1986): 5-20, bib.
       The shrine at Notre Dame de Saut d'Eau, and its exploitation by political leaders.

612   Laguerre, Michel [Saturnin]. "Nativism in Haiti: The politics of Voodoo." M.A. thesis (anthropology), Roosevelt University (Chicago), 1973, 179 pp.

613   Laguerre, Michel Saturnin. "The place of Voodoo in the social structure of Haiti." *Caribbean Quarterly* (Mona, Jamaica) 19, no. 3 (1973): 36-50, bib.
       On the transformation of Vodou from a messianic cult into a religion fostering village unity and national independence.

614   Laguerre, Michel [Saturnin]. "Le tambour et la danse religieuse dans la liturgie chrétienne en Haïti." *Revue du Clergé Africain* 27, no. 6 (1972): 587-603. English translation. "The drum and religious dance in the Christian liturgy in Haiti." *Freeing the Spirit* (Washington, D.C.) 1, no. 2 (1972): 11-15.

615   Laguerre, Michel [Saturnin]. *Urban life in the Caribbean: A study of Haitian urban community*. Cambridge, Mass.: Schenkman Publishing Co., 1982, 214pp., bib., maps, illus.
       Includes Vodou and urban life, and the mediating role of Vodou priests.

616   Laguerre, Michel [Saturnin]. "Vodou daprè dives épok koloni an." *Sel. Jounal Ayisyin Alétrangé* (New York) 6, no. 41 (1978): 9-13.
       In Creole.

616a   Laguerre, Michel S[aturnin]. *Voodoo and politics in Haiti*. London: Macmillan, 1989, 152 pp., illus.
       The interaction between Vodou and politics from the colonial to the post-Duvalier era. An important study of the politicization of Vodou and Vodouization of politics, including the emergence of secret societies from the earlier Maroons.

617   Laguerre, Michel [Saturnin]. "Voodoo as religious and political ideology." *Freeing the Spirit* (Washington, D.C.) 3, no. 1 (1974): 23-28.

Vodou as a politico-religious movement that was a critical factor in the success of the Haitian revolution.

618   Laguerre, Michel [Saturnin]. *Voodoo heritage*. Sage Library of Social Research, 98. Beverly Hills, Calif.: Sage Publications, 1980, 231 pp., illus., glossary.

Two hundred forty-nine Vodou songs collected in the Belair slum of Port-au-Prince; pp. 11-15, foreword by V. D. Rubin; pp. 181-207, appendix of *vèvè* or ritual drawings used in training *houngans*, with their accompanying invocations and "magical prayers."

619   Laguerre, Michel [Saturnin]. "Voodoo oral tradition as spiritual revelation." Paper, Afro-American Religious History Group, American Academy of Religion annual meeting, San Francisco, 29 December 1977.

620   Laguerre, Michel [Saturnin]. "You lis liv sou vodou." *Sel. Jounal Ayisyin Alétrangé* (New York) 6, no. 42 (1978): 34-38.

In Creole. A selective bibliography on Vodou.

621   Lamartinière, Honorat Michel. "Les danses folkloriques haïtiennes." *Publications du Bureau d'Ethnologie de la République d'Haïti* (Port-au-Prince), 2d ser., no. 11 (1955), 155 pp.

622   Lanternari, Vittorio. *Religions of the oppressed*. London: MacGibbon & Kee, 1963, 343 pp. (Many other editions and translations).

Pp. 165-69, Haiti, reprinted in *Black society in the New World*, edited by R. Frucht (New York: Random House, 1971, pp. 308-12).

623   Lapaix, Jean Leon. "Origenes, causas y efectos del vudu." *Avance* (Chile) 2, no. 60 (1973): 28-30.

624   Laroche, Maximilien. *Le miracle et la métamorphose: Essai sur les littératures du Québec et d'Haïti*. Montreal: Éditions du Jour, 1970, 242 pp.

Includes Vodou possession.

625   Larose, Serge. "The meaning of Africa in Haitian Vodou." In *Symbols and sentiments: Cross-cultural studies in symbolism*, edited by I. Lewis. London and New York: Academic Press, 1977, pp. 85-116.

626   Latorre Cabal, Hugo. *La revolución de la iglesia latino-americana*. English translation. *The revolution of the Latin American church*. Norman: University of Oklahoma Press, 1978, 192 pp.

Pp. 86-87, on Duvalier's political use of Vodou, supported by the Catholic hierarchy but strongly challenged by younger post-Conciliar priests.

627   Latortue, François. "Haïti et la Louisiane." *Revue de la Société d'Histoire et de Géographie d'Haïti* (Port-au-Prince), no. 126 [38] (March 1980): 5-14; no. 127 [38] (June 1980): 39-47.

628   Lauwerysen, Herman. "Vodoun in Haiti: Onderzoek naar de magico-religieuze polariteit in een afro-amerikaanse volksreligie." Vol. 2. Thesis for Licentiate in Missions (theology), Catholic University of Louvain, 1974, 189 pp., bib. Mimeo.

629   Lecale, Errol. *Zombie*. London: New English Library, 1974.
       A novel portraying Vodou in sensational and negative terms.

630   Leconte, Padern. "Les conditions de la désintégration du vaudou haïtien." Thèse de Licence (ethnologie), Université d'État d'Haïti, 1962.

631   Léger, Jacques-Nicolas. *Haïti: Son histoire et ses détracteurs*. New York: Neale Publishing Co., 1907, 411 pp., illus. English translation. *Haiti: Her history and her detractors*. New York: Neale Publishing Co., 1907, 372 pp., illus.
       By a distinguished diplomat and statesman. Pp.'346-60, a brave defense of Haiti at a difficult time in its history, against sensational reports of cannibalism and of Vodou, the importance of which he tends to minimize.

632   Légitime, François Denis. *La vérité sur le vaudou*. Port-au-Prince: Imprimerie de l'Abeille, 1903, 67 pp.

633   Leigh-Fermor, Patrick [Michael]. "Voodoo rites in Haiti." *World Review* (London), October 1950, pp. 39-49.

634   Leiris, Michel. "Martinique, Guadaloupe, Haïti." *Les Temps Modernes* (Paris), no. 52 [5] (February 1950): 1345-68.
       Pp. 1350-55 on Haitian Vodou.

635   Leiris, Michel. "Note sur l'usage de chromolithographies par les vaudouisants d'Haïti." In *Les Afro-Américains*. Mémoires de l'Institut Français de l'Afrique Noire, no. 27. Dakar: IFAN, 1952 [1953 on cover], pp. 201-7 + 3 plates.

636   Leiris, Michel. "Sacrifice d'un taureau chez le houngan, Jo Pierre-Gilles." *Haïti, poètes noirs*. *Présence Africaine* 12, no. 4 (1951): 22-36.

Pp. 33-34, extracted in *Voodoo in Haiti*, by A. Métraux (entry 725), pp. 174-75.

637 Lekis, Lisa. "The dance as an expression of Caribbean folklore." In *The Caribbean: Its culture*, edited by A. C. Wilgus. Gainsville: University of Florida Press, 1955, pp. 43-73.
Pp. 66-70, Vodou, and its dance forms.

638 Lescot, Elie. *Avant l'oubli: Christianisme et paganisme en Haïti et autres lieux*. Port-au-Prince: Imprimerie Henri Deschamps, 1974, 532 pp., illus.
Mainly describes the institutionalization of the Catholic Church, with some material on the interaction between the church and folk religious traditions such as Vodou. By a president of Haiti deposed in 1946.

639 Lescouflair, A. "Jésus ou Legba?" *Le Temps*, 31 January 1934.
On Milo Rigaud's work.

639a Lester, D. "Voodoo death: Some new thoughts on an old phenomenon." *American Anthropologist* 74, no. 3 (June 1972): 386-90.

639b Lex, Barbara W. "Voodoo death: New thoughts on an old explanation." *American Anthropologist* 76 (1974): 818-23.

640 Leyburn, James G[raham]. *The Haitian people*. Caribbean Series, 9. New Haven, Conn.: Yale University Press, 1941. Rev. ed. 1966, 342 pp, map, bib. Spanish translation. *El pueblo haitiano*. Buenos Aires, 1946.
Pp. 131-65, Vodou – a classic account, scholarly, objective, and understanding, with a sound socioeconomic interpretation of political history; pp. 166-74, religious borrowings; and see index for listings under "Vodou."

640a Ligan, Samson. "La thème de la religion dans *Gouverneurs de la rosée* de Jacques Roumain." Dissertation, University of Bordeaux III, 128 pp.

641 Locke, Ralph G. *The priest is the tree: Possession trance in Haitian Voodoo*. Occasional Papers of the Experimental Learning Laboratory, no. 3. Durham, N.C.: Duke University, 1982.

642 Loederer, Richard A. *Wudu-Feuer auf Haiti*. Vienna and Leipzig: A. Wolf, 1932, 216 pp., illus., maps. English translation. *Voodoo fire in Haiti*. Garden City, N.Y.: Doubleday, Doran & Co., 1935, 274 pp., illus., maps.; London: Jarrolds, 1935, 283 pp., illus.

One of the more lurid accounts in the genre of W. B. Seabrook.

643   Logan, Rayford W. *Haiti and the Dominican Republic*. London: Oxford University Press, 1968, viii + 220 pp., map.

        Pp. 173-83, "Religion: Hispaniola, Santo Domingo, and the Dominican Republic"; pp. 176-78, Vodou.

644   Longuet, Yves Jacques. "Possession and vaudou." *Conjonction* (Port-au-Prince) 13 (February 1948): 52-57.

645   Loughlin, Elmer H. "The truth about Voodoo." *Natural History* 63, no. 4 (1954): 168-79, illus.

        A medical doctor's sympathetic account, with many photos of a Rada ceremony.

646   Louis-Jean, Antonio. *La crise de possession et la possession dramatique*. Ottawa: Éditions Lémeac, 1970, 173 pp., illus., bib.

        On the sources of Haitian dance and theater in Vodou, as an example of the sacred origins of dance and drama.

647   Lowenthal, Ira P. "Ritual performance and religious experience: A service for the gods in southern Haiti." *Journal of Anthropological Research* 34, no. 3 (1978): 392-414.

        Examines the offertory ritual in the participants' own terms as a coherent religious event in their subjective experience.

648   Lundhal, Mats. *Peasants and poverty: A study of Haiti*. New York: St. Martins Press; London: Croom Helm, 1979.

        Pp. 352-54, 358 (notes, p. 364), 430, 598, Vodou – all from an economic perspective.

649   Mabille, Pierre. "Les loas parlent en govis: Sorcellerie et voyance dans la religion vaudou." *Les Lettres Nouvelles* (Paris), no. 64 [6] (October 1958): 409-16.

        By a doctor, based on his experience as hospital superintendent in Port-au-Prince in 1940.

650   McConnell, H. Ormonde. *Haiti diary, 1933-1970*. Cincinnati, Ohio: United Methodist Commission on Relief, 1977.

        P. 16, instances of converts from Vodou to Christianity – those to Protestant forms seldom reverting as compared with Catholic converts.

651   Madiou, Thomas, *fils*. *Histoire d'Haïti*. 4 vols. Port-au-Prince: Imprimerie J. Courtois, 1847-1904; 2d ed. of first 3 vols. only. Port-au-Prince: Imprimerie E. Chenet, 1922.

The most important history, by a mulatto Haitian. Vol. 1, p. 72-73, Derance, a Vodou-inspired rebel in the 1790s; p. 97, a similar rebel in 1793; vol. 2, p. 91, Toussaint L'Ouverture and Dessalines in relation to Vodou.

652   Magloire, Gaby. "Houngan–Le rôle privilégié d'un dignitaire d'une religion spontanée." Licentiate dissertation (sociology), University of Louvain, 1972, 97 pp.

652a Makouta-Mboukou, Jean Pierre. "La vision de Dieu chez Jacques Roumain." Thèse de License, Faculté de Théologie Protestante (Paris), 1974.
      Refers to entry 838.

653   Malenfont, [Colonel]. *Des colonies et particulièrement celle de Saint-Dominigue*. Paris: Audibert, 1814.
      Pp. 217-20, encounters with Vodou priests, priestesses, and members during a military expedition of 1792 in the Plaine du Cul-de-Sac; reprinted in A. Métraux, *Voodoo in Haiti* (entry 725), pp. 44-45.

654   Manigat, J. F. Thalès. "Conférence sur le vaudoux." Cap-Haïtien, 1897.
      Part of an anti-Vodou campaign.

655   Mannington, George. *The West Indies with British Guiana and British Honduras*. London: L. Parsons; New York, 1925, xv + 304 pp., illus.
      Pp. 267f., Vodou–the common critical outline.

656   Manolesco, Jean. *Vaudou et magie noire*. Montreal: Éditions du Jour, 1972, 143 pp.

657   Marcelin, Milo. "Bibliographie: Écrivains haïtiens et le vodou." *Optique* (Port-au-Prince), no. 30 (August 1956), pp. 61-70.

658   Marcelin, Milo. "Cent croyances et superstitions." *Optique* (Port-au-Prince), no. 7 (September 1954), pp. 48-56.

659   Marcelin, Milo. "Coutumes funéraires." *Optique* (Port-au-Prince), no. 11 (January 1955), pp. 45-59.
      On the Vodou cult of the dead.

660   Marcelin, Milo. "Danses et chants vodou." *Optique* (Port-au-Prince), no. 12 (February 1955), pp. 29-37.

661   Marcelin, Milo. "Écrivains étrangers et le vodou." *Optique* (Port-au-Prince), no. 32 (October 1956), pp. 53-57.
       A bibliography.

662   Marcelin, Milo. "Les fêtes en Haïti." *Optique* (Port-au-Prince), no. 16 (June 1955), pp. 33-45.

663   Marcelin, Milo. "Folklorico haitiano: Creencias y supersticiónes." *Archivos Venezolanos de Folklore* (Caracas) 1, no. 2 (1952): 414-19. Issued separately. Caracas: Universidad Central de Venezuela, Faculdad de Filosofía y Letras, 1952, 8 pp.

663a   Marcelin, Milo. "Les grands dieux du vaudou haïtien." *Journal de la Société des Américanistes de Paris* (Paris) 36 (1947): 51-135.

664   Marcelin, Milo. "Jésus ou Legba." *Le Temps* (Paris), 15 November 1933.

665   Marcelin, Milo. *Mythologie vodou (rite arada)*. Preface by Morisseau-Leroy. Vol. 1. Port-au-Prince: Les Éditions Haïtiennes, 1949, 137 pp. Vol. 2. Pétionville, Haïti: Éditions Canapé-Vert, 1950, 201 pp.
       An important study of the divinities in the Rada rite and their relation to Catholic saints.

666   Marcelin, Milo. *Nouvelles études: Legba Ayizan*. Collection Folklore. Pétionville, Haïti, 1954, 42 pp., illus., bib.

667   Marcelin, Milo. "El vodou haitiano; sus dioses y sus emblemas." *Sociedad Folklorica de Mexico Annuario* (Mexico City) 10 (1955): 149-65.

668   Marcelin, Milo. "Le vodou: Religion populaire." *Optique* (Port-au-Prince), no. 14 (April 1955), pp. 37-44; no. 15 (May 1955), pp. 39-49; no. 17 (July 1955), pp. 45-51; no. 19 (September 1955), pp. 47-50.

669   Marks, Herbert. "Voodoo in Haiti." In *Afro-Caribbean religions*, edited by B. E. Gates. London: Ward Lock Educational, 1980, pp. 58-66.
       A convenient summary account.

670   Mars, Louis. "La crise de possession dans le vaudou." *La Vie Médicale* (Paris), Noël 1952, pp. 81-88.
       The author was foreign minister in the 1950s and is a son of Jean Price-Mars.

671 Mars, Louis. *La crise de possession dans le vaudou: Essai de psychiatrie comparée.* Preface by G. Devereux. Port-au-Prince: Bibliothèque de l'Institut d'Ethnologie, 1946, 15 + 105 pp.

672 Mars, Louis. *La crise de possession: Essais de psychiatrie comparée.* Port-au-Prince: Imprimerie de l'État, for Bureau d'Ethnologie, 1946, xvi + 103 pp. New ed., 1955, 103 pp.

Regards possession as pathological, but much valuable detail.

672a Mars, Louis. "La crise de possession et la personnalité humain en Haiti." *Revue de Psychologie des Peuples* (Le Havre) 17, no. 1 (1962): 6-22. Reprinted in *Revue de la Faculté d'Ethnologie* (Port-au-Prince) 8 (1964): 37-62.

673 Mars, Louis. "Les crises de loas, les hiéroglyphes cinétiques et l'ethnodrame." *Revue de la Faculté d'Ethnologie* (State University of Haiti) 11 (1966): 22-25.

674 Mars, Louis. "Délire mystique à thème vaudouique." *Les Griots: Revue Scientifique et Littéraire d'Haïti* (Port-au-Prince), no. 2 (1938), pp. 281-85.

675 Mars, L[ouis]. "L'ethnopsychiatrie et la schizophrénie en Haïti." *Psychopathologie Africaine* (Dakar) 5, no. 2 (1969): 235-55.

A psychiatric analysis of Vodou.

676 Mars, Louis. *La lutte contre la folie.* Port-au-Prince: Imprimerie de l'État, 1937.

677 Mars, Louis. "Nouvelle contribution à l'étude de la crise de possession." *Psyché*, no. 60 (October 1951), pp. 640-69. Reprinted in *Les Afro-Américains*. Mémoires de l'Institut Français de l'Afrique Noire, no. 27. Dakar: IFAN, 1952 [1953 on cover], pp. 213-33.

A detailed study and classification of various cases; appendixes on the dramatic aspects.

678 Mars, Louis. "Une nouvelle étape dans la réflexion sur les théolepsies en Haïti." *Cahiers des Religions Africaines*, no. 20 [10] (1976) [i.e., 1978]: 203-10. Reprinted in *L'Ethnographie* 76, no. 3 (1980): 283-90.

On the "crises of possession" in Haitian Vodou; the significance for communication theory and interdisciplinary study.

679 Mars, Louis. "Phenomena of 'possession.'" *Tomorrow* (New York) 3, no. 1 (1954): 61-73.

680   Mars, Louis. "La psychopathologie du vaudou." *Psyché: Revue Internationale des Sciences de l'Homme et de Psychanalyse*, nos. 23-24 (September-October 1948): 1064-88.

681   Mars, Louis. "Le symbolisme dans la religion vodouique et les philosophies de l'Occident." *Psychopathologie Africaine* (Dakar) 6, no. 1 (1970): 67-70.

682   Mars, Louis. "Syndrome maniaque et croyances vaudouiques." *Bulletin du Service d'Hygiène*, March 1938.
       Cited by D. Bellegarde (entry 342), p. 86.

683   Mars, Louis. *Témoignages I: Essai ethnologique-psychologique.* Madrid: Taller Gráfico Cies Hermosilla, 1966, 77 pp.
       Pp. 7-9, 12-49, 56-58, 62-71, a new analysis of Vodou in terms of "ethnodrama," as both drama and religion.

684   Mars, Louis, and Devereux, Georges. "Haitian Voodoo and the ritualization of the nightmare." *Psychoanalytic Review* 38, no. 4 (1951): 334-42.

685   Mathews, Basil. "Vodun and Catholicism." *Catholic World* (New York) 158 (1943): 65-72.
       Vodou is not a distinct religion but a cult that could be incorporated into Catholicism; by a Benedictine monk.

686   Mathison, Richard R. *Faiths, cults, and sects of America: From atheism to Zen.* Indianapolis: Bobbs-Merrill Co., 1960, 384 pp.
       Pp. 223-34, Vodou – of the "prime blacks" imported from the West Indies to Louisiana.

686a   Maupoil, Bernard. "Le culte du vaudou: M. J. Herskovits et l'ethnographie afro-américain." *Les Cahiers d'Outre-Mer* (Talence) 3 (1937): 195-205.

687   Maximilien, Louis. "Voodoo, gnosis, and Catholicism." *Tomorrow* (New York) 3, no. 1 (1954): 85-90.
       Rejects views of Vodou as wierd, diabolical, or cabalistic.

688   Maximilien, Louis. *Le vodou haïtien: Rite radas-canzo.* Port-au-Prince: Imprimerie de l'État, [1945], xxviii + 225 pp. Reprint. Port-au-Prince: Imprimerie H. Deschamps, 1982, 224 pp. + plates.
       A sympathetic and detailed account, by a Haitian.

689   Mennesson-Rigaud, Odette. "À propos du vodou." *Bulletin du Bureau d'Ethnologie* (Port-au-Prince) 3, no. 16 (1958): 50-53.

By a French woman, long resident in Haiti and accepted by Vodou members as virtually a priestess.

690   Mennesson-Rigaud, Odette. "Étude sur le culte des Marassas en Haïti." *Zaïre* (Louvain) 6, no. 6 (1952): 597-621, illus., glossary.
      A good study of the cult of the twins, who are regarded as having supernatural power akin to that of the *loa*.

691   Mennesson-Rigaud, Odette. "The feasting of the gods in Haitian Vodu." English translation by A. and R. Métraux. *Primitive Man* 19, nos. 1-2 (1946): 1-58.

692   Mennesson-Rigaud, Odette. "Noël vodou en Haïti." In *Haïti: Poètes noirs*. *Présence Africaine* (Paris) 12, no. 4 (1951): 37-60, illus..
      Rural Christmas ceremonies for protection against evil.

693   Mennesson-Rigaud, Odette. "Notes on two marriages with vodoun loa." In *Divine horsemen: The living gods of Haiti*. London and New York: Thames & Hudson, 1953, Appendix A, pp. 263-70.
      On mystical marriage in Vodou between a *loa* and a devotee.

694   Mennesson-Rigaud, Odette. "Le rôle du vaudou dans l'indépendance d'Haïti." *Présence Africaine*, nos. 18-19 (February-May 1958), pp. 43-67.
      Vodou's role in Haitian independence.

695   Mennesson-Rigaud, Odette. "Vodou haïtien: Quelques notes sur les réminiscences africaines." In *Les Afro-Américains*. Mémoires de l'Institut Français de l'Afrique Noire, no. 27. Dakar: IFAN, 1952 [1953 on cover], pp. 235-38.
      On the relation of dances, rituals, and loas in Vodou to the origins of slaves in different parts of Africa.

696   Mennesson-Rigaud, Odette, and Denis, Lorimer. "Cérémonie en l'honneur de Marinette." *Bulletin du Bureau d'Ethnologie* (Port-au-Prince), 2d ser., no. 3 (July 1947), pp. 13-21.
      Marinette is a she-devil *loa* with the screech-owl as emblem. See A. Métraux (entry 725), pp. 117-18 for a summary.

697   Mennesson-Rigaud, Odette, and Denis, Lorimer. "Quelques notes sur la vie mystique de Marie-Noël." *Bulletin du Bureau d'Ethnologie* (Port-au-Prince), 2d ser. (March 1947), pp. 30-34.
      On a remarkable dream of a "queen-chorister" to the grand *houngan* of Port-au-Prince.

698   Mercier, Paul. "La 'possession' comme fait sociale." *La Revue Internationale* (Paris), no. 3 (1946), pp. 287-99.

699   Merwin, Bruce W. "A Voodoo drum from Hayti." *University of Pennsylvania Museum Journal* 8, no. 2 (1917): 123-25.
       Describes the cult; extract in W. B. Seabrook (entry 852), p. 296.

700   Métraux, Alfred. "L'Afrique vivante en Haïti." *Présence Africaine* 12, no. 4 (1951): 13-21.

701   Métraux, Alfred. "Chants vodou." *Les Temps Modernes* (Paris), no. 52 [5] (February 1950): 1386-93, bib.
       Discussion, with eleven texts extracted from various publications.

702   Métraux, Alfred. "La comédie rituelle dans la possession." *Diogène* (Paris), no. 11 (July 1955), pp. 1-24. English version. "Dramatic elements in ritual possession." *Diogenes* (Paris), no. 11 (July 1955), pp. 18-36.
       Spirit possession illustrated by the nature of Vodou trance.

703   Métraux, Alfred. "The concept of soul in Haitian Vodu." *Southwestern Journal of Anthropology* 2, no. 1 (1946): 84-92.
       Includes hiding the soul to avoid witchcraft, and a ceremony to restore an enfeebled soul.

704   Métraux, Alfred. "Les croyances animistes dans le vodou haïtien." In *Les Afro-Américains*. Mémoires de l'Institut Français de l'Afrique Noire, no. 27. Dakar: IFAN, 1952 [1953 on cover], pp. 239-44.
       Vodou as of African, mostly Dahomean, origin.

705   Métraux, Alfred. "Croyances et pratiques magiques dans la Vallée de Marbial, Haïti." *Journal de la Société des Américanistes* (Paris), n.s. 42 (1953): 135-98.
       Pp. 165-71, on divination by dream symbolism.

706   Métraux, Alfred. "Le culte du vodou en Haïti." *Le Monde Religieux: L'Afrique Païenne et Juive* (Lezay) 26 (1956-57): 148-58.

707   Métraux, Alfred. "Le culte vodou en Haïti." *La Revue de Paris* 60 (August 1953): 119-29.

708   Métraux, Alfred. "Les dieux et les esprits dans le vodou haïtien." *Bulletin: Société Suisse des Américanistes* (Geneva), no. 10 (September 1955), pp. 2-16; no. 11 (March 1956), pp. 1-9.

709   Métraux, Alfred. "Divinités et cultes vodou dans la vallée de Marbial (Haïti)." *Zaïre* (Louvain) 8, no. 7 (1954): 675-707.

710   Métraux, Alfred. "Documents sur la transe mystique dans le vaudou." *Ethnologica* (Cologne), n.s., no. 2 (1960), pp. 530-41.

710a   Métraux, Alfred. "Jeux du sexe et de la mort dans le vodou." *La Nouvelle Revue Française* (Paris) 125 (1963): 796-809.

711   Métraux, Alfred. *Haïti: La terre, les hommes, et les dieux*. Neuchâtel: La Baconnière, 1957, 109 pp. English translation. *Haiti: Black peasants and Voodoo*. New York: Universe Books; Toronto: Burns & MacEachern; London: G. G. Harrap, 1960, 109 pp., illus., map.
        Pp. 58-83, Vodou; pp. 84-90, possession; pp. 92-95, sacred waterfall; pp. 96-99, sorcery and zombies.

712   Métraux, Alfred. "Histoire du vodou depuis la guerre de l'indépendence jusqu'à nos jours." *Présence Africaine*, no. 16 (October-November 1957), pp. 135-49.

713   Métraux, Alfred. "Le mariage mystique dans le vodou." *Cahiers du Sud* (Marseilles) 337 [43] (October 1956): 410-19.
        Between a *loa* and a devotee.

714   Métraux, Alfred. "Médecine et vodou en Haïti." *Acta Tropica* (Basel) 10, no. 1 (1953): 28-68.

715   Métraux, Alfred. "Le Noël vodou en Haïti." *Bulletin de la Société Neuchâteloise de Géographie* (Neuchâtel), n.s., no. 10 [51, no. 5] (1954-55): 95-118.
        A comparison of two different Vodou ceremonies at Christmas, seeking protection against evil.

716   Métraux, Alfred. "Origines e historia de los cultos vodú." *Casa de las Américas* (Havana), nos. 36-37 [6] (May-August 1966): 42-62.
        Spanish translation of chap. 1 of "Le vaudou haïtien ... zombis." *Les Lettres Nouvelles* (Paris), no. 64 [6] (October 1958). Also available in English in chap. 1 of *Voodoo in Haiti* (New York: Oxford University Press, 1959), pp. 25-57.

717   Métraux, Alfred. "Réactions psychologiques à la christianisation de la Vallée de Marbial (Haïti)." *Revue de Psychologie des Peuples* 8, no. 3 (1953): 250-67.

718   Métraux, Alfred. "La religion vodou en Haïti." *Panorama du Monde et des Sciences* (Paris), no. 2 (Summer 1953), pp. 9-15.

719   Métraux, Alfred. "Les rites de naissance dans le vodou haïtien." In *Mélanges Pittard*. Brive (Corrèze): Chastrusse & Co., 1957, pp. 229-33.

720   Métraux, Alfred. "Les rites d'initiation dans le vodou haïtien." *Tribus* (Stuttgart), n.s., nos. 4-5 (1954-55), pp. 177-98.

721   Métraux, Alfred. "Rites funéraires des paysans haïtiens." *Arts et Traditions Populaires* (Paris) 2, no. 4 (1954): 289-306.
       On the Vodou cult of the dead.

722   Métraux, Alfred. "Le vaudou haïtien: Sociétés de sorciers et zombis." *Les Lettres Nouvelles* (Paris), no. 64 [6] (October 1958): 395-407.

723   Métraux, Alfred. "Le vodou et christianisme." *Les Temps Modernes* (Paris), no. 136 [12] (June 1957): 1848-83.
       Includes the symbiosis between Catholicism and Vodou; pp. 1861-70, attitude of the Church, and successful anti-idolatry campaign in Marbial Valley; pp. 1877-83, Vodou's relation to Protestantism.

724   Métraux, Alfred. "Vodou et protestantisme." *Revue d'Histoire des Religions* 144, no. 2 (1953): 198-216.
       See also his *Voodoo in Haiti* (entry 725) and review in *American Anthropologist*, October 1961, p. 1129, as being inadequate on Protestantism.

725   Métraux, Alfred. *Le voudou haïtien*. 5th ed. Paris: Gallimard, 1958, 357 pp., illus. English translation. *Voodoo in Haiti*. New York: Oxford University Press; London: A. Deutsch, 1959, 400 pp., illus. 2d ed. New York: Schocken Books, 1972.

726   Métraux, Alfred, and Schulman, Fernande. "Jeux de sexe et de la mort dans le vodou." *La Nouvelle Revue Française* (Paris), no. 125 [21] (1963): 796-809.

727   Métraux, Rhoda. "Some aspects of hierarchical structure in Haiti." In *Acculturation in the Americas*, edited by S. Tax. Chicago: University of Chicago Press, 1952. Reprint. New York: Cooper Square Publications, 1967, pp. 185-94.
       P. 187 (notes 5 and 7), leadership in Vodou; pp. 190-92, hierarchical structures within Vodou sanctuaries.

728   Metzger, E. "Haïti. III. Vaudoux Verehrung und Kannibalismus." *Globus* (Brunswick) 47 (1885): 252-53.

729 Michel, Rose Lhérisson. *La grande famille haïtienne: Christianisme et vodou*. Port-au-Prince: Imprimerie des Antilles, 1970, 28 pp.

729a Mikell, Gwendolyn. "When horses talk: Reflections on Zora Neale Hurston's Haitian anthropology." *Phylon* (Atlanta) 43, no. 3 (September 1982): 218-30.
Describes Hurston's training and critiques her anthropology. See Z. N. Hurston (entry 559).

730 Mintz, Sidney W[ilfred]. Introduction to *Voodoo in Haiti*, by A. Métraux. 2d English ed. New York: Schocken Books, 1972, pp. 1-14, bib.
A good evaluation of Métraux's work on Vodou, with further comments.

731 Mirel, E. "Voodoo and politics." *Science Newsletter* (Washington, D.C.) 83 (11 May 1963), p. 299.

732 Missions Advanced Research and Communications Center. *Status of Christianity: Haiti*. Monrovia, Calif.: Missions Advanced Research and Communications Center, 1972, 8 pp.

732a Moissan, Catherine. *Pampa, vaudou, samba: En Amerique avec la tournée Louis Jouvet*. Collection des Voyages de Lettres. Paris: Fasquelle Éditeurs, 1947, 217 pp.

733 Montilus, [Robert] Guérin. *Dieux en diaspora: Les loa haïtiens et les vodun du royaume d'allada (Sud Dahomey). Étude ethnologique comparative*. Paris: UNESCO, 1971, 202 pp.

733a Montilis, Gérin [Montilus, Robert Guérin]. "Fini Ak Kont Sa a: Vodou Ayisyin soti Daomé." *Sel. Jornal Ayisyin Alétrangé* (New York) 6, no. 42 (1978): 28-33.
In Creole. The death of Atale: Haitian Vodou came from Dahomey.

734 Montilus, Robert Guérin. "Haïti: Un cas témoin de la vivacité des religions africaines en Amérique et pourquoi?" In *Colloque de Cotonou: Les religions africaines comme source de valeurs de civilisation*. Paris: Présence Africaine, 1972, pp. 297-309.

734a Montilus, Robert Guérin. *Mythes, écologie, acculturation en Haiti: Essai sur la réinterpretation des mythes du Golfe de Guinée dans le Vaudou haitien*. Collection: Archives et documents. Paris: Institut d'Ethnologie, Sorbonne, 1974.

735   Montilus, Robert Guérin. "La pratique religieuse haïtienne dans ses dimensions historiques et sociologiques." In *Études sur le vodou*, by R. G. Montilus, et al. Sondeos, 2. Cuernavaca, Mexico: Centro Inter-Cultural de Documentación, 1966, pp. 3-20. Reprinted from *Rond-Point* (Port-au-Prince), no. 8 (June-July 1963), pp. 2-19.

736   Montilus, [Robert] Guérin. "Les repas sacrés haïtiens – Essai d'interprétation théologique." Mémoire de Théologie, Paris, 1968.

737   Montilus, [Robert] Guérin. *Les repas sacrificiels du vodou haïtien: Contexte historique et rituel (essai).* Mémoire d'Ethnologie, Institut d'Ethnologie. Paris: Musée de l'Homme, 1969, 189 pp.

738   Montilis, Gérin [Montilus, Robert Guérin]. "Sa yo rélé vodou? Sa loua yo yé?" *Sel. Jounal Ayisyin Alétrangé* (New York) 6, no. 41 (1978): 3-8.
        In Creole. What is Vodou? Who are the Vodou spirits?

739   Montilus, [Robert] Guérin, et al. *Études sur le vodou.* Sondeos, 2. Cuernavaca, Mexico: Centro Inter-Cultural de Documentación, 1966, 163 pp.
        Essays reprinted from various journals, etc., and sharing a more positive nonpolemic approach to Vodou. See L. Bijou (entry 350), F. Gayot (entry 526), R. G. Montilus (entry 735), J. Parisot (entry 763), P. Pompilus (entry 794), J.-M. Salgado (entry 845), and W. Smarth (entry 871).

740   Moral, Paul. *Le paysan haïtien: Étude sur la vie rurale en Haïti.* Paris: Maisonneuve & Larose, 1961, 375 pp. Reprint. Port-au-Prince: Fardin, [1977?].
        Doctoral dissertation, University of Paris, 1961.

741   Morand, Paul. *Magie noire.* Paris, 1928.

742   Moreau de Saint Méry, Médéric Louis Elie. *Description topographique . . . de la partie française de l'isle Saint-Domingue. . . .* 2 vols. Philadelphia, 1797-98. New ed. Edited by B. Maurel and E. Taillemite. Paris: Larose, 1958.
        The basic primary source. A learned West Indian (b. Martinique, 1750) who was an eye-witness in Haïti. Vol. 1, pp. 44-51, etc., describes Vodou immediately before the slave revolt – extracted and translated in J. J. Williams (entry 928), pp. 59-68. The first detailed account of the new, more unified form of Negro religion that developed after ca. 1760 (summary in A. Métraux [entry 725], pp. 36-38). Pp. 210-11, on the Don Pedro dance or cult (Métraux, idem, pp. 38-39); pp. 651-53, Macandel, the miracle-working rebel, 1757.

743   Morris, Joe Alex. "Doctors vs. witchcraft." *Saturday Evening Post*, 16 September 1961.

744   Mortel, Roger. *Le mythomanie sociale en Haïti: Essais de psychologie*. Port-au-Prince: Imprimerie du Collège Vertières, 1947.
See especially pp. 5-7, 30-31, 40-43.

745   Motta, R. [Protest and conformism in the Vodou rite.] *Ciência e Trópico* (Recife) 7, no. 2 (1979): 255-62, bib.; English and French summaries.
In Portuguese.

746   Mudimbe, Valentin Y. "Et Dieu que devient-il?" *Cahiers des Religions Africaines* (Kinshasa), no. 15 [8] (January 1974): 135-41.
A review article of L. Hurbon's *Dieu dans le vaudou haïtien* (entry 555), by an African scholar appreciative of Hurbon's work, but ultimately rejecting his methodology.

747   Mulrain, George M[acdonald]. *Theology in folk culture: The theological significance of Haïtian folk religion*. Frankfurt and Bern: Peter Lang, 1984, 423 pp.
Pt. 2, theological issues. Pp. 79-110, eschatology. By a Trinidadian Methodist minister who has worked in Haiti.

748   Mumper, Sharon E. "Global report: A world-wide survey." *Evangelical Missions Quarterly* 23 (January 1987): 92-97.
Pp. 92-93, subsection "Voodoo on the defensive."

749   Muñoz, Nélida Agosto de. "Haitian Voodoo: Social control of the unconscious." *Caribbean Review* (San Juan) 4, no. 3 (July-September 1972).
How individuals' unconscious thoughts are controlled through spirit possession.

750   Murray, Gerald F[rancis]. "Population pressure, land tenure, and Voodoo: The economics of Haitian peasant ritual." In *Beyond the myths of culture: Essays in cultural materialism*. Edited by E. B. Ross. New York and London: Academic Press, 1980, pp. 295-321.
Effects of the demands of Vodou ritual on the land-tenure system.

751   Newell, William W. "Myths of Voodoo worship and child sacrifice in Hayti." *Journal of American Folklore* 1, no. 1 (1888): 16-30.

752   Newell, William W. "Reports of Voodoo worship in Hayti and Louisiana." *Journal of American Folklore* 2, no. 4 (1889): 41-47.

Vodou in the New Orleans area.

753   Nicholls, David. *From Dessalines to Duvalier: Race, colour, and national independence in Haiti*. Cambridge Latin America Studies, 34. Cambridge: Cambridge University Press, 1979, 384 pp., map.

       Pp. 132-34, Vodou; pp. 134-36, the "Pan-African movement"; pp. 135-38, "the ethnological movement"–Dorsainvil, Holly, J. Price-Mars; pp. 158-64, "the literary movement"–J. Roumain, C. Brouard; pp. 167-72, "noirisme" on the black heritage or negritude–L. Denis, F. Duvalier; pp. 181-83, the "anti-superstition campaign."

754   Nicholls, David. "Idéologie et mouvements politiques en Haïti (1915-1946)." *Annales: Économies, Sociétés, Civilisations* (Paris) 30, no. 4 (1975): 654-79, bib. references.

       Vodou, passim, in the course of discussing various social and cultural movements of a nationalistic nature. Similar to entries 753 and 756.

755   Nicholls, David. "Ideology and political protest in Haiti, 1930-1946." *Journal of Contemporary History* 9 (October 1974): 3-26.

       Pp. 6, 8, passing references to Vodou; pp. 11-14, the Catholic "anti-superstition campaign."

756   Nicholls, David. "Religion and politics in Haiti." *Canadian Journal of Political Science* 3, no. 3 (1970): 400-414.

       Brief account of the early period; fuller account from the 1920s; detailed account of the Duvalier period, 1957-66.

757   Niles, Blair. *Black Hayti: A biography of Africa's eldest daughter*. New York: G. P. Putnam's Sons, 1926, 325 pp.

       One of many books of average and below-average quality that appeared during the twenties, normally putting emphasis on the political instability of the country and the dark aspects of Vodou.

758   Oddon, Yvonne. "Une cérémonie funéraire haïtienne." In *Les Afro-Américains*. Mémoires de l'Institut Français de l'Afrique Noire, no. 27. Dakar: IFAN, 1952 [1953 on cover], pp. 245-48.

       The Vodou ceremony of *wété mo nâ dlo*, to restore the soul of the dead from the aquatic to the terrestrial realm.

759   Oriol, Jacques. *Les survivances du totémisme dans le vodou haïtien*. Port-au-Prince: Bureau d'Ethnologie, 1967, 32 pp., bib.

       Reviews the literature and describes totemic survivals, but not by field study.

760 Oriol, Jacques; Viaud, Léonce; and Aubourg, Michel. "Le mouvement folklorique en Haïti." *Bulletin du Bureau d'Ethnologie* (Port-au-Prince) 2, no. 9 (April 1952).

761 Owen, Mary A[licia]. "Voodoo." In *Encyclopaedia of religion and ethics*. Vol. 12. Edinburgh: T. & T. Clark, 1921, pp. 640a-641b.

Reflects the loose popular reference to "devil-worship" and "fetishism" associated with Negro slave religion in the U.S. and West Indies; associated in the index with cannibalism, lycanthropy, serpent-worship, and vampires. An example of ignorance and misrepresentation in a major learned encyclopedia; throws little light on religion in Haiti.

762 Paré, Jean-Michel. "Dimension politique du fait religieux en Haïti." *Nouvelle Optique* (Montreal), nos. 6-7 (1972), pp. 5-29.

763 Parisot, Jean. "Vodou et adaptation." *Pastorale et Vodu: Église en Marche* (Port-au-Prince), no. 2 (December 1963), pp. 15-26. Reprinted in *Études sur le vodou*, by R. G. Montilus et al. Sondeos, 2. Cuernavaca, Mexico: Centro Inter-Cultural de Documentación, 1966, pp. 96-109.

A more tolerant attitude toward spirit possession.

764 Parisot, Jean. "Vodou et christianisme." In *Des prêtres noirs s'interrogent*. Paris: Éditions du Cerf, 1957, pp. 213-59. 1966 ed. Paris: Éditions du Cerf, pp. 213-58 [p. 240 has been abbreviated].

By a Catholic priest.

765 Parsons, Elsie Clews. "El culto de los Espiritus en Haiti." *Archivos del Folklore Cubano* (Havana) 4, no. 4 (1929): 334-55; 5, no. 3 (1930): 193-205.

766 Parsons, Elsie Clews. "Spirit cult in Hayti." *Journal de la Société des Américanistes* (Paris) 20 (1928): 157-79.

A valuable account of many *loa*, their names, texts of associated songs, details of rituals and healers; also dissociates "zombies" from reports of human cannibalism.

767 Paul, Emmanuel-Casséus. "Bilan spirituel du Boyéisme." *Revue de la Société Haïtienne d'Histoire, de Géographie, et de Géologie* (Port-au-Prince), no. 87 [23] (1952): 1-15; no. 89 [23] (1952): 37-47; no. 90 [24] (1952): 30-38; no. 91 (1953), pp. 43-49.

Boyer was president of Haiti, 1820-45.

768 Paul, Emmanuel-Casséus. "Carnaval, rara, vodou." *Optique* (Port-au-Prince), no. 23 (January 1956).

769 Paul, Emmanuel-Casséus. "Considérations sur le dogme du vodou." *Bulletin du Bureau d'Ethnologie* (Port-au-Prince), 2d ser., no. 12 (1955).

770 Paul, Emmanuel-Casséus. *L'ethnologie en Haïti*. Port-au-Prince: Imprimerie de l'État, 1949.

771 Paul, Emmanuel-Casséus. *Ethnologie et christianisme* (Port-au-Prince) 34 (December 1956).

772 Paul, Emmanuel-Casséus. "La notion du *mana* dans la culture haïtienne." *Optique* (Port-au-Prince), no. 30 (August 1956), pp. 49-52. Also as "Dans le vodou haïtien," in *Selected papers of the Fifth International Congress of Anthropological and Ethnological Sciences*, Philadelphia, 1956.

773 Paul, Emmanuel-Casséus. *Panorama du folklore haïtien: Présence africaine en Haïti*. Port-au-Prince: Imprimerie de l'État, 1962, 323 pp., illus. Reprint. Port-au-Prince: Fardin, 1978.
        Includes Vodou myths and beliefs; see especially pp. 230-31, 248-81.

774 Paul, Emmanuel-Casséus. "Représentations religieuses dans le vodou." *Bulletin du Bureau d'Ethnologie*, 2d ser., no. 12 (1955), pp. 47-54.

775 Paul, Emmanuel-Casséus. "Le sacrifice de l'igname." *Le National*, 25 July 1953.

776 Paul, Emmanuel-Casséus. "Le vaudou est-il une religion monothéiste ou polythéiste?" *Bulletin du Bureau d'Ethnologie* (Port-au-Prince), 3d ser., no. 27 (April 1961), pp. 3-22.

777 No entry.

778 Pelton, Robert Wayne. *The complete book of Voodoo*. New York: G. P. Putnam's Sons, [ca. 1972], 254 pp., illus., bib. (pp. 247-54).
        In Haiti and New Orleans – analyzed in depth.

779 Pelton, Robert Wayne. *Voodoo secrets from A. to Z.* South Brunswick, N.Y.: Barnes; London: Yoseloff, 1974, 138 pp., illus.

780 Pelton, Robert Wayne. *Voodoo signs and omens*. South Brunswick, N.Y.: Barnes; London: Yoseloff, 1974, 284 pp., bib. (pp. 277-84).

780a   Perkins, Kenneth. *Voodoo'd*. New York: Harper & Brothers, 1931, 289 pp.

         A "mystery story."

781   Peters, Carl Edward. *La croix contre l'asson*. Port-au-Prince: La Phalange, 1960, 298 pp.

         By a Catholic priest. "Asson" is the net-covered calabash rattle of the Vodou priest.

782   Peters, Carl E[dward]. *Lumière sur le houmfort*. Port-au-Prince: Chérquit, 1941, 55 pp.

         Violently attacks Vodou, as part of the "anti-superstition campaign."

783   Peters, C[arl] E[dward]. *Le service des 'loas.'* Port-au-Prince: Imprimerie Telhomme, 1956, 108 pp.

         On the Vodou services called *manger-mort* in honor of the gods and the dead. See summary of pp. 71-75 in A. Métraux (entry 725), pp. 264-65. Critical of spirit possession.

784   Philippe, Jeanne. "Bilinguisme, syncrétisme religieux dans la vocabulaire des troubles mentaux en Haïti." *Conjonction* (Port-au-Prince, Institut Français d'Haïti) 132 (December 1976-January 1977): 45-58.

         The influence of bilingualism and religious syncretism on the perception and experience of mental disorders in Haiti.

785   Philippe, Jeanne, and Romain, Jean-Baptiste. "*Indisposition* in Haiti (with brief comments on the occurrence, etiology, and treatment of *indisposition*, by Claude Charles)." *Social Science and Medicine* (Oxford) 13B, no. 2 (1979): 129-33, 135-36.

         "Indisposition" is a syndrome falling between psychic and somatic ailments, here interpreted as "one of several types of dissociative states commonly used by Haitians."

786   Pierre, André. "Ma théologie vaudou: L'artiste André Pierre parle à Roger Gaillard." *Le Nouveau Monde: Le Quotidien National et International d'Haïti* (Port-au-Prince), no. 2578 [18] (19 February 1975): 1, 3.

787   Pierre, R[oland]. "Caribbean religion: The Voodoo case." *Sociological Analysis* 38, no. 1 (1977): 25-36, bib.

788   Pierre, Roland. "La notion de salut dans le vaudou haïtien." 2 vols. Thèse de doctorat 3è cycle (sciences religieuses), Faculté de Théologie Catholique de Strasbourg, 1970, 1:332 pp.; 2:73 pp.

789 Planson, Claude. *À la découverte du vaudou*. Paris: Éditions de Vecchi, 1978, 223 pp.

By a French theatrical director concerned with drama and the sacred, married to a Vodou priestess, and himself initiated into the grade of *hounsi kanzo*.

790 Planson, Claude. *Le vaudou*. Paris: MA Éditions, 1987, 188 pp.
Defends Vodou.

791 Planson, Claude. *Vaudou: Un initié parle*. Collection "Dieu." Paris: Jean Dullis, 1974, 326 pp., illus., bib.

A vivid, intimate, and comprehensive account, with appendixes containing texts (prayers, songs, etc.), ritual calendar, glossary, tables on *loa* and initiation societies.

792 Planson, Claude (text), and Vannier, Jean-François (photos). *Vaudou/Voodoo rituels et possessions/rituals and possessions*. Paris: Pierre Horay Éditeur, 1975, 79 pp, many illus.

Text in French and English.

793 Pollak-Eltz, Angelina. "Culto vodun en Haïti." In *Cultos afroamericanos*. Caracas: Universidad Catolica Andrés Bello, 1972, 270 pp.

See also entry 76.

794 Pompilus, Pradel. "Le vaudou dans la littérature haïtienne." *Rond-Point* (Port-au-Prince), no. 8 (June-July 1963). Reprinted in *Études sur le vodou*, by R. G. Montilus, et al. Cuernavaca, Mexico: Centro Inter-Cultural de Documentación, 1966, pp. 69-83.

795 Pressoir, Catts. *Le protestantisme haïtien*. 3 vols. Histoire de la Nation Haïtienne. [Port-au-Prince]: Imprimerie de la Société Biblique et des Livres Religieux d'Haïti, 1945, 1:257 pp. Reprint. (3 vols. in 2.) Port-au-Prince: M. Vilaire, 1976, 1977.

Chap. 2 (pp. 16-32), "Le paganisme haïtien" – on Vodou.

796 Price, Hannibal. *De la réhabilitation de la race noire*. Port-au-Prince: Verrolot, 1900.

Includes a positive account of Vodou.

797 Price-Mars, Jean. "Africa in the Americas." *Tomorrow* (New York) 3, no. 1 (1954): 75-84.

Surveys the historical and geographical origins of Vodou. Price-Mars founded the Haitian school of ethnology and became director of the new Bureau d'Ethnologie.

798   Price-Mars, Jean. *Ainsi parla l'oncle . . . Essais d'Ethnographie*. Paris and Port-au-Prince: Imprimerie de Compiègne, 1928. Reprint. 1929, 243 pp. Reprint. Paris: Édition B. Grasset, 1947. 2d ed. New York: Parapsychology Foundation, 1954, 245 pp. New ed., with introduction by R. Cornevin (pp. 11-42). Collection Caraïbes. Ottawa: Éditions Leméac, 1973, 314 pp. Spanish translation. *Así habló el tío*. Havana: Casa de las Américas, 1968, xxxvii + 298 pp., bib., pp. 295-99. English translation, with introduction and notes. *So spoke uncle*. Translated by Magdeline W. Shannon. Washington, D.C.: Three Continents, 1983, 252 pp., illus.

This famous book includes the first open and objective defense of Vodou as a genuine religion. The rest is a rather poor ethnographic picture of peasant life, but the work was the seminal book for the "negritude" movement through its positive evaluation of the African heritage and the new culture created in Haiti.

799   Price-Mars, Jean. "Le culte des marassas." *Afroamérica* (Mexico City) 1, nos. 1-2 (1945): 41-49.

The cult of twins in Vodou.

800   Price-Mars, Jean. "Le culte du vaudou en Haïti, par M. J. Verschueren: Essai critique." *Revue de la Société Haïtienne d'Histoire et de Géographie* (Port-au-Prince), October 1948.

801   Price-Mars, Jean. *De Saint-Domingue à Haïti: Essai sur la culture, les arts, et la littérature*. Paris: Présence Africaine, 1959, 170 pp.

802   Price-Mars, Jean. *Une étape de l'évolution haïtienne*. Port-au-Prince: Imprimerie de la Presse, 1929, 208 pp.

Exposition and defense of Vodou similar to *Ainsi parla l'oncle* (entry 798) – as genuine animism and not superstition.

803   Price-Mars, Jean. *Formation ethnique: Folk-lore et culture du peuple haïtien*. Port-au-Prince: V. Valgin, 1959, 151 pp. Reprint. Port-au-Prince: Imprimerie N. A. Théodore, 1956, 151 pp.

804   Price-Mars, Jean. "Lemba-petro: Un culte secret." *Revue de la Société d'Histoire et de Géographie d'Haïti* (Port-au-Prince), no. 18 [9] (January 1938): 12-31.

"Petro" is a local name for Vodou blood-sacrifice ceremonies.

805   Price-Mars, Jean. "Puissance de la foi religieuse chez les Nègres de Saint-Domingue dans l'insurrection générale des esclaves de 1791 à 1803." *Revue d'Histoire des Colonies* (Paris) 42, no. 1 (1954): 5-13.

806   Price-Mars, Jean. "Le sentiment et le phénomène religieux chez les Nègres de Saint-Domingue." *Bulletin de la Société d'Histoire et de Géographie d'Haïti* (Port-au-Prince) 1 (May 1925).

The author had served as ambassador to the Dominican Republic.

807   Price-Mars, Jean. "Simples remarques de psychiatrie sur les crises vaudouesques." *Les Annales de Médecine Haïtienne* (Port-au-Prince) 8 (1930).

808   Price-Mars, Jean. "Sociologie religieuse: La République d'Haïti." *Revue de la Société Haïtienne d'Histoire et de Géographie* (Port-au-Prince), no. 71 [19] (1948): 1-21.

809   Price-Mars, Jean. "Les survivances africaines dans la communauté haïtienne." *Études Dahoméennes: Institut Français de l'Afrique Noire* (Porto Novo) 6 (n.d.): 5-10. Also in *Les Afro-Américains*. Mémoires de l'Institut Français de l'Afrique Noire, no. 27. Dakar: IFAN, 1952 [1953 on cover], pp. 249-53.

A general survey; p. 252, religious survivals.

810   Price-Mars, Jean. "Le vodou haïtien: L'ouvrage du Dr. Louis Maximilien." *Haiti Journal*, November 1945.

811   No entry.

812   Prichard, Hesketh [Vernon]. *Where black rules white: A journey across and about Hayti.* 3d ed. Westminster: A. Constable, 1900, 288 pp., illus. Reprint. London and New York: T. Nelson, 1908, etc. Reprint. Shannon: Irish University Press, 1972, 288 pp., illus.

Chap. 4 (pp. 74-101, 274-75), Vodou worship and sacrifice, the priest being "a Borgia in poisons . . . an actor, a colossal quack, and a terrorist."

813   *Pro Mundi Vita.* Dossiers for Latin America. Series "Informes" (Spanish only). *Haïti*, no. 19 (1980).

814   Ravenscroft, Kent, Jr. "Spirit possession in Haiti: A tentative theoretical analysis." B.A. Honors thesis, Yale University, 1962.

815   Ravenscroft, Kent, [Jr.]. "Voodoo possession: A natural experiment in hypnosis." *International Journal of Clinical and Experimental Hypnosis* 13, no. 3 (1965): 157-82.

816   Rémy, Rémus. *Vaudou, magie, et sorcellerie.* Port-au-Prince, 1937.

817   Rigaud, Milo. *Jésus ou Legba, ou Les dieux se battent*. École du Symbolisme Afro-Haïtien. Poitiers, 1933, 245 pp.
See entry 639 for review by A. Lescouflair.

818   Rigaud, Milo. "Le röle du vaudou dans l'indépendence d'Haïti." *Présence Africaine*, nos. 17-18 (February-March 1958), pp. 43-68.

819   Rigaud, Milo. *La tradition vaudoo et le vaudoo haïtien: Son temple, ses mystères, sa magie*. Paris: Éditions Niclaus, 1953, 433 pp., photos by Odette Mennesson-Rigaud. English translation. *Secrets of Voodoo*. New York: Arco, 1969. Reprint. 1971, 219 pp., illus.
By a poet, painter, and novelist with intimate knowledge of Vodou and many speculative theories. Pp. 144-46 (Eng. trans.), a fairly complete list of the *loa*; pp. 167-204, exorcism of the "dead" who have been sent against a person.

820   Rigaud, Milo. *Vè-vè, diagrammes rituels du vodou*. Trilingual ed. (French, English, and Spanish). New York: French and European Publications, 1974, 587 pp., mainly illus.

821   Riou, Roger. "Medicine or Voodoo?" *Worldmission* 17 (1966): 26-32.
A Catholic missionary account.

822   Robert, Paul. *Catholicisme et vaudou*. Collection Sondeos, 82. Cuernavaca, Mexico: Editions du CIDOC, 1971, 516 pp.
A collection of studies and pastoral letters by the bishop of Gonaïves, a leader in the "anti-superstition" campaign, on the missionary problem in relation to Vodou, regarded as paganism.

823   Robert, Paul. *Superstition et religion en Haïti*. N.p., n.d.

824   Robert, Paul. *Texte du rapport sur la superstition*. Port-au-Prince, 1947.

824a Robinson, G. R. "Voodoo on the hearth." *Popular Gardening* (London) 12 (May 1961): 22.

825   Rodman, Selden. *Haiti: The black republic. The complete study and guide*. New York: Devin-Adair Co., 1954, 168 pp. 2d rev. ed. Old Greenwich, Conn.: Devin-Adair Co., 1961. Rev. ed. 1973, 168 pp., illus.
Pp. 61, 64-75 (1st ed.), the Catholic and Vodou religions, especially good on Vodou, with fine illustrations (see between pp. 42-43); pp. 76-77, the Protestant Episcopal church and Vodou.

826 Rodman, Selden. *The miracle of Haitian art*. Garden City, N.Y.: Doubleday & Co., 1965. Reprint. 1974, 95 pp., illus.

A Haitian poet and art critic, who traces the origins of Haitian folk art in Vodou vèvè or symbolic drawings.

827 Rodriguez, Manuel Tomás. *Papa Legbá (la crónic del voudú o pacto con el diablo)*. Ciudad Trujillo: Imprimerie Arte y Cine, 1945, 190 pp. 2d ed. Santo Domingo, 1962, 195 pp.

828 Romain, Charles Poisset. "Introduction à la sociologie du protestantisme en Haïti." *Conjonction* (Port-au-Prince), nos. 141-42 (1979), pp. 35-48.

Pp. 40-47, various remarks about the relation of Protestantism and Vodou, and the former's break with Haitian tradition.

829 Romain, Jean-Baptiste. *Africanismes haïtiens: Compilations et notes*. Port-au-Prince: Imprimerie de l'État, 1978, 102 pp., illus.

830 Romain, Jean-Baptiste. "Généralités sur le vodou haïtien." *Revue de la Faculté d'Ethnologie* (State University, Haiti) 15 (1970): 1-14.

830a Romain, Jean-Baptiste. "Introduction au vaudou haïtien." *Conjonction* (Port-au-Prince) 21, no. 1 (1970): 3-17.

831 Romain, Jean-Baptiste. *Quelques moeurs et coutumes des paysans haïtiens*. Port-au-Prince: Imprimerie de l'État, 1958.

Pp. 151-217, the popular religion of the region of Milot; by the dean of the Faculty of Ethnology in Haiti.

832 Romain, Jean-Baptiste. "Survivances africaines dans la culture d'Haïti." In *Cultural traditions and Caribbean identity*, edited by J. K. Wilkerson. Gainsville: Center for Latin American Studies, University of Florida, 1980, pp. 233-42; English summary (pp. 243-44); Spanish summary (pp. 245-46).

833 Ronceray, Hubert de. "Enquête empirique au Belair." *Conjonction* (Port-au-Prince), no. 119 (February-March 1973), pp. 19-29.

A black ghetto in downtown Port-au-Prince.

834 Ronceray, Hubert de. "El vudu en la sociedad haitiana." *Advance* 2, no. 69 (November 1973): 31-33.

835 Rotberg, Robert Irwin. "Vodun and politics of Haiti." In *The African diaspora*, edited by M. L. Kilson and R. I. Rotberg. Cambridge, Mass.: Harvard University Press, 1976, pp. 342-65.

836 Rotberg, Robert [Irwin], and Clague, Christopher K. *Haiti – The politics of squalor*. Boston: Houghton Mifflin, 1971, 456 pp.

Pp. 164-65, Vodou rediscovered by Haitian writers and supported by Duvalier.

837 Roumain, Jacques. *À propos de la campagne "anti-superstitieuse."* Port-au-Prince: Imprimerie de l'État, 1937. Reprint. 1942, 26 pp.

By one of the founders of the Bureau d'Ethnologie in Haiti and a protégé of A. Métraux. See D. Nicholls (entry 753), p. 160.

838 Roumain, Jacques. *Gouverneurs de la rosée*. Paris: Éditeurs Français Réunis, 1944. English translation. *Masters of the dew*. New York: Reynal & Hitchcock, 1947, x + 180 pp. Reprinted, with an introduction by J. M. Dash (pp. 5-21). Caribbean Writers Series. London: Heinemann, 1978, 192 pp.

An outstanding novel. Pp. 8-11, 64-72, description of a Vodou thanksgiving service among extremely poor peasants.

839 Roumain, Jacques. *Le sacrifice du tambour-assotor*. Publication du Bureau d'Ethnologie de la République d'Haïti, 1. Port-au-Prince: Imprimerie de l'État, 1943, 71 pp.

Assotor is a large sacred drum inhabited by a *loa*. See summary in A. Métraux (entry 725), pp. 168-70, 184-85.

840 Rousseau, Alfred. "Un enterrement à la campagne." *Le Soir* (Port-au-Prince), 4 May 1907.

On the Vodou cult of the dead.

841 Rubin, V[era D.], and Schaedel, R. P., eds. *The Haitian potential: Research and resources in Haiti*. New York and London: Teachers College Press, 1975.

See E. Douyon (entry 487).

842 Saint-Jean, Serge. *Naïfs d'Haïti et vaudou*. Port-au-Prince: Imprimerie des Antilles, 1972, 52 pp.

Vodou art, primitivism, and twentieth-century art in Haiti.

843 St. John, Spencer [Buckingham]. *Hayti, or the black republic*. London: Smith, Elder & Co., 1884. Reprint. 1889, 343 pp., map. Reprint. London: F. Cass, 1972. French translation. *Haïti, ou La république noire*. Paris: Plon, 1886, xv + 336 pp.

British consul for ten years in the 1870s; chap. 5 (pp. 182-228), "Vaudoux worship and cannibalism." Made Haiti infamous as a land of human sacrifice and cannibalism, but did bring it to the attention of the outside world. Pp. 197-204, account of an alleged anthropophagy; pp. 254-55, Catholicism and Vodou.

843a   Salgado, Antoine. *Le phénomène des zombies dans la culture haïtienne*. Port-au-Prince: Imprimerie des Antilles, 1982, 146 pp., illus.
         A general discussion.

844   Salgado, Jean-Marie [O.M.I.]. "Appréciation du vodou à la lumière de la révélation." In *Études sur le vodou*, by R. G. Montilus, et al. Sondeos, 2. Cuernavaca, Mexico: Centro Inter-Cultural de Documentación, 1966, pp. 121-59.

845   Salgado, Jean-Marie. *Le culte africain du vaudou et les baptisés en Haïti: Essai de pastorale*. Urbania, Nova Series 2. Rome: Editiones Urbanianae, 1963, xviii + 117 pp. Selection reprinted in *Études sur le vodou*, by R. G. Montilus, et al. Cuernavaca, Mexico: Centro Inter-Cultural de Documentación, 1966, pp. 21-61.

846   Salgado, Jean-Marie. "Données ethnologiques; vodou primitif: Culte de serpent? Culte de l'Être Suprême?" In *Études sur le vodou*, by R. G. Montilus, et al. Cuernavaca, Mexico: Centro Inter-Cultural de Documentación, 1966, pp. 21-61.

846a   Salgado, Jean Marie. *Hauts-lieux sacrés dans le sous-sol d'Haiti (1947-1980)*. Port-au-Prince: Les Ateliers Fardin, 1980, 243 pp.

847   Salgado, Jean-Marie. "Survivance des cultes africains et syncrétisme en Haïti." In *Devant les sectes non-chrétiennes*, by Museum Lessianum. Louvain: Desclée de Brouwer, 1962, pp. 225-52.

848   Savain, Pétion. *La case de Damballah*. Port-au-Prince, 1939.
         A novel on Haitian life; includes much on Vodou (e.g., songs, pp. 208-12).

849   Scarpa, Antonio. "Appunti di etnoiatria haitiana." *Episteme: Revista Critica* ... (Milan) 7, no. 4 (1973): 298-303.
         Notes on Haitian ethnomedicine.

850   Scofield, John. "Haiti–West Africa in the West Indies." *National Geographic Magazine* 119, no. 2 (1961): 226-59, illus.
         Pp. 226, 253, 256-59, Vodou, with good color photos.

851   Seabrook, William B[uehler]. *Geheimnisvolles Haiti: Rätsel und Symbolik des Wodu-Kultes*. Munich: Matthes & Seitz, 1982, 252 pp.

852   Seabrook, William B[uehler]. *The magic island*. London: George G. Harrap & Co., 1929, 320 pp., illus.; New York: Literary Guild of

America, 1929, 336 pp. Reprint. New York: Paragon House, 1989, 336 pp., illus., + 35 plates of author's photographs.

An influential if somewhat sensational book; pp. 276-79, extract from J. C. Dorsainvil (entry 479); p. 296, extract from B. W. Merwin (entry 699); pp. 299-302, extract from A. C. Holly (entry 549); pp. 302-3, extract from E. Aubin (entry 459); pp. 308-15, extracts from a *houngan*'s book of secret formulas. . . .

853   Seabrook, William B[uehler]. "Le vaudou, culte secret." *La Revue de Paris* (Paris), 15 May 1929, pp. 364-78.

853a   Sertima, Ivan van. "The voodoo gallery: African presence in the ritual and art of Haiti." *Journal of African Civilizations* (New Brunswick, Rutgers University) 3, no. 2 (November 1981): 78-104, plates.

Vodou's dynamic force in Haitian history and differences between Haitian and Dahomean cults – approached through Haitian art.

854   Servan, Anthony. "Obeah and Voodoo." *Blackwood's Magazine*, no. 1636 [271] (February 1952): 110-20.

855   Simpson, George Eaton. "Acculturation in northern Haiti." *Journal of American Folklore*, no. 254 [64] (1951): 397-403.

856   Simpson, G[eorge] E[aton]. "The belief system of Haitian Vodun." *American Anthropologist* 47, no. 1 (1945): 35-59. Reprinted in *Religious cults of the Caribbean*. . . . Río Piedras: Institute of Caribbean Studies, University of Puerto Rico, 1970, pp. 234-56.

857   Simpson, George Eaton. *Black religions in the New World*. New York: Columbia University Press, 1978, 415 pp.

Pp. 62-71 (plus notes, pp. 329-31).

858   Simpson, George E[aton]. "Discussion [of paper by J. Price-Mars, 'Le processus d'une culture']." In *Acculturation in the Americas* . . . , edited by S. Tax. Chicago: University of Chicago Press, 1952, pp. 148-51.

Pp. 149-51, the relation of peasant families to Vodou, and the latter as derived from African and Catholic religions and provincial French witchcraft.

859   Simpson, George Eaton. "Étude comparée du syncrétisme religieux à Haïti et à la Jamaïque." *Bulletin du Bureau d'Ethnologie* (Port-au-Prince), 3d ser., no. 14 (1958), pp. 31-48.

860 Simpson, George Eaton. "Four Vodun ceremonies." *Journal of American Folklore*, no. 232 [59] (April-June 1946): 154-67. Reprinted in *Religious cults of the Caribbean.* . . . Río Piedras: Institute of Caribbean Studies, University of Puerto Rico, 1970, pp. 273-86.

Ceremonies of degradation, transmission, renunciation, and dismissal (i.e., when converted from Vodou to Christianity).

861 Simpson, George Eaton. "Haitian magic." *Social Forces* 19, no. 1 (1940): 95-100.

Contemporary magical practices associated with Vodou in northern Haiti.

862 Simpson, George E[aton]. "Ideas about ultimate reality and meaning in Haitian vodun." *Ultimate Reality and Meaning* 3, no. 3 (1980): 187-99; with reply by Erica Bourguignon, pp. 232-38.

A sympathetic survey of Vodou – its personal view of the divine and concern with this present life.

863 Simpson, George Eaton. "Loup-Garou and loa folktales from northern Haiti." *Journal of American Folklore* 218 [55] (1942): 219-27.

864 Simpson, George Eaton. "Magical practices in northern Haiti." *Journal of American Folklore* 266 [67] (1954): 395-403.

Descriptive reporting.

865 Simpson, George Eaton. "Peasant songs and dances in northern Haiti." *Journal of Negro History* 25, no. 2 (1940): 203-15.

Pp. 212-13, Vodou music and its differences from ordinary *bal* music.

866 Simpson, George Eaton. "Two Vodun-related ceremonies." *Journal of American Folklore* 239 [61] (1948): 49-52.

867 Simpson, George Eaton. "Vodun and Christianity." In *Religious cults of the Caribbean.* . . . Río Piedras: Institute of Caribbean Studies, University of Puerto Rico, 1970, pp. 287-88.

868 Simpson, George E[aton]. "The Vodun cult in Haiti." *African Notes* (Ibadan) 3, no. 2 (1966): 11-21.

Vodou as combining African, Catholic, and French provincial magical elements with local additions to form a religious system that has in fact served the needs of the peasant masses.

869 Simpson, G[eorge] E[aton]. "The Vodun service in northern Haiti." *American Anthropologist* 42, no. 2:1 (1940): 236-54. Reprinted in

Religious cults of the Caribbean. . . . Río Piedras: Institute of Caribbean Studies, University of Puerto Rico, 1970, pp. 257-72.

A descriptive account.

870   Skrzypek, Marian. [Voodoo–A "peripheric" religion of Haiti.] *Euhemer-Przeglad Religionznowczy* 28, no. 4 (1984): 69-82.

Original text in Polish. Edited abstract from the journal.

871   Smarth, William. "Sevi loa se sevi Satan?" *Pastorale et Vodu: Église en Marche* (Port-au-Prince), no. 2 (December 1963), pp. 29-39.

In Creole. Spirit possession as not necessarily evil.

872   Smat, Lusyin [Smarth, Lucien]. "Kek not pou-n abodé etid vodou." *Sel. Jounal Ayisyin Alétrangé* (New York) 6, no. 42 (1978): 25, 27.

In Creole. Some notes for the study of Vodou.

873   Smat, Ouiliam [Smarth, William]. "Eské legliz mandé pou-n krazé vodou." *Sel. Jounal Ayisyin Alétrangé* (New York) 6, no. 42 (1978): 3-7.

In Creole. Does the church ask us to destroy Vodou?

874   Smat, Ouiliam [Smarth, William]. "Rapo Jézi-Kri ak vodou." *Sel. Jounal Ayisyin Alétrangé* (New York) 6, no. 42 (1978): 7-14.

In Creole. Relation of Jesus Christ to Vodou.

875   Smucker, Glenn R. "The social character of religion in rural Haiti." In *Haiti–to-day and to-morrow: An inter-disciplinary study*, edited by C. R. Foster and A. Valdeman. Lanham, Md.: University Press of America, 1984, pp. 35-56.

876   Snow, L. F. "'I was born just exactly with the gift': An interview with a Voodoo practitioner." *Journal of American Folklore*, no. 341 [86] (1973): 272-81.

877   Sobel, Mechal. *Trabelin' on: The slave journey to an Afro-Baptist faith.* Contributions in Afro-American and African Studies, 36. Westport, Conn.: Greenwood Press, 1979, 454 pp., illus.

Pp. 48-57, and notes 38-41 on pp. 378-79, Vodou from Haiti in Louisiana.

878   Sosis, Howard Justin. "The colonial environment and religion in Haiti: An introduction to the black slave cults in eighteenth century Saint-Domingue." Ph.D. dissertation (religion), Columbia University, 1971, 489 pp.

African religions developed into Vodou cults with only nominal Christian influences; two groups of cults – Rada (the oldest) and Pêtro (named from a cult leader of the 1760s).

879   Souffrant, Claude. "Le cas haïtien: Un catholicisme de résignation (analyse d'un recueil des cantiques catholiques haïtiens)." In *Les religions africaines comme source de valeurs de civilisation*, by the Colloque de Cotonou. Paris: Présence Africaine, 1972, pp. 212-25.

Analysis of a collection of Creole hymns published in 1954; relation of Catholicism and Vodou, passim.

880   Souffrant, Claude. "Un catholicisme de résignation en Haïti: Sociologie d'un recueil de cantiques religieux." *Social Compass* 17, no. 3 (1970): 425-38.

Analysis of Catholic Creole religious texts shows the social values that religion inculcates, although the religion itself can be explained only by the social structure.

881   Souffrant, Claude. "Catholicisme et négritude à l'heure du Black Power." *Parole et Mission* 46 (1969): 377-89. Reprinted in *Présence Africaine* 75 (1970): 131-40.

Pleads for respect for Vodou and other "traditional religions," as a basis of indigenous unity and strength greater than Catholicism.

881a   Souffrant, Claude. "Le fatalisme religieux du paysan haïtien." *Europe: Revue Mensuelle* (Paris) 49, no. 50 (January 1971): 27-41.

882   Souffrant, Claude. "Idéologies afro-américaines du développement: Langston Hughes et le cas d'Haïti." *Présence Africaine* (Paris), no. 103 (1977), pp. 129-44.

882a   Souffrant, Claude. "Idéologies religieuses et développement social autour de deux romans haïtiens: 'Gouverneurs de la rosée' de Jacques Roumain et 'Les arbres musiciens' de Jacques Stephen Alexis." Mémoire, École Pratique des Hautes Études (Paris), 1973.

882b   Souffrant, Claude. *Une négritude socialiste: Religion et développement chez Jacques Roumain, Jacques Alexis, et Langston Hughes*. Paris: Éditions l'Harmattan, 1978, 238 pp.

883   Souffrant, Claude. "La religion du paysan haïtien: De l'anathème au dialogue." *Social Compass* 19, no. 4 (1972): 585-97, bib.

Vodou as much Christian as folk Catholicism in Europe in the Middle Ages or among modern Latin American peasantry, but repressed as pagan until more recent recognition of its values.

884 Souffrant, Claude. "Vaudou et développement chez Jean Price-Mars." *Présence Africaine* (Paris), no. 71 (3d Quarter 1969), pp. 9-18.

885 Stebich, Ute. "Voodoo and art." In *Haitian art*. New York: Brooklyn Museum, 1978, pp. 54-93, illus.

885a Sterlin, Philippe. *Première communication portant sur une étude des vèvès*. Port-au-Prince: Centre de Production de Matériel Educatif, 1954, 8 pp.

886 Sterlin, Philippe. *Vèvès vodou*. Série I. Port-au-Prince: Imprimerie P. Sterlin, 1953, 63 pp., illus.
       Color drawings, with comments, of ritual symbols for African divinities (*vèvès*).

887 Sterlin, Philippe. *Vèvès vodou*. Série II. Port-au-Prince: Imprimerie de l'État, 1954, 48 pp.
       Vèvès are Vodou symbols.

888 Stoddard, T[heodor] L[othrop], ed. *Religions and politics in Haiti*. Institute for Cross-Cultural Research Studies, 1. Washington, D.C.: The Institute, 1966.

889 Stowe, Leland. "Haiti's Voodoo tyrant." *Reader's Digest*, no. 500 [83] (December 1963): 49-53.
       On President Duvalier, described as an "authority on the mumbo-jumbo sorceries" of Vodou, which he exploited for political purposes (pp. 50-51).

890 Sullivan, R. "Putting a hex on Voodoo." *New York Times Magazine*, November 1962, pp. 136-37.

891 Sylvain, Bénito. "La lanterne et le voudoux." *La Fraternité*, 7 October 1890.
       Denies Vodou is important in Haiti.

892 Sylvestre, Fritz. "A sociological analysis of Haitian Voodoo." M.A. thesis, Howard University (Washington, D.C.), 1962, 112 pp.

893 Taft, Edna. *A puritan in Voodoo-land*. Philadelphia: Penn Publishing Co., 1938, 407 pp.

894 Tauxier, Louis. "L'origine exacte du vaudou dans l'île magique." *Revue de Folklore Français et de Folklore Colonial* (Paris) 4-5 (1932): 243-46.

895 Temple, Helen. *A balm in Gilead: Stories from the Caribbean*. Kansas City: Nazarene Publishing House, 1978, 63 pp.

Pp. 9-19, the death curse. Based on a true story involving a Vodou priest – from the missionary point of view.

895a Terrall, Mary. "The structure of the Vodou belief system." Honors thesis, Harvard University, 1974, 64 pp.

896 Terry, Richard R[unciman]. *Voodooism in music and other essays*. Essay Index Reprint Series. London: Burns, Oates & Washbourne, 1934, 146 pp. Facs. reprint. Freeport, N.Y.: Books for Libraries, 1971.

Pp. 1-17, "Voodooism in music"–attacking various claims for Negro spirituals, jazz, etc., as Negro creations with an African background; the latter is found in the "degenerate" and "subversive" cults of Haiti and San Domingo.

897 Thébaud, Frantz. "Katholizismus, Vaudou, und Ideologie im sozio-kulturellen Entwicklungsprozess der Republic Haiti." In *Aspekte der Entwicklungssoziologie*. Kölner Zeitschrift für Soziologie und Sozialpsychologie, Sonderheft 13. Cologne and Opladen: Westdeutscher Verlag, 1969, pp. 122-35.

Fiction – rather sensationalist versions of Vodou, influenced by W. B. Seabrook.

898 Thoby-Marcelin, [Émile] Philippe. "Les grands dieux du voudou haïtien." Introduction by A. Métraux. *Journal de la Société des Américanistes* (Paris), n.s. 36 (1947): 51-135.

Individual divinities, with songs associated with each – a major, detailed study.

899 Thoby-Marcelin, [Émile] Philippe, and Chenet, Jean. "La double vie d'Hector Hyppolite, artiste et prêtre vodou." *Conjonction* (Port-au-Prince) 16 (August 1948): 40-44; 17 (October 1948): 37-41.

900 Thoby-Marcelin, [Émile] Philippe, and Marcelin, [Leonce Perceval] Pierre. *La bête de Musseau*. New York: Éditions de la Maison Française, 1946. English translation. *The beast of the Haitian hills*. New York: Farrar & Rinehart, 1946. Reprint. London: V. Gollancz, 1951, 224 pp.

A novel aiming to reveal the "superstitions" of Vodou.

901 Thoby-Marcelin, [Émile] Philippe, and Marcelin, [Leonce Perceval] Pierre. *Le crayon de dieu*. Paris: La Table Ronde, 1952, 254 pp. English translation. *The pencil of God*. Boston: Houghton Mifflin; London: V. Gallancz, 1951 [1952], 204 pp.

A novel in the context of Vodou.

902   Thoby-Marcelin, [Émile] Philippe, and Marcelin, [Leonce Perceval] Pierre. *Canapé-vert.* New York: Éditions de la Maison Française, 1944, 255 pp. English translation. New York: Farrar & Rinehart, 1944, xxvii + 225 pp.

903   Thompson, Robert Ferris. *The flash of the spirit: African and Afro-American art and philosophy.* New York: Random House, 1983, xvii + 317 pp., illus.
       Chap. 3 (pp. 163-91): "Vodun religion and art in Haiti"–the Dahomean/Yoruba or "Rara" section of Vodou; chap. 2 (pp. 103-31): Kongo art and religion in the Americas–Cuba, Brazil, Haiti, and southern U.S.

904   Thompson, Robert Ferris. "The flash of the spirit: Haiti's Africanizing vodun art." In *Haitian art*, edited by U. Stebich. New York: Brooklyn Museum, 1978, pp. 26-37, illus.

905   Trouillot, Duverneau. *Bosquejo etnográfico del vaudou.* Puerto Principe, 1885.
       Cited from Jean Price-Mars, *Así habló el tío* (entry 798), p. 139.

906   Trouillot, Duverneau. *Le vodoun: Apperçu historique et évolutions.* Port-au-Prince: Imprimerie R. Ethéart, 1885.

906a   Trouillot, Hénock. "La guerre de l'indépendence d'Haiti: Les grandsprêtres du vodou contre l'armée française." *Revista de Historia de América* (Mexico City) 72, no. 2 (1971): 259-327; (1972): 73-74, 75-130.

907   Trouillot, Hénock. "Introduction à une histoire du vodou." *Revue de la Société Haïtienne d'Histoire, de Géographie, et de Géologie* (Port-au-Prince), no. 115 [34] (January-March 1970): 33-182. Reprinted separately. Port-au-Prince: Imprimerie des Antilles, 1970, 152 pp.
       Origins of Vodou and relation to the Haitian revolution; cannibalism, cult of the dead, dances, and socioreligious classification of the cult.

908   Trouillot, Hénock. "La pensée du docteur Jean Price-Mars." *Revue de la Société Haïtienne d'Histoire, de Géographie, et de Géologie* (Port-au-Prince), special issue (1956).

909   [Turner, Harold Walter.] "Voodoo." *Encyclopaedia Britannica*, 1974. Micropaedia, vol. 10, p. 494b.

910   Underhill, Edward Bean. *The West Indies: Their social and religious condition.* London: Jackson, Wolford & Hodder, 1862, 493 pp., illus.

Reprint. Westport, Conn.: Negro Universities Press, 1970, pp. 114-15, 158-63.

911   Valentin, Marina. "Freedom for Haiti." *Wesleyan World* (U.S.), February 1975, p. 3.

Note on Vodou by an American Wesleyan missionary.

912   Van der Kooft, H. "Vodou in chiesa." *Nigrizia* 102, no. 1 (1984): 57-58.

"Vodou in church."

913   Ventura, Michael. "Hear that long snake moan." *Whole Earth Review*, no. 54 (Spring 1987), pp. 28-43; no. 55 (Summer 1987), pp. 82-92. Reprinted from *Shadow dancing*, by M. Ventura, 1985, and from *L.A. Weekly*.

Rock' n' Roll derives from a nineteenth-century Vodou celebration in New Orleans; Vodou is a healthier religion than that of the "christianists."

914   Verschueren, Joseph [Op-Hey, Henri, pseud.]. "Quelques remarques sur l'essai critique du Dr. Price-Mars concernant 'Le culte du vaudoux en Haïti.'" *Revue de la Société Haïtienne d'Histoire et de Géographie* (Port-au-Prince), no. 73 [20] (1949): 26-40.

By a Belgian priest.

915   Verschueren, Joseph [Op-Hey, Henri, pseud.]. *La République d'Haïti*. Vol. 3, *Le culte du vaudoux en Haïti: Ophiolâtrie et animisme*. Wetteren, Belgium: Scaldis; Paris: P. Lethielleux, 1948, 467 pp., illus.

In spite of its impressive size, this work contains little novelty. Its passages on Vodou are obviously biased and over-credulous. Pp. 12-23, 293-385.

916   Viademonte, H. M. "El vudu haitiano." *Missiones Extranjeras* (Burgos), 1963, pp. 304-6.

917   Viatte, Auguste. "Notes de lecture sur la négritude et le vodou." *Ethnographie*, n.s., no. 76 [119, no. 1] (1978): 139-44.

On publications on Vodou: pp. 140-41, on J. Kerboull, *Voodoo and magic practices* (entry 583).

918   Viaud, Léonce. "Le houmfor." *Bulletin du Bureau d'Ethnologie* (Port-au-Prince), 2d ser., no. 12 (1955), pp. 30-35.

919   Viaud, Léonce, and Aubourg, Michel. "Une cérémonie du culte pétro." *La Voix des Jeunes*, March 1946, p. 7.

920   Viaud, Léonce, and Aubourg, Michel. "La doctrine des griots." *Les Griots*, February 1948, p. 5.

921   Vincent, Sténio. *Efforts et résultats*. Port-au-Prince, [ca. 1938].
       P. 257, criticism of Vodou as of the "noiristes," by a president of Haiti.

922   Wade, Davis E. "The ethnobiology of the Haitian zombie." *Journal of Ethnopharmacology* 9 (1983): 85-104.

923   Walendowska-Zapendowska, Barbara. "Éléments africains des religions syncrétiques dans les Antilles (le cas du culte haïtien du vaudou)." Thesis, Adam Mickiewicz Faculty of Philosophy and History, 1971. Abstract in *Africana Bulletin* (Warsaw) 19 (1974): 148-52.

924   Walendowska-[Zapendowska], Barbara. [The vodou cult of Haiti: A developing belief system.] *Etnografia Polska* 23, no. 1 (1979): 55-80.
       In Polish. The African components predominate in this fluid belief system, since they reconcile the sacred and the profane; Christian elements are inserted in a magical way, out of the Christian context.

925   Walker, Sheila S[uzanne]. *Ceremonial spirit possession in Africa and Afro-America: Forms, meanings, and functional significance. . . .* Leiden: E. J. Brill, 1972, 179 pp.
       Vodou, passim.

926   "The whistle and the whip." *Tomorrow* (New York) 3, no. 1 (1954): 91-94.

926a   Welland, James. "Negroes." In *Man, myth, and magic*. Edited by R. Cavendish. Reference edition, vol. 7. New York and London: Cavendish Marshall, 1985, pp. 1957-61, illus.
       P. 1961, Vodou in general, with extract from A. C. Holly.

927   Williams, Geraint. "Voodoo unmasked: The reality behind the image." *Traveller* 11, no. 2 (1981): 28-31, illus.
       A defense of Vodou as a "democratic, sensitive and sincere religion."

928   Williams, Joseph J[ohn]. *Voodoos and obeahs: Phases of West Indian witchcraft*. New York: L. Macneagh, Dial Press, 1932, xix + 257 pp. Reprint. London: George Allen & Unwin, 1933, xix + 257 pp, bib. Reprint. New York: AMS Press, 1970.

Chap. 3 (pp. 56-107), Vodou in Haiti; pp. 59-68, long extracts (translated if necessary) from valuable early sources, such as S. B. St. John, Price-Mars, and especially Moreau de Saint-Méry.

929   Williams, Sheldon. *Voodoo and the art of Haiti*. Nottingham, U.K.: Morland Lee, [1969], 112 pp.

930   Wilmeth, Marlyn Walton, and Wilmeth, J. Richard. "Theatrical elements in Voodoo: The case for diffusion." *Journal for the Scientific Study of Religion* 16, no. 1 (1977): 27-37.
         A popular theatrical tradition, *commedia dell'arte*, facilitated the adoption by Vodou of dramatic elements (costumes, props, etc.) not found in the African background.

931   Wilson, Edmund. "Voodoo in literature." *Tomorrow: Quarterly Review of Psychical Research* (New York) 3, no. 1 (1954): 95-102.
         Originally an introduction to Thoby-Marcelin's novel, *The pencil of God* (entry 901), reviewing modern fiction in Haiti.

932   Wipfler, W[illia]m L. "Religious syncretism in the Caribbean: A study of the persistence of African and Indian belief." *Occasional Bulletin, Missionary Research Library* (New York) 19, no. 1 (1968): 1-13.
         Pp. 6-13, Vodou in Haiti.

932a   Wirkus, Faustin E., and Dudley, Taney. *The white king of La Gonave*. Garden City, N.Y.: Garden City Publishing Co., [1931?], 553 pp., illus.
         A white American who became a lieutenant in the Haitian gendarmerie on La Gonave Island for fourteen years, and being uncorruptible, was elected local king and admitted to Vodou secrets as reincarnating their patriot-emperor, Faustin.

933   Wirkus, Faustin E., and Lanier, H[enry] W[ysham]. "The black pope of Voodoo." *Harper's Magazine* (New York) 168 (December 1933): 38-49; 168 (January 1934): 189-98.

934   Wittkower, E[ric] D. "Spirit possession in Haitian Vodun ceremonies." *Transcultural Psychiatric Research* [*Review*] 14 (1963): 53-55.

935   Wittkower, E[ric] D.; Douyon, Lamarck; and Bijou, Legrand. "Spirit possession in Haitian vodun ceremonies." *Acta Psychothérapeutica, Psychosomatica et Orthopaedagogica* (Basel) 12, no. 1 (1964): 72-80.
         By a psychiatrist.

936   Wolfe, Fritz. *L'initiation dans le vaudou et la célébration de l'eucharistie*. Rome: Pontifical Gregoriani University, 1970, 79 pp.
       Extracted from his dissertation in the Faculty of Theology.

937   Wolff, M. S. "Notes on the Vodoun religion in Haiti with reference to its social and psycho-dynamics." *Revue Internationale d'Ethnopsychologie Normale et Pathologique* (Tangiers) 1, no. 2 (1956): 209-40.

938   Zellon, James. *Voodoo exposed*. Port-au-Prince: Imprimerie Modèle, 1940, 51 pp.

939   "Zombis." *Haïti Littéraire et Sociale*, December 1905, p. 534.

Jamaica

Of Jamaica's two million people, some 80% are black and about 15% are mulatto, so there is an extensive base for Afro-Jamaican and similar religious movements, dating from as far back as the first independent Baptists under George Liele in 1783.

The following items offer general surveys: L. E. Barrett, a Jamaican scholar (entries 948 and 950); R. Bastide (entry 952); J. Bradford (entry 966); J. M. Davis (entry 999, a contemporary hostile Christian view); F. Henriques (entry 1034); Z. N. Hurston (entry 1047); Jamaica Government (entry 1054); M. Kerr (entry 1058, a classic study); I. Morrish (entry 1087); F. J. Osborne and G. I. Johnstone (entry 1097, the best–but unpublished–history of Christianity in the Caribbean); A. Pollak-Eltz (entry 1104, in Spanish); G. E. Simpson (entry 1135); the three United Kingdom, Department of Education and Science reports (entries 1151-1153).

For the early Native Baptists: on Moses Baker see his autobiography (entry 944) and C. V. Black (entry 962); on George Liele see B. Brown (entry 975), J. W. Davis (entry 1000), J. P. Gates (entry 1026), C. Gayle (entry 1027, an important item), E. A. Holmes (entry 1042), the *Journal of Negro History* (entry 1064, primary sources), and A. Pringle (entry 1106, a contemporary view). For missionary attitudes see G. Blyth (entry 964, hostile), G. A. Catherall (entry 987, sympathetic), F. A. Cox (entry 994), S. Green (entry 1030), E. A. Payne (entry 1101), M. Turner (entry 1148), and H. M. Waddell (entry 1156).

For Myallism see F. Cundall (entry 995) and M. Schuler (entry 1126). On Obeah see R. T. Banbury (entry 945, for the mid-century position) and M. W. Beckwith (entry 954, chap. 8).

On the Revival of the 1860s: N. L. Erskine, a Jamaican theologian (entry 1018, pp. 98-106); *Evangelical Christendom* (entry 1052); R. Lovett (entry 1076, a missionary view); and F. J. Osborne and G. I. Johnstone (entry 1097).

On Bedwardism: M. W. Beckwith (entry 955, pp. 40-45), A. A. Brooks (entry 973, a sophisticated official history–few copies known), W. F. Elkins (entry 1009, pp. 19-25), *Jamaica Historical Society Bulletin* (entry 1131, official documents), M. Lopez (entry 1075, fiction), R. M. Pierson (entry 1103, well-documented), and *Woodstock Letters* (entry 1057, Catholic, contemporary).

For Revival/Revival Zion: H. G. De Lisser (entry 1001), E. Seaga – later Prime Minister (entry 1129), and G. E. Simpson (entry 1138).

For Pocomania/Pukumina: D. W. Hogg (entries 1038 and 1041), and W. J. Makin (entry 1077).

For Kumina/Cumina: E. K. Brathwaite (entry 970), M. W. Lewis (entry 1070), and J. G. Moore and G. E. Simpson (entry 1085).

For Convince/Bongo/Flenkee/Fankee: D. W. Hogg (entry 1037).

940 "Alexander Bedward – Obituary." *Jamaica Mail* (Kingston), 11 November 1930.

Bedward died on 8 November.

941 "Ashanti influence in Jamaica." *Journal of American Folklore* 47 (1934): 391-95.

The "Coromantyns," or Gold Coast Africans, traced to the Ashanti; likewise Jamaican Obeah.

942 Augier, F. R., and Gordon, Shirley C., comps. *Sources of West Indian history*. London: Longmans, 1962, 308 pp.

Pp. 147-49, the Council order of 1807 aimed at suppression of Native Baptists.

943 Austin, Diane J. "Born again . . . and again and again: Comunitas and social change among Jamaican Pentecostalists." *Journal of Anthropological Research* 37, no. 3 (1981): 226-46, bib.

Comunitas indicates subordinate social position rather than acting as an agent of social change.

944 Baker, Moses. "An account of Moses Baker . . . (drawn up by himself . . .)." *Evangelical Magazine* (London), no. 11 (September 1803), pp. 365-71.

An autobiography of M. Baker incorporated into a letter to a friend in England.

945 Banbury, R. Thomas. *Jamaica superstitions, or The Obeah book: A complete treatise of the absurdities believed in by the people of the island*. Kingston: M. C. DeSouza (printer), 1894, iv + 38 pp., illus.

First written about 1860. On Obeah, Myallism, duppies, and other folk beliefs; background to all religious developments.

946 *Baptist Magazine* (London, Baptist Missionary Society). News items and letters from Jamaica:

7 (April 1815): 168-69, letter from John Rowe, Falmouth, 29 December 1814, on Moses Baker not having baptized or administered communion for several years; his profligate son now converted.

9 (February 1817): 74-75, report on Mr. Lee Compere (the second Baptist missionary from England) after invitation to Kingston from several thousand Native Baptists, with extracts from his letter of 6 July 1816 on their ignorance and warm response.

11 (February 1819): 96, letter from a Moravian missionary praising Baker and the "clever and gifted black preachers."

11 (October 1819): 455, letter from a "gentleman in Kingston" on the 10,000 to 12,000 Baptists and their orderly prayer meetings, despite a lack of ministers.

14 (February 1822): 87, James Coultart's eulogistic report on the aged and infirm Baker after attending worship he had led.

947   Barnett, Sheila. "Jonkonnu: Pitchy patchy." *Jamaica Journal* (Kingston), no. 43 [1979], pp. 18-32, illus.

The original Jonkonnu figure, derived from both African and British elements, and thus a symbol of creolization; his relation of Myallism, Kumina, Pocomania, Obeah, etc.

948   Barrett, Leonard E[mmanuel]. "African roots in Jamaican indigenous religion." *Journal of Religion* 35, no. 1 (1978): 7-26.

Myal, Kumina, Liele's Baptist Church, the 1860-61 Revival; Pukumina and Revival cults described, and differences between Revival and North American Pentecostalism arriving since 1929.

949   Barrett, Leonard E[mmanuel]. "Portrait of a Jamaican healer: African medical lore in the Caribbean." *Caribbean Quarterly* (Mona, Jamaica) 19, no. 3 (1973): 6-19, illus.

Mammy Forbes, succeeded by her daughter Mother Rita, at Blake's Pen balmyard.

950   Barrett, Leonard E[mmanuel]. *The sun and the drum: African roots in Jamaica folk tradition*. Kingston: Sangster's Book Stores; London: Heinemann, 1976, 128 pp., illus.

A more popular presentation, with Afro-Jamaican cults, passim, but especially pp. 25-27, Kumina and Myal; p. 27, "Pukumina" as "Pocomania"; pp. 54-55, Mother Forbes as healer; pp. 55-68, her daughter, Mother Rita Adams, as successor; pp. 72-89, Obeah; pp. 101-10, theoretical conclusions concerning psychic phenomena.

951   Barrett, Lindsay. *Song for Mumu: A novel*. London: Longmans, 1967, 154 pp.

Fiction on the "Black Soul" theme.

952 Bastide, Roger. *Les Amériques noires*. Paris: Payot, 1967. English translation. *African civilizations in the New World*. London: C. Hurst, 1971, 232 pp.
  Pp. 102-4, 162-68, and notes, p. 170, Jamaican religions.

953 Baytop, Adrianne Roberts. "James Baldwin and Roger Mais – The Pentecostal theme." *Jamaica Journal* (Kingston), no. 42 (September 1978), pp. 14-21, illus.
  A comparison of their writings, especially as to the religious content.

954 Beckwith, Martha Warren. *Black roadways: A study of Jamaican folk life*. Chapel Hill: University of North Carolina Press, 1929, 243 pp., illus., bib. Reprint. New York: Negro Universities Press, 1969.
  Chap. 8, Obeah; chap. 9, the Myal people; chap. 10, the Revivalists (pp. 167-71, Bedwardism); chap. 11, the Pukkermerians.

955 Beckwith, Martha Warren. "Some religious cults in Jamaica." *American Journal of Psychology* 34, no. 1 (1923): 32-45.
  The Revivalists, the Isaiahs, and pp. 40-45, Bedwardism.

956 Bilby, Kenneth M. "How the 'older heads' talk: A Jamaican Maroon spirit possession language and its relationship to the Creoles of Suriname and Sierra Leone." *Nieuwe West-Indische Gids* (The Hague) 57, nos. 1-2 (1983): 37-88, bib.
  Pp. 70-72, recorded "spirit language," with translations; pp. 72-85, list of words common in possession speech.

957 Bilby, Kenneth M. "The Kromanti dance of the Windward Maroons of Jamaica." *Nieuwe West-Indische Gids* (The Hague) 55, nos. 1-2 (1981): 52-101.
  Details in Moore Town area, and relation of the dance to Afro-Jamaican cults.

958 Bilby, Kenneth M. "Partisan spirits: Ritual interaction and Maroon identity in eastern Jamaica." M.A. thesis, Wesleyan University, 1979.

959 Bilby, Kenneth M., and Fu-Kiau, Kia Bunseki. *Kumina: A Kongo-based tradition in the New World*. Cahiers du CEDAF (Brussels), 3d ser., Linguistique B, 1983.

960 Bilby, Kenneth M., and Leib, Elliott. "From Kongo to Zion: Three black musical traditions from Jamaica" [sleeve-liner notes]. *From Kongo to Zion*. Heartbreak Record no. 17. Cambridge, Mass.: Heartbreak Records, 1983.

961   Black, Clinton V[ane de Brosse]. *History of Jamaica*. London: Collins, 1958. Rev. ed. *The story of Jamaica from prehistory to the present*. 1965, 256 pp., illus.

Chap. 17, the Morant Bay rebellion, and G. W. Gordon, mulatto founder of an independent Baptist church, in which he ordained Paul Bogle – see pp. 172, 173. By the Jamaican government archivist.

962   Black, Clinton V[ane de Brosse]. *Living names in Jamaica's history*. Caribbean Home Library. Kingston: Jamaica Welfare, 1943, 24 pp., illus., photos.

Pp. 1-5, Moses Baker.

963   Bleby, Henry. *Death struggles of slavery ... during the two years preceding Negro emancipation*. London: Hamilton, Adams & Co., 1853, 304 pp. 3d ed. 1868.

Pp. 110-20, Sam Sharpe and the Native Baptists in the Christmas rebellion, 1831. By a Wesleyan missionary who knew Sharpe.

964   Blyth, George. *Reminiscences of missionary life with suggestions to churches and missionaries*. Edinburgh: Wm. Oliphant & Sons; Glasgow: D. Robertson; London: Partridge & Oakey, 1851, 256 pp., illus.

Pp. 86-87, 158-62, his hostile reactions to the Native Baptists. By a Presbyterian missionary.

965   Bowen, Calvin. "Jamaica's John Canoe." *Caribbean Commission Monthly Information Bulletin* (Port of Spain) 8, no. 1 (1954): 10-12, illus.

966   Bradford, John. "Jamaica – A religious perspective." Department of Education and Science, course no. N187, member's report. London: Department of Education and Science, 1973, 28 pp. + 2 pp. Appendix by Jamaica Catholic Educational Association. Mimeo.

Surveys most religious groups in historical context and current forms.

967   Brathwaite, Edward Kamau. "Caliban, Ariel, and Unprospero in the conflict of creolization: A study of the slave revolt in Jamaica in 1831-2." In *Comparative perspectives on slavery in New World plantation societies*, edited by V. Rubin and A. Tuden. New York: Annals of the New York Academy of Science, vol. 292, 1977, pp. 41-62.

Especially pp. 54-60 on the variety of Afro-Christian churches, and on Sam Sharpe and the revolt of 1831.

968 Brathwaite, Edward [Kamau]. *The development of Creole society in Jamaica, 1770-1820*. Oxford: Clarendon Press, 1971, 374 pp., maps, bib. Reprint. 1979.

Pp. 253-55, and index, black Baptists–George Liele, Moses Baker, George Gibb, George Lewis; pp. 218-20, 224, religion of the slaves, Obeah men (and see index, "Obeah"); all discussed as part of a distinctive Jamaican society that is at the same time part of the wider New World black culture.

969 Brathwaite, Edward [Kamau]. *The folk-culture of the slaves in Jamaica*. London and Port of Spain: New Beacon Books, 1979, 25 pp.
Originally part of entry 968.

970 Brathwaite, Edward Kamau. "Kumina–The spirit of African survival in Jamaica (with commentary by Olive Lewin)." *Jamaica Journal*, no. 42 [12, nos. 1-2] (1978): 44-63.

Focused on an interview with Mrs. Imogene Kennedy, "queen" or priestess of the Kumina cult, treated as a "living fragment of an African religion" that is now "a life-form of African/Maroons," with commentaries on the text and its African background, comparison with Martha Beckwith's work in the 1920s, and consideration of the future of Jamaican culture. Brief comments by Olive Lewin and Marjorie Whylie.

971 Brathwaite, Edward Kumau. "'Kumina': The spirit of African survival in the Caribbean." In *African dispersal?* edited by A. C. Gulliver. Occasional Paper 5, Afroamerican Studies Program, Boston University, 1979, pp. 57-72.

972 Brodber, Erna. *A study of yards in the city of Kingston*. Working Paper Series, 9. Kingston: Institute of Social and Economic Research, University of the West Indies, 1975.

973 Brooks, A. A. *History of Bedwardism, or, The Jamaica Baptist Free Church, Union Camp, August Town, St Andrew, Ja, B.W.I.* Kingston: Press of P. J. Benjamin Mfg. Co., 1909, 25 pp., photo. 2d rev. ed. Kingston: Jamaica Gleaner, 1917, 39 pp., photo.

A very literate official history by a sophisticated Negro who was converted to Bedwardism in 1907, upon returning from missionary work on the Mosquito coast, Nicaragua. The 2d ed. added some sections (pp. 20-23), a chapter on "God and the War" (pp. 32-35), some minor updating, and a photo of the church. The only copies traced are in the Jamaica Institute; photocopies are now held at Lexington (Kentucky) Theological Seminary, at the Centre at Selly Oak Colleges, and by the remnant of the Bedwardites in Kingston.

974   Brooks, Walter H. "The priority of the Silver Bluff Church and its
      promoters." *Journal of Negro History* 7, no. 2 (1922): 172-96.
            In relation to the question of the first Negro independent
      church.

975   Brown, Beverly. "George Liele: Black Baptist and Pan-Africanist,
      1750-1826." *Savacou* (Mona; a journal of the Caribbean Artists'
      Movement), nos. 11-12 (September 1975), pp. 58-67.

976   Buchner, J. H. *The Moravians in Jamaica: History of the mission of
      the United Brethren's Church to the Negroes in the island of Jamaica.*
      London: Longman Brown & Co., 1854, 175 pp., illus. Facs. reprint.
      Black Heritage Library. New York: Arno Press, 1977.
            Pp. 46-53, George Lewis, a Baptist employed then rejected by
      the Moravians, began his own "'Negroes' home religion and
      meeting"; pp. 138-43, Myallism and Obeah, reprinted in F. Cundall
      (entry 995), p. 587.

977   Burchell, William Fitz-er. *Memoir of Thomas Burchell, twenty-two
      years a missionary in Jamaica.* London: Benjamin L. Green, 1849, 416
      pp., illus.
            Pp. 86-87, brief reference to Baptist missionary Burchell's
      refusal to recognize Moses Baker's church as Christian, and to the
      later "reconstruction" of Baker's congregation within the Baptist fold.

978   Burkett, Randall K[eith]. *Black redemption: Churchmen speak for the
      Garvey movement.* Philadelphia: Temple University Press, 1978, 197
      pp.
            Pp. 3-18, introduction on the religious dimensions of the
      movement; mostly speeches and articles on this dimension by ten
      churchmen, including G. A. McGuire (pp. 157-80).

979   Burkett, Randall K[eith]. *Garveyism as a religious movement: The
      institutionalization of a black civil religion.* ATLA Monograph Series,
      13. Metuchen, N.J. and London: Scarecrow Press, for American
      Theological Library Association, 1978, xxvi + 216 pp., illus.
            Treats Garvey as the preeminent black theologian of the early
      twentieth century; religious analysis of the *Ritual* and *Catechism*,
      speeches and sermons; the religious dimension of the Universal
      Negro Improvement Association explains much of its appeal; the
      relation to the African Orthodox Church; examines the careers of
      over twenty Negro churchmen affiliated with the U.N.I.A.

980   Campbell, Joyce. "Jamaican folk and traditional dances." *Jamaica
      Journal* 10, no. 1 (1976): 8-9.

Includes references to the religious origins and continuing religious use, as in Revival and Kumina.

981 Campbell, M[avis]. "The Maroons of Jamaica: Imperium in Imperio?" *Pan-African Journal* 6, no. 1 (1973): 45-55.

982 Carley, Mary Manning. *Jamaica: The old and the new.* London: George Allen & Unwin, 1963, 212 pp., illus., map.
A popular account: p. 134, Native Baptists; pp. 135, 137, Pocomania; p. 136, Obeah; pp. 138-39, Rastafari; p. 139, Bedwardites.

983 Carlile, [Gavin]. *Thirty-eight years' mission in Jamaica: A brief sketch of the Rev. Warrand Carlile.* London: James Nisbet & Co., 1884, 204 pp.
By one of Warrand Carlile's sons. Pp. 27-28, Myallism; pp. 51-52, 105-7, Obeah; pp. 113-27, the 1860s Revival – sections reprinted in F. J. Osborne and G. I. Johnstone (entry 1097), pp. 143-47.

984 Cassidy, Frederic Gomes. *Jamaica talk: Three hundred years of the English language in Jamaica.* London: Macmillan & Co.; New York: St. Martin's Press; [Kingston]: Institute of Jamaica, 1961, 468 pp., map.
Pp. 235-40, Kumina cult; pp. 140-46, Obeah and Myallism; pp. 247-55, duppies and spirits; pp. 256-62, John Canoe.

985 Catherall, Gordon A. "The Baptist Missionary Society and Jamaican emancipation, 1814-1845." M.A. thesis, University of Liverpool, 1966, 182 pp., table, illus.
By a Baptist minister; pp. 11-21, 29-30, Liele, Baker, and the first English missionary.

986 Catherall, Gordon A. "British Baptist involvement in Jamaica, 1783-1865." Ph.D. dissertation, University of Keele, 1970, 318 pp.
Pp. 48-75, the Native Baptists: pp. 54-60, G. Liele; pp. 60-67, M. Baker. Pp. 76-83, Native and British Baptists; pp. 278-93, Gordon and Bogle in the Morant Bay rebellion.

987 Catherall, G[ordon] A. "The Native Baptist Church." *Baptist Quarterly* (London) 24, no. 2 (1971): 65-73.
Jamaica Native Baptist Free Church.

988 Chevannes, [Alston] Barry [Barrington]. "Revival and black struggle." *Savacou* (Mona; a journal of the Caribbean Artists' Movement), no. 5 (June 1971), pp. 27-39.

The Native Baptist movement; pp. 32-33, Myallism; pp. 33-34, Great Revival; pp. 34-37, Bedwardism, especially relations with the government.

989   Chevannes, [Alston] Barry [Barrington]. "Revivalism: A disappearing religion." *Caribbean Quarterly* (Mona, Jamaica) 24, nos. 3-4 (1978): 1-17.

     On the African Methodist Episcopal Zion Church of Kingston–its members, beliefs, worship, polity, healing, etc., and its absorption by American evangelical churches.

990   Clarke, Colin G. *Kingston, Jamaica: Urban development and social change, 1692-1962.* Berkeley: University of California Press, 1975, 270 pp., maps, illus., bib.

     Pp. 24-25, 51-52, 66-67, 104-5, outlines of the religious history of the African population; p. 224 (fig. 70), map of the distribution of "other Christians"; pp. 119-26, 130-31, 138, Rastafarians; p. 79, the Dung Hill (Dungle).

991   Clarke, C[olin] G. "Population pressure in Kingston Jamaica: A study of unemployment and overcrowding." *Transactions of the Institute of British Geographers*, 1966, pp. 165-82.

     P. 177, squatters who "scuffle" for a living, especially in the "Dungle"; p. 179, Rastafarians.

992   Clarke, John; Dendy, Walter; and Philippo, James M[ursell]. *The voice of Jubilee, a narrative of the Baptist mission, Jamaica from its commencement.* . . . London: John Snow, 1865, 359 pp.

     Pp. 30-39, on earliest Baptist work: especially pp. 30-32, George Liele; pp. 33-36, Moses Baker; p. 37, George Lewis.

992a   Clipham, E. F. "Andrew Fuller and the Baptist mission." *Foundations: A Baptist Journal of History and Theology*, January-March 1967, pp. 4-18.

     Uses correspondence concerning the early native Baptist preachers. Fuller was secretary of the Baptist Missionary Society.

993   Coke, Thomas. *A history of the West Indies . . . with an account of the missions . . . established . . . by the Society.* . . . 3 vols. Liverpool: Nuttall, Fisher & Dixon (Printers), 1808.

     Vol. 1, footnote to p. 410, the Methodist Dr. Coke's brief testimony to the earliest Baptist work in Jamaica–extract quoted in G. A. Catherall (entry 986), p. 54.

994   Cox, F. A. *History of the Baptist Missionary Society from 1792 to 1842.* 2 vols. London: T. Ward & Co.; G. & J. Dyer, 1842.

Vol. 2, pp. 12-17, George Liele and the "independent" and "native Baptists"; pp. 17-22, 35-36, Moses Baker and the first Baptist missionaries, and their persecutions.

995   [Cundall, Frank.] "The editor: On Myalism." *Journal of the Institute of Jamaica* (Kingston) 2, no. 6 (1899): 586-88.
Historical survey of references, with texts quoted from E. Long (entry 1072), B. Edwards (entry 1008), M. G. Lewis (entry 1069), J. Phillippo (entry 1102), J. H. Buchner (entry 976), and C. Rampini (entry 1107, p. 142).

996   Curtin, Philip D[eArmand]. *Two Jamaica's: The role of ideas in a tropical colony, 1830-1865.* Cambridge, Mass.: Harvard University Press, 1955. Reprint. 1970, 270 pp., illus., bib.
Pp. 28-38, African religious inheritance and Afro-Christian sects (Native Baptists, pp. 32-34); pp. 162-72, missions, Afro-Christian sects, Obeah, Myal, and the 1861 Revival.

997   Dallas, R[obert] C[harles]. *The history of the Maroons.* 2 vols. London: Longmans & Rees, 1803, 359 + 514 pp., maps, illus. Reprint. London: F. Cass, 1968.
Vol. 1, pp. 92-93, brief description of the Maroon religion.

997a   Dance, Daryl C. *Folklore from contemporary Jamaicans.* Knoxville: University of Tennessee Press, 1985, 229 pp., bib., illus.
Includes tales about duppies, religion, and Rastafarians.

998   D'Anna, Andrea. *Le religioni afroamericane.* Bologna: Editrice Nigrizia, 1972.
Pp. 83f., Myallism, Obeah, Angelism, Convince cult, and Rastafari.

999   Davis, J. Merle. *The Church in the new Jamaica.* New York and London: International Missionary Council, 1942, 100 pp.
Pp. 41-47, 50, "irresponsible sects" (Pocomania, Revivalism); pp. 44-47, "the African psychic heritage" (Obeah). A responsible but very hostile Christian view at that time.

1000   Davis, John W. "George Liele and Andrew Bryan, pioneer Negro Baptist preachers." *Journal of Negro History* 3, no. 2 (1918): 119-27.

1001   De Lisser, H[erbert] G[eorge]. *Twentieth century Jamaica.* Kingston: Jamaica Times, 1913, 208 pp., illus.
P. 134, Bedwardites; pp. 134-44, full description of a Revivalist meeting in a back street in Kingston, by a native Jamaican critical of this kind of religion.

1002   Dreher, Melanie Creagan. "Working men and ganja: Commonalities and variations in rural Jamaican communities." Ph.D. dissertation (anthropology), Columbia University, 1977, 461 pp.

Stresses social structure factors, rather than ganja as representing a deviant subculture or expressing psychological or cultural chacteristics of individual users; found among lower socioeconomic levels of adult men in the rural working class.

1003   Dreher, M[elanie] C[reagan], and Rogers, C. M. "Getting high: Ganja man and his socio-economic milieu." *Caribbean Studies* (Río Piedras, University of Puerto Rico) 16, no. 2 (1976): 219-31.

Compares an urban Rastafarian "yard" in Kingston with a Pentecostal "revivalist sect" in a rural mountain village, before 1974; by a nursing-scientist and an anthropologist.

1004   Duncker, S. J. "The free coloured and their fight for civil rights in Jamaica, 1800-1830." M.A. thesis, University of London, 1961.

1005   Dunning, T. G. "George Liele: Negro slavery's prophet of deliverance." *Baptist Quarterly* 20, no. 8 (1964): 340-51, 361.

1006   Dutton, Geoffrey. *The hero as murderer: The life of Edward John Eyre, Australian explorer and governor of Jamaica, 1815-1901.* London: Collins Cheshire, 1967, 416 pp., illus., maps.

Pp. 253-82, G. W. Gordon and Paul Bogle in the Morant Bay revolt. In this sympathetic study, Eyre is rehabilitated (by an Australian scholar) as an ill-judged man.

1007   Eaton, George E. *Alexander Bustamente and modern Jamaica.* Kingston: Kingston Publishers, 1975, 276 pp.

Pp. 20-25, a succession of messianic leaders–M. Garvey, A. Bedward (pp. 21-22), Solomon Hewitt or "Brother Sol of the Cross" (pp. 22-23), Alexander Bustamente as Prime Minister; p. 241, M. Manley as successor.

1008   Edwards, Bryan. *The history, civil and commercial, of the British colonies in the West Indies.* 2d ed. London: Stockdale, 1794.

Vol. 2, p. 107: on Obeah; cf. the "Myal men," quoted in F. G. Cassidy (entry 984), pp. 241-42, and F. Cundall (entry 995), p. 586.

1009   Elkins, W. F. *Street preachers, faith healers and herb doctors in Jamaica, 1890-1925.* Caribbean Studies Series. Brooklyn, N.Y.: Revisionist Press, 1976.

Pt. 1, on "messianic healers"–pp. 10-18, Bedward; pp. 19-25, C. C. Higgins; pp. 26-33, Holiness People (of I. Tate), Dowie's Zionism, and Pokomania; pp. 33-41, Black Princes–Makarooroo and

Shervington – with back-to-Africa ideas; pp. 42-48, prophets in 1914 in Smith's Village – D. Bell, S. Hewitt.

1010   Elkins, W. F. "'Warrior Higgins,' a Jamaican street preacher." *Jamaica Journal* 8, no. 4 (1974): 28-31, illus.

By the general secretary of the Paraclesian Society, Stanford, Calif., on a Jamaican and his Royal Millennium Baptist Missionary Society, founded in Kingston in 1899; his association with Alexander Bedward; and his death in 1902. Based on contemporary press reports.

1010a   Elkins, W. F. "William Lauron DeLaurence and Jamaican folk religion." *Folklore* 97, no. 2 (1986): 215-18.

DeLaurence (1868-1936), emphasizing both magical features and divine immanence, influenced traditional Obeah by presenting a more modern "science," especially through his *Sixth and seventh books of Moses*, despite its banning in both the colonial and the independence periods.

1011   Emerick, Abraham J. *Jamaica duppyism*. Woodstock, Md.: privately printed, 1916.

A Jesuit study.

1012   Emerick, Abraham J. *Jamaica Mialism*. Woodstock, Md.: privately printed, 1916, as extract from *Woodstock Letters*, 1915, pp. 39-50.

For long extracts see J. J. Williams (entry 1164): pp. 39ff. (Williams, pp. 154-55); pp. 47f. (Williams, pp. 156-58); pp. 190ff. (Williams, pp. 202-6).

1013   Emerick, Abraham J. *Obeah and duppyism in Jamaica*. Woodstock, Md.: privately printed, 1915.

1014   EPICA Taskforce. *Jamaica: Caribbean challenge*. Washington, D.C.: EPICA [Ecumenical Program for Interamerican Communication and Action] Taskforce, 1979, 119 pp., illus.

Pp. 21-23, G. W. Gordon, Paul Bogle, and Morant Bay; pp. 26-28, "the impact of Marcus Garvey"; pp. 41, 42, 77, 94-95, Rastafarians; pp. 92-95, religion in Jamaica.

1015   "Epiphany (Theophany) feast of the Ethiopian church in Jamaica." *One Church/Yedinaya Tserkov* (New York) 26, no. 3 (1972): 129-31.

1016   Erickson, Arvel B. "Empire or anarchy: The Jamaican rebellion of 1865." *Journal of Negro History* 44, no. 2 (1959): 99-122.

A full and balanced account of Governor Eyre's relation to the Morant Bay events, as background to the influence of G. W. Gordon, Paul Bogle, and the Baptists.

1017   Erskine, Noel Leo. "Black religion and identity: A Jamaican perspective." Ph.D. dissertation (theology), Union Theological Seminary, 1978, 248 pp.
        A historical approach. Chap. 3, slave religion including Myallism and Obeah; chap. 4, the failure of the churches to satisfy the blacks after emancipation; chap. 5, black "people's religion" developed in between the African and Christian heritages.

1018   Erskine, Noel Leo. *Decolonizing theology: A Caribbean perspective.* Maryknoll, N.Y.: Orbis Books, 1981, 130 pp.
        Pp. 98-106, Revivalism (Bedwardism and Revivalists in general); pp. 106-13, Rastafarians; pp. 114-15, notes on these.

1019   Ferguson, R. H. "An open letter to ministers of religion." *Daily Gleaner* (Kingston), 12 October 1932. Also, editorial reply, "Pocomanism," 13 October 1932.
        Both attack "these orgiastic revival dances," but the editorial finds the remedy in legal rather than clerical action; full text in J. J. Williams (entry 1164), pp. 172-75.

1020   Findlay, G. G., and Holdsworth, W. W. *The history of the Wesleyan Methodist Missionary Society.* Vol. 2. London: Epworth Press, 1921, 534 pp.
        P. 48, note 1, Liele's Baptist churches; pp. 373-74, Myallism as the new form of Obeah; pp. 374-75, the 1862 Revival.

1021   Foner, Nancy. *Status and power in rural Jamaica: A study of educational and political change.* New York: Teachers College Press, 1973, 172 pp.
        See index under names of individual churches – Pentecostal, Church of God, Baptist, Methodist, etc.; pp. 95-99, Obeah; pp. 73-77, church affiliation; pp. 101-3, church court cases.

1022   Forsythe, Dennis. "Repression, radicalism, and change in the West Indies." *Race* 15, no. 4 (1974): 401-29.
        Pp. 404-5, strong reactions to Rastafarians quoted from the local press; p. 407, quotation from a *Gleaner* editorial 2 May 1921 attacking Bedwardism; p. 413, news report on Claudius Henry being suppressed; p. 421, brief report of the Bedward arrest, etc., in 1921. The whole article relates the suppression of radicals, including Marcus Garvey, passim; originally a pamphlet of the New Jamaica Study Group, Montreal.

1023   Galloway, Ernestine Royals. "Religious beliefs and practices of Maroon children of Jamaica." Ed.D. dissertation, New York University, 1981, 469 pp.

In Accompong, children six to twelve years old. Includes account of early Christian Maroon groups. Obeah beliefs survive among children; the "Procomania [*sic*] Church" Sunday service and New Year's festivals described.

1024   Gardner, William James. *A history of Jamaica from its discovery by Christopher Columbus to the present time.* London: Eliot Stock, 1873. Reprint. London: F. Cass, 1971, 510 pp., map.

Pp. 187-91, Obeah; pp. 191, 460, Myallism; pp. 343-45, Liele and Baker; pp. 465-66, the Great Revival; pp. 471-94, the 1865 rebellion of Bogle and Gordon (viewpoint hostile to them), with incidental references to Native Baptists; by a missionary.

1025   Garvey, Marcus. [Condemnation of religious revivalism.] *Black Man* 1 (March 1936): 16; 2 (January 1937): 12-13.

1026   Gates, John Parmer. "George Liele: A pioneer Negro preacher." *Chronicle* (Chester, Pa., American Baptist Historical Society) 6, no. 3 (1943): 118-29.

1027   Gayle, Clement [H. L.]. *George Liele: Pioneer missionary to Jamaica.* Kingston: Jamaica Baptist Union, 1982, vii + 47 pp.

Establishes Liele as the father of the Baptist Church in Jamaica, although he is neglected by most church historians. By the lecturer in church history, United Theological College.

1028   Gerloff, Roswith Ingebord Hildegard. "The case for British black theologies: The black church movement in Britain in its transatlantic, historical, and cultural connexions." Ph.D. dissertation (theology), University of Birmingham, [in preparation, 1989].

1029   Gradussov, Alex. "Kapo, cult leader – sculptor – painter." *Jamaica Journal* 3, no. 2 (1969): 46-51, illus. Reprinted in *Freeing the Spirit* (Washington, D.C.) 3, no. 1 (1974): 29-31.

Mallica Reynolds, or "Kapo" (b. 1911), founder of his own Zion Revival group, after a vision – mainly on his development as an artist.

1030   Green, Samuel. *Baptist mission in Jamaica: A review of the Rev. W. G. Barrett's pamphlet.* London: Houlston & Stoneham; G. & J. Dyer, 1842, 32 pp.

A defense of Baptist churches, with no clear distinction between mission-connected and Native Baptists – see pp. 15-20 more especially.

1031   Hart, Ansell. *The life of George William Gordon*. Cultural Heritage Series, 1. Kingston: Institute of Jamaica, 1972, 130 pp.
Quotes extensively from contemporary sources.

1032   Hemming, William E. "Bedward's remnants mourning still." *Jamaica Times* (Kingston), 6 August 1949.

1033   Henderson, George E. *Goodness and mercy: A tale of a hundred years. By George E. Henderson, Pastor 1876-1926 Brown's Town Baptist Church. Jamaica B.W.I.* Kingston: Gleaner Co., Printers, 1931, 169 pp. Reprint. Owen Sound, Ontario: Richardson, Bond & Wright, 1967, 173 pp.
Pp. 100-104, the Revival in Jamaica, 1860-61, as the root of later "revivalism."

1034   Henriques, [Louis] Fernando. *Family and colour in Jamaica*. London: Eyre & Spottiswoode, 1953, 196 pp.
Pp. 60-62, 76-80, 168-71, Myallism, Pocomania, Revivalism, Bedward and messianism; Obeah, passim (see index).

1035   Henry, A. E. T. "Dip dem Missa Bedward, dip dem. ..." *Sunday Gleaner* (Kingston), 10 November 1968, p. 8.
On the attempts of the Bedwardites to fly.

1036   Hill, Richard. *Lights and shadows of Jamaican history; being three lectures delivered in aid of the mission schools of the colony*. Kingston: Ford & Gall, 1859, 164 pp., map.
Pp. 77-80, 83-86, Moses Baker (quoting his own accounts); p. 80, briefly on George Liele.

1037   Hogg, Donald W[illiam]. "The Convince cult in Jamaica." In *Papers in Caribbean Anthropology*, compiled by S. W. Minty. Yale University Publications in Anthropology, 58. New Haven, Conn.: Department of Anthropology, Yale University, 1960, (separate pagination) 24 pp. + 6 plates.
On Flenkee, Fankee, or Bongo cult, 1956; Christian and African elements; criticizes M. J. Herskovits on Afro-American cults.

1038   Hogg, Donald W[illiam]. "Elegy for a Christian pagan." *Caribbean Review* 2, no. 2 (1970): 1-10.
Outline of the life of Francis Walker (1884-1960), a Jamaican Pocomania leader, who tried to combine his cult with being an elder in the Presbyterian church.

1039   Hogg, Donald W[illiam]. "Jamaican religions." Ph.D. dissertation (anthropology), Yale University, 1964, 474 pp., bib. (pp. 450-66).

See especially pp. 34-165.

1040   Hogg, Donald W[illiam]. "Magic and 'science' in Jamaica." *Caribbean Studies* (Río Piedras, University of Puerto Rico) 1, no. 2 (1961): 1-5.

1041   Hogg, Donald W[illiam]. "A West Indian shepherd." *In Context* (New Haven, Conn., Yale University) 4, no. 2 (1956): 12-15.
        On "Shepherd Randy," a leader of a Pocomania band, incorporating Christian, African, and Hindu elements, and his elevation to the rank of "Father."

1042   Holmes, Edward A. "George Liele: Negro slavery's prophet of deliverance." *Baptist Quarterly* 20, no. 8 (1964): 340-51, 361 (references). Reprinted in *Foundations* (Rochester, American Baptist Historical Society) 9, no. 4 (1966): 333-45.
        On the first Negro congregation in the U.S. gathered by Liele in 1775; a good survey.

1043   Hopkin, John Barton. "Music in the Jamaican Pentecostal churches." *Jamaica Journal* (Kingston), no. 42 (September 1978), pp. 23-40, illus., music scores.
        A detailed study, with a general account of Jamaican Pentecostalism and its features, marked by emphasis on religious experience that is both immediate and communal.

1044   Hovemyr, Anders. "The Native Baptist Church of Jamaica: An outline of the beginning of its history with special reference to the ministry of George Liele." B.D. thesis, Baptist Theological Seminary (Ruschlikon, Switzerland), 1976.
        Largely based on the work of G. A. Catherall (entry 986).

1045   Hovemyr, Anders. "Negerbaptister – pionjärer – missionärer apropä USA: s 200-Arsjubileum." *Svensk Missionstidskrift* 64, no. 3 (1976): 171-75.
        George Liele, ca. 1750-1826; based on chap. 2 of his thesis (entry 1044).

1046   Hovemyr, Anders. "Pioneer black Baptist churches in America." *Quarterly Review* (Nashville) 39, no. 2 (1979): 72-75.
        On George Liele, the foundation of the Silver Bluffs and Savannah black congregations, and his mission in Jamaica.

1047   Hurston, Zora N[eale]. *Tell my horse*. New York: J. B. Lippincott & Co., 1938, 290 pp., illus., maps. Reprinted as *Voodoo gods: An enquiry into native myths and magic in Jamaica and Haiti*. London: J. M. Dent & Sons, 1939, 290 pp., illus., maps.

Pt. 1, Jamaica: pp. 9-11, Pocomania; pp. 41-60, Nine Night ceremonies, including pp. 56-60, Kumina.

1048   Hurwitz, Samuel J., and Hurwitz, Edith F. *Jamaica: A historical portrait*. London: Pall Mall Press, 1971, 273 pp.

P. 69, Liele; pp. 147-49, Bogle and the Morant Bay revolt; pp. 190-91, Rastafarians and M. Garvey. Very simplified accounts.

1049   Hutton, Joseph Edmund. *A history of Moravian missions*. London: Moravian Publication Office, [ca. 1922], 550 pp., bib., maps.

Pp. 220-22, Obeah and Myallism; pp. 224-27, the Great Revival of 1858-60.

1050   Jacobs, H. P. "Dialect, magic, and religion." In *Ian Fleming introduces Jamaica*, edited by M. Cargill. Kingston: Sangster's Book Stores; London: A. Deutsch, 1965, pp. 79-96.

Pp. 79-84, African influences, especially on language; pp. 85-86, magic; pp. 89-92 and illus. facing p. 33, Rastafarians; pp. 92-96, Pocomania, Revival, Kumina, etc.

1051   Jamaica Committee. *Facts and documents relating to the alleged rebellion in Jamaica, and the manner of repressions; including notes on the trial of Mr. Gordon*. Jamaica Papers, 1. London: Jamaica Committee, 1866.

By the committee formed in London to bring Governor Eyre to justice. Copy at Spurgeon's College, London.

1052   "Jamaica: Extraordinary   religious   awakening."   *Evangelical Christendom: Its State and Prospects* (London) 15 [n.s. 2] (1 January 1861): 31-35; (1 August 1861): 498-99.

Two reports on the 1860 revival.

1053   Jamaica Government. *Jamaica heritage*. Edited by Alex Gradussov. Kingston: Ministry of Finance and Planning, [1970], 64 pp., illus.

Pp. 18-20, "African religious influence," especially Obeah and Pocomania; three photos of Bedward; pp. 36, 52, Marcus Garvey, with photo.

1054   Jamaica Government. "Religion in Jamaica." Facts on Jamaica, Series 3. Kingston: Jamaica Tourist Authorities, n.d. [in use, 1976], 18 pp. Mimeo.

Pp. 5-6, Native Baptists; pp. 8-13, Great Revival, Revival Zion, Pocomania, Kumina, Rastafari (latter given more than its share of space); pp. 17-18, Ethiopian Orthodox Church arrival, 1970-71.

1055 Jamaica Government. *Report of mission to Africa.* Kingston: Government Printer, 1961, 23 pp.

Pp. 1-13, majority report by the six non-Rastafarians; pp. 15-23, minority report by the three Rastafarians – Filimorie Alvaranga, Douglas Mack, and Mortimo Planno. This was the official mission of inquiry, April-June 1961, into the possibilities of repatriation to Africa.

1056 Jamaican High Commission. *Jamaica.* London: Jamaican High Commission, 1973, 88 pp., illus.

Pp. 15-16, "Rastafari cult as a politico-religious movement" with a biblical basis but opposed to Western Christianity – a sympathetic statement; pp. 46-47, music and text of "Guinea war," a Kumina song; pp. 23, 59, 61, 63, Edna Manley's statue of Paul Bogle, treated as a national hero.

1057 "Jamaica's Negro prophet." *Woodstock Letters* (Woodstock, Md.) 23 (1894): 120-25 (reprinted from *Sun* [New York], 13 November 1893); 354-66 (reprinted from various Kingston newspapers).

A pastoral charge by the Catholic Bishop Gordon in 1893; his public interchange of acrimonious letters with the Anglican Bishop Nuttall concerning Bedwardism and other matters.

1057a Johnson, Howard. Introduction to *Boy in a landscape: A Jamaican picture,* by Trevor Fitz-Henley. Gordon Town, Jamaica, 1980.

1058 Kerr, Madeline. *Personality and conflict in Jamaica.* Liverpool: Liverpool University Press, 1952, 221 pp., illus. Reprint. London: Collins; Kingston: Sangster's Book Stores, 1963, 220 pp.

A classic study of Jamaican society – religion, politics, etc. Pp. 137-55, folklore. See index for Pocomania, Revivalism, Kumina, visions.

1059 Kuper, Adam. *Changing Jamaica.* London and Boston: Routledge & Kegan Paul, 1976, 163 pp., maps.

Pp. 87-88, churches in a village near Christiana; pp. 94-99, 104-6, 140, 141, Rastafarians and their political significance.

1060 Lanternari, Vittorio. "Dreams as charismatic stimulants: Their bearing on the rise of new religious movements." In *Psychological anthropology,* edited by T. Williams. The Hague: Mouton, 1976, pp. 321-35.

Pp. 226-29, prophet Kapo's dreams and Afro-Christian cult in Kingston.

1061 Lanternari, Vittorio. "Religious movements in Jamaica." In *Black society in the New World*, edited by R. Frucht. New York: Random House, 1971, pp. 308-12. Reprint of pp. 158-65 of the English translation of *The religions of the oppressed*. New York: A. A. Knopf, 1963 (pp. 133-38 in Mentor Books ed.).

1062 Leigh-Fermor, Patrick [Michael]. *The traveller's tree: A journey through the Caribbean islands*. New York: Harper, 1950, 403 pp., illus., maps. Reprint. London: Arrow Books, 1961, 286 pp., illus., maps.

   Chap. 13, Jamaica: pp. 342-46 (1950), Pocomania; pp. 348-52, Rastafari; p. 361, brief reference to Myallism; illustrations (no pagination).

1063 Leslie, Charles. *A new history of Jamaica, from the earliest accounts*. 2d ed. London: J. Hodges, 1740, 340 pp. maps.

   Mentions two gods, Naskew and Timnew, connected with Kumina cult – the earliest mention of the latter.

1064 "Letters showing the rise and progress of early Negro churches in Georgia and the West Indies." *Journal of Negro History* 1, no. 1 (1916): 69-92.

   Mostly written by George Liele and Andrew Bryan; some quoted from the *Baptist Annual Register*, 1790-93 and 1801-2. On Savannah and Kingston.

1065 Lewin, Olive. "Cult music: Notes and introduction." *Jamaica Journal* 3, no. 2 (1969): 14-15.

   Five examples of hymns or choruses from Zion, Pocomania, and Revival cults; music only.

1066 Lewin, Olive. "Folk music of Jamaica: An outline for classification." *Jamaica Journal* 4, no. 2 (1970): 68-72.

   Musical texts, with notes on each, classified into secular and religious, and the latter divided as follows: 1) Revival, (a) Zion, (b) Pukko; 2) Kumina; 3) Rastafarian; 4) Gumbay (at St. Elizabeth).

1067 Lewin, Olive. "Jamaican folk music." *Caribbean Quarterly* (Mona, Jamaica) 14, nos. 1-2 (1968): 49-56.

   Pp. 53-55, music and worship; pp. 54-55, revival or spirit cults, Kumina, Rastafarians.

1068 Lewis, Gordon K[enneth]. *The growth of the modern West Indies*. London: MacGibbon & Kee; New York: Monthly Review Press, 1968, 506 pp.

   Pp. 194-96, Jamaica popular religion, and elites' religion.

1069   Lewis, Matthew Gregory. *Journal of a West India proprietor, kept during a residence in the island of Jamaica (1815-1817)*. London, 1834. Another ed. as *Journal of residence ... in the West Indies*. London, 1845. Reprinted as *India proprietor, 1815-17*. London: G. Routledge & Sons, 1929, 356 pp., illus.

References to Obeah ceremonies and Myal dance (e.g., pp. 88, 134, 148f., 354f.); see also extract in F. Cundall (entry 995), pp. 586-87.

1070   Lewis, Maureen Warner. "The nkuyu: Spirit messengers of the Kumina." *Savacou* (Mona; a journal of the Caribbean Artists' Movement) 13 (1977): 57-78 (pp. 83-86, notes). Also separate publication. Mona: Savacou Publications, 1977.

An interview with Miss Queenie Kumina, a leader in Kumina.

1071   Livingstone, William Pringle. *Black Jamaica: A study in evolution*. London: Sampson Low, Marston & Co., 1899, 298 pp.

P. 64, Native Baptists; pp. 19, 47, 110, "Obeahism" as a "black thread of mischief," coupled with superstition – a brief, superficial, conventional Western account.

1072   Long, Edward. *The history of Jamaica*. 3 vols. London: Lowndes, 1774.

Vol. 2, p. 416 on Myallism; contains the earliest instance of the word *myal*. Cited in F. G. Cassidy (entry 984), p. 241, and other extracts in F. Cundall (entry 995) and J. J. Williams (entry 1164), pp. 181-82.

1073   Long, Joseph K. "Jamaican medicine: Choices between folk healing and modern medicine." Ph.D. dissertation (anthropology), University of North Carolina at Chapel Hill, 1973, 293 pp.

Rural lower classes and their use of balmyards, etc. for healing, especially of psychic disorders.

1074   Long, Joseph K. "Medical anthropology, dance, and trance in Jamaica." *Bulletin of the International Committee on Urgent Anthropological and Ethnological Research* 14 (1972): 17-23.

Five aspects of Jamaican culture for attention: 1) of balmyards and their herbalistic religious and psychotherapeutic value; 2) Maroon villages supposedly of Ashanti origin; 3) the Kumina cult village of Airy castle; 4) "Pocomania" revivalist cult; 5) remnants (if any outside the Balm) of Obeah and Myallism.

1075   Lopez, M. *De mericle at Mona: A story of Alexander Bedward and some Jamaica sketches*. Kingston: Mutual Printing Co., [1921?], 31 pp.

Fiction, in patois; pp. 5-11, "De mericle at Mona" (reprinted from the *Daily Gleaner*) – a healing in Mona river water.

1076   Lovett, Richard. *The history of the London Missionary Society*. Vol. 2. London: Henry Froude; Oxford University Press, 1899, 778 pp.
         Vol. 2, pp. 381-87, the "Great Revival" of 1861, as seen by missionaries.

1077   Makin, William J[ames]. *Caribbean nights*. London: Robert Hale, 1939, 287 pp.
         Pp. 94-134, mainly on Pocomania and Obeah. By the editor of the *Jamaica Standard*.

1078   Marriott, Louis. *Bedward*. New version of Mariott's play, *The Shepherd* (1960). Presented at Little Theatre, Kingston, September 1984 – duration, 2 hours, 40 mins.
         See review by M. Reckord (entry 1110).

1079   Marsden, Peter. *An account of the island of Jamaica: With reflections on the treatment . . . of the slaves, etc.* Newcastle, 1788.
         Reveals the typical European attitude to "the obeah-man."

1080   Martin, Tony. *Race first: The ideological and organizational struggles of Marcus Garvey and the Universal Negro Improvement Association*. Contributions in Afro-American and African Studies, 19. Westport, Conn.: Greenwood Press, 1976, 421 pp.
         A useful new study of Garvey; pp. 71-73, 120, African Orthodox Church; chap. 4 (pp. 67-80), religion, showing the messianic aspects of Garveyism, his religious interest and tolerance; p. 74, on his disapproval of Jamaican folk religion; pp. 74-77, Garveyism and Islam. Many source references.

1081   Mathieson, William Law. *The sugar colonies and Governor Eyre, 1849-1866*. London: Longmans, Green & Co., 1936, 243 pp.
         Pp. 139-43, Native and other Baptists; pp. 158-60, 164-65, W. G. Gordon and P. Bogle in relation to the Native Baptists; pp. 168-69, the 1861 Revival.

1082   Moore, Joseph G[raessle]. "Music and dance as expressions of religious worship in Jamaica." In *African religious groups and beliefs*. Meerut, India: Archana Publications, for the Folklore Institute (Berkeley, Calif.), 1982, pp. 265-89.

1083   Moore, Joseph G[raessle]. "Religion of Jamaican Negroes: A study of Afro-Jamaican acculturation." Ph.D. dissertation (anthropology), Northwestern University, 1954, 284 pp.

Mainly on Revival and Kumina cults in Morant Bay.

1084   Moore, Joseph G[raessle]. "Religious syncretism in Jamaica." *Practical Anthropology* 12, no. 2 (1965): 63-70.
      Against a background of Anglican and evangelical Protestant churches.

1085   Moore, Joseph G[raessle], and Simpson, George E[aton]. "A comparative study of acculturation in Morant Bay and West Kingston, Jamaica." *Zaire* (Brussels) 11, nos. 9-10 (1957): 979-1019; 12, no. 1 (1958): 65-87.
      Kumina cult, surviving from tribal farm in St. Thomas and W. Kingston with spirit possession.

1086   Morrish, Ivor. *The background of immigrant children*. Unwin Education Books, 4. London: Allen & Unwin, 1971, 256 pp.
      Chap. 2 includes African influences and Rastafarians: p. 35, Native Baptists; pp. 42-46, cults, Obeah, and Pocomania; pp. 46-48, Rastafarians.

1087   Morrish, Ivor. *Obeah, Christ, and Rastaman: Jamaica and its religion*. Cambridge: James Clarke, 1982, 122 pp., maps.
      Pp. 40-45, Obeah and duppies; pp. 45-48, Myallism; pp. 49-51, Bedwardism; pp. 51-55, Pocomania; pp. 55-58, Zionism and Revivalism; pp. 59-67, Kumina, and various ceremonies (wakes, John Canoe, marriage, etc.); pp. 68-91, Rastafarians.

1088   Napier, Robert. "The first arrest of Bedward." *Jamaica Historical Society Bulletin* 11, no. 1 (1957): 13-14.

1089   *Negro Churchman* 1-9 (1923-31). Reprint. 2 vols. (*1923-1926* and *1927-1931*). Millwood, N.Y.: Kraus Reprint, 1977, original discontinuous pagination.
      Official monthly journal of the McGuire's African Orthodox Church, founded January 1923 under his editorship. Relevant materials on Jamaica, Africa, etc., passim.

1090   Nettleford, Rex M. *Mirror, mirror: Identity, race, and protest in Jamaica*. Kingston: Sangster; London: William Collins, 1970, 256 pp. Reprinted, with a new preface (pp. 8-16), as *Identity, race, and protest in Jamaica*. New York: William Morrow, 1972, 256 pp.
      Pp. 39-111, 218-21, 233, 253, Rastafari; p. 77, Zionism; pp. 77, 194, Pocomania; M. Garvey, see index; pp. 44, 75, 108-9, Ethiopian Orthodox Church.

1091   Nettleford, Rex M. "Pocomania in dance-theatre." *Jamaica Journal* 3, no. 2 (1969): 21-24, illus. Reprinted in *Freeing the Spirit* (Washington, D.C.) 3, no. 1 (1974): 16-19.

      A Pocomania festival as a source for the National Dance Theatre Company presentation of Jamaican folk-ritual dance.

1092   Newman, Richard. Review of *Black pioneers in a white denomination*, by M. D. Morrison-Reed (Boston: Skinner House, 1980). *Newsletter of the Afro-American Religious History Group of the American History Group of the American Academy of Religion* 5, no. 2 (1981): 12-13.

1093   Norris, Katrin. *Jamaica: The search for an identity*. London: Institute for Race Relations; Oxford University Press, 1962, 104 pp.

      Pp. 43-60, "The call of Africa," and pp. 96-98, Rastafarians; Appendix (pp. 102-3), a fifteen-year-old schoolgirl's essay, "A visit to an obeah man."

1094   O'Gorman, Pamela. "The introduction of Jamaican music into the established churches." *Jamaica Journal* 9, no. 1 (1975): 40-44, 47.

      P. 42, influence of Rastafari, Revival, and Pocomania, with texts of a Rastafarian and a Revival song – seen as "lower class sects."

1095   Olivier, [Sidney Haldane], Lord (Baron Olivier). *The myth of Governor Eyre*. London: Hogarth Press, 1933, 348 pp., map.

      G. W. Gordon, especially in chaps. 6, 8, 17, 18; Paul Bogle, especially chap. 8; both also passim; the Morant Bay "rebellion" of 1865.

1096   Open University. *Sectarian beliefs*. Tape no. D283 13/14. Milton Keynes: Marketing Division, Open University, [1975?], 20 minutes x 2.

      Three deacons of the Miracle Revival Fellowship, East London (Walthamstow) talk about their experience; mainly West Indian immigrant members, and Pentecostal.

1097   Osborne, Francis J., and Johnstone, Geoffrey I. "Coastlands and islands: First thoughts on Caribbean church history." Kingston: Jamaica: United Theological College of the West Indies, 1972, 261 pp., map. Mimeo.

      Pp. 143-47, the 1860 revival; pp. 141, 145, Myallism; pp. 51-55, 123, 137-43, Native Baptist Church. An important history.

1098   Patterson, Horace Orlando. *The sociology of slavery: An analysis of the origins, development, and structure of Negro slave society in Jamaica*. London: MacGibbon & Kee, 1967, 310 pp., map.

Chap. 7: "Witchcraft, sorcery, and religion"; pp. 185-95, Obeah and Myallism.

1099   Patterson, Sheila [Caffyn]. *Dark strangers: A sociological study of the absorption of a recent West Indian group in Brixton, South London*. London: Tavistock, 1963, 470 pp. Abridged ed. Harmondsworth: Penguin Books, Pelican Book, 1965, 380 pp.

Pp. 302-6 (1965 ed.), religious associations – Revival, Pocomania, Rastafari, the first two types not transplanting to Britain.

1100   Payne, Ernest A[lexander]. "Baptist work in Jamaica before the arrival of the missionaries." *Baptist Quarterly* (London), n.s. 8 (January 1934): 20-26.

Includes the full text of George Liele's church covenant.

1101   Payne, Ernest A[lexander]. *Freedom in Jamaica: Some chapters in the story of the Baptist Missionary Society*. London: Carey Press, 1933, ix + 112 pp., illus. Rev. and enl. ed. 1945, 120 pp., illus.

Pp. 18-19 (first ed.), George Liele's pioneer work; pp. 26-28, Sam Sharpe and the 1832 revolt.

1102   Philippo, James [Mursell]. *Jamaica: Its past and present state*. London: J. Snow; New York: James M. Campbell, 1843, xvi + 487 pp., illus. Reprint. Westport, Conn.: Negro Universities Press, 1970, 487 pp., illus.

By a Baptist missionary. Pp. 239-66, Myallism and Obeah. Section on Myallism reprinted in Cundall (entry 995).

1103   Pierson, Roscoe M[itchell]. "Alexander Bedward and the Jamaica Native Baptist Free Church." *Lexington Theological Quarterly* (Lexington, Ky.) 4, no. 3 (1969): 65-76. Reprinted in *Black apostles: Afro-American clergy confront the twentieth century*, edited by R. K. Burkett and R. Newman. Boston: G. K. Hall & Co., 1978, pp. 1-10.

A history based on newspaper and other research in Jamaica – a good account, well-documented.

1104   Pollak-Eltz, Angelina. "Myalismo, obeah y el convince cult de Jamaica." In *Cultos afroamericanos*. Caracas: Universidad Catolica Andrés Bello, 1972, pp. 143-51.

Includes Pocomania, Revivalism, Rastafari, etc.

1105   "Press lies about us claim Bedwardites." *Star* (Kingston), 6 March 1965.

On reports of internal dissension.

1106   Pringle, Alex. *Prayer for the revival of religion in all the Protestant churches and for the spread of the Gospel among heathen nations recommended.* Edinburgh: Schaw & Pillans, 1796.

Especially pp. 104-11, on George Liele and his Jamaican Baptist Church.

1107   Rampini, Charles J. G. *Letters from Jamaica: The lands of streams and woods.* Edinburgh: Edmonston & Douglas, 1873, 182 pp.

Pp. 131f., 135, 142, on Obeah men as distinguished from Myal men – extracted in J. J. Williams (entry 1164), pp. 196-97, 198-99. Section on Myallism reprinted in Cundall (entry 995).

1107a   Rashford, John. "The cotton tree and the spiritual realm in Jamaica." *Jamaica Journal* (Kingston) 18, no. 1 (February-April 1985): 49-57, bib., illus.

As a shrine or sanctuary in Myallism and Obeah.

1108   Reckord, Mary. "The Jamaica slave rebellion of 1831." *Past and Present*, no. 40 (July 1968), pp. 108-25. Reprinted in *Black society in the New World*, edited by R. Frucht. New York: Random House, 1971, pp. 50-66. Also similar title in *Jamaica Journal* 3, no. 2 (1969): 25-31.

The basic organization and ideology of the revolt lay in the Negro syncretist and Baptist groups, assisted by Wesleyan and Baptist missions, although missionaries opposed the actual revolt. Pp. 112-15, Native Baptists, especially Sam Sharpe; p. 123, Nat Turner's 1831 revolt in the U.S.

1109   Reckord, Mary. "Missionary activity in Jamaica before emancipation." Ph.D. dissertation, University of London, 1964, 384 pp., maps.

P. 15, note 1, Liele, Baker, and the Negro Baptist Church: Baker's letters to Dr. Ryland (Baptist Missionary Society); pp. 117-22, Obeah men and Myal men; pp. 122-25, Native Baptist and other independent groups; pp. 302-8, 324-26, Sam Sharpe and Native Baptists in the 1831 Christmas rebellion.

1110   Reckord, Michael. "On the wings of song: 'Bedward flies high.'" *Daily Gleaner* (Kingston), 26 September 1984, p. 6.

A favorable review of L. Mariott's play, *Bedward* (entry 1078).

1111   Reid, V[ictor] S[tafford]. *New day.* New York: Alfred A. Knopf, 1949. Reprint. London: Heinemann Educational Books, 1973, 358 pp.

A first, and famous, novel, with the Morant Bay "uprising" of 1865 as background, and showing the influence of Native Baptist Christianity over successive generations.

1112   "Reports of the arrest and trial of Alexander Bedward." *Jamaica Post* (Kingston), 23 January, 30 April, 1 May, 2 May 1895.

Accounts of Bedward's first arrest and trial.

1113   Rippon, John, ed. *Baptist Annual Register*. London: Dilley, Button & Thomas, 1790-1802, as follows. References to Liele or Native Baptists: 1, no. 1 (1790-93): 332-44, 473-84, 540-45; nos. 3-4 (1798-1802): 366-67, 974-75, 1144-45. Some reprinted in entry 1064, pp. 69-92.

1114   Robb, Alex[ander]. *The gospel to the Africans: A narrative of the life and labours of the Rev. William Jameson in Jamaica and Old Calabar.* London: Hamilton Adams & Co., 1861. 2d ed. Edinburgh: Andrew Elliot, 1862, 299 pp., illus.

Pp. 34-36, descriptions and evaluations of Native Baptists under Moses Baker and Gibb; their emphasis on prayer, dreams, and baptism; their "puerilities and superstitions ... mixed up with the religion of heaven" – as found in 1837.

1115   Roberts, W. Adolphe. "Bedward the revivalist." *Sunday Gleaner* (Kingston), 31 January 1960.

Reminiscences from an interview conducted some fifty-three years previously.

1116   Roberts, W. Adolphe. *Six great Jamaicans: Biographical sketches.* Kingston: Pioneer Press, 1957, 122 pp., illus.

Pp. 25-50, uncritical biography of G. W. Gordon; pp. 75-77, Alexander Bedward.

1117   Rusling, G. W. "A note on early Negro Baptist history." *Foundations* (Rochester, Journal of the American Baptist Historical Society) 11, no. 4 (1968): 362-68.

Supplies information supplementing E. A. Holmes (entry 1042) and the text of Liele's "Covenant of the Anabaptist Church" of 1795, with discussion. See also M. Sobel (entry 1143), pp. 149-52 and 394, note 15.

1118   Russell, Horace O. "The missionary outreach of the West Indian church to West Africa in the nineteenth century." D.Phil. thesis, University of Oxford, 1972, 516 pp. (pp. 425-515, sources and bib.).

Pp. 33ff., Liele; pp. 42-46, Baker. By a Jamaican scholar.

1118a   Ryman, Cheryl. "Kumina: Stability and change." *Research Review* (Kingston) 1 (1984): 81-128, illus.

Presented as a new Afro-Jamaican religion to be regarded as a "denomination" in its own right; its history, forms, and functions.

1119   Ryman, Cheryl, and Hall, Beverly. [Notes on accompanying long-playing record, containing music of seven dance/drumming forms.] *Jamaica Journal* 10, no. 1 (1976): 2-4, 6-7.

Includes references to religious use, as in Revival, Zionism, Pukumina, Myal, etc.

1120   Sackett, Sam. "Make a burnt offering unto the Lord." *Christian Century* 97, no. 3 (1980): 60-62.

On the Jamaican Zion Coptic Church, its island off Florida, and marijuana; conflict with U.S. officials over marijuana, taxes, etc.; apparent harassment by residents and the government.

1121   The Saint [pseud.]. "Tattered flock awaits return of dead leader." *Star* (Kingston), 24 June 1963, p. 6.

The Bedwardites; includes an interview with a disciple of Bedward and a report of current internal dissension.

1122   Salkey, Andrew. *A quality of violence*. London: New Authors, 1959, 205 pp. Reprint. London: New English Library, 1962, 159 pp. Reprint. London and Port of Spain: New Beacon Books, 1978, 207 pp.

A novel: pp. 44-63 (1959 and 1978), the fictional account of a Pocomania service during a severe drought at the turn of the century has been described as "an unauthentic middle class attempt to reestablish African cultural elements."

1123   Schafer, Daniel Lee. "The Maroons of Jamaica: African slave rebels in the Caribbean." Ph.D. dissertation (history), University of Minnesota, 1973, 345 pp.

Includes the religious life of the four remaining Maroon villages.

1124   Schlesinger, Benjamin, and Maxwell, John. *August Town, Jamaica: A community study*. Kingston: Institute of Social and Economic Research, University of the West Indies, 1966, 66 pp., map.

P. 3, August Town as historically associated with Alexander Bedward; pp. 14-16, religious groups: includes Bethlehem Tabernacle, Bryce Hill Road (Revivalist; older, poor, less educated people).

1125   Schuler, Monica Elaine. *"Alas, alas, Kongo": A social history of indentured African immigration into Jamaica, 1841-1865*. Baltimore: Johns Hopkins University Press, 1980, 186 pp. (bib., pp. 165-77).

Includes Kumina (as brought from Africa), Myallism, and Baptists.

1126   Schuler, Monica [Elaine]. "Myalism and the African religious tradition in Jamaica." In *Africa and the Caribbean: The legacies of a link*, edited by M. E. Craham and F. W. Knight. Baltimore and London: Johns Hopkins University Press, 1979, pp. 65-79.
        A historian on Myallism as a millennial movement, its changes over time, and continuities with Revivalism and Rastafarianism (pp. 65-79).

1127   Seaga, Edward [Phillip George]. "Healing in Jamaica." In *True experiences in exotic ESP*, edited by Martin Ebon. Signet Mystic Books. New York: New American Library, 1953. Reprint. 1968, pp. 98-108.
        Folk and balmyard healing as influential outside the middle and upper classes.

1128   Seaga, Edward [Phillip George]. "Introduction and notes." *Folk music of Jamaica*. Ethnic Folkways Library Album no. P453. Edited by H. Courlander. New York: Folkways Records and Service Corp., 1956, 7 pp., illus.
        Spirit cults: Kumina (as "Afro"), Zion-Way Baptist, and Pukumina (as "Christianized").

1129   Seaga, Edward [Phillip George]. "Revival cults in Jamaica: Notes toward a sociology of religion." *Jamaica Journal* (Kingston) 3, no. 2 (1969): 3-13, illus., tables. Reprinted in *Freeing the Spirit* (Washington, D.C.) 2, no. 4 (1973): 24-35. Reprinted as "All God's children got the spirit." *Encore: American and Worldwide News* (New York) 2, no. 9 (1973): 60-61, illus. (excerpted).
        Mainly on Pocomania and Zion.

1130   Seaga, Edward [Phillip George]. "River Maid, River Maid." *Jamaica Journal* 3, no. 2 (1969): 16-20, illus. Reprinted in *Freeing the Spirit* (Washington, D.C.) 3, no. 1 (1974): 20-22.
        A prize poem relating the possession experiences of River Maid, a principal functionary in Pocomania Revival.

1131   "The second arrest of Bedward." *Jamaica Historical Society Bulletin*, no. 15 [2] (September 1960): 245-48.
        A collection of the official documents concerning Bedward's arrest in 1921: the Governor's orders for and the Resident Magistrate's report on the arrest during the Bedwardites' "march on Kingston."

1132   Semmel, Bernard. *Jamaican blood and Victorian conscience: The Governor Eyre controversy*. Studies in Society. London: MacGibbon & Kee, 1962; Boston: Houghton Mifflin Co., 1963 [i.e., 1962], 188 pp.

English reaction to the uprising of 1865: supports the interpretation of Lord Olivier. Serves as context for G. W. Gordon, Paul Bogle, and the Native Baptists.

1133   Sibley, Iney Knibb. *The Baptists of Jamaica*. Kingston: Jamaica Baptist Union, 1965, 91 pp., illus., bib.
An outline: pp. 1-3, G. Liele and M. Baker and their appeal to the Baptists in England; pp. 50-53, the Baptists in relation to the Morant Bay "revolt" of 1866.

1134   Simpson, George Eaton. "The acculturative process in Jamaican revivalism." In *Men and cultures*, edited by A. F. C. Wallace. Philadelphia: University of Pennsylvania Press, 1960, pp. 332-41.
Afro-American religious cults in Kingston in the 1950s.

1135   Simpson, George Eaton. *Black religions in the New World*. New York: Columbia University Press, 1978, 415 pp.
Pp. 98-102, 111-17 (and notes, pp. 290-91, 338-40, 368), Jamaica.

1136   Simpson, George Eaton. "Culture change and reintegration found in the cults of West Kingston, Jamaica." *Proceedings of the American Philosophical Society* 99, no. 2 (1955): 89-92.

1137   Simpson, George Eaton. "Introduction and notes." *Jamaican cult music*. Album P461. New York: Ethnic Folkways Library, 1954, 10 pp., illus.
Detailed account of the various types found in West Kingston, with some information on the cults' history – Revivalism, Rastafari, Kumina, and John Canoe.

1138   Simpson, George Eaton. "Jamaican Revivalist cults." *Social and Economic Studies* (Kingston) 5, no. 4 (1956): 321-442.
With a bibliography of ninety-five items.

1139   Simpson, George E[aton]. "The nine-night ceremony in Jamaica." *Journal of American Folklore*, no. 278 [70] (October-December 1957): 329-35. Revised and enlarged in *Caribbean papers*. Cuernavaca, Mexico: Centro Intercultural de Documentación, 1970, pp. 201-7.

1140   Smith, Ashley [Alexander]. "Pentecostalism in Jamaica." *Jamaica Journal*, no. 42 (September 1978), pp. 3-13.

1141   Smith, Ashley [Alexander]. "Pentecostalism in Jamaica: A challenge to the established churches and society." Kingston: Hope United Church, 1975. Mimeo.

1142   Smith, Sandra E. H. "Afro-Christian cults in Jamaica and Trinidad." Research paper (for professor T. O. Ranger), University of California, Los Angeles, History Department, Winter 1973, 32 pp. Mimeo.

        By a West Indian graduate student: a survey of the African legacy and its adaptations in Myallism, Obeah, and various forms of Revivalism and Kumina in Jamaica, and in Shango, the Rada cult, and the Spiritual Baptists or Shouters in Trinidad – together with ancestral, spirit-possession, and water-rite features, and their interaction with Christianity. Copy held in the Centre, Selly Oak Colleges, Birmingham.

1143   Sobel, Mechal. *Trabelin' on: The slave journey to an Afro-Baptist faith*. Contributions in Afro-American and African Studies, 36. Westport, Conn.: Greenwood Press, 1979, 454 pp., illus.

        Pp. 104-7, 149-52, 188-89, 388 (note 7), 394 (note 15), on George Liele.

1144   Stewart, J. *An account of Jamaica and its inhabitants*. London, 1808. 2d ed. *View of the past and present state of the island of Jamaica*. Edinburgh: Oliver & Boyd, 1817. Reprint. 1823.

        Pp. 256ff., Obeah, as countered by Christianity (extracts in J. J. Williams (entry 1164), pp. 184-85.

1145   T., W. W. *A letter from Jamaica*. London, 1860.
        On the subject of religious revivals.

1146   Tanna, Laura. "Kumina: The Kongo connection." *Sunday Gleaner Magazine* (Kingston), 5 December 1982, pp. 2-3.

1147   [Taylor, Adam?] *General Baptist Repository* (London, New Connexion of General Baptists) 1 (1802), Supplement [ca. 1805?]: 229-40 [misprint for 289-300].

        Contains one version of George Liele's Church Covenant: see G. W. Rusling (entry 1117) for text and discussion. See also M. Sobel (entry 1143), pp. 149-52.

1148   Turner, Mary. *Slaves and missionaries: The disintegration of Jamaican slave society, 1787-1834*. Blacks in the New World Series. Urbana: University of Illinois Press, 1982, 223 pp.

Native and Black Baptists and other independent groups, passim: especially pp. 11-18, 57-59, 72-73, 92-95, 148-55 (Sam Sharpe), 199-200; also pp. 54-57, Obeah. Based on archival research.

1149   Underhill, Edward Bean. *Life of James Mursell Philippo, missionary in Jamaica*. London: Yates & Alexander, 1881, 437 pp.

Pp. 311-14, Phillipo's summary of the revival of 1860-61.

1150   Underhill, Edward Bean. *The West Indies: Their social and religious condition*. London: Jackson, Walford & Hodder, 1862, 493 pp., illus. Reprint. Westport, Conn.: Negro Universities Press, 1970.

A Baptist visitor's report; p. 115, "nightly orgies and indecent dances of the Vaudoux"; pp. 159-62, Vodou rites; pp. 191-207, 231-32, Native Baptists in Jamaica; pp. 312-13, secession from the Sturge Town Baptist Church by those rejecting Obeah practices, which had developed there; pp. 388-90, Moses Baker's independent church.

1151   United Kingdom, Department of Education and Science. "Background report: Short course N174, Jamaica, 1971." London: The Department, 1971. Mimeo.

Pp. 33-53, religion: pp. 33-35, list of 127 names of denominations; pp. 43-47, Rastafari; pp. 48-50, Pocomania; pp. 50-51, Anansi-Tacoma folk-cycle.

1152   United Kingdom, Department of Education and Science. "Background report: Short course N187, Jamaica, 1972." London: The Department, 1973. Mimeo.

Pp. 79-108, churches and religion: pp. 96-101, Rastafari.

1153   United Kingdom, Department of Education and Science. "The nine nights at Ochos Rios." Topic reports from Jamaica, group J9, topic 2. London: The Department, 1972, 8 pp. Mimeo.

The nine-night funeral ceremonies.

1154   [United Kingdom Government.] *Report of the Jamaica Royal Commission of Inquiry respecting certain disturbances in the island of Jamaica and the measures taken in the course of their suppression.* 1866.

1155   United States, Department of the Army. *Area handbook for Jamaica*. American University, Foreign Area Studies. Edited by I. Kaplan. DA PAM 550-177. Washington, D.C.: United States Government Printing Office, 1976, 332 pp.

Pp. 116-20, religious life, including the main "cults" and the Rastafarians; p. 78, M. Garvey, and A. Bedward.

1156   Waddell, Hope Masterton. *Twentynine years in the West Indies and Central Africa.* London: T. Nelson & Sons, 1863, 681 pp., illus. Reprint, with introduction by G. I. Jones. London: F. Cass, 1970, 681 pp., illus.

      Selections on Native Baptist Church, the Baptist Church (English), and Myallism.

1157   Watson, Jack. *The West Indian heritage: A history of the West Indies.* London: John Murray, 1979, 210 pp., illus., maps.

      Pp. 68-71, African slaves, importance of Obeah as a political influence; p. 138, Vodou; pp. 173-74, Rastafarians. Note p. 69, engraving of Obeah man.

1158   Wedenoja, William [Andrew]. "Modernization and the Pentecostal movement in Jamaica." In *Perspectives on Pentecostalism: Case studies from the Caribbean and Latin America,* edited by S. D. Glazier. Washington, D.C.: University Press of America, 1980, pp. 27-48.

      American-originated Pentecostalism has been reinterpreted to meet Jamaican needs and values, and become a truly "revolutionary" religion.

1159   Wedenoja, William Andrew. "Religion and adaptation in rural Jamaica." Ph.D. dissertation (anthropology), University of California (San Diego), 1978, 536 pp.

      Afro-Christian revival cults and balmyards, and more recent Pentecostalism.

1160   "West Indian Negro mystic cult called 'Pocomania.'" *Black Man* 1, no. 12 (1936): 16-17.

1161   Whitley, W[illiam] T[homas]. *A history of British Baptists.* London: Charles Griffin & Co., 1923, 381 pp.

      P. 255, brief reference to Liele and M. Baker as independent Baptist pioneers, and to a *Pocket companion* being printed for members by Liele's assistant.

1161a   Williams, Anthony John. "The role of the prophet in millennial cults: Politico-religious movements in Jamaica, 1800-1970." B.Litt. thesis, University of Oxford, 1974.

1162   Williams, Joseph John. *The Maroons of Jamaica.* Anthropological Series, Boston College Graduate School, vol. 3, no. 4 (serial no. 12). Chestnut Hill, Mass.: Boston College, 1938, pp. 379-480.

      Pp. 398-401, 478-79, Obeah.

1163   Williams, Joseph J[ohn]. *Psychic phenomena of Jamaica*. New York: Dial Press, 1934, 309 pp., bib (pp. 286-99). Facs. reprint. Westport, Conn.: Greenwood Press, 1979.

Distinguishes Obeah from Myallism, spiritism, Revivalism, Bedwardism.

1164   Williams, Joseph J[ohn]. *Voodoos and Obeahs: Phases of West Indian witchcraft*. New York: L. Macneagh, Dial Press, 1932. London: George Allen & Unwin, 1933, xix + 257 pp., bib. Reprint. New York: AMS Press, 1970.

Chap. 5 (pp. 142-208), Myallism and its relation to Obeah, Bedwardites (pp. 156-57, 159, as "decadent Myalists"), Revivalism, the laws dealing with Obeah (pp. 159-71); pp. 172-75, extract from R. H. Ferguson (entry 1019); pp. 181-82, extract from E. Long (entry 1072); pp. 184-85, extract from J. Stewart (entry 1144); pp. 196-97, 198-99, extract from C. J. G. Rampini (entry 1107); pp. 210-12, "Voodoo"; pp. 212-20, 234-36, Obeah, Myallism, and Revivalism.

1165   Wilson, Bryan R[onald]. *Magic and the millennium: A sociological study of religious movements of protest among tribal and third-world peoples*. London: Heinemann Educational Books; New York: Harper & Row, 1973, 547 pp. Reprint. Frogmore, St. Albans: Granada Publishing Co., Paladin Books, 1975.

Pp. 59-60, Pocomania; pp. 63-69, Rastafarians; pp. 123-25, syncretism and thaumaturgical demand – based on G. E. Simpson, M. J. Herskovits, and M. G. Smith.

1166   Wright, Philip. *Knibb "the Notorious": Slaves' missionary, 1803-1845*. London: Sidgwick & Jackson, 1973, 264 pp., illus.

Pp. 76-79, 202-83, Native Baptists; pp. 222-25, Myallism and Obeah (based on H. M. Waddell [entry 1156]).

1167   Wynter, Sylvia. *The ballad of a rebellion*. Kingston: Graphic Arts, 1965.

A play sponsored by the government and chronicling the triumphs of a national hero, Paul Bogle; this part was played by a Rastafarian.

1168   Wynter, Sylvia. "Garvey and Bedward." *Sunday Gleaner* (Kingston), 12 March 1972.

A comparison between Marcus Garvey and his contemporary, prophet A. Bedward.

1169   Wynter, Sylvia. *The hills of Hebron*. London: Jonathan Cape, 1962, 283 pp.

Vivid fictional presentation of rural religion in Jamaica, with overtones of the Bedwardites; Pocomania members appear occasionally (as on p. 113), and a Rastafarian arrest (pp. 268-70). The central figure is a black messianic Christ who founds a new community, Hebron, for poor and oppressed followers.

1170   Wynter, Sylvia. "Jokonnu in Jamaica: Towards the interpretation of folk dance as a cultural process." *Jamaica Journal* 4, no. 2 (1970): 34-48.

Jokonnu or John Canoe, a declining rural dance festival dating from the seventeenth century, with its African origins and religious connotations; pp. 40-41, 45 Myallism; pp. 45-46, the Revival and Pocomania; pp. 46-47, Kumina, Convince, Gumbay, Revival Zion, Pocomania, and Rastafari.

Lesser Antilles

As explained earlier, these small densely populated islands with many different kinds of political status are here grouped under the term Lesser Antilles, which is taken as including the Netherlands Antilles and also Barbados. The limited materials are arranged according to the alphabetic order of the islands, and then alphabetically again by author within each island. Islands are absent from the following list when no specific materials have been available.

For general surveys see A. Pollak-Eltz (entry 1175, briefly, in Spanish, and more especially on Spiritual Baptists and Shouters) and R. Sereno (entry 1176 on Obeah as declining).

On Dominica see I. Ball (entry 1178) on "Dreads" as an offshoot of the Rastafarians, the articles in *Race Today* (entries 1179, 1181-1182, 1184-1186, 1189-1190) on the Desmond Trotter murder charge, G. E. Simpson (entry 1187) for a summary, and R. Singh (entry 1188).

On Grenada, see H. Bell (entry 1191), a sympathetic but superficial survey. See A. Pollak-Eltz (entry 1194) on Shango, and her entries under Trinidad and Tobago, where works dealing with Shango in both Grenada and Trinidad are placed. For Carriacou, a small dependency of Grenada, see G. E. Simpson (entry 1197), and especially M. G. Smith (entry 1200) for a full autobiography of N. Paul.

On Guadeloupe see L. Hurbon (entry 1201) on African religious traditions seeking new legitimation in Mahikari, the Japanese Buddhist-Christian immigrant movement. A. Pollak-Eltz (entry 1202, in Spanish) deals with Martinique also.

On Martinique see G. Alexis (entry 1204) on the African background and P. Massajoli (entry 1208) on the Amerindian cultural influences (included as an unusual study although religion is not especially examined). M. M. Horowitz and M. Klass (entry 1207) study the Maldevidan cult in the

General

Catholic Indian population; compare V. S. Naipaul (entry 1210) for a casual account.

On Montserrat, see J. D. Dobbin's studies of ancestor-related possession cults (entry 1211) and S. D. Glazier's review of Dobbin's work (entry 1212).

On Netherlands Antilles see A. F. Marks (entry 1216), but especially G. J. Kruijer (entry 1215 – see English summary, p. 251).

On St. Lucia see G. E. Simpson (entry 1223) on Shango-type cults; see J. C. Beck's account of a "typical West Indian" individual (entry 1218) and R. D. Abraham's review of Beck's work (entry 1217).

For St. Vincent, the material is mainly on Shouters or Spiritual Baptists and the Streams of Power movement from Europe; see G. E. Simpson (entry 1230), a survey based on J. H. Henney (entry 1227) and C. Gullick (entry 1225). The Black Caribs are treated under Particular Movements, although many have in effect become Spiritual Baptists this century.

On the Virgin Islands see E. A. Weinstein (entry 1235), chiefly on the Obeah aspect.

General

1171   Debien, Gabriel. "La christianisation des esclaves des Antilles Françaises aux XVIIe et XVIIIe siècles." *Revue d'Histoire de l'Amérique Française* (Montreal) 20, no. 4 (1967): 525-55; 21, no. 1 (1967): 99-111.

1172   Hurbon, Laënnec. "Le nom du père et le recours aux esprits aux Antilles." In *Actes du 2e Séminaire Inter-Caraïbe sur l'Inadaptation Juvénile – La Question du Père*. Pointe-à-Pitre, Guadeloupe: Services et Clubs de Prévention, 1981, pp. 89-106.
        Religion in the French Antilles.

1173   Hurbon, Laënnec. "Le poids des pratiques magico-religieuses dans la culture antillaise." In *Actes du 1er Séminaire Inter-Caraïbe sur l'Inadaptation Juvénile*. Pointe-à-Pitre, Guadeloupe: Services et Clubs de Prévention, 1980, pp. 196-211.
        Religion in the French Antilles.

1174   Hurbon, Laënnec. "Sectes religieuses, loi, et transgression aux Antilles." *Le CARE* (Pointe-à-Pitre, Centre Antillais de Recherches et d'Études), May 1981, pp. 79-107.

1175   Pollak-Eltz, Angelina. "Los Shouting Baptists en las Antillas Francescas." In *Cultos afroamericanos*. Caracas: Universidad Andrés Bello, 1972, pp. 141-43, 169-73.

  Surveys Shango and the Shouters in anglophone Antilles, and the cults in Guadeloupe and Martinique.

1176   Sereno, Renzo. "Obeah: Magic and social structure in the Lesser Antilles." *Psychiatry* (Washington, D.C.) 11, no. 1 (1948): 15-31.

  Pp. 15-16, 21-31, the practice of Obeah, its important healing and other functions, its recent decline; based on field work on many islands.

Antigua

1177   "Antigua's Rasta movement." *Caribbean Contact* (Port of Spain, Trinidad) 4, no. 7 (1976): 15. Reprinted in *Christian Action* (Caribbean Council of Churches) 2, no. 10 (1976): 3.

  About 1,000 young Rastafarians in Antigua, with schemes for craftwork, agriculture, and fishing, and some government assistance.

Dominica

1178   Ball, Ian. "Emergency goes on as sect keeps island in fear." *Daily Telegraph* (London), 7 March 1981, p. 7.

  News report on the "Dreads" of Dominica, in armed conflict with the government, and described as "the most violent offshoot of the Rastafarian sect."

1179   "Desmond Trotter – Dominica." *Race Today* 9, no. 4 (1977): 89.

  Outline of the murder case and of efforts to free Trotter, a Rastafarian leader in Dominica, in 1974.

1180   [The "Dreads" – various articles.] *Caribbean Monthly Bulletin* 9 (May-June 1975): 43-48; (September 1975): 29.

  Summarized in G. E. Simpson, *Black religions in the New World* (entry 1187), pp. 128-30.

1181   "Free Desmond Trotter." *Race Today* 7, no. 5 (1975): 103.

  Convicted for murder.

1182   "Free Desmond Trotter." *Race Today* 8, no. 2 (1976): 34-35.

Dominica

Letter from prison by Desmond Trotter, together with introduction to the situation.

1183 "Get this man out of jail." *Caribbean Contact* (Port of Spain) 4, no. 2 (1976): 1 and back page, illus.
Protest against the wrongful life imprisonment of Desmond Trotter.

1184 "It dread in Dominica." *Race Today* 7, no. 1 (1975): 4-5.
On the Desmond Trotter murder case.

1185 "Murder trial in Dominica." *Race Today* 6, no. 9 (1974): 258-59.
The background and detail of the Desmond Trotter murder conviction.

1186 "Reports from . . . Dominica." *Race Today* 7, no. 10 (1975): 232.
Further on the Dominica banning of Rastafarian hairstyles.

1187 Simpson, George Eaton. *Black religions in the New World*. New York: Columbia University Press, 1978, 415 pp.
Pp. 128-30, the Rastafari-like "Dreads."

1188 Singh, Rickey. "Trotter's message from prison." *Caribbean Contact* 6, no. 11 (1979: 1, 16, illus.
Desmond Trotter (or Ras Kabinda), a Rastafarian leader framed on a murder charge by the Dominican government police in 1974. Singh is editor of this journal, which has campaigned for Trotter's release.

1189 "Trotter defence committee banned." *Race Today* 7, no. 11 (1976): 231.
The agitation to reprieve Trotter, convicted of murder.

1190 "Trotter reprieved." *Race Today* 8, no. 4 (1976): 80.
The outcome of the murder conviction.

Grenada (and Carriacou)

1191 Bell, [Henry] Hesketh J[oudou]. *Obeah: Witchcraft in the West Indies*. London: S. Low, Marston, Searle & Rivington, 1889, viii + 200 pp. 2d ed. 1893. Reprint. New York: Greenwood Press; Negro University Press, 1970, 200 pp.

Mainly on Grenada: under half is on religion or "obeah," and this is rather superficial observation by a sympathetic colonial servant.

1192   Fichte, Hubert. "Revolution und Magie: Ammerkungen zum Shangokult auf Grenada." In *Petersilie: Santo Domingo, Venezuela, Miami, Grenada*. Die Afroamerikanischen Religionen, 3. Frankfurt am Main: S. Fischer Verlag, 1980, pp. 167-93.

1193   Fichte, Hubert (text), and Mau, Leonore (photos). *Petersilie: Santo Domingo, Venezuela, Miami, Grenada*. Die Afroamerikanischen Religionen, 4. Frankfurt am Main: S. Fischer Verlag, 1980, 403 pp., many color plates, with notes.
        Text (pp. 167-93), on Grenada.

1194   Pollak-Eltz, Angelina. "The Shango cult in Grenada, British Westindies [*sic*]." In *Proceedings, VIIIth International Congress of Anthropological and Ethnological Sciences, 1968, Tokyo and Kyoto*. Vol. 3. Tokyo: Science Council of Japan, pp. 59-60.

1195   Pollak-Eltz, Angelina. "Shangokult und Shouterkirche in Grenada." *Anthropos* 65, nos. 5-6 (1970): 814-32.

1196   Redhead, W. A. "Truth, fact, and tradition in Carriacou." *Caribbean Quarterly* (Mona, Jamaica) 16, no. 3 (1970): 61-63.
        Critical of M. G. Smith's account of the coexistence of Christianity and the ancestor cult in *Kinship and community in Carriacou* (entry 1198).

1197   Simpson, G[eorge] E[aton]. *Black religions in the New World*. New York: Columbia University Press, 1978, 415 pp.
        Pp. 82-83, Shango cult; pp. 83-86, Norman Paul's movement; pp. 102-3, Big Drum or Nation Dance; pp. 140-42, N. Paul's personal history and experiences.

1198   Smith, M[ichael] G[arfield]. *Kinship and community in Carriacou*. Caribbean Series, 5. New Haven, Conn., and London: Yale University Press, 1962, xiv + 347 pp.
        Chap. 7 (pp. 138-63): "Death and the afterlife: Co-existence of Christianity and the ancestor cult"; pp. 147-52, Obeah; pp. 152-63, funeral rites–on an island north of Grenada. See W. A. Redhead's criticism (entry 1196) and M. G. Smith's reply (entry 1199).

Grenada

1199   Smith, M[ichael] G[arfield]. "A note on truth, fact, and tradition in Carriacou." *Caribbean Quarterly* (Mona, Jamaica) 17, nos. 3-4 (1971): 128-38.

1200   Smith, Michael Garfield, recorder. "Dark Puritan." *Caribbean Quarterly* (Mona, Jamaica) 5, no. 1 (1957): 34-47; no. 2 (1958): 85-98; no. 4 (1958): 284-91; 6, no. 1 (1959): 48-59. Reprinted as *Dark Puritan*. Kingston: Department of Extra-Mural Studies, University of the West Indies, 1963, 139 pp., illus.
         The autobiography of Norman Paul, a healer, diviner, and seer on Carriacou, a small dependency of Grenada; his relations with Seventh Day Adventists and Baptists, and with "Oshun," his own cult. As told to M. G. Smith in 1952-53, and with an introduction by Smith.

Guadeloupe

1201   Hurbon, Laënnec. "Le double fonctionnement des sectes aux Antilles: Le cas du Mahikari en Guadeloupe." *Archives de Sciences Sociales des Religions*, no. 50 [25, no. 1] (1980): 59-75.
         On the African religious tradition seeking new legitimation in Mahikari, the Japanese Buddhist-Christian movement, which has a congenial worldview.

1202   Pollak-Eltz, Angelina. "Religion y magia en las Antillas Francescas." In *Cultos afroamericanos*. Caracas: Instituto de Investigaciones Historicas, Universidad Catolica Andrés Bello, 1972, pp. 169-73.
         Syncretism of European beliefs and magical practices.

1203   Singaravelou. "Indian religion in Guadeloupe, French West Indies." *Caribbean Issues* (St. Augustine) 2, no. 3 (1976): 39-51.
         A syncretism of nineteenth-century north and south Hindu practices (not affected by later reforms in India) with some Islamic and more Catholic elements.

Martinique

1204   Alexis, Gerson. "Avatars du vodou en Martinique." *Conjonction* (Port-au-Prince, Institut Français d'Haïti), no. 126 (June 1975), pp. 33-48.
         African religious survivals internalized, operating subconsciously, and emerging in the form of psychological conflicts.

Martinique

1205   Alexis, Gerson. *Voudou et quimbois: Essai sur les avatars du voudou à la Martinique*. Port-au-Prince: Les Éditions Fardin, 1976, 71 pp.
        Popular religion, especially Vodou and magic practitioners.

1206   Horowitz, Michael M. "The worship of south Indian deities in Martinique." *Ethnology* 2, no. 3 (1963): 339-46.
        Detailed description of rituals and of the similarities with practices in south India – preserving continuity with the country of origin and not syncretized with the simultaneous Catholic practice.

1207   Horowitz, Michael M., and Klass, Morton. "The Martiniquan East Indian cult of Maldevidan." *Social and Economic Studies* 10, no. 1 (1961): 93-100.
        The Catholic East Indians' combination of Catholic theology with ritual derived from their original south Indian villages to form a cult of the chief god Maldevidan coexisting with their Catholic practice.

1208   Massajoli, Pierleone. "Amerindian elements in the Creole culture of Martinique." *L'Universo* (Florence) 3 (1979): 561-88, illus., map.
        An unusual inquiry; although not focused on the religious dimension, it provides important background.

1209   Masse, Raymond. *Les Adventistes du septième jour aux Antilles françaises: Anthropologie d'une espérance millénariste*. Montreal: Centre de Recherches Caraïbes; Ste. Marie, Martinique: Fonds Saint Jacques, 1978, 107 pp.
        Pp. 39-44, on continuing beliefs in magic and in exorcism of evil spirits. Argues that Adventism channels social and political dissent into religious millenarianism.

1210   Naipaul, V[idiadhar] S[urajprasad]. *The middle passage: Impressions of five societies . . . in the West Indies and South America*. London: A. Deutsch, 1962, 232 pp. Harmondsworth: Penguin, 1969, 256 pp., map.
        Maldevidan cult in the Catholic Indian population.

Montserrat

1211   Dobbin, Jay D. *The Jombee dance of Montserrat: A study of the trance ritual in the West Indies*. Columbus: Ohio State University Press, 1986, 202 pp., illus.
        Discusses the possible African origins in terms of G. E. Simpson's categories of neo-African or ancestor cult, and by

Montserrat

comparison with Kumina and Convince in Jamaica, Carriacou Big Drum, and the Kele cult on St. Lucia; the relation with Christianity is examined in terms of syncretism, parallelism, and stratification (all three relations are found). By a Catholic priest.

1212 Glazier, Stephen D[avey]. Review of *The Jombee dance of Montserrat*, by J. D. Dobbin (entry 1211). *Journal of American Folklore* 100 (1987): 363-65.

1213 Métraux, Rhoda. "Montserrat, B.W.I.: Some implications of suspended cultural change." *Transactions, New York Academy of Sciences*, 2d ser. 20, no. 2 (1957): 205-11.
P. 209, on the appeal of Protestant "sects."

1214 Philpott, Stuart B. *West Indian migration: The Montserrat case*. London School of Economics Monographs on Social Anthropology, 47. London: Athlone Press, 1973, 210 pp.
Pp. 26-27, general decline, and influence of Obeah; pp. 154-64, "Ceremonial and belief"–belief in "jumbies" and Obeah, wakes, "jumbie dances," in which ancestor spirits communicate important messages.

Netherlands Antilles

1215 Kruijer, G. J. "Kerk en religie op de Bovenwindse Eilanden der Nederlandse Antillen." *West-Indische Gids* (The Hague) 34, no. 4 (1953): 238-51; English summary (p. 251).
In St. Martins, St. Eustatius, and Saba in the Leeward Islands, economic advance is associated with decline in magic; Afro-European religious forms similarly associated with poorer social and economic conditions.

1216 Marks, A. F. *Man, vrouw en huishoudgroep: De Afro-Amerikaanse familie in de samenleving van Curacao*. Verhandelingen van het Koninklijk Instituut voor Taal-, Land-, en Volkenkunde, 77. 1976.
Includes meetings of a Vodou character, with slightly orgiastic elements and trance, but without the spirits or divinities of Afro-American cults elsewhere.

St. Lucia

1217　Abrahams, Roger D. Review of *To windward of the land: The occult world of Alexander Charles* (entry 1218). *Nieuwe West-Indische Gids* (The Hague) 57, nos. 1-2 (1983): 102-5.

1218　Beck, Jane C. *To windward of the land: The occult world of Alexander Charles*. Bloomington and London: Indiana University Press, 1979, 1 + 309 pp.
　　　A folk-healer's own account of his life, as told to Beck, a folklorist; including Obeah beliefs and practices.

1219　Bosquet, Earl. "Who says Rastas are criminals? ... the situation in St. Lucia." *Caribbean Contact* (Port of Spain) 4, no. 1 (1976): 19, illus.
　　　Rastas as craft workers and agriculturalists, with effects seen in fall of the crime rate, yet increasing conflict with the police over marijuana. No connection with Ethiopian Orthodox Church.

1220　*Calling Rastafari* (newspaper of the Iyanola Rasta Improvement Association, set up by the Dreads in St. Lucia).

1221　Crowley, Daniel J[ohn]. "Supernatural beings in St. Lucia." *Caribbean* (Port of Spain, Caribbean Commission) 8, nos. 11-12 (1955): 241-44, 264-65.
　　　Pp. 264-65, Obeah and Obeah men.

1221a　Kremser, M. "Das Blut-, Trank-, und Speiseopfer- am Beispiel des Kélé-Kultes in St. Lucia/Kleine Antillen." *Mitteilungen der Anthropologischen Gesellschaft in Wien* 117 (1987): 125-40; English summary.

1222　Simmons, Harold F. C. "Notes on folklore in St. Lucia." In *Iouanaloa: Recent writing from St. Lucia*. Castries, St. Lucia: Department of Extra-Mural Studies (June 1963): 41-49.
　　　Pp. 44-47, Kele ceremony as ancestral sacrificial worship without possession features, commencing ca. 1867 with the arrival of Ekiti people from Nigeria; banned by the Catholic Church in 1954. By a St. Lucian artist and scholar.

1223　Simpson, George Eaton. "The Kele (Chango) cult in St. Lucia." *Caribbean Studies* (Río Piedras, University of Puerto Rico) 13, no. 3 (1973): 110-16. Shorter version in *Black religions in the New World*. New York: Columbia University Press, 1978, pp. 103-6, 337.

St. Lucia

> A ceremony asking the African ancestors for protection and blessings, with ritual similar to Shango and other Afro-American cults, but a simpler belief system.

St. Vincent (except Black Caribs)

1224　Goodman, Felicitas D. "Glossolalia: Speaking in tongues in four cultural settings." *Confina Psychiatrica* (Basel) 12, no. 2 (1969): 113-29.

> As ascribed to the Holy Spirit–in Streams of Power (St. Vincent), U.S. Midwest tent revival, Texas Protestant Church, and Mexican Pentecostal Church.

1225　Gullick, Charles [John Montgomery Rowley]. "Shakers and ecstasy." *New Fire* (Oxford Society of St. John the Evangelist), no. 9 (1971), pp. 7-11.

> On the "Shakers" or Spiritual Baptists of St. Vincent–their services and possession behavior described in detail.

1226　Henney, Jeannette H[illman]. "Functions of Shakerism." In *Trance, healing, and hallucination*, edited by F. D. Goodman, et al. New York and London: John Wiley & Sons, 1974, pp. 96-102.

1226a　Henney, Jeannette H[illman]. "Sex and status of women in St. Vincent." In *A world of women: Anthropological studies of women in the societies of the world*. Edited by E. Bourguinon. New York: Praeger, 1980, pp. 161-83.

> Describes Spiritual Baptist service; concludes that men rather than women need and receive compensatory status in the Spiritual Baptists.

1227　Henney, Jeannette H[illman]. "The Shakers of St. Vincent: A stable religion." In *Religion, altered states of consciousness, and social change*, edited by E. Bourguignon. Columbus: Ohio State University Press, 1973, pp. 219-63.

1228　Henney, Jeannette H[illman]. "Spirit possession belief and trance behavior in a religious group in St. Vincent, British West Indies." Ph.D. dissertation (anthropology), Ohio State University, 1968, 227 pp.

> "The 'mourning' ceremony of the Spiritual Baptists, in which ritual isolation induced . . . holy hallucination."

1229   Henney, Jeannette H[illman]. *Trance behavior among the Shakers of St. Vincent*. The Ohio State University Cross-Cultural Study of Dissociational States, Working Paper no. 8, 1967.

1230   Simpson, G[eorge] E[aton]. *Black religions in the New World*. New York: Columbia University Press, 1978, 415 pp.
        Pp. 121-23 (and notes, pp. 340-41), the Shakers and Streams of Power–both based on J. H. Henney.

Virgin (and associated) Islands

1231   Cochran, Hamilton. "Obeah in the Virgin Islands." *VI View* 3, no. 9 (1968): 30-41.

1232   Levo, John [Ernest]. *The hurricane*. London: Hutchinson, 1930, 288 pp.
        A novel by an English clergyman, reflecting the religious life of the Virgin Islanders.

1233   Levo, John [Ernest]. *Virgin Islands*. London: Hutchinson, 1933, 291 pp.
        A novel reflecting the religious life.

1234   Trevor, J. C. "Aspects of folk culture in the Virgin Islands." Ph.D. dissertation, University of Cambridge, 1959.
        Pp. 87-115, 467, Obeah; pp. 115-21, witchcraft beliefs.

1235   Weinstein, Edwin A. *Cultural aspects of delusion: A psychiatric study of the Virgin Islands*. New York: Free Press; London: Collier-Macmillan, 1962, 215 pp., map.
        Pp. 145-56, Obeah or witchcraft and its therapeutic value; pp. 163-64, Obeah in the French community; p. 179, briefly on Obeah, religion, and death among Puerto Ricans; pp. 197-99, Obeah in relation to psychosis, with case studies in support.

Windward Islands

1236   Beck, Jane C. "The implied Obeah man." *Western [Journal of] Folklore* (Berkeley, California Folklore Society) 2 (January 1976): 23-33.
        Based on a study in the Windward Islands, but applicable generally in the West Indies. Obeah is the recognized source of all

Windward Islands

power, and is "implied" as the basis for any individual success, which thus arouses suspicion, in contrast to the acknowledged Obeah man who serves the community.

Puerto Rico

In a population of about three million, some 15% are black and another 10% mulatto. While ostensibly a Catholic country, Protestant social influence is strong, but the Pentecostal community, which includes many indigenous churches, is the largest religious tradition after Catholicism, and spreads out from Christian forms into the spiritism that pervades much of the popular religion. The study of popular religion is the preoccupation in many of the items collected here, and studies of particular movements serve to illustrate religious forms that are widespread throughout the community. There are also immigrant movements such as Sri Chinmoy and Rastafarians, but no available studies of these.

For general surveys see J. A. Keefe and R. Nash (entry 1261) for a theoretical and general survey of religion; J. A. Steward, et al. (entry 1290) is a landmark survey with a rural emphasis.

For case studies see S. Cook (entry 1246) on the Cilicia Temple; A. Harwood (entry 1260) for six case studies of urban churches; J. D. Koss (entry 1267) for a young woman possessed by her grandfather's spirit; and M. M. Tumin and A. S. Feldman (entry 1291) for a rural area.

For Pentecostalism see E. Benz (entry 1242, in German) on the Mita religion; V. Garrison (entry 1257) for comparison with Catholicism; and A. L. La Ruffa (entries 1271 and 1273).

On spiritism see T. Andino (entry 1240, in Spanish); J. Bram (entry 1245); J. D. Koss (entry 1263 in Spanish, or entry 1264 in English) on the European spiritualist origins; E. Seda Bonilla (entry 1284) for a rural area; and M. Singer and R. Garcia (entry 1287).

On the Puerto Rican diaspora, in New York see M. A. Borello and E. Mathias (entry 1243, also on healing); V. Garrison (entry 1255); I. Lubshansky, et al. (entry 1275); R. Poblete and T. F. O'Dea (entry 1279); and A. M. Stevens-Arroyo (entry 1289). In Hartford, Conn., see M. Singer and R. Garcia (entry 1287). In the northeast U.S. see M. Gaviria and R. M. Wintrob (entry 1258).

On healing, mental healing, and psychiatry see E. Seda Bonilla (entries 1285-1286); M. Gaviria and R. M. Wintrob (entry 1258); I. Lubshansky, et al. (entry 1275); and L. H. Rogler and A. B. Hollingshead (entry 1281).

1237   Agosto [de Muñoz], N[élida]. "The Mita congregation: An anthropological study of a religious community in Puerto Rico." D.Phil. thesis (social anthropology), University of Oxford, 1981.

1238   Alegria, Ricardo E. *La fiesta de Santiago Apóstol en Loiza Aldesa.* Colección de Estudios Puertorriqueños. Madrid: Artes Gráficas, 1954, xxxv + 76 pp.
        The Negro population as most faithful supporters of the festival of Santiago, interpreted as a syncretism between Catholicism and the Yoruba divinity, Shango.

1239   Amorin, Deolino. *Africanismo y espiritismo.* Buenos Aires: Editorial Constancia, 1958.

1240   Andino, Telesforo. *El espiritismo en Puerto Rico y la reforma.* San Juan: Tipografia San Juan, 1937, 234 pp.
        A detailed presentation of spiritist concepts, as complementary to both philosophy and theosophy.

1241   Babín, María Teresa. *Panorama de la cultura Puertorriqueña.* New York: Las Americas Publishing Co., 1958, 500 pp., illus., bib.

1242   Benz, Ernst. *Der Heilige Geist in Amerika.* Düsseldorf and Cologne: E. Diederichs Verlag, 1970, 231 pp.
        Chap. 6 (pp. 89-112), Mita and the Pentecostal movement in Puerto Rico. The Mita congregation in San Juan as visited by the author in the late 1960s.

1243   Borello, Mary Ann, and Mathias, Elizabeth. "Botánicas: Puerto Rican pharmacies." *Natural History* (New York) 86, no. 7 (1977): 64-73, illus.
        In New York City–the *botánicas* that sell paraphernalia for spiritism and Santería; description of a mediumistic session.

1244   Bradford, William Penn. "Puerto Rican spiritism: Contrasts in the sacred and the profane." *Caribbean Studies* (Río Piedras, University of Puerto Rico) 24, nos. 3-4 (1978): 48-55, bib.
        Description by direct observation, but no systematic study.

1245   Bram, Joseph. "Spirits, mediums, and believers in contemporary Puerto Rico." *Transactions, New York Academy of Sciences,* 2d ser. 20, no. 4 (1958): 340-47.

On the origins of spiritism; Kardec's influence in Puerto Rico; mediums and other features.

1246   Cook, Scott. "The Prophets: A revivalistic folk religious movement in Puerto Rico." *Caribbean Studies* (Río Piedras, University of Puerto Rico) 4, no. 4 (1965): 20-35.
        Cilicia Temple in Caquas, similar to Rastafari and Shango: as fundamentalism, spiritualism, folk culture, and Catholicism.

1247   Cook, Scott. "Some sociocultural aspects of two revivalistic religious groups in a Puerto Rican municipio." Graduate thesis, University of Puerto Rico, Institute of Caribbean Studies, Interamerican Program of Advanced Social Science Studies, 1963.

1248   Cruz, Nicky. *Satan on the loose*. Tappan, N.J.: Fleming H. Revell Co., 1973, 158 pp.; London: Oliphants, 1973, 153 pp.
        Chaps. 2-4 describe the author's parents in Puerto Rico–practicing healing, etc., through their psychic and spirit powers.

1249   Dohen, Dorothy. *Two studies of Puerto Rico: Religion data; the background of consensual union*. CIDOC: Sondeos, 3. Cuernavaca, Mexico: Centro Intercultural de Documentación, 1966, 155 pp., maps, bib.
        A well-documented statistical study of the main variables in religious behavior in 1958.

1250   Fenton, Jeremy. *Understanding the religious background of the Puerto Rican*. CIDOC: Sondeos, 52. Cuernavaca, Mexico: Centro Intercultural de Documentación, 1969, 72 pp., bib.
        Catholic, Protestant, Pentecostal, and spiritist forms of religion, and the needs met, both in Puerto Rico and New York.

1251   Figueroa, José E. "The cultural dynamic of Puerto Rican spiritism: Class, nationality, and religion in a Brooklyn ghetto." Ph.D. dissertation (sociology), City University of New York, 1981, 270 pp.
        In Williamsburg, Brooklyn, among Puerto Rican workers, with the liberating aspect of religious creativity countering religious escapism, and so contributing to national self-awareness and working-class consciousness.

1252   Fitzgerald, William A. "A survey of religious conditions in Puerto Rico, 1899-1934." Ph.D. dissertation, Fordham University, 1934.

1253   Garcia, Michael A[nthony]. "The effects of spiritualism and Santeria as a cultural determinant in New York: Puerto Rican women as reflected by their use of projection." Ph.D. dissertation (clinical psychology), Adelphi University, 1979, 173 pp.

1254   Garrido, Pablo. *Esotería y fervor populares de Puerto Rico*. Madrid: Ediciónes-Cultura Hispánica, 1952, 250 pp., illus., map, music.

Folk practices of a religious origin, and the beliefs and customs of the "espiritistas."

1255   Garrison, Vivian. "Doctor, *espiritista*, or psychiatrist? Health-seeking behaviour in a Puerto Rican neighbourhood in New York City." *Medical Anthropology* 1, nos. 2-3 (1977): 65-180.

Folk healers – their clients, the disorders and their treatments.

1256   Garrison, Vivian. "The 'Puerto Rican syndrome' in psychiatry and *espiritismo*." In *Case studies in spirit possession*, edited by V. Garrison and V. Crapanzo. New York: John Wiley, 1977, pp. 383-449.

1257   Garrison, Vivian. "Sectarianism and psychosocial adjustment: A controlled comparison of Puerto Rican Pentecostals and Catholics." In *Religious movements in contemporary America*, edited by I. I. Zaretsky and M. P. Leone. Princeton, N.J.: Princeton University Press, 1974, pp. 298-329.

No single characteristic distinguished one group from the other, unless it be conscious choice of the minority religion (Pentecostalism) in a Catholic milieu.

1258   Gaviria, Moisés, and Wintrob, Ronald M. "Supernatural influences in psychopathology: Puerto Rican folk beliefs about mental illness." *Canadian Psychiatric Association Journal* (Ottawa) 21, no. 6 (1976): 361-69.

Studied in two Connecticut cities; includes folk healers, spiritism, etc.

1259   Gonzalez, Justo L. *The development of Christianity in the Latin Caribbean*. Grand Rapids: W. B. Eerdmans, 1969, 136 pp.

P. 111, Mita movement in Arecibo, from the Iglesia de Dios Pentecostal (or Assemblies of God). Mita, as a "goddess," claims to reincarnate the Holy Ghost and has thousands of followers.

1260   Harwood, Alan. *RX – Spiritist as needed: A study of a Puerto Rican community mental health resource*. Contemporary Religious Movements. New York: Wiley-Interscience, 1977, 251 pp., bib.

Case studies of individuals and of six urban "spiritualist" churches; pp. 43-52, Mesa Blanca and Santería as variant spiritist traditions; pp. 57-72, description of a major ritual; pp. 182-83, spiritism as a religion; pp. 183-88, spiritism as a form of therapy.

1261   Keefe, Joseph A., and Nash, Robert. "Religion and education in the Puerto Rican culture." *Journal of Education* (Boston) 150, no. 2 (1967): 23-34, bib.

1262   Koss, Joan D. "Artistic expression and creative process in Caribbean possession cult rituals." In *The visual arts, plastic and graphic*, edited by J. M. Cordwell. The Hague: Mouton, 1979, pp. 373-410, illus.
        As seen in spiritism.

1263   Koss, Joan D. "El porque de los cultos religiosos: El caso del espiritismo en Puerto Rico." *Revista de Ciencias Sociales* (Río Piedras, University of Puerto Rico, Colegio de Ciencias Sociales) 16, no. 1 (1972): 61-72, bib.
        Reasons for growth of cults, with special reference to spiritualism, its European birth, and Puerto Rican developments.

1264   Koss, Joan D. "Religion and science divinely related: A case history of spiritism in Puerto Rico." *Caribbean Studies* (Río Piedras, University of Puerto Rico) 16, no. 1 (1976): 22-43.
        History of spiritism from the eighteenth century in Europe and in Puerto Rico, with its relation to folk religion and healing.

1265   Koss, Joan D. "Social process and behaviour change in Puerto Rican spiritist cults." In *Caribbean cults: Individual and social change*, edited by D. W. Hogg and J. D. Koss. San Juan: University of Puerto Rico Press, 1975.
        Written in 1967.

1266   Koss, Joan D. "Social process, healing, and self-defeat among Puerto Rican spiritists." *American Ethnologist* 4, no. 3 (1977): 453-60.
        The long-term effects on the healing mediums themselves: the initial beneficial results may be reversed by the dynamics of the cult group itself.

1267   Koss, Joan D. "Spirits as socializing agents: A case study of a Puerto Rican girl reared in a matricentric family." In *Case studies in spirit possession*, edited by V. Garrison and V. Crapanzano. New York: John Wiley, 1977, pp. 365-82.

1268   Koss, Joan D. "Terapéutica del sistema de una secta en Puerto Rico." *Revista de Ciencias Sociales* (Río Piedras, University of Puerto Rico, Colegio de Ciencias Sociales) 14, no. 2 (1970): 259-78, bib.

1269   Koss, Joan D. "The therapist-spiritist training project in Puerto Rico: An experiment to relate the traditional healing system to the public health system." *Social Science and Medicine* 14B, no. 4 (1980): 255-66, bib.

Practitioners of each system now refer patients to one another.

1270   Lange, Yvonne Marie. "Santos: The household wooden saints of Puerto Rico." Ph.D. dissertation (religion), University of Pennsylvania, 1975, 973 pp., illus.

Chiefly among Hispanic stock in the mountainous hinterland; covers the Catholic "celestial hierarchy"; origins, making, and functions.

1271   La Ruffa, Anthony L. "Culture change and Pentecostalism in Puerto Rico." *Social and Economic Studies* (Mona, Jamaica) 18, no. 3 (1969): 273-81.

1272   La Ruffa, Anthony L. "Pentecostalism in Puerto Rican society." In *Perspectives on Pentecostalism: Case Studies from the Caribbean and Latin America*, edited by S. D. Glazier. Washington, D.C.: University Press of America, 1980, pp. 49-65.

Mainly on the Miñi Miñi Church of God (American-connected); concludes that Pentecostalism adapts both to poor, deprived peoples and to the more affluent in a consumer society, and thus does not criticize the social order.

1273   La Ruffa, Anthony L. *San Cipriano: Life in a Puerto Rican community.* Library of Anthropology. New York: Gordon & Breach, 1971, 149 pp., illus.

Pp. 73-83, folk religion – fiestas, spiritualism, and witchcraft; pp. 84-86, Protestantism; pp. 86-87, two "prophetic churches"; pp. 87-107, Pentecostalism (as in a Church of God congregation); pp. 107-12, a new locally founded Church of God; pp. 113-35, Pentecostal beliefs, rites, and religious experiences.

1274   Lewis, Gordon [Kenneth]. *Puerto Rico: Freedom and power in the Caribbean.* London: Merlin Press, 1963, 626 pp.

Pp. 271-80, religion; pp. 272-73, Pentecostalism a nativist reaction against American Protestantism as being middle-class; p. 275, spiritualism; useful on the general religious situation.

1275   Lubshansky, Isaac; Egri, Gladys; and Stokes, Janet. "Puerto Rican spiritualists view mental illness: The faith healer as a para-professional." *American Journal of Psychiatry* 127, no. 3 (1970): 312-27.

Two healing case studies analyzed in psychiatric terms; based on twenty Puerto Rican spiritualist temples in the Bronx, New York

City, operating publicly–either as store-front types emphasizing healing religion, or as Kardecist types with a "scientific religion."

1276 Michtom, Madeleine. "Becoming a medium: The role of trance in Puerto Rican spiritism as an avenue to mazeway resynthesis." Ph.D. dissertation (cultural anthropology), New York University, 1975, 425 pp.

Uses A. F. C. Wallace's concept of "mazeway resynthesis" to study the social and cognitive functions of possession-trance among all social classes. Learning to become a medium involves new social and personal identities.

1276a Morales-Dorta, José. *Puerto Rican espiritismo: Religion and psychotherapy*. New York: Vantage Press, 1976, 106 pp.

Origins and structure of spiritism; description of a séance; relation to mental-health care among New York Puerto Ricans.

1277 Osorio, Edison H. "Eine prophetische Symbolhandlung in Puerto Rico." In *Kirche, Benzin, und Bohnensuppe: Auf den Spuren dynamischer Gemeinden*. Zurich: Theologisch Verlag Zurich, 1971, pp. 122-28.

1278 Otero Yañez, Teresa. *El espiritismo en Puerto Rico*. San Juan, 1963.

1279 Poblete, Renato, and O'Dea, Thomas F. "Anomie and the 'Quest for Community': The formation of sects among the Puerto Ricans of New York." *American Catholic Sociological Review* 21, no. 1 (1960): 18-36.

1280 Ramírez, Ana Maria Díaz. "Religion in the melting pot of the Caribbean: San Juan, Puerto Rico." *New World Outlook*, n.s. 35, no. 9 [65, no. 5] (1975): 8-15, illus.

Pp. 8-10, the Mita religion; p. 11, the Catholic Cursillo movement; pp. 11-12, a healing charismatic group; p. 12, Pentecostalism.

1281 Rogler, Lloyd H., and Hollingshead, August B. "The Puerto Rican spiritualist as a psychiatrist." *American Journal of Sociology* 67, no. 1 (1961): 17-21.

1282 Safa, Helen Icken. *The urban poor of Puerto Rico: A study in development and inequality*. New York: Holt, Rinehart & Winston, 1974, 116 pp.

Pp. 70-73, religion–references to "sects" and their influence, especially Seventh Day Adventism.

1283   Salgado, Ramona Matos. "The role of the Puerto Rican spiritist in helping Puerto Ricans with problems of family relations." D.Ed. dissertation (anthropology), Columbia University, 1974, 237 pp.

1284   Seda Bonilla, Eduardo. *Interacción social y personalidad en una communidad de Puerto Rico*. San Juan: Ediciones Juan Ponce de León, 1964, 167 pp. English translation. *Social change and personality in a Puerto Rican agrarian reform community*. Evanston, Ill.: Northwestern University Press, 1973, 187 pp., bib.

        Includes spiritism in Nocora, a sugar-cane community on the north coast, in 1948 and 1959.

1285   Seda Bonilla, Eduardo. "Spiritualism and psychodrama." *Revista Inter-Americana de Psicología* 2, no. 3 (1968): 189-96.

        Presentation and analysis of spiritualist treatment of a patient in a catatonic state.

1286   Seda Bonilla, Eduardo. "Spiritualism, psychoanalysis, and psychodrama." *American Anthropologist* 71, no. 3 (1969): 493-97, bib.

        The relation between the concepts of "fluid" in spiritualism and of "libido" in psychoanalysis, and between the spiritualist session and psychodrama.

1286a   Singer, Merrill, and Borrero, M. C. "Indigenous treatment for alcoholism: The case of Puerto Rico spiritism." *Medical Anthropology* (Pleasantville, N.Y.) 8, no. 4 (1984): 246-73.

1287   Singer, Merrill, and Garcia, Roberto. "La guérison spirite dans une communauté portoricaine." *Mouvements Religieux* (Sarreguemines, France, Bulletin de l'Association d'Étude et d'Information sur les Mouvements Religieux), no. 45 (January 1984), pp. 1-5. (French translation from English original.)

        Spiritist healing movements and "centres," recently being influenced by Cuban Santería "temples"; case study of the "Centre de Notre Père Lanzare" of "Marta de Jesus" among Puerto Ricans at Hartford, Conn.

1288   Stevens-Arroyo, Antonio M. "The indigenous elements in the popular religion of Puerto Ricans." Ph.D. dissertation (religion, history), Fordham University, 1981, 281 pp.

1289   Stevens-Arroyo, Antonio M. "Religion and the Puerto Ricans in New York." In *Puerto Rican perspectives*, edited by E. Mapp. Metuchen, N.J.: Scarecrow Press, 1974, pp. 119-30.

1290   Steward, Julian H., et al. *The people of Puerto Rico: A study in social anthropology*. Urbana: University of Illinois Press, 1956. Reprint. 1969, 540 pp., illus., maps. 2d ed. Indianapolis: Bobbs Merrill, 1971.

A landmark study focused on the rural and poorer populace. See index under: magic, Pentecostal church, spiritualism, visions, witchcraft.

1291   Tumin, Melvin M., and Feldman, Arnold S. "The miracle at Sabana Grande." *Public Opinion Quarterly* (Princeton, N.J.) 19, no. 2 (1955): 125-39.

Sociological study of results of an appearance of a saint to children in a rural village in 1953; a mass response concerned with healing, despite strong Catholic Church opposition.

1292   Universidad de Puerto Rico. *Primer ciclo de conferencias públicas sobre temas de investigación social*. Río Piedras: Centro de Investigaciones Sociales, Universidad de Puerto Rico, 1969, 192 pp.

Nine public lectures given in 1967-68, including one on spiritualism as a religion.

1293   Vidal, Theodoro. *Santeros puertorriqueños*. San Juan: Ed. Alba, 1979.

1294   Wagenheim, Kal. *Puerto Rico: A profile*. New York and London: Praeger Publishers, 1970, 286 pp.

Pp. 159-66, "religion"–popular unorthodox Catholicism, Pentecostalism, spiritism, and Mita's "home-grown church" from 1940.

Suriname

In a population of about half a million, about 37% are Creole and about 11% are Bush Negroes or Maroons, who represent "the most highly developed independent societies and cultures in Afro-America, except perhaps for Haiti," and now tend to adopt the term *Bosnegers*. They are in several groups – the Saramaka and the Djuka (about 15,000 to 20,000 each), and the Aluku, the Matawai, and the Paramaka (each about 2,000).

For general surveys see A. Pollak-Eltz (entry 1356, in Spanish) and G. E. Simpson (entry 1369, based on Herskovits, Wooding, and de Groot). For Winti, the religion of the coastal Creoles, see E. C. Green (entry 1317), J. G. Platvoet (entry 1355, using Schoonheym and Wooding), P. E. Schoonheym (entry 1366), and J. Voorhoeve (entry 1396, English translation from a report made in the late 1950s). Note that *obiaman* refers to spiritual healers, and not, like *Obeah* in much of the West Indies, to practitioners of harmful magic, for which the term here is *wisi*.

For all study of Suriname Bush Negroes, R. Price (entry 1360), a bibliographic essay and history of the study, is essential. C. de Beet and H. U. E. Thoden van Velzen (entry 1299) is an important survey of prophet movements since the eighteenth century.

On the Matawai prophet-evangelist Johannes King and his work among the Djuka (his father was a Djuka) for the Moravians without creating an independent church, see his own writings (entries 1336-1338), G. A. Freytag (entry 1309), A. Schulze (entry 1367), and J. Voorhoeve (entry 1399).

On the messianic Saramaka prophet Anake see I. Albitrouw, a local Moravian mission evangelist (entry 1295, Dutch translation from 1890s original), L. Junker (entry 1332, a first-hand account), J. Voorhoeve and H. C. van Renselaar (entry 1400), and Thoden van Velzen and W. van Wetering (entry 1384, pp. 119-24).

On the Djuka prophet Afaka see J. W. Gonggryp (entry 1311) and J. W. Gonggryp and C. N. Dubelaar (entry 1314). For the Djuka *Gaan Gadu* or *Gaan Tata* cult from 1885 see Thoden van Velzen (especially entry 1380 and also entries 1379 and 1382) and Thoden van Velzen and W. van Wetering (entry 1384). On the new Djuka prophet, Akalali or Aklari, from 1972, see Thoden van Velzen and W. van Wetering (entry 1387) and Thoden van Velzen (entry 1379, pp. 111-14). C. N. Dubelaar (entry 1305) reviews the literature on the new script of Afaka.

The only material on the Amerindians is A. J. Butt Colson (entry 1301), who describes a short-lived prophet movement among the Waiyana Indians, and we include a missionary's comment.

Some 15% of the population is Javanese and Islamic. See A. de Waal Malefijt (entries 1401-1402) for a syncretized Islam with a new form of the *slametan* rite and new specialists.

1295   Albitrouw, Izaak. *Tori foe da bigin foe Anake: Verslag van een messianistische beweging.* Edited, with an introduction by Miriam [de Beet-]Sterman. Translated into Dutch by R. van Es-Redmond. Bronnen voor de Studie van Bosneger Samenlevingen, 2. Utrecht: Centrum voor Caraïbische Studies, Rijksuniversiteit Utrecht, 1978, 147 pp., map, bib.

    Original text and translation of an account by prophet Anake, by a local Moravian Mission evangelist, Albitrouw, of the 1890s.

1296   Albitrouw, Izaak. *Zendingsarbeid in Aurora onder de Saramaker Bosnegers van 1891 tot 1896.* Edited, with an introduction by Miriam [de Beet-]Sterman. Bronnen voor de Studie van Bosneger Samenlevingen, 3. Utrecht: Centrum voor Caraïbische Studies, Instituut voor Culturele Antropologie, Rijksuniversiteit Utrecht, 1979, 168 pp., map, illus.

    The Suriname text of the Moravian Mission evangelist Albitrouw (pp. 15-108) followed by Dutch translation (pp. 109-50) – includes Anake, the Saramaka prophet.

1297   Anderson, Alan B. "Recent acculturation of Bush Negroes in Surinam and French Guiana." *Anthropologica*, n.s. 22, no. 1 (1980): 61-84, map, bib.

    Acculturation to the coastal society, and away from Africanisms; pp. 70-71, on religious aspects.

1298   Bechler, Th. "Menzen zur Beute und die starken zum Raube: Zwei bilder aus der Buschlandmission in Suriname." In *Alle Welte.* Missionsstunden aus der Brüdergemein, 5. Herrnhut: Missionsbuchhandlung der Missionsanstalt der Evang. Brüder-Unität, 1906, pp. 57-74.

    On Anake.

1299   Beet, Chris de, and Thoden van Velzen, H[endrik] U[lbo] E[ric]. "Bush Negro prophetic movements: Religions of despair?" *Bijdragen tot de Taal-, Land-, en Volkenkunde* 133, no. 1 (1977): 100-135, illus., map, bib.

Outlines earliest Saramaka prophet movements, from 1772, using missionary sources, as well as later movements (Johannes King, Gaan Tata, and Akalali cults); criticizes deprivation, etc., theories (especially that of J. Voorhoeve and H. C. van Renselaar [entry 1400]), pp. 113-28 by showing the relative prosperity of the Djuka. An important article.

1299a   Bekier, Bozena Ewa. *Perserverence of African beliefs in the religious ideas of Bosnegers in Surinam.* Hemisphere Studies on Culture and Societies, no. 1, Contributions. Wroclaw: Polskiej Akademi Nauk, 1985, pp. 93-108.

Religious ideas were pivotal among escaped slaves and have changed less than among other blacks.

1300   *Berichten uit de Heiden-Wereld uitgegeven door het Zendings-genootschap der Broedergemeente te Zeist*, 1895, pp. 12-42.

Cited in H. U. E. Thoden van Velzen (entry 1379) as including material on the Gaan Gadu cult.

1301   Butt Colson, Audrey J. "The sky pilot." *Sunday Times Colour Magazine* (London), 5 July 1964, p. 38.

The Aramawali movement of prophet Pidima among the Waiyana in the early 1960s – near West Indies Mission.

1302   Caffe, E. D. "Worstelen tussen culturen: De rol van winti in het leven van de Afro-Surinamer." *Religieuza Bewegingen in Nederland*, no. 12 (1986), pp. 7-22.

1303   Dalby, [Terry] David [Pereira]. "The indigenous scripts of West Africa and Surinam: Their inspiration and design." *African Language Studies* (London), no. 9 (1968), pp. 156-97.

Pp. 192-94, the Afaka or Djuka script, and its relation to West African scripts.

1304   Dosker, Henry E. "John King, the apostle of Surinam." *Missionary Review of the World*, n.s. 9, no. 7 (1896): 519-23.

An outline biography, quoting his account of his conversion vision.

1305   Dubelaar, C. N. "Het Afakaschrift in de Afrikanistiek." *Nieuwe West-Indische Gids* (The Hague) 47, no. 3 (1970): 294-303, illus.

Review article on T. D. P. Dalby (entry 1303).

1306 Dubelaar, C. N., and Gonggryp, J. W. "Het Afakaschrift." *Nieuwe West-Indische Gids* (The Hague) 46 (1968): 232-60.

1307 Elst, Dirk Hendrik van der. "The Bush Negro tribes of Surinam, South America, a synthesis." Ph.D. dissertation (anthropology), Northwestern University, 1970, 377 pp.
     Pp. 174-81, ideology; pp. 182-206, spirit beings; pp. 207-28, *Kunu* (avenging spirits); pp. 229-71, lesser gods, and the dead; pp. 272-313, various practices and beliefs; pp. 314-35, religious change; pp. 336-53, worldview. Based only on the literature.

1308 Fortune, Gwendoline. "The Surinamese Maroons and their tradition of independence." *Black Art* (Los Angeles) 5, no. 4 (1983): 40-47, illus.

1309 Freytag, Gottfried A. *Johannes King der Buschland-Prophet: Ein Lebensbild aus der Mission der Brüdergemeine in Suriname. Nach seinen eigenen Aufzeichnungen Dargestellt.* Hefte zur Missionskunde, 20. Herrnhut: Missionsbuchhandlung, 1927, 88 pp.
     Johannes King, a Bush Negro prophet in Suriname, late nineteenth century, who had much influence in Moravian missionary extension without creating an independent church. A very good account.

1310 Goeje, C. H. de. "Negers in Amerika." *De West-Indische Gids* (The Hague) 28 (1947): 217-22.
     Includes a first-hand account of the burial of a Vodou god.

1311 Gonggryp, J. W. [Gonggrijp – alternative spelling]. "The evolution of a Djuka-script in Surinam." *Nieuwe West-Indische Gids* (The Hague) 40 (1960): 63-72.
     A Bush-Negro script with origins or development in the messianic movement of Afaka, ca. 1910.

1312 Gonggrijp, J. W. "De geschiedenis van het Djoeka-schrift van Afaka." *Opbouw* (Paramaribo), December 1958, pp. 24-29.
     See entry 1311 for English version.

1313 Gonggryp, J. W., and Dubelaar, C. N. "De geschriften van Afaka in zijn Djoeka-schrift." *Nieuwe West-Indische Gids* (The Hague) 42 (1964): 213-54.

1314 Gonggryp, J. W., and Dubelaar, C. [N.]. "Pater Morssink en Afaka." *Opbouw* (Utrecht), Kerstnummer (1960), pp. 1-11.

On the Afaka messianic movement among Bush Negroes; pp. 6-11, examples of a new, revealed script, with texts and translations into Dutch.

1315 Green, Edward [Crocker]. "Living with the Matawai Bushnegers." *Surinam Adventure* (Paramaribo) 4, no. 12 (1972): 17.
Includes Johannes King.

1316 Green, Edward Crocker. "The Matawi Maroons: An acculturating Afro-American society." Ph.D. dissertation (anthropology), Catholic University of America, 1974, 341 pp.
Includes Johannes King.

1317 Green, Edwin [elsewhere, Edward] C[rocker]. "*Winti* and Christianity: A study in religious change." *Ethnohistory* 25, no. 30 (1978): 251-76, bib.
Incompatibility between African and Moravian belief-systems as one reason for lack of syncretism in the religion of Afro-Americans in Suriname, as compared with other areas.

1318 Groot, Sylvia W. de. *Djuka society and social change: History of an attempt to develop a Bush Negro community in Surinam, 1917-1926.* Assen: Van Gorcum; Atlantic Highlands, N.J.: Humanities Press, 1969, 256 pp.
Pp. 6-11, 20-29, Djuka history and religion, in the course of an account of the 1917-26 attempt to develop the Bush Negro community.

1318a Groot, Silvia W. de. "Maroon women as ancestors, priests, and mediums in Suriname." *Slavery and Abolition* (London) 7, no. 2 (September 1980): 160-74.
Their importance in a matrilineal society.

1319 Groot, Sylvia W. de. "Migratiebewegingen der Djoeka's in Suriname van 1845 tot 1863." *Nieuwe West-Indische Gids* (The Hague) 44, nos. 1-2 (1965): 133-51.

1320 Groot, Sylvia W. de. *Van isolatie naar integratie: De Surinaamse Marrons en hun afstammelingen. Officiële documenten betrefeffende de Djoeka's (1845-1865).* Verhandelingen van het Koninklijk Instituut voor Taal-, Land-, en Volkenkunde, 41. The Hague: Martinus Nijhoff, 1963, 100 pp.

1321 "Guiana." *Evangelical Christendom: Its state and prospects* (London) 17 [n.s. 4] (2 February 1863): 100.
Report on "a remarkable movement" under John King.

1322 Herskovits, Melville J[ean], and Herskovits, Frances S. *Rebel destiny: Among the Bush Negroes of Dutch Guiana*. New York: McGraw Hill; London: Whittlesey House, 1934, 366 pp., illus. Reprint. 1971. Facs. reprint. Amsterdam: S. Emmering, 1974.

Chap. 5, "The shrine to the river gods"; chap. 13, "The gods speak"; chap. 17, Obeah – as a gift from the gods for warning and healing, through Obiamen who can control it.

1323 Herskovits, Melville J[ean], and Herskovits, Frances S. *Suriname folklore*. Columbia University Contributions to Anthropology, 27. New York: Columbia University Press, 1936. Selections reprinted in *The New World Negro*, by M. J. Herskovits. Bloomington: Indiana University Press, 1966, pp. 267-319.

Passim, the religion of the black urban population (i.e., Creole or Winti religion of coastal blacks).

1324 Hurault, Jean. "Analyse comparative d'ouvrages sur les noirs refugiés de Guyane: Saramaka et Aluku (Boni)." *L'Homme* (Paris) 20, no. 2 (1980): 119-27.

Discusses R. Price (entry 1361).

1325 Hutton, Joseph Edmund. *A History of Moravian missions*. London: Moravian Publishing Office, [ca. 1922], 550 pp., bib., maps.

Pp. 121-25, on the Bush Negro mission, 1765-1813, at first successful, then abandoned; outlines of Bush Negro religion.

1326 Jones, J[ohan] F[rits]. "Christus en Kwakoe in Suriname." *Wereld en Zending: Tijdschrift voor Missiologie* (Amsterdam) 5, no. 1 (1976): 17-20.

Afro-American syncretist religion, including Winti, Gaan Gadu cult, etc.

1327 Jones, Johan Frits. "Kwakoe en Christus: Een keschouwing over de ontmoeting van de Afro-Amerikaanse cultuur en religie met de Hernhutter zending in Suriname." Dissertation, University Protestant Faculty in Brussels, 1981, 157 pp.

1328 Jones, Johan Frits. "De ontmoeting van het Christelijk geloof en de West-Afrikaanse religie in Suriname." Thesis, University Protestant Faculty in Brussels, 1966.

1329 Junker, L. "De godsdienst der Boschneggers." *Onze Aarde* (Amsterdam) 7 (1934): 331-36, illus.

1330 Junker, L. "De godsdienst der Boschneggers." *De West-Indische Gids* (Amsterdam) 7 (1925-26): 81-95, 127-37, 153-64.

Saramaka religion.

1331   Junker, L. "Godsdienst, zeden, en gebruiken der Boschnegers." *De West-Indische Gids* (Amsterdam) 6 (1924-25): 73-81.
        On Saramaka religion; notes *tiki bribi* shrines still existing in the twentieth century. The author has been described as a "paternalistic part-time government official."

1332   Junker, L. "Primitief communisme." *De West-Indische Gids* (Amsterdam) 22 (1940): 277-83.
        A "first-hand account" of Anake's movement among the Saramaka.

1333   Kahn, Morton [Charles]. "The Bush Negroes of Dutch Guiana." *Natural History* (New York) 28, no. 3 (1928): 243-52.
        An American physician who collected carvings, etc., and tended toward sensational accounts. Pp. 251-52, religion.

1334   Kahn, Morton [Charles]. *Djuka: The Bush Negroes of Dutch Guiana*. New York: Viking Press, 1931, 233 pp., illus. Reprinted, with an introduction by Blair Niles. New York: AMS Press, 1979, 233 pp., illus., plates, bib.
        Chap. 9 (pp. 133-60), "Medicine and magic." Not well-regarded by anthropologists.

1335   Kahn, Morton [Charles]. "Notes on the Saramaccaner Bush Negroes of Dutch Guiana." *American Anthropologist* 31 (1929): 468-90 + 6 plates.
        Pp. 482-84, religion, and burial ceremonies – "voodoo and obeiah [*sic*] is universal," and "a great god called 'Gran Gadu' . . . also several minor gods" and "spirits which are called 'wintee' . . . and 'wishi,' and many others." An unreliable account.

1336   King, Johannes. "Het eerste visioen van Johannes King (naar het handschrift uit Herrnhut meegedeeld in moderne spelling)." *Vox Guyanae* (Paramaribo) 3, no. 1 (1958): 15-41.
        Pp. 34-40, Jan Voorhoeve discusses existing manuscripts of King.

1337   King, Johannes. "Koiri ini hemel." In *Kri, kra! proza van Johannes King*, edited by T. Doelwijt. Paramaribo: Bureau Volkslectuur, 1973, pp. 25-38.
        Selected from J. King (entry 1336).

1338   King, Johannes. *Life at Maripaston*. Edited by H. F. de Ziel. Verhandelingen van het Koninklijk Instituut voor Taal-, Land-, en

Volkenkunde, 64. The Hague: M. Nijhoff, 1973, 142 pp., illus.; English summary (pp. 13-49) and Sranan text (pp. 51-142).

King, a Bush Negro convert of the Moravians and independent missionary, wrote this self-justification concerning his quarrel with his elder brother, the chief; includes Surinamese religious history. Pp. 1-11, introduction by the Surinamese editor.

1339   Köbben, A[ndre] J. F. "Continuity in change: Cottica Djuka society as a changing system." *Bijdragen: Tot de Taal-, Land-, en Volkenkunde (Anthropologica 10)* 124, no. 1 (1968): 56-89.
        Pp. 70-79, Djuka religion, and missions.

1340   Köbben, A[ndre] J. F. "Opportunism in religious behaviour." In *Explorations in the anthropology of religion*, edited by W. E. A. Van Beek and J. H. Scherer. Verhandelingen van het Koninklijk Instituut voor Taal-, Land-, en Volkenkunde, 74. The Hague: M. Nijhoff, 1975, pp. 46-54, map.
        Mainly on Suriname Bush Negro religion.

1341   Leerdam, H. "Onze Boslandbewoners: Het godsdienstig leven XXXVI." *Dagblad "De West"* (Paramaribo), 18 April 1957.
        On Bush Negro religious life.

1342   Legêne, P. M. *De zwarte profeet uit het oerwoud.* Zeist: Lendingsgenootschap der Evangelische Broedergemeente, n.d.
        On Johannes King.

1343   Lenoir, John D. "Surinam national development and Maroon cultural autonomy." *Social and Economic Studies* 24, no. 3 (1975): 308-17.
        Pp. 314-16, on the Paramaccan Maroons' assimilation to Christianity since the 1870s, without adopting the Christian worldview, producing new syncretist movements, or abandoning Obeah beliefs. A "negative instance" renewal movement.

1343a   Lier, R. van. *Bonuman: Een studie van zeven religieuze specialisten in Suriname.* YICA Publication 60. Leiden: Institute of Cultural and Social Studies, Leiden University, n.d. [early 1980s?], 132 pp.
        Life history of seven religious specialists in Suriname.

1344   Lier, Willem F. van. "Aantekeningen over het geestelijk leven en de samenleving der Djoeka's Aukaner Boschnegers in Suriname." *Bijdragen tot de Taal-, Land-, en Volkenkunde* (The Hague) 99, no. 2 (1940): 129-294, bib.
        Notes on the spiritual life and society of the Djukas in Suriname – by the government's agent among the Djuka.

1345   Linde, Jan Marinus van der. *Het visioen van Herrnhut en het apostolaat der Moravische Broeders in Suriname, 1735-1863.* Paramaribo: C. Kersten & Co., 1956.

A Utrecht (Theological Institute) doctoral thesis, in which Johannes King is discussed. Portion reprinted as "Johannes King, *ca.* 1830-1898" in *Dagblad "De West"* (Paramaribo), 9 April 1956.

1346   Martin, K. *Bericht über eine Reise nach Niederländisch West-Indien und darauf gegründete studien.* Leiden: Brill, 1888.

P. 61, detailed description of *Gran Gado* or *tiki bribi* shrines in Saramaka villages on the middle Suriname River.

1347   *Missionary Review of the World,* n.s. 10, no. 11 (1897): 814.

The Moravian mission to the Bush Negroes, with special mention of John King as a "native evangelist."

1348   Mitrasing, F. E. M. *Surinam, land of seven peoples: An ethnohistorical study.* Paramaribo, 1981.

1349   Müller, Th. "Uit hit Jaarverslag van 1921 over Suriname." *Berichten uit de Heiden-Wereld,* 1922, pp. 66-71.

Reports a "Jesus-Maria" movement among the Saramaka in 1921.

1350   Naipaul, V[idiadhar] S[urajprasad]. *The middle passage: Impressions of five societies . . . in the West Indies and South America.* London: A. Deutsch, 1962, 232 pp. Reprint. Harmondsworth: Penguin, 1969, 256 pp., map.

Pp. 180-82 (1962), a Bush Negro "spiritualist" dance in Berlin village; pp. 185-86, Afaka's script.

1351   Panhuys, L. C. van. "The heathen religion of the Bush-Negroes in Dutch Guiana." In *Actes du IVè Congrès Internationale d'Histoire des Religions . . . 1912.* Leiden: E. J. Brill, 1913, pp. 53-57.

Brief details of sixteen gods or spirits; charms and Obeahs; dances, "other superstitions," secret societies; p. 57, Chief Oseisie's decree of 1895 establishing only one god and prohibiting Obeah (i.e., a new religious movement?).

1352   Panhuys, L. C. van. "A most remarkable Obeah from Suriname." *Ethnos* 12, nos. 1-2 (1947): 93-94, illus.

A Bush Negro magic healing legband containing early eighteenth-century Danish shillings.

1353 Penard, F. P., and Penard, A. P. "Surinaansch bijgeloof: Iets over *winti*en andere natuurbegrippen." *Bijdragen tot de Taal-, Land-, en Volkenkunde van Nederlandsch-Indië* (The Hague) 67 (1913): 157-83.
Pp. 170-83, *Winti* (wind) rites, dances, and songs.

1354 Pierce, B. E. "Afro-American and Christian religious systems of lower status Creoles in Paramaribo, Surinam." Paper presented at Northeastern Anthropological Association, Buffalo, April 1972. Digest in *Abstracts in Anthropology* 3, no. 3 (1972): no. 1135.
There is a distinctive combination of African and Christian elements in the religion of the *Nengre* (lower status Creoles).

1355 Platvoet, Johannes Gerhardus. *Comparing religions: A limitative approach. An analysis of Akan, Para-Creole, and IFO-Sananda rites and prayers*. The Hague: Mouton Publishers, 1982, 356 pp. Originally a doctoral dissertation (theology), University of Utrecht, 1982.
Pp. 44-48, 121-56, on the religion of the Para-Creoles (distinct from Bush Negroes); pp. 175-200, comparisons; pp. 201-15, prayers.

1356 Pollak-Eltz, Angelina. "Negros cimarrones y Negros urbanos en Surinam." In *Cultos afroamericanos*. Caracas: Instituto de Investigaciones Historicas, Universidad Catolica Andrés Bello, 1972, pp. 213-31. (Spanish translation of Dutch original, rev. and enl.).
Bush Negro religion synthesizes many African religions, but has few European and Christian elements.

1357 Price, Richard. "Afro-Surinamese religions." In *The encyclopedia of religion*, edited by M. Eliade. Vol. 1. New York: Macmillan, 1987, pp. 105-7.

1358 Price, Richard. "Avenging spirits and the structure of Saramaka lineages." *Bijdragen tot de Taal-, Land-, en Volkenkunde* 129 (1973): 86-107.
Religious organization among the Bush Negroes (Saramaka) on the Pikilio.

1359 Price, Richard. *First time: The historical vision of an Afro-American people*. Johns Hopkins Studies in Atlantic History and Culture. Baltimore and London: Johns Hopkins University Press, 1983, 189 pp., illus., maps.
See especially pp. 5-12 on the role of religion in the formation of Maroon societies – in the shape of an ancestral cult, shrine, and ideology. Pp. 44, 69, ancestral shrines (photos).

1360 Price, Richard. *The Guiana Maroons*. Baltimore: Johns Hopkins University Press, 1976, 184 pp.

A bibliographic essay, essential for all study of the Maroons or Bush Negroes in Suriname. Pp. 20-22, the religious systems.

1361   Price, Richard. *Saramaka social structure: Analysis of a Maroon society in Surinam*. Caribbean Monograph Series, 12. Río Piedras: Institute of Caribbean Studies, University of Puerto Rico, 1975, 179 pp.

Pp. 38-43, divination. The only full study in English of a Bush Negro society.

1362   Ratelband, K. "Een boschnegerschrift van Westafrikaanschen oorsprong." *De West-Indische Gids* (Amsterdam) 26 (1944): 193-208.

The Afaka script, as derived from the Vai script in Liberia. This thesis is refuted by T. D. P. Dalby and by C. N. Dubelaar and J. W. Gonggryp.

1363   Schmidt, Rasmus. *Bericht des Bruders Rasmus Schmidt von der Mission unter den Freidnegern in Neu-Bambey in Suriname vom Jahr 1843*. Nachrichten aus der Brüdergeneine, 1846, pp. 514-41.

Pp. 527-37, Tiop's *Gran Gado* or pole cult from 1843 among the Saramaka, as reported by the local Moravian missionary.

1364   Schmidt, Rasmus. *Bericht des seligen Bruders Rasmus Schmidt vom dem Freineger Gemeinlein zu Bambey in Suriname vom Jahr 1844*. Nachrichten aus der Brüdergeneine, 1847, pp. 596-631.

Pp. 618, 630-31, Moravian missionary Schmidt's report on the Gran Gado cult.

1365   Schneider, H. G. "Die Buschneger Surinames." *Beiblatt Allegemeines Missions Zeitschrift von D. G. Warneck* 20, no. 2 (1893): 17-30.

Pp. 21-22, on the prevalence of the *tiki bribi* (Gran Gado) cult among the Saramaka.

1366   Schoonheym, Peter E. *Je geld of . . . je leven; een sociaal-economische benandering van de religie der Para-Creolen in Suriname*. Utrecht: Instituut voor Culturele Antropologie, 1980, 166 pp.

Especially pp. 44-50, 78-79, 111, 112, 122, 137, 138, on combination of Christianity and primal religion, and economic aspects of religion.

1367   Schulze, Adolf. "Johannes King, der Buschland-prophet." In *Das Buch der deutschen Weltmission*, edited by J. Richter. Gotha: L. Klotz, 1935, pp. 290-93.

1368 Schweintz, Paul de. "A bright spot on a dark continent." *Missionary Review of the World* 20, no. 11 [n.s. 10, no. 11] (November 1897): 809-16.

P. 814, on John King the "Matuari [*sic*] Bush-Negro" as evangelist.

1369 Simpson, George Eaton. *Black religions in the New World.* New York: Columbia University Press, 1978, 415 pp.

Pp. 204-7, Winti, and religion among the Djuka. Based on M. J. and F. S. Herskovits, C. J. Wooding, and S. W. de Groot.

1370 Sitte, Fritz. *Schwarze Gotter: Abenteuer in Surinam.* Heidelberg: Ueberreuter, 1976, 156 pp.

1371 Spalburg, J[ohn] G[eorge]. *De Tapanahoni Djuka rond de eeuwwisseling: Het dagboek van Spalburg (1896-1900).* Bronnen voor Studie van Bosneger Samenlevingen, 5. Utrecht: Centrum voor Caraïbische Studies, Instituut voor Culturele Antropologie, Rijksuniversiteit Utrecht, 1979, 129 pp., map.

With introductions on the missionary background by C. de Beet (pp. 1-13) and on the Djuka by H. V. E. Thoden van Velzen (pp. 14-28). Pp. 17-28, discussion of tribal cults, especially Gaan Gadu, as recorded by missionary Spalburg in his journal, which follows, in its original Dutch text.

1372 Staehelin, F. *Die Mission der Brüdergemeine in Suriname und Berbice im achtzehnten Jahrhundert: Eine Missionsgeschichte hauptsächlich in Auszugen aus Briefen und Originalberichten ... 1765-1813.* 3 vols. Herrnhut: Verlag von C. Kerten & Co. (and elsewhere), 1923-19, 424 pp., 320 pp., and 310 pp.

Cited by H. U. E. Thoden van Velzen as containing many notes by missionaries on new movements among the Saramaka every few years.

1373 Stedman, J[ohn] G[abriel]. *Narrative of a five-year's expedition ... from the year 1772 to 1777.* 2 vols. London: Printed for J. Johnson and J. Edwards, 1796. Reprint. 1806. Abridged ed., edited by C. Bryant. London: Folio Society, 1965, 239 pp. New critical ed., edited by R. and S. Price. Baltimore: Johns Hopkins University Press, 1985, xcvii + 708 pp.

For the coastal or Winti religion.

1374 Stephen, Henri J. M. *Winti: Afro-surinaamse religie en magische rituelen in Suriname en Nederland.* Amsterdam: Karnak, 1985, 132 pp.

1375   Suparlan, Parsudi. "The Javanese in Surinam: Ethnicity in an ethnically plural society." Ph.D. dissertation (anthropology), University of Illinois (Urbana), 1976, 401 pp.
Chap. 6, variations in Javanese religion.

1376   "Suriname: Zwei geistergeschichten aus Suriname." *Missionsblatt der Brüdergemeine* 47 (1883): 62-63.
Anonymous Moravian missionary's account of the *Gran Gado* or *tiki bribi* cult in a Saramaka village in the 1880s.

1377   Sweet, R. "Africaners weren beschaving af: En zelfs fanatieke nationalistische groepen zitten stil." *De Ploeg* (Paramaribo) 11, no. 1 (1961): 6-10, 27-30.

1378   Thoden van Velzen, H[endrick] U[lbo] E[ric]. "Beroering onder de Bosnegers." *Kabul* (Utrecht), no. 5 (May 1974), pp. 2-10.
On Aklari's new messianic movement.

1379   Thoden van Velzen, Bonno [Hendrik Ulbo Eric]. "Bush Negro regional cults: A materialist explanation." In *Regional cults*, edited by R. P. Werbner. London: Academic Press, 1977, pp. 93-118, map, bib., and see pp. xxvii-xxix for editorial comment.
The Gaan Tata (or Gaan Gadu, etc.) cult, 1885-1972; a neoprimal movement with an active, moral, High God; pp. 111-14, replacement by Akalali's new cult. The economic factor involved.

1380   Thoden van Velzen, H[endrik] U[lbo] E[ric]. "The Gaan Gadu cult material forces and the social production of fantasy." *Social Compass* 32, no. 1 (1985): 93-109.
Around 1890, in Djuka villages of the Tapanahoni river with fierce antiwitchcraft campaigns. The material forces shaping the cult and the collective fantasies produced by cult adepts, with no place in ordinary social discourse. While linked to the world of economic goods and to the entrenched positions of power, it also enjoys its own relative autonomy.

1381   Thoden van Velzen, H[endrik] U[lbo] E[ric]. [Introduction on the Djuka.] In *De Tapanahoni Djuka rond de eeuwwisseling: Het dagboek van Spalburg (1896-1900)*, by J. G. Spalburg. Bronnen voor Studie van Bosneger Samenlevingen, 5. Utrecht: Centrum voor Caraïbische Studies. Instituut voor Culturele Antropologie, Rijksuniversiteit Utrecht, 1979, pp. 17-28.
Tribal cults as recorded by Spalburg.

1382   Thoden van Velzen, H[endrik] U[lbo] E[ric]. "The origins of the Gaan Gadu movement of the Bush Negroes of Surinam." *Nieuwe West-Indische Gids* (The Hague) 52 (June 1978): 81-130.

1383   Thoden van Velzen, Bonno [Hendrik Ulbo Eric]. "Why disorder?" In *Rule and reality: Essays in honor of Andre J. F. Kobben*. Series no. 8. Amsterdam: Antropologisch-Sociologisch Centrum, Universiteit van Amsterdam, 1975, pp. 134-54, map.

1384   Thoden van Velzen, H[endrik] U[lbo] E[ric], and Wetering, W[ilhelmina] van. "Affluence, deprivation, and the flowering of the Bush Negro religious movements." *Bijdragen tot de Taal-, Land-, en Volkenkunde* 139, no. 1 (1983): 99-139.
        Pp. 109-19, 124-25, Gaan Gadu movement; pp. 119-24, Anake's new cargo movement replacing Gaan Gadu; pp. 124-29, the Na Ogii anti-Gaan Gadu movement under Atjaimikule; pp. 129-32, conclusions on all three movements – new religious ideas cannot be derived from economic changes.

1385   Thoden van Velzen, H[endrik] U[lbo] E[ric], and Wetering, W[ilhelmina] van. "Female religious responses to male prosperity in turn-of-the-century Bush Negro societies." *Nieuwe West-Indische Gids* (The Hague) 56, nos. 1-2 (1982): 43-68.
        Describes new religious movements in relation to the new male affluence and employment elsewhere as wage earners.

1386   Thoden van Velzen, H[endrik] U[lbo] E[ric], and Wetering, Wilhelmina van. *The Great Father and the danger: Religious cults, material forces, and collective fantasies in the world of the Surinamese Maroons*. Dordrecht: Foris, 1988, 451 pp.

1387   Thoden van Velzen, H[endrik] U[lbo] E[ric], and Wetering, W[ilhelmina] van. "On the political impact of a prophet movement in Surinam." In *Explorations in the anthropology of religion*, edited by W. E. A. van Beek and J. H. Scherer. Verhandelingen van het Koninklijk Instituut voor Taal-, Land-, en Volkenkunde, 74. The Hague: M. Nijhoff, 1975, pp. 214-33, map.

1388   Thoden van Velzen, H[endrik] U[lbo] E[ric], and Wetering, W[ilhelmina] van. "Voorspoed, Angsten en Demonen" [Prosperity, anxiety, and demons]. *Antropologische Verkenningen* 1, no. 2 (1982): 85-118.
        Economic ups and downs have left clear traces in Afro-Surinamese thought. As in western Europe, the impact of modern capitalism contributed to a rise of demon beliefs. In a period of stabilization that followed, these aspects wore off and beliefs were

routinized. Though some traits tend to fade away and new accretions evolve, a tribal faith will not necessarily show less persistence over time than world religions do.

1389   Treu, W. "Bericht des seligen Bruders Treu von seiner Begleitungsreise des nach Bambey ... 1846." *Nachrichten ans der Brüdergemeine*, 1847, pp. 366-95.

     P. 395, Moravian missionary's report on later period and spread of *Gran Gado* cult, of Tiopo.

1390   Vandercook, John W. "White magic and black." *Harper's Magazine* 151 (October 1925): 548-54.

     By a sympathetic American.

1391   Vernon, Diana. "Bakuu: Possessing spirits of witchcraft on the Tapanahony." *Nieuwe West Indische Gids* (The Hague) 54, no. 1 (1980): 1-38.

     Among the Djuka-a new type of spirit pantheon in a mediumistic cult, recently expanding.

1392   Voorhoeve, Jan. "Church Creole and pagan cult languages." In *Pidginization and creolization of languages*, edited by D. Hymes. Cambridge: Cambridge University Press, 1971, pp. 305-15.

     By a Dutch linguist.

1393   Voorhoeve, Jan. "Johannes King, 1830-1899." In *Emancipatie 1863-1963, biographieën*. Paramaribo: Surinaamse Historische Kríng, 1964, pp. 53-66.

1394   Voorhoeve, Jan. "Johannes King: Een mens met groot overtuiging." *Kerkbode van Evangelische Broedergemeente in Suriname* 52, no. 51 (28 December 1958); 53, no. 1 (4 January 1959); 53, no. 2 (11 January 1959); 53, no. 3 (18 January 1959); 53, no. 4 (25 January 1959).

1395   Voorhoeve, Jan. "Johannes King: Een mens met groot overtuiging, Plus Minus 1830-1899." *Dagblad "De West"* (Paramaribo), 22 and 24 May 1963.

1396   Voorhoeve, Jan. "The *Obiaman* and his influence in the Moravian parish." *Bijdragen tot de Taal-, Land-, en Volkenkunde* 139, no. 4 (1983): 411-20.

     English translation from a report by Voorhoeve in the late 1950s to Moravian Brethren, discovered later in Suriname. The spirit-healer, or Obiaman, in the Afro-American religion, Winti, of the Creoles, treated as a distinct system coexisting with Christianity rather than as a syncretism.

1397   Voorhoeve, Jan. "Op zoek naar de handschriften van Johannes King." *Vox Guyanae* (Paramaribo) 3, no. 1 (1958): 34-40.
The search for the complete diaries of J. King.

1398   Voorhoeve, Jan. "Tori vo dem bigin vo Anakee en moro fara." *Kerkbode de Evangelische Broeder-gemeente in Suriname* 52, no. 13 (30 March 1958); no. 23 (8 June 1958); no. 24 (15 June 1958); no. 25 (22 June 1958); no. 27 (6 July 1958); no. 37 (14 September 1958); no. 43 (26 October 1958); no. 44 (2 November 1958); no. 46 (16 November 1958); no. 47 (30 November 1958).

1399   Voorhoeve, Jan. "Het wonder van Johannes King"; and "Profeten der Wanhoop." In *Kondre sa jere (het land zal het horen) – 200 jaar zending onder de bosnegers van Suriname.* Zeist: Seminarie der Evangelische Broedergemeente, 1965, pp. 42-47, 48-52.
On Johannes King, and a survey of Anake, Atijamarikoele, Wensi, and Colin.

1400   Voorhoeve, Jan, and Renselaar, H. C. van. "Messianism and nationalism in Surinam." *Bijdragen tot de Taal-, Land-, en Volkenkunde* 118, no. 2 (1962): 193-216.
Important comparison of movement focused on the slave Colin in Coronis district (1836), the late nineteenth-century Saramakan Bush Negro movement led by Anake, and mid-twentieth-century nationalism.

1401   Waal Malefijt, Annemarie de. "Animism and Islam among the Javanese in Surinam." *Anthropological Quarterly* 37, no. 3 (1964): 149-55. Reprinted in *Peoples and cultures of the Caribbean*, edited by M. M. Horowitz. Garden City, N.Y.: Natural History Press, 1971, pp. 553-59.
Regarded as both syncretistic and "new": *slametan* rite and *dukuns* (specialists).

1402   Waal Malefijt, Annemarie de. *The Javanese of Surinam: Segment of a plural society.* Assen: Van Gorcum, 1963, 206 pp., illus., map.
Pp. 151-75, religion (a syncretized Islam); pp. 159-65, 173-75, 180-83, spirits and the Slametan rite, an indigenous development.

1403   Walker, Sheila S[uzanne]. *Ceremonial spirit possession in Africa and Afro-America: Forms, meanings, and functional significance for individuals and social groups.* Leiden: E. J. Brill, 1972, 179 pp., bib.
Winti in Suriname, passim. P. 88, difference from possession in Haiti – more bargaining with the Winti, and culturally unacceptable forms of possession when the Winti is opposed.

1404   Weiss, H. *Ons Suriname: Handbook voor Zendings studie*. Zeist: Nederlandschen Studenten-Zendingsbond, 1911, 186 pp., illus.

P. 69, Bush Negro movement of 1711 (from Staehelin); p. 84, Gran Tata; p. 85, "Atjarinsi Kode," the first important medium of the "Diku" of "Graan Gossu Kossu Kwaami" Spirit. A new medium (Andre Pakosi) appearing, 1979-.

1405   Westerloo, Gerard van (text), and Diepraam, Willem (photos). *Frimangron*. Amsterdam: Arbeiderspers, 1975, 224 pp., illus., maps.

Chap. 4 (pp. 77-123), Bush Negroes and Akalali; chap. 9 (pp. 199-217), "God dwells in front, the spirits live behind" – the Creole Moravian community.

1406   Wetering, W[ilhelmina] van. "Dynamics of witchcraft accusations in Tapanahoni Djuka society." In *Structure, function, and process*, edited by P. Kloos and A. J. F. Köbben. Assen: Van Gorcum, 1972. Revised as "Witchcraft among the Tapanahoni Djuka." In *Maroon societies: Rebel slave communities in the Americas*, edited by R. Price. Garden City, N.Y.: Anchor Books, 1973, pp. 370-88.

1407   Wetering, Wilhelmina van. "Hekserij bij de Djuka: Een sociologische benadering" [Witchcraft among the Djuka: A sociological approach]. Ph.D. thesis, University of Amsterdam, 1973.

1408   Wetering, W[ilhelmina] van. "Religieuze bewegingen bij de Bosnegers." *Iros (Informatietijdschrift over Ontwikkelingsvraag-stukken van Suriname)* (Rotterdam) 2, no. 3 (1977): 21-28.

Includes the social reform aspects for the whole field.

1409   Wooding, Charles J[ohan]. "Durkheim's opposition sacred-profane, absolute or not?" In *Rule and reality: Essays in honor of Andre J. F. Köbben*. Series no. 8. Amsterdam: Antropologisch-Sociologisch Centrum, Universiteit van Amsterdam, 1975, pp. 185-98, diagram.

Uses the primal religion, Winti, of the Para people in Suriname as a test case. Pp. 188-97, specifically on Winti.

1410   Wooding, Charles J[ohan]. *Evolving culture: A cross-cultural study of Suriname, West Africa, and the Caribbean*. Washington, D.C.: University Press of America, 1981, xiv + 329 pp.

Chap. 5 (pp. 85-111), the supernatural world (pp. 108-11), integration of African gods into a new system, Winti; chap. 6, "Secret rites" (of Winti); chap. 7, "Dance"; chap. 8, "Rites"; chap. 9, "Case histories"; chap. 10 (pp. 260-68), "Religious change"; chap. 11 (pp. 271-81), Afro-American cross-cultural comparisons; pp. 279-81, prophet movements.

1411 Wooding, Charles Johan. "Geesten en Goden bij winti: Rechtzetting" [Spirits and gods in Winti: Rectification]. *Vrije Stem* (Paramaribo), no. 5521 (4 September 1979), p. 5; no. 5567 (27 October 1979), p. 3.
Two articles in the daily paper.

1412 Wooding, Charles Johan. "Winti." *De Gids* (Amsterdam) 133 (1970): 286-88.

1413 Wooding, Charles J[ohan]. "The Winti–Cult in the Para-District." *Caribbean Studies* (Río Piedras, University of Puerto Rico) 12, no. 1 (1972): 51-78.
Treated as an Afro-American religion in which women play a major role, and where reinterpreted African elements are more prominent than in cults elsewhere in the Caribbean; a major study, in some detail.

1414 Wooding, Charles Johan. *Winti: Een afroamerikaanse godsdienst in Suriname*. Meppel: Krips Repro. b.v., 1972.
A doctoral thesis on Winti as an amoral, non-salvific, pragmatic polytheistic healing cult in Creole folk religion, with elements from several West African religions and Christianity.

1415 Zamuel, H. S. "Johannes King, ca. 1830-1899: Profiel van een Surinaamse boslandprofeet." Doctoral dissertation (theology), University of Utrecht, 1975, 81 pp.

1416 Zeefuik, Karel August. "De winti en het daarmeede samenhangende complex van magische en religieuze handelingen en verschijnselen in Suriname." Doctorandus [M.A.] thesis (theology), Rijkuniversiteit te Utrecht, 1963, 61 pp.

Trinidad and Tobago

In a population of about one million, some 43% are black, 16% are mulatto, and about 40% are Asians known as "East Indians," originally imported as plantation labor, mostly Hindus and chiefly villagers and peasants from south India, and therefore with a religion akin to the primal type. There are small indigenous Afro-Christian bodies and spirit-possession cults, and other movements from Jamaica (Rastafarians), from the U.S. (African Methodist Episcopal and Pentecostal churches), from Europe (Streams of Power, via St. Vincent), and also Baha'i, Divine Light Mission, Ethiopian Orthodox Church, etc. Studies of the Spiritual Baptists or Shouters, and of Shango, the Yoruba-related possession cult, dominate the literature.

General works include S. D. Glazier (entry 1436, suggests a process of juxtaposition rather than syncretism); A. Pollak-Eltz (entry 1453, in German, includes Grenada); G. E. Simpson (entry 1456, for acculturation and the interaction between Shango and the Shouters); U.S. Government, Department of the Army (entry 1465); and S. A. Vertovec (entry 1467).

For case studies see A. T. Carr (entry 1420, on the Rada cult); F. Mayhew (entry 1445, a Spiritual Baptist pastor's autobiography); and J. Stewart (entry 1464, on Spiritual Baptists).

On the African contribution (Yoruba and Dahomey) see J. D. Elder (entry 1424); M. W. Lewis (entry 1442); and C. McDaniel (entry 1444).

On the Amerindian contribution see S. D. Glazier (entry 1425).

On Shango see F. Henry (entry 1438); F. Mischel (entry 1447); W. and F. Mischel (entry 1449); G. E. Simpson (entry 1461, a brief survey, and entry 1462, more fully); and C. Ward (entry 1469).

On the Spiritual Baptists or Shouters see S. D. Glazier (entries 1429 and 1426, and for their missionary outreach in North and South America, entry 1427), and C. Ward and M. H. Beaubrun (entry 1470). This movement was banned by the colonial government, 1917-51, and the banning documents and a court case are included in M. J. and F. S. Herskovits (entry 1440, dealing with the movement in detail).

On Pentecostalism, see S. D. Glazier (entry 1433, on why it is replacing Rada and Obeah).

Although some "East Indians" hold leadership positions among the Spiritual Baptists, the literature on them focuses on their Hindu rites, with some reference to borrowings and syncretism. See M. Klass (entry 1441) and B. M. Schwartz (entry 1454, on adaptations).

On music see A. P. Merriam, et al. (entry 1446, the Rada songs).

On healing see G. E. Simpson (entry 1459) and C. Ward (entry 1469).

1417   Borofsky, Robert. "Obeah in Trinidad." M.A. thesis, Brandeis University, 1968.

1418   Brathwaite, Lloyd. "The problem of cultural integration in Trinidad." *Social and Economic Studies* 3, no. 1 (1954): 82-96. Reprinted in *Consequences of class and colour*, edited by D. Lowenthal and L. Comitas. Garden City, N.Y.: Doubleday, Anchor, 1973, pp. 241-60.

Pp. 251-53 (pp. 89-90 in 1954 article), Shango, and its limited return to public favor as part of the cultural heritage.

1419   Brewer, Peter. "Let me introduce you to the Baptists of Trinidad (1815-1900)." *Missionary Herald* (London, Baptist Missionary Society), January 1976, pp. 5-7.

Early independent Baptists, settled in Trinidad after service with the British in the 1812-14 war versus the U.S.

1420   Carr, Andrew T. "A Rada community in Trinidad." *Caribbean Quarterly* (Mona, Jamaica) 3, no. 1 (1953): 35-54, illus.

"Rada" (i.e., native of Dahomey) preserves much Dahomean practice, although the cultists regard themselves as Catholics. A descriptive survey by an author of Mandingo ancestry who grew up associated with Rada.

1421   Clement, Dorothy C. "Shango: A modernizing cult in Trinidadian society." M.A. thesis, University of North Carolina at Chapel Hill, 1969.

1422   Crowley, Daniel J[ohn]. "Plural and differential acculturation in Trinidad." *American Anthropologist* 59, no. 5 (1957): 817-24.

Pp. 821-23, on the religious aspects, magic, and festivals.

1423   D'Anna, Andrea. *Le religioni afroamericane*. Bologna: Editrice Nigrizia, 1972.

Pp. 77-79, Shango, Rada, and Shouters.

1424 Elder, J. D. "The Yoruba ancestor cult in Gasparillo: Its structure, organization, and social function in community life." *Caribbean Quarterly* (Mona, Jamaica) 16, no. 3 (1970): 5-20, tables.

In Trinidad – compared with Yoruba cults in Nigeria; following W. R. Bascom.

1425 Glazier, Stephen D[avey]. "Aboriginal influences on Spirit Baptist ritual." Paper presented at 44th International Congress of Americanists, Manchester 1982. Digest in *Abstracts of the Congress*, p. 263.

1426 Glazier, Stephen D[avey]. "African cults and Christian churches in Trinidad: The Spiritual Baptist case." *Journal of Religious Thought* 39 (Fall-Winter 1982): 17-25.

1427 Glazier, Stephen D[avey]. "Baptist outreach from Trinidad." *Cultural Survival Quarterly* 7 (1983): 38-40, illus.

1428 Glazier, Stephen D[avey]. Commentary on "Trance induction and hallucination in Spiritualist Baptist mourning," by C. Ward and M. H. Beaubrun (entry 1470). *Journal of Psychological Anthropology* 3, no. 2 (Spring 1980): 231-33.

1429 Glazier, Stephen D[avey]. "Heterodoxy and heteropraxy in the Spiritual Baptist faith." *Journal of the Interdenominational Theological Center* (Atlanta) 8, no. 1 (Fall 1980): 89-101.

Belief and ritual systems in a polytheistic setting.

1430 Glazier, Stephen D[avey]. "Leadership roles, church organisation, and ritual-change among the Spiritual Baptists of Trinidad." Ph.D. dissertation (anthropology), University of Connecticut (Storrs), 1981, 171 pp.

1431 Glazier, Stephen D[avey]. *Marchin' the pilgrims home: Leadership and decision-making in an Afro-Caribbean faith.* Contributions to the Study of Religion, 10. Westport, Conn.: Greenwood Press, 1983, 165 pp., bib.

On the Spiritual Baptists, with special examination of the influence of leadership.

1432 Glazier, Stephen D[avey]. "Mourning in the Afro-Baptist traditions: A comparative study of religion in the American South and in Trinidad." *Southern Quarterly* 23, no. 3 (1985): 141-56.

The Spiritual Baptists as the case study in Trinidad.

1433   Glazier, Stephen D[avey]. "Pentecostal exorcism and modernization in Trinidad, West Indies." *Trans-Cultural Psychiatric Research Review* (Montreal) 16 (1979): 82-83. Reprinted in *Perspectives on Pentecostalism: Case Studies*. Washington, D.C.: University Press of America, 1980, pp. 67-80.

Pentecostalism as more satisfying than Obeah and movements like Rada, and adapted to Creole culture while also valuing the American connection.

1434   Glazier, Stephen [Davey]. "The ritual mosaic: Playful celebration in Trinidad Shango." *Play and Culture* 1, no. 3 (1988): 216-25.

1435   Glazier, Stephen D[avey]. *Spiritual Baptist music of Trinidad*. Ethnic record FE 4234. New York: Folkways Record and Service Corp., 1980

1436   Glazier, Stephen D[avey]. "Syncretism and separation: Ritual change in an Afro-Caribbean faith." *Journal of American Folklore*, no. 387 [98] (1985): 49-62.

Based on thirty Spiritual Baptist congregations and a number of Shango cult centers, between 1976 and 1982; suggests "ritual juxtaposition" occurs rather than integrated syncretism.

1437   Guggenheim, Hans. "Tribalism in Trinidad." *MD Medical Newsmagazine* (New York) 9, no. 2 (1965): 138-43, illus.

Rada cult practices – drawings with commentaries.

1437a   Henry, Frances. "Religion and ideology in Trinidad: The resurgence of the Shango religion." *Caribbean Quarterly* (Kingston) 29, nos. 3-4 (September-December 1983): 63-69.

After serious decline in the 1960s, a major recovery as Shango became more middle class, open to nonblacks, affected by black militancy, and more accepted by Christian denominations.

1438   Henry, Frances. "Social stratification in an Afro-American cult." *Anthropological Quarterly* 38, no. 2 (1965): 72-78, bib.

Shango in Trinidad; status determined by the nature of one's experience of possession; three levels: cult leaders, active participants, and marginal individuals.

1439   Henry, Frances. "Stress and strategy in three field situations." In *Stress and response in fieldwork*, edited by F. Henry and S. Saberwal. New York: Holt, Rinehart & Winston, 1969, xi + 79 pp., map.

Methodological procedures, including those used in a six-month study of Shango.

1440   Herskovits, Melville J[ean], and Herskovits, Frances S. *Trinidad village*. New York: A. A. Knopf, 1947, 351 + xxv pp., illus. Reprint. New York: Octagon Books, 1964. Selections reprinted in *The New World Negro*. Bloomington: Indiana University Press, 1966, 370 pp.

Pp. 190-223 (pp. 329-53 in 1966 selection), the Shouters, with detailed descriptions; pp. 268-74, court case; pp. 300-317, funerals, divination, and magic; pp. 321-39, Shango-worship; pp. 340-48, official documents banning Shouters, Obeah, and Bongo.

1441   Klass, Morton. *East Indians in Trinidad: A study of cultural persistence*. New York: Columbia University Press, 1961, 265 pp.

Chap. 5, religion, especially pp. 156-57, 169-83; pp. 179-80, Obeah, not a "new movement," but see pp. 178-80 for borrowings and syncretism.

1442   Lewis, Maureen Warner. "Yoruba religion in Trinidad – Transfer and reinterpretation." *Caribbean Quarterly* (Mona, Jamaica) 24, nos. 3-4 (1978): 18-32.

1443   Lovelace, Earl. *The wine of astonishment*. London: Andre Deutsch, 1982. Reprinted, with an introduction by Marjorie Thorpe (pp. vii-xiv). Caribbean Writers Series. London: Heinemann, 1983, xiv + 146 pp.

Fiction: on the survival of Spiritual Baptists in rural Trinidad in the 1940s-1950s.

1444   McDaniel, Cecilia. "The Trinidadian Yoruba: An enquiry into a belief system." *Renaissance 2: A Journal of Afro-American Studies* (New Haven, Conn., Yale University) 3 (1973): 6-13.

1445   Mayhew, Frank [Aubrey McDonald]. "My life." *Caribbean Quarterly* (Mona, Jamaica) 3, no. 1 [1953]: 13-23, photo, illus.

A pastor of the Shouters, or Spiritual Baptists, of Trinidad, and some of his "revealed" songs.

1446   Merriam, Alan P.; Whinery, Sara; and Fred, B. G. "Songs of a Rada community in Trinidad." *Anthropos* 51, nos. 1-2 (1956): 156-74.

A study of thirty-one Dahomean songs preserved in the Rada cult, noted in 1953-54 by A. T. Carr (entry 1420).

1447   Mischel, Frances [Osterman]. "African 'Powers' in Trinidad: The Shango cult." *Anthropological Quarterly* 30, no. 2 (1957): 45-59.

Rites and divinities of the Shango cult.

1448   Mischel, Frances Osterman. "A Shango religious group and the problem of prestige in Trinidadian society." Ph.D. dissertation (anthropology), Ohio State University, 1958, 188 pp.

Shango as one among other religious groups providing means for attaining otherwise inaccessible prestige; Shango organization, rites, beliefs, and divinities in detail; spirit possession and the prestige hierarchy receive detailed attention.

1449   Mischel, Walter, and Mischel, Frances [Osterman]. "Psychological aspects of spirit possession." *American Anthropologist* 60, no. 2 (1958): 249-60.

Description and analysis of the Shango cult, using learning theory.

1450   Niehoff, Arthur. "The spirit world of Trinidad." *Shell Trinidad* 5, no. 7 (1959): 17-19.

Folk religion and Obeah in southern Trinidad.

1451   Parks, Alfrieta Velois. "The conceptualization of kinship among the Spiritual Baptists of Trinidad." Ph.D. dissertation (anthropology), Princeton University, 1981, 188 pp.

Based on research in Moruga.

1452   Pollak-Eltz, Angelina. *Afro-Amerikaanse Godsdiensten en culten.* Roemond: Romen & Zonen, 1970, 221 pp., illus. Spanish translation. *Cultos afroamericanos.* Caracas: Instituto de Investigaciones Historicas, Universidad Catolica Andrés Bello, 1972, 268 pp.

Pp. 134-40 (Spanish translation), Shango in Trinidad and Grenada, also Spiritual Baptists.

1453   Pollak-Eltz, Angelina. "Shango-Kult und Shouter-Kirche auf Trinidad und Grenada." *Anthropos* 65, nos. 5-6 (1970): 814-32.

Pp. 819-22, Shango in Trinidad (based on G. E. Simpson [entry 1461]); pp. 823-26, Shango in Grenada; pp. 826-29, Spiritual Baptists; pp. 829-31, their interactions.

1454   Schwartz, Barton M. "Differential socio-religious adaptation." *Social and Economic Studies* (Mona, Jamaica) 16, no. 3 (1967): 237-48.

The Sanatan Dharma Maha Sabha sect in a mainly East Indian village in southwest Trinidad – as an adaptation of traditional and more sophisticated Hinduism to the local situation.

1455   Schwartz, Barton M. "Ritual aspects of caste in Trinidad." *Anthropological Quarterly* 37, no. 1 (1964): 1-15.

Ritual expressing caste identity being modified toward securing direct rewards, and Hindu theology largely ignored.

1456   Simpson, George Eaton. "The acculturative process in Trinidadian Shango." *Anthropological Quarterly* 37, no. 1 (1964): 16-27, bib. Original form in *Congreso Internacional de Americanistas 35, Mexico 1962: Actas y Memorias*. Vol. 3. Mexico City: Instituto Nacional de Antropología e Historia, 1964, pp. 297-98.
       Trinidadian Shango and Shouter religions now in interaction through increased social contact.

1457   Simpson, George Eaton. "Baptismal, 'mourning,' and 'building' ceremonies of the Shouters in Trinidad." *Journal of American Folklore* 79, no. 314 (1966): 537-50.
       Beliefs and practices of the Spiritual Baptists and their relation to Shango.

1458   Simpson, George Eaton. *Black religions in the New World*. New York: Columbia University Press, 1978, 415 pp.
       Pp. 73-99, 117-21, 287-90 (plus notes, pp. 331-32, 340, 368) on Trinidad.

1459   Simpson, George Eaton. "Folk medicine in Trinidad." *Journal of American Folklore*, no. 298 [75] (October-December 1962): 326-40. Reprinted in *Religious cults of the Caribbean*. ... Río Piedras: Institute of Caribbean Studies, University of Puerto Rico, 1970. Reprinted in *Caribbean papers*. Cuernavaca, Mexico: Centro Intercultural de Documentación, 1970.
       Includes the explanations of sickness of Rada, Shango, and the Spiritual Baptists.

1460   Simpson, George Eaton. "The Shango cult in Nigeria and in Trinidad." *American Anthropologist* 64, no. 5 (1962): 1204-19. Reprinted in *Religious cults of the Caribbean*. ... Río Piedras: Institute of Caribbean Studies, University of Puerto Rico, 1970, pp. 112-26.
       A comprehensive account, by cultural themes, of similarities and differences.

1461   Simpson, George Eaton. *The Shango cult in Trinidad*. Caribbean Monograph Series, 2. Río Piedras: Institute of Caribbean Studies, University of Puerto Rico, 1965, 140 pp., illus., bib. Reprinted in *Religious cults of the Caribbean*. ... Río Piedras: Institute of Caribbean Studies, University of Puerto Rico, 1970.
       Acculturation in the psychological, sociological, and psychiatric dimensions of the cult.

1462   Simpson, George Eaton. "Shango cult in Trinidad." *African Notes* (Ibadan) 3, no. 1 (1965): 11-21, bib.

A public lecture at Ibadan, 1965, giving a general survey.

1463   Stewart, John. "Mission and leadership among the Merikin Baptists of Trinidad." *LAAG* [Latin American Anthropology Group, within American Anthropological Association]. Vol. 1. Washington, D.C., 1976, pp. 17-25.

    LAAG contributions to Afro-American Ethnohistory in Latin America and the Caribbean.

1464   Stewart, John. "Where goes the indigenous black church?" In *Is Massa day dead?* edited by Orde Coombs. New York: Doubleday, Anchor, 1974, 260 pp.

    Pp. 189-204, lower-class Baptists, and case study of Pastor Lea's independent church.

1465   United States Government, Department of the Army. *Area handbook for Trinidad and Tobago.* Prepared by Foreign Area Studies, American University. Edited by Jan K. Black, et al. DA PAM 550-178. Washington, D.C.: U.S. Government Printing Office, 1976, 304 pp.

    Pp. 103-6, religious life.

1466   Vertovec, Steven A[llen]. "The East Indians of Trinidad – Their social, cultural, and religious context." Paper submitted to the Faculty of Anthropology and Geography, Nuffield College, University of Oxford, in partial fulfillment of transfer to D.Phil. status, May 1984, v + 155 pp.

    Chap. 3, "Religious pluralism": p. 82, Pentecostalism; pp. 83-106, black religions; pp. 111-17, Hindu forms; pp. 117-19, "Folk beliefs" and Hindu-Christian/Hindu-African syncretism.

1467   Vertovec, Steven Allen. "Hinduism and social change in village Trinidad." D.Phil. thesis (social anthropology), University of Oxford, 1988, 390 pp. Publication expected as *Hinduism and social change.* London: Macmillan.

    Contains relevant themes as in entry 1466.

1468   Walker, Sheila S[uzanne]. *Ceremonial spirit possession in Africa and Afro-America: Forms, meanings, and functional significance for individuals and social groups.* Leiden: E. J. Brill, 1972, 179 pp.

    Shango (Trinidad), passim.

1469   Ward, Colleen. "Therapeutic aspects of ritual trance: The Shango cult in Trinidad." *Journal of Altered States of Consciousness* 5, no. 1 (1979-80): 19-29.

1470 Ward, Colleen, and Beaubrun, Michael H. "Trance induction and hallucination in Spiritualist Baptist mourning." *Journal of Psychological Anthropology* (New York) 2, no. 4 (1979): 479-88, bib.

Studied in relation to ritual healing and mourning in Trinidad, from a "psycho-anthropological perspective."

1471 Warner, Maureen. "African feasts in Trinidad." *Bulletin of the African Studies Association of the West Indies* (Kingston) 4 (December 1971): 85-94.

Yearly religious feasts, secular feasts (birth, marriage, funerals, etc.) as in the late nineteenth and early twentieth centuries.

1472 Wood, Donald [Peter John]. *Trinidad in transition: The years after slavery*. London: Oxford University Press, for Institute of Race Relations, 1968, 318 pp.

Pp. 38-39, the first Trinidad Baptists, independent of missions, formed from Christian Negroes who had fought for Britain in the 1812 war and been disbanded in the Bahamas.

Venezuela

This country of some 14 million people is officially Roman Catholic, but this is seen more in the widespread folk Catholicism than in Church practice. The population being 64% mestizo (Spanish-Indian), 10% black, and perhaps 3% Indian (an uncertain figure, but amounting to several hundred thousand Indians), together with influences from the Caribbean island world, means that there is great and increasing religious variety. The growing María Lionza cult exemplifies this in its syncretism of Amerindian, African, Catholic, and Spiritist elements. From the Caribbean have come Kumina, Santería, Spiritual Baptists, Shango, Rastafarians, occultisms, etc., and from Brazil, various forms of spiritism, including Umbanda. There are large movements on which no information has been secured, such as the Iglesias Nativas Venezolanas de Apure or "Bethel Church" among mestizos in Apure state since 1925. The varied and prolific research work of the Venezuelan Vienna-trained anthropologist, Angelina Pollak-Eltz of the Catholic University of Andrés Bello, dominates the following materials.

For general works see A. Pollak-Eltz (entry 76, 1970 in Dutch, 1972 in Spanish; entry 1498, in English with French and Spanish summaries, on the three main cultural traditions; and entry 1512).

For the African contributions see F. Pérez Fernández (entry 1497, in Spanish) and A. Pollak-Eltz (entry 1523, on Afro-Catholic syncretism, and entry 1525, on syncretism).

For Amerindian movements, the literature is minimal. The Hallelujah religion among the Pemon in the east has most material on its forms in Guyana (q.v.), where it originated. See, however, R. Ave-Lallemant (entry 1477, an early traveler's report), J. Clarac de Briceño (entry 1480), A. Pollak-Eltz (entry 1511), F. Sierksma (entry 1532, on the Yaruro Indians), and D. J. Thomas (entry 1539, on the San Miguel movement among the Pemon since 1971).

On the María Lionza cult see J. Clarac de Briceño (entry 1478, with English summary, and entry 1482), P. Dauguet (entry 1485, detailed, in French), A. Pollak-Eltz (entry 1499, the first version of her main work, in

German with English, French, and Spanish summaries; entry 1502, in Spanish; and entry 1521, an extended study, in Spanish), M. A. Perera (entry 1496, in Spanish), G. E. Simpson (entry 1533, based on Pollak-Eltz), and M. V. (entry 1541, popular, descriptive).

On spiritism see J. Clarac de Briceño (entry 1481).

On Pentecostalism see A. Pollak-Eltz (entry 1519, mainly Catholic forms, but useful as background).

On immigrant religions see A. Pollak-Eltz (entry 1521 and entry 1507, on Santería, in German with Spanish summary) and S. D. Glazier (entry 1487, on Spiritual Baptists, largely as in Trinidad, in Spanish).

On healing see A. Pollak-Eltz (entry 1503 and especially entry 1517).

On Brotherhoods or Cofradias see J. P. Sojo (entry 1534) and M. Acosta Saignes (entry 1473).

1473   Acosta Saignes, Miguel. "Las cofradías coloniales y el folkore." *Cultura Universitara* (Caracas, Universidad de Venezuela) 47 (January-February 1955): 79-102.
        Includes the black Christian brotherhoods, in which African divinities were equated to Catholic saints.

1474   Acosta Saignes, Miguel. *Estudios de folklore venezolano*. Caracas: Instituto de Antropología e Historia, Universidad Central de Venezuela, 1962, 289 pp., illus.
        Includes a festival of the African cult of San Benito in Betijocque.

1475   Acosta Saignes, Miguel. *Vida de los esclavos negros en Venezuela*. Caracas: Hespérides, 1967, 410 pp., illus.

1476   Aretz, Isabel, and Ramon y Rivera, Luis Felipe. "Aspectos del culto de María Lionza." *Boletin Indigenista Venez* (Caracas) 6-7, nos. 1-4 (1958).

1477   Ave-Lallemant, Robert [Christian Berthold]. *Reise durch Nord-Brasilien im Jahre 1859*. 2 vols. Leipzig: Brockhaus, 1860. Portuguese translation. *Viagem pelo norte de Brasil no ano de 1859*. 2 vols. Rio de Janeiro: Instituto Nacional do Livro, 1961.
        Vol. 2, pp. 154-56 (Portuguese translation, vol. 2, pp. 120-23), on new religion under Venantius, upper Rio Negro, Venezuela, in 1857 (based on Capt. J. Firmino).

1478   Clarac de Briceño, Jacqueline. "El culto de María Lionza." *América Indígena* (Mexico) 30, no. 2 (1970): 359-74; English summary.
        History and social range; causes, and similarities with Macumba in Brazil and Peyote in North America.

1479   Clarac de Briceño, Jacqueline. *Dioses en exilio: Representaciones y prácticas simbólicas en la Cordillera de Mérida*. Colección Rescarte, 2. Caracas: Fundarte, 1981, 263 pp., maps.
Pp. 12-15, 141-45, 162-73, 211-19, as most relevant sections.

1480   Clarac de Briceño, Jacqueline. "Influencia indígena americana en la mitología afroamericana." *Boletín Antropológico* (Mérida), no. 3 (September-October 1983), pp. 28-38, illus.

1481   Clarac de Briceño, Jacqueline. "Re-estructuración en la Cordillera de Mérida en relación al capitalismo y al urbanismo emergente." *Boletín Antropológico* (Mérida), no. 2 (1982), pp. 43-48, illus.
Pp. 47-48, new spiritist and syncretist cults like María Lionza, and their causes.

1482   Clarac de Briceño, Jacqueline. "Una religión en formación en una sociedad petrolera." *Boletín Antropológico* (Mérida), no. 4 (November-December 1983), pp. 29-35, illus.
The cult of María Lionza in the process of development as a characteristic twentieth-century Venezuelan religion.

1483   Clarac de Briceño, Jacqueline, and Pollak-Eltz, Angelina, consultants. *María Lionza*. Film. Mérida: Departamento de Cine, Universidad de Los Andes, 1983.

1484   Cuervo, Maria Lourdes. "La santería en Venezuela." Tesis de grado, Universidad Católica Andrés Bello (Caracas), 1978.

1485   Dauguet, P. "Le culte de Maria Lionza." *Ethno-Psychologie: Revue du Psychologie des Peuples* (Le Havre) 33, no. 2 (1978): 117-40.
Based on study at their sacred mountain, near Chevaco, Garacuy state: exorcism, healings, historico-mythical basis; positive evaluation as a remarkable "indo-africano-catholic" syncretism, with the last element as the base.

1486   Garmendia, Hernán. *El mito de María Lionza*. Barquisimeto, 1964, 103 pp.

1487   Glazier, Stephen D[avey]. "Organización social y económica de los Bautistas Espirituales con atención especial a sus misiones en Venezuela." *Revista Montalbán* (Caracas), no. 15 (1985), pp. 5-41.
Beliefs and practices, baptism, economic activities, overseas missions from Trinidad.

1488   Gramcko, Ida. *María Lionza*. Barquisimeto, 1955. Reprint. 1964.

1489   Jiménez Sierra, E. *La Venus venezolana*. Caracas: Ed. Chicuramay, 1971, 80 pp.
        On María Lionza.

1490   León, Ed. "María Lionza, una leyenda que se convirtió en culto." *El Universal* (Caracas), 30 July 1967.

1491   Lozano, Rafael. "La fiesta de San Juan Bautista en las montañas de María Lionza." *Imágenes* (Caracas), no. 55 [9] (1972): 5-8.

1492   Madriz Galindo, Fernando. *Folklore de Barlovento*. Cumaná, Venezuela: Ediciones de la Universidad de Oriente, 1964, unpaged, illus.
        Black folklore as told by a local Barlovento man; includes proverbs, festivals, and legends of the supernatural.

1492a   Mahlke, Reiner. "Der Kulte der Maria Lionza in Venezuela." Master's dissertation (theology), Philipps University (Marburg), 1987.

1493   "Maria Lionza." *Archivo Venezolano de Folklore* (Caracas) 4-5 (1957-58): 28 pp.

1493a   Martín, Gustavo. *Magia y religión en la Venezuela contemporánea*. Caracas: La Biblioteca, Universidad Central de Venezuela, 1983, 298 pp., bib., illus.
        Popular religion and magic cults deal with the "tension between Nature and Culture" and flourish in undeveloped areas.

1494   Oxford Lopez, Eduardo. "El Estado Yaracuy, señorío de María Lionza." *El País* (Caracas), 20 June 1947.

1495   Parra, José. *María Lionza, mito yaracuyano*. Caracas: Ministerio de Educación, Dirección de Cultura y Bellas Artes, 1954, [9 pp.], illus.
        An illustrated poem.

1496   Perera, Miguel A. "Aspectos socio-estructurales y geográficos del culto de María Lionza." *Boletín de la Sociedad Venezolana de Espeleología* (Caracas) 9, no. 17 (1978): 49-71.

1497   Pérez Fernández, Françoise. "Por el mundo ceremonioso, mágico e iluminado del Negro." *Revista Shell* (Caracas), March 1959, pp. 36-41, illus.

1498   Pollak-Eltz, Angelina. "African, Amerindian, and Spanish traditions in the folk-culture of Venezuela." In *Culture traditions and Caribbean identity: The quest of patrimony*, edited by J. K. Wilkerson. Gainesville: Center for Latin American Studies, University of Florida, 1980, pp. 217-20; Spanish and French summaries (pp. 230, 231).

1499 Pollak-Eltz, Angelina. "Afrikanische Relikte in der Volkskultur Venezuelas." In *Materialen des Arnold-Bergsträsser-Instituts für Kulturwissenschaftliche Forschung.* Freiburg im Breisgau, 1966, 339 pp., bib.; English, French, and Spanish summaries.
Origin and history of former Negro slaves in Venezuela, and of African traits in the present-day population.

1500 Pollak-Eltz, Angelina. "El Baile de los Diablos en Patanemo." *Revista Venezolana de Folklore* (Caracas), n.s. 3 (1970): 7-8.
On Afro-Christian rites found in the "Dance of the Devils."

1501 Pollak-Eltz, Angelina. "El culto de María Leonza [*sic*] en Venezuela." *América Latina* (Rio de Janeiro) 9, no. 1 (1966): 95-115; English and Spanish summaries (pp. 114-15).
The worship of an Indian girl, which appeared in Sorte, combining Amerindian, African, and Catholic elements.

1502 Pollak-Eltz, Angelina. "El culto de María Lionza." *Revista Zona Franca* (Caracas) 58 [4] (July 1968): 14-22.

1503 Pollak-Eltz, Angelina. "Curanderismo y curanderos en Venezuela." *Anthropos* (Los Teques, Instituto Superior Salesiano de Filosofía y Educación) 1 (1981): 54-78.
Popular medicine, magic and witchcraft, herbalists, spiritist healers ("curanderos"); pp. 70-72, José Gregorio Hernandez; pp. 72-76, healing in María Lionza cult.

1504 Pollak-Eltz, Angelina. "The devil dances in Venezuela." *Caribbean Studies* (Río Piedras, University of Puerto Rico) 8, no. 2 (1968): 65-73.
Many African elements preserved in a Christian context; also Spanish elements.

1505 Pollak-Eltz, Angelina. "Devoción y culto vicioso de San Benito." *Revista Educación* (Caracas), no. 32 (1945).

1506 Pollak-Eltz, Angelina. "Dr José Gregorio Hernandez, der grosse venezolanische Wunderheiler, Volksmedizin und Volkskatholismus in Venezuela." *Curare* 5, no. 3 (1982): 15-16.

1507   Pollak-Eltz, Angelina. "Einflüsse der Kubanischen Santería in Venezuela." *Jahrbuch für Geschichte von Staat, Wirtschaft und Gesellschaft: Lateinamerikas* (Vienna) 21 (1984): 303-22; Spanish summary (p. 322).

1508   Pollak-Eltz, Angelina. "Expresiones de la religiosidad entre los Negros de Yaracuy." *Anthropos* (Los Teques, Venezuela) 2 (1982): 80-98.
        Pp. 96-97, briefly outlines the cults of María Lionza and J. G. Hernandez.

1509   Pollak-Eltz, Angelina. *Folklore y cultura en los pueblos negros de Yaracuy.* Caracas: Editorial Arte (printer), 1984, 107 pp.
        Pp. 28-31, popular Catholicism; p. 32, María Lionza and José Hernandez cults; pp. 33-38, fiesta of San Juan.

1510   Pollak-Eltz, Angelina. *Folk medecine in Venezuela.* Acta Ethnologica et Linguistica. Vienna: University of Vienna, 1982.
        Similar to entry 1517.

1511   Pollak-Eltz, Angelina. "Indianische Relikte im Volksglauben der Venezolaner." In *Indiana,* edited by G. Kutscher, et al. Contributions to Ethnology . . . of Indian America, 3. Berlin: Ibero-Amerikanisches Institut Preussischer Kulturbesitz, 1975, pp. 133-45, bib.
        The indigenous Indian contributions to the syncretistic Catholic folk culture of Venezuela; pp. 142-45, the same situation in the cult of María Lionza.

1512   Pollak-Eltz, Angelina. "Magico-religious movements and social change in Venezuela." *Journal of Caribbean Studies* (Kingston) 2, nos. 2-3 (1981): 162-80.
        A general survey, against the background of folk Catholicism: Pentecostalism, spiritism, Trincadistas, Santería (from Cuba after 1960), Shango and Vodou (both imported), the cult of Dr. J. G. Hernandez, María Lionza – their social functions, interactions, and political significance.

1513   Pollak-Eltz, Angelina. "Magic, sorcery, and witchcraft among Afrovenezuelan peasants." *Africa* (São Paulo, Revista do Centro de Estudos Africanos) 1, no. 1 (1978): 69-81, bib.

1514   Pollak-Eltz, Angelina. "María Leonza: Ein Afro-Indischer Kult in Venezuela." *Weiner Völkerkundliche Mitteilungen* (Vienna) 14-15 (1967-68): 43-67.

1515   Pollak-Eltz, Angelina. "María Lionza, mito y culto venezolano."
        Reportajes (Caracas) 2, no. 7 (1968): 30-36.

1516   Pollak-Eltz, Angelina. *María Lionza, mito y culto venezolano.*
        Caracas: Instituto de Investigaciones Históricas, Universidad
        Católica Andrés Bello, 1972, 73 pp., bib. Reprinted in *Montalban*
        (Caracas) 2 (1973): 509-76. Rev. and enl. ed. *María Lionza – Mito y
        culto venezolano.* Caracas: Universidad Católica Andrés Bello, 1985,
        90 pp.

1517   Pollak-Eltz, Angelina. *La medicina popular en Venezuela.* Estudios,
        Monografías y Ensayos, 86. Caracas: Academia Nacional de la
        Historia, 1987, 314 pp., illus.
            Pp. 61-71, María Lionza cult; pp. 73-77, overlap with popular
        Catholicism; pp. 79-87, cult of J. G. Hernandez as a "saint" and his
        assimilation into both the María Lionza cult and the Hallelujah
        religion of the Pemon; pp. 209-11, tobacco in María Lionza healing
        rites; pp. 224-28, María Lionza – suppression, influence, and changing
        forms; pp. 254-74, its cult centers in Caracas and Sorte; pp. 291-93,
        María Lionza prayers.

1518   Pollak-Eltz, Angelina. "El Negro en Venezuela." *Boletín del Museo
        Hombre Dominicano* (Santo Domingo) 9, no. 13 (1980): 293-314, bib.

1519   Pollak-Eltz, Angelina. "Pentecostalism in Venezuela." *Anthropos* 73,
        nos. 3-4 (1978): 461-82, bib.
            A comprehensive account of Pentecostalism itself and of its
        forms and functions in Venezuela, with accounts of various
        Pentecostal groups, both upper- and lower-class – chiefly as related to
        the Catholic Church, but useful background for Venezuelan folk
        religion. P. 478, the Christian Gnostic Church of Mexican S. A.
        Weor, from the 1950s, as a marginal Protestant group.

1520   Pollak-Eltz, Angelina. *Regards sur les cultures d'origine africaine du
        Vénézuela.* Montreal: Centre de Recherches Caraïbes, 1977, 60 pp.
            An overview of the common features of the cultures of the
        Caribbean islands and coastlands, including the African religious
        influences.

1521   Pollak-Eltz, Angelina. "Relictos africanos en culto a los santos
        católicos; el culto de María Lionza; prácticas afroamericanos en
        Venezuela." In *Cultos afroamericanos.* Caracas: Instituto de
        Investigaciónes Históricas, Universidad Católica Andrés Bello, 1972,
        pp. 191-212.

1522   Pollak-Eltz, Angelina. "Research commentary: El culto de María Leonza [*sic*] en Venezuela." *Caribbean Studies* (Río Piedras, University of Puerto Rico) 7, no. 4 (1968): 45-53.

1523   Pollak-Eltz, Angelina. "Semejanzas estructurales en la religiosidad popular entre Africa occidental y Venezuela." *Cuadernos Afro-Americanos* (Caracas, Universidad Central de Venezuela) 1, no. 1 (1975): 125-34, bib. Also in *Megafón: Revista Interdisciplinaria de Estudios Latinoamericanos* (Argentina), nos. 9-10.
        Catholic and African religious syncretism.

1524   Pollak-Eltz, Angelina. "Synkretistische Kulte in Volkskatholizismus Venezuelas." *Ethnomedizin* (Hamburg) 4, nos. 3-4 (1976-77): 341-56.

1525   Pollak-Eltz, Angelina. "Tradiciones africanas en Chuao, Estada Aragua." *Boletín del Museo del Hombre Dominicano* 8, no. 12 (1979): 307-25, bib., plates.
        A four-hundred-year-old village in central Venezuela and its two festivals – Corpus Christi and San Juan – as evidence of popular Afro-Venezuelan syncretism.

1526   Pollak-Eltz, Angelina. "Urgent anthropological research in Venezuela." *R.E. Review of Ethnology* (Vienna) 8, nos. 11-19 (1982): 136-38.
        P. 137, Hallelujah religion spreading in mission villages.

1527   Pollak-Eltz, Angelina. "Velorio de la Cruz de Mayo en Altarico, Yaracuy." *Artesanía y Folklore Venezolano* (Caracas), no. 33 [6] (1981): 40-41.

1528   Pollak-Eltz, Angelina. *Vestigios africanos en la cultura del pueblo venezolano*. CIDOC: Sondeos, 76. Cuernavaca, Mexico: Centro Intercultural de Documentación, 1971, various pagings, bib. Reprint. Serie de Religiones Comparadas, 19. Universidad Católica Andrés Bello, 1972, 171 pp., bib.
        African elements in Venezuelan village Catholic religion; there are recent additions in the cult of María Lionza.

1529   Pollak-Eltz, Angelina. "The Yoruba religion and its decline in the Americas." *Verhandlungen des 38 Internationalen Amerikanistenkongresses, Stuttgart-München, 12 bis 18 August 1968.*

1530   Ramón y Rivera, Luis Felipe. "América indígena y española en una fiesta merideña." *El Farol* (Buenos Aires, Standard Oil Co.) 211 [26] (1964): 17-20, illus.

A Christmas festival in the state of Mérida, Venezuela, with syncretism of worship of Christ and an Indian totemic post.

1531   Rodrigues Cardenas, Manuel. "María Lionza." *El Nacional* (Caracas), 11 November 1951.

1532   Sierksma, F[okke]. *Een nieuwe hemel en een nieuwe aarde: Messianische en eschatologische bewegingen en voorstellingen bij primitieve volken*. The Hague: Mouton, 1961, 312 pp., bib.
        Pp. 171-85, Yaruro Indian movement in Venezuela.

1533   Simpson, George Eaton. *Black religions in the New World*. New York: Columbia University Press, 1978, 415 pp.
        Pp. 163-70 (plus notes 349-50) on María Lionza cult (based on A. Pollak-Eltz).

1534   Sojo, Juan Pablo. "Cofradías etno-africanas en Venezuela." *Revista de Cultura Universitaria* (Caracas) 1 (May-June 1947): 97-103.
        Black brotherhoods.

1535   Sojo, Juan Pablo. "La encantada princesa María Lionza." *El País* (Caracas), 31 October 1947.

1536   Sojo, Juan Pablo. "El Negro y la brujería." *Revista de Folklore* (Caracas) 1, no. 1 (1947).

1537   Sosa, Antonio Juan; Sosa, Maria Helena; and Hernandes, Mercedes. "El culto a María Lionza, una religión venezolana." *SIC (Sons, Idées, Couleurs, Formes)* (Caracas), no. 354 [36] (1973): 158-60.

1538   Tamayo, Francisco. "El mito de María Lionza." *Boletín del Centro Histórico Larense* (Barquisimeto) 2, no. 5 (1943): 1-8.

1539   Thomas, David John. "El movimiento religioso de San Miguel entre los Pemon." *Antropológica* (Caracas) 43 (1976): 3-52; English and Spanish summaries.
        A movement among the Pemon Indians in southwestern Venezuela, since 1971, syncretizing Indian and Catholic elements, and both drawing upon and seeking to replace earlier movements, Hallelujah and Cho-chimuh. A detailed, first-hand report.

1540   United States Government, Department of the Army. *Area handbook for Venezuela*. Foreign Area Studies Division, American University. Edited by T. E. Weil, et al. DA PAM 550-71. Washington, D.C.: Government Printing Office, 1971, 523 pp.

Pp. 186-89, folk religion, María Lionza cult, and the Afro-Venezuelan cult of St. John (eastern coastal area).

1541 V., M. "El culto María Lionza." *Momento* (Caracas), no. 287 (14 January 1962), pp. 8-12, 64-65, illus.

Popular account of a visit to various María Lionza cult devotees and patients in search of healing on Mt. Sorte, the area of the cult's origin.

1542 Veracoechea, Ermila de. "Tres cofradías de Negros en la Iglesia de 'San Mauricio' en Caracas." *Montalbán* (Caracas) 5 (1976): 33-76.

Three semi-independent black brotherhoods: San Juan Bautista (founded 1611), Nuestra Señora de Guia (1701), and Santísimo Sacramento (1751), with religious, social, and economic functions among the "Tarí nation" and lasting into the nineteenth century; based on archival research, with textual extracts.

1543 Viet-Thané, Beatriz. *Doctrina de la Asociación civil y filosófica, culto aborigen de María Lionza*. Caracas, 1970.

1544 Viet-Thané, Beatriz. *María Lionza y yo*. Caracas, 1963.

1545 Williams, Anthony J. "Concepts of ethnicity in Venezuelan spirit cults." Paper presented at the 44th International Congress of Americanists, Manchester 1982. Digest in *Abstracts of the Congress*, p. 262.

Contemporary beliefs about María Lionza spiritism and analysis of myths about María Lionza.

1546 Williams, Anthony J. "The social and moral context of illness and healing: The case of the María Lionza cult in contemporary Venezuela." D.Phil. thesis (anthropology), University of Oxford, 198?

1547 Williams, Anthony [J.], and [Butt] Colson, Audrey [J.]. "A study of affliction and illness, health and healing in the Venezuelan religious cult of María Lionza." Final report, University of Oxford, 1981.

1548 No entry.

Other Territories

Other territories, such as the Cayman Islands and Caicos and Turks Islands, do not readily fall within previous groupings. It would not be surprising if there were movements of which published reports have not reached us. But see entries 12-13 in the Theory section, and entry 104a.

Particular Movements

Black Caribs

The people known as Black Caribs (known to themselves as Garif or Garifuna), are treated separately for several reasons. They are distributed over five countries (St. Vincent, and on the Caribbean littoral of Belize, Guatemala, Honduras, and Nicaragua) and they represent what is virtually a new ethnic group formed since the early seventeenth century by a fusion of Arawak/Carib and African peoples, at first in St. Vincent.

Since 1797, when the British transplanted most of them to an island off Honduras, their independence has been eroded and their original synthesis of Amerindian elements has been extended to include Afro-American and white influences. They are important as representing a synthesis rather than a syncretism. Their religion is very much part of the sociocultural system, and is new in this context rather than as a specific movement. While the Amerindian influence was predominant in their earlier history (and their strong resistance to Christian missions), since the mid-nineteenth century many have become at least nominally Christian, and in a Catholic form – except in Belize, where many are now Protestant, and in St. Vincent, where most are nominally Anglican but in practice are Spiritual Baptists (see C. Gullick, entry 1225).

On their distinct identity see C. J. Gullick (entry 1567).

For general items see R. Bastide (entry 1550, in French), P. Massajoli (entry 1575, in Italian, on Belize), A. Pollak-Eltz (entry 1577, in Spanish), and G. E. Simpson (entry 1579, in English).

For history see N. L. Gonzalez (entry 1561) and C. J. Gullick (entry 1565, on St. Vincent era).

For religion see E. Conzemius (entry 1557), C. J. Gullick (entries 1568 and 1569, the latter on the relation to the churches), N. L. Solien (entry

Black Caribs

1563), and D. M. Taylor (entry 1580, the most detailed study, but mainly on the shamanistic and ancestral cult elements).

For Indian influences, see the theme of the Couvade in the literature.

For Obeah or later Afro-American influence see N. L. Gonzalez (entry 1562, based on Livingston in Guatemala).

On the soul see R. Coelho (entry 1554, in French).

On rituals see R. Coelho (entry 1555, in Spanish, on Belize).

On healing see E. Conzemius (entry 1557).

1549   Adams, R[ichard] N[ewbold]. "Livingston and the Black Carib culture." In *Cultural surveys of Panama – Nicaragua – Guatemala – El Salvador – Honduras*. Washington, D.C.: Pan American Sanitary Bureau, 1957, 669 pp., maps.

At Livingston in Guatemala, after 1945.

1550   Bastide, Roger. *Les Amériques noires*. Paris: Payot, 1967. English translation. *African civilizations in the New World*. London: C. Hurst; New York: Harper & Row, 1971, 232 pp.

Pp. 76-83 (English trans.), Black Caribs, their history and real fusion of Indian and African elements, with the former predominant.

1551   Bateman, Rebecca. "African frontiersmen: The Black Carib of St. Vincent Island." *Papers in Anthropology* (Norman, Okla.) 22, no. 1 (1981): 119-29.

1552   Beaucage, Pierre, and Samson, Marcel. *Historio del pueblo Garífuna y su llegeda a Honduras en 1796*. N.p.: Editorial Paulino Valladares, [1967?], 22 pp.

Summary account of research on the Garifunas (Afro-Caribs) on the north coast of Honduras.

1553   Coelho, Ruy Galvão de Andrade. "The Black Carib of Honduras: A study in acculturation." Ph.D. dissertation (anthropology), Northwestern University, 1955, 315 pp. Spanish translation. *Los Negros caribes de Honduras*. Tegucigalpa, Honduras: Editorial Guaymuras, 1981, 208 pp.

On the resilience of this Afro-Indian culture in reinterpreting African and Indian features in a consciously selective syncretic culture and religion.

1554   Coelho, Ruy [Gavão] de [Andrade]. "Le concept de l'âme chez les Caraïbes noirs." *Journal de la Société des Américanistes* (Paris) 41, no. 1 (1952): 21-30.

1555   Coelho, Ruy [Galvão] de [Andrade]. "As festas dos Caribes negros." *Anhembi* (São Paulo) 9, no. 25 (1952): 54-72.
        Syncretist rites in the then British Honduras.

1556   Coelho, Ruy [Galvão] de [Andrade]. "Os Karaíb negros de Honduras." *Revista do Museu Paulista* (São Paulo), n.s. 15 (1964): 4-212, bib.

1557   Conzemius, Edward. "Ethnographic notes on the Black Carib (Garif)." *American Anthropologist* 30, no. 2 (1928): 183-205.
        The "Garif" (their own term) on the Central American Caribbean coast since 1798; pp. 200-205, their religion (mostly Catholic outwardly, but with pre-Christian inner content), Obeah, and a curing festival described in detail.

1558   Conzemius, Edward. "Sur les Garif ou Caraïbes noires de l'Amérique Centrale." *Anthropos* 25 (1930): 859-77.
        Pp. 876-77, religion.

1559   D'Anna, Andrea. "I riti dei Caraibi neri." In *Le religione afroamericane*. Bologna: Editrice Nigrizia, 1972, pp. 59-62.

1560   Davidson, William V. "The Caribs (Garifuna) of Central America: A map of their realm and a bibliography of research." *National Studies* (Belize City) 2, no. 6 (1974): 15-25, map.

1560a   Foster, Byron. "Spirit possession in southern Belize." *Belizean Studies* (Belize City) 10, no. 2 (1982): 18-23.
        Women's behavior during a Garifuna healing rite and its social effects.

1561   Gonzalez, Nancie L[oudon Solien]. "From Black Carib to Garifuna: The coming of age of an ethnic group." In *Actes du 42e Congrès International des Américanistes, Paris, 1976*. Vol. 6. Paris: Société des Américanistes, Musée de l'Homme, 1979, pp. 577-88.

1561a   Gonzalez, Nancie L[oudon Solien]. "Garifuna traditions in historical perspective." *Belizian Studies* (Belize City) 14, no. 2 (1986): 11-26.
        The Black Caribs as culturally flexible, with borrowings from Afro-American and other sources.

1562   Gonzalez, Nancie L[oudon] Solien. "Obeah and other witchcraft among the Black Caribs." In *Systems of North American witchcraft and sorcery*, edited by D. E. Walker, Jr. Anthropological

Black Caribs

Monographs, 1. Moscow: University of Idaho, 1970, pp. 95-108, maps.

Includes shamans (*buwiye*) and their spirits, as well as Obeah men; the contrasts and likenesses between them; studied in Guatemala.

1563 [Gonzalez], Nancie L[oudon] Solien. "West Indian characteristics of the Black Carib." *Southwestern Journal of Anthropology* 15, no. 3 (1959): 300-307. Reprinted in *Peoples and cultures of the Caribbean*, edited by M. M. Horowitz. Garden City, N.Y.: Natural History Press, 1971, pp. 133-42.

Pp. 136-37, on religion; passim, Honduras and Belize – African heritage in syncretism with Catholicism.

1564 Gullick, C[harles] J[ohn] M[ontgomery] R[owley]. "Afro-Indians." In *Past and present in the Americas*, edited by J. Lynch. 44th International Congress of Americanists, 1982. Manchester: Manchester University Press, 1984, pp. 156-67.

A theoretical discussion of the various Afro-American groups, including the Black Caribs.

1565 Gullick, C[harles] J[ohn] M[ontgomery] R[owley]. "The Caribs of St. Vincent, historical background and research bibliography." *National Studies* (Belize City) 3, no. 3 (1975): 22-27, map.

1566 Gullick, Charles John Montgomery Rowley. "The changing society of the Black Caribs." 2 vols. B. Litt. thesis, University of Oxford, 1969, cxlviii + 557 pp., maps.

Revised as entry 1568.

1567 Gullick, C[harles] J[ohn] M[ontgomery] R[owley]. "Confused identity in the Caribbean." *Geographical Magazine* (London) 54, no. 9 (1982): 522-23, illus., map.

The distinction of Black Caribs as Afro-Indians from Afro-Americans and Amerindians, and therefore as neither "red" nor "black" – the history of Black Carib identity and that which threatens it.

1568 Gullick, C[harles] J[ohn] M[ontgomery] R[owley]. *Exiled from St. Vincent: The development of Black Carib culture in Central America.* Malta: Progress Press, 1976.

Pp. 13-15, 44-49, 85-91, 117-19, religion examined at successive periods of their history, showing progressive responses to outside influences both black and white. A revision of his thesis, entry 1566.

1568a Gullick, C[harles] J[ohn] M[ontgomery] R[owley]. *Myths of a minority: The changing traditions of the Vincentian Caribs*. Studies of Developing Countries, 30. Assen: Van Gorcum, 1986, 211 pp., illus.

On the remaining Black Caribs of St. Vincent, as distinct from mainland Black Caribs.

1569 Gullick, C[harles] J[ohn] M[ontgomery] R[owley]. "Pilgrimage, cults, and holy places. Carib religious trips: Some anthropological visions." *DYN: Journal of the Durham University Anthropological Society* 6 (1981): 1-13.

Historical and religious survey of Black Caribs – the varieties of religious survivals and syncretisms, and the relation to Catholics, Anglicans, Methodists, and Spiritual Baptists.

1570 Gullick, Charles John Montgomery Rowley. "Tradition and change among the Caribs of St. Vincent." D.Phil. thesis, University of Oxford, 1974.

1571 Hadel, Richard E[ugene]. "Carib folksongs and Carib culture." Ph.D. dissertation (anthropology), University of Texas at Austin, 1972, 369 pp.

The Catholic aspects of Carib culture; by a Jesuit.

1572 Hadel, Richard E[ugene]. "Words of some Carib songs." *Natural Studies* 2, no. 6 (1974): 26-30.

1573 Hain, H. [Letter to Methodist Society, London, 15 April 1853.] London: Methodist Missionary Society Archives.

Describes Carib Easter celebrations in 1853 in British Honduras [later Belize].

1574 Kerns, Virginia Baker. "Daughters bring in: Ceremonial and social organization of the Black Carib of Belize." Ph.D. dissertation (culture), University of Illinois at Urbana, 1977, 377 pp.

1575 Massajoli, Pierleone. "Popoli e civiltà dell'America Centrale: I Caribi neri." *L'Universo: Revista Bimestrale di Divulgazione Geografica* (Florence, Italy, Instituto Geografico Militare) 51, no. 5 (1971): 1121-62, illus., maps, bib.

The Black Caribs, including their religion and shamanism.

1576 Palacio, Joseph O. "Carib ancestral rites: A brief analysis." *National Studies* (Belize City) 1, no. 3 (1973): 3-8.

Black Caribs

1577   Pollak-Eltz, Angelina. *Afro-Amerikaanse Godsdienste en Culten.*
       Roemond: Romen & Zonen, 1970, 221 pp., illus. Spanish translation.
       Cultos afroamericanos. Caracas: Instituto de Investigaciones
       Historicas, Universidad Católica Andrés Bello, 1972, 268 pp.
           Pp. 152-56 (Spanish trans.), Black Caribs.

1578   Sanford, Margaret. "Revitalization movements as indicators of
       completed acculturation." *Comparative Studies in Society and History*
       16, no. 4 (1974): 504-18.
           Uses the Belize Black Carib identity movement of T. V. Ramos
       in the 1940s as a case study for her theoretical discussion, showing
       that return to older practices may indicate advanced acculturation.

1579   Simpson, George Eaton. *Black religions in the New World.* New York:
       Columbia University Press, 1978, 415 pp.
           Pp. 106-10 (plus notes, p. 338), Black Caribs.

1580   Taylor, Douglas MacRae. *The Black Carib of British Honduras.*
       Viking Fund Publications in Anthropology, 17. New York: Wenner-
       Gren Foundation, 1951, 175 pp., map, illus.
           The main study of religion. Pp. 102-12, traditional beliefs
       concerning the supernatural; pp. 113-36, religious rites and practices,
       magic; pp. 137, 140-43, religious syncretism: the ancestor-cult theme,
       with Arawak elements predominating. See also review article by
       Thomas Leon, "Les Caraïbes noires du Honduras Britannique," *Les
       Cahiers d'Outre-Mer* 30 [8] (1955): 196-202.

1581   United States Government, Department of the Army. *Area handbook
       for Guatemala.* Prepared by Foreign Area Studies, American
       University, Washington, D.C. Edited by John Dombrowski, et al. DA
       PAM 550-78. Washington, D.C.: U.S. Government Printing Office,
       1970, 361 pp., maps.
           Pp. 88-89, Black Caribs – brief reference to their religion in
       Livingston, Guatemala.

1582   Wells, Marilyn McKillop. "Circling with the ancestors: *Hugulendii*
       symbolism in ethnic group maintenance." *Belizean Studies* 8 (1980):
       1-9.
           Hugulendii is a dance among the Black Caribs.

1583   Wells, Marilyn McKillop. "Spirits see red: The symbolic use of
       Guseue among the Garif (Black Carib) of Central America."
       Anthropological Quarterly 55, no. 1 (1982): 44-55. Also in *Belizean
       Studies* (Belize City) 10, nos. 3-4 (1982): 10-16.

Guseue is a deep red powder for coloring the body or for food seasoning; pp. 52-53, mutual relationships between Garif and Catholic religious ceremonies.

Rastafari

This movement is treated separately because there is a great deal of literature devoted especially to it, and because of its unusual features, its growth, historical and religious importance, and its wide diffusion. Materials that include but are not confined to Rastafari must be sought in other sections (e.g., K. Norris, entry 1093; W. R. Scott, *Going to the Promised Land: Afro-American immigrants in Ethiopia, 1930-1935*, under Afro-American in vol. 5 of this series, *Latin America*; and other articles under Dominica – entries 1178-1190). Items referring to the United Kingdom and other areas outside the Caribbean are included where available. The "foundation document" and first overall survey is the official report by M. G. Smith, et al. (entry 1871).

For general surveys see L. E. Barrett (entry 1591), E. E. Cashmore (entries 1632-1634), Catholic Commission for Racial Justice (entry 1638), K. De Albuquerque (entry 1656), J. Fox and C. Jones (entry 1683), International Rastafarian Conference (entry 1720), M. Jackson (entry 1724), T. R. Malloch (entry 1771), and G. E. Simpson (entry 1868).

For the back-to-Africa theme see L. A. Garrison (entry 1690), D. Jenkins (entry 1728), K. J. King (entry 1744, on a Barbadian black Jew), J. S. Pobee (entry 1812), and R. G. Weisbord (entry 1901).

For Marcus Garvey and background see L. E. Barrett (entry 1591), R. Kuhl (entry 1749), and I. J. Tafari (entry 1880); for a denial of Tafari's assertion of the continuity of Rastafarianism with Garveyism, see A. and L. Mansingh (entry 1774).

For Nyabinghi tradition see J. B. Emtage (entry 1667), R. A. Hill (entry 1709), L. P. Howell [G. G. Maragh] (entry 1715), Order of Nyabinghi (entry 1796), and F. Philos (entry 1808).

For Claudius Henry see A. B. Chevannes (entry 1640).

For Rastafarianism in the Caribbean elsewhere than in Jamaica see E. Bosquet (entry 1600), H. Campbell (entry 1621), and items mentioned in the Dominica section (entries 1178-1190).

Beyond the Caribbean:

Canada: *Caribbean Contact* (entry 1717), V. Harris (entries 1610, 1701, and 1783), and C. D. Yawney (entry 1919).

Ethiopia: Sheshamane community (entries 1862-1863) and B. Shlachter (entry 1864).

Ghana: L. A. Goffe (entry 1697).

Rastafari

New Zealand: G. Campbell (entry 1619), "Gangs a legacy" (entry 1687), C. Hogg (entry 1711), P. Kitchin (entry 1746), N. Legat (entry 1759), and D. Lomas (entry 1765).

United Kingdom: M. Brake (entry 1603, as popular subculture), M. J. C. Calley (entry 1617), E. E. Cashmore (entry 1634), Catholic Commission for Racial Justice (entry 1638), L. A. Garrison (entry 1691), and R. Miles (entry 1782).

United States: M. Fineman (entry 1676).

For variants, relation to the law, black power, criminal elements, etc., see J. Anderson (entry 1585, U.S.), J. Brown (entry 1609, U.K.), M. Fineman (entry 1676, U.S.), C. Hogg (entry 1711, distinctions), D. Humphrey and G. Latibeaudiere (entry 1716, U.K.), and J. Plummer (entry 1811, U.K.).

For the place of women see Sister Ilaloo (entry 1719), W. Lane (entry 1756), M. Rowe (entry 1844), M. Silvera (entry 1865), and C. D. Yawney (entry 1920).

For economics and politics see N. G. Callam (entry 1616), and C. Stone (entry 1879).

For food and health see J. Landman-Bogues (entry 1755) and C. Montague and C. D. Yawney (entry 1784).

For language see V. Pollard (entries 1814-1815), Ras Dizzy I (entry 1824), and Ras Michael (entry 1828).

For marijuana see K. M. Bilby (entry 1592, an anthropologist), H. A. Fraser (entry 1684), and F. Hickling (entry 1707, a Rastafari medical doctor).

For music (reggae, etc.) see G. White (entry 1904, on Count Ossie, drummer, pioneer of Rastafari music in 1960) and especially E. Brodber and J. E. Greene (entry 1607), C. Brooks (entry 1608, himself a Rastafari), S. Clarke (entry 1645), A. D'Anna (entry 1652, in Italian, on Peter Tosh), B. Ford (entry 1680), D. Hebdige (entry 1704, in U.K.), J. A. Hellstrom (entry 1706, in Swedish), L. K. Johnson (entry 1731), P. O'Gorman (entry 1795), V. Reckord (entry 1833), and the Wailers (entry 1775, song texts).

For Bob Marley see A. Boot and V. Goldman (entry 1597), S. Davis (entry 1653), L. K. Johnson (entry 1729), C. Salewicz and A. Boot (entry 1852, the funeral), N. Spencer (entry 1874), and T. White (entry 1908).

On conversions see E. E. Cashmore and B. Troyna (entry 1637, in U.K.), "I was a Rastafarian" (entry 1723, in U.K., to Rastafari and then to Jehovah's Witnesses), and B. Troyna (entry 1886).

On relation to Hinduism see A. and L. Mansingh (entry 1774).

On relation to Christianity, Bible, and Churches see I. Boyne (entry 1602, World Council of Churches, sympathetic), L. A. Breiner (entry 1605, Bible), Catholic Commission for Racial Justice (entry 1638), L. Isaac and A. Forrest (entry 1721), L. Lagerwerf (entry 1753), Order of Nyabinghi (entry 1796, a Rastafari "reasoning"), and T. G. Vincent (entry 1895, on the African Orthodox Church).

1584 Allen, Oscar. "Youth: The crescent rose at the margins." In *New mission for a new people*, edited by D. I. Mitchell. New York: Friendship Press, 1977, pp. 114-17.
      P. 114 explains the term *dread* as used by Rastafarians.

1585 Anderson, Jack. "Rude Boys worry officials: Rastafarians get violent." *Goshen News* (Goshen, Ind.), 29 June 1983; 30 June 1983.
      A columnist's report on "criminal elements" identifying themselves as Rastafarians in the U.S.

1586 "Antigua's Rasta movement." *Caribbean Contact* (Port of Spain) 4, no. 7 (1976): 15. Reprinted in *Christian Action* (Caribbean Council of Churches) 2, no. 10 (1976): 3.
      About a thousand young Rastafari in Antigua with government-assisted work schemes.

1587 ASAWI [The African Studies Association of the West Indies]. "A summary of the international seminar on Marcus Garvey, Kingston, Jamaica." *Black Scholar* 4, no. 5 (1973): 58-60.
      P. 60, the continuing influence of Garvey among Rastafarians.

1588 Baku, Shango. *3 plays of our time*. Belmont, Trinidad: Baku Publications, 1984, 116 pp., illus.
      Includes *Revo (A hilarious comedy)*, 3-50; *Ruby my dear (A hard play)*, 51-92; *One bad casa (Scripted for improvisation)*, 93-114. By a Rastafari actor, writer, media journalist, etc.

1589 Baku, Shango. *Writings from the dread level*. London, 1976. 2d ed. Belmont, Trinidad: Baku Publications, 1984, 20 pp., illus.

1590 Barkun, Michael. *Disaster and the millennium*. New Haven, Conn.: Yale University Press, 1974, 246 pp., bib.
      Pp. 174-75, 227, Rastafarians as an unusual millenarian movement in being urban.

1591 Barrett, Leonard E[mmanuel]. *The Rastafarians: A study in messianic cultism in Jamaica*. Caribbean Monograph Series, 6. Río Piedras: Institute of Caribbean Studies, University of Puerto Rico, 1968 (issued 1969), 238 pp., illus., bib. (pp. 231-38). Reprinted as *The Rastafarians: The Dreadlocks of Jamaica*. Kingston: Sangster's Bookstores; London: Heinemann Educational Books, 1977, 272 pp. Also reprinted as *The Rastafarians: Sound of cultural dissonance*. Boston: Beacon Press, 1977, 272 pp.; rev. ed., Beacon Paperback 795, Boston: Beacon Press, 1988, xviii + 302 pp.

Rastafari

A major study by a Jamaican scholar.

1591a   Bilby, Kenneth M. "Black thought from the Caribbean: Ideology at home and abroad." *Nieuwe West-Indische Gids* (The Hague) 57, nos. 3-4 (1983): 201-14, bib.

Review essay on J. Owens (entry 1800), P. B. Clarke (entry 1644), John Plummer (entry 1811), and D. Hebdige (entry 1705).

1591b   Bilby, Kenneth M. "The half still untold: Recent literature on Reggae and Rastafari." *Nieuwe West-Indische Gids* (The Hague) 59, nos. 3-4 (1985): 211-17.

Critical review essay on I. Morrish (entry 1785), M. Faristzaddi (entry 1675), H. Johnson and J. Pines (entry 1728a), and Y. S. Nagashima (entry 1787).

1592   Bilby, Kenneth [M.]. "The holy herb: Notes on the background of cannabis in Jamaica." In *Caribbean Quarterly Monograph*, 1985, pp. 82-95.

The historical diffusion of cannabis within and from Africa; with the name derived from India; its use among Rastafari; many useful references. By an anthropologist.

1593   Bilby, Kenneth [M.], and Leib, Elliott. *From Kongo to Zion*. HB 17. Somerville, Mass.: Heartbeat Records, 1983.

Record with accompanying pamphlet; on music and drumming.

1593a   Bishton, Derek. *Black heart man*. London: Chatto and Windus, 1986, 135 pp., illus.

Pp. 21-41, important account of author's visit to Sheshamane in 1981; pp. 43-63, the Maroons of Accopong; pp. 86-92, Marcus Garvey; pp. 95-98, Bedward; pp. 99-100, Morant Bay Revolt; pp. 105-8, Myallism; pp. 109-19, Howell and the Pinnacle community–all informative and vivid surveys.

1594   Bishton, Derek, and Homer, Brian, eds. *Talking blues: The black community speaks about its relationship with the police*. Birmingham: All Faiths for One Race (AFFOR), 1978, 47 pp., illus.

Pp. 8, 12, 15, 36, Rastafari–brief references only; pp. 39-46, the churches–good statements from ministers.

1594a   Bishton, Derek, and Reardon, John. *Home front*. London: Jonathan Cape, 1984, 160 pp., illus.

Social life, including Rastafarians, in Handsworth, Birmingham.

1595 Blake, W. A. "Beliefs of the Ras Tafari cult." November 1961, 19 pp. Mimeo.
Held at United Theological College, Kingston.

1596 Bones, Jah. *One love: Rastafari: History, doctrine, and livity.* London: Voice of Rasta Publishing House, 1985, 83 pp., illus.
A leading Rastafari in London, who upholds the return-to-Africa policy.

1597 Boot, Adrian, and Goldman, Vivian. *Bob Marley: Soul rebel – natural mystic.* London: Eel Pie; Hutchinson, 1981, [text, 19 pp.; illus., 75 pp.]. Reprint. New York: St. Martins Press, 1982.

1598 Boot, Adrian, and Green, J. *Bob Marley and the Wailers.* London, New York, and Sydney: Wise Publications, 1976, 90 pp., songs with music, illus.
Concerned with analysis of Jamaican society.

1599 Boot, Adrian, and Thomas, Michael. *Jamaica: Babylon on a thin wire.* London: Thames & Hudson, 1976, 96 pp., illus.
Pp. 69, 72-85, 88-93, on Rastafarians.

1600 Bosquet, Earl. "Who says Rastas are criminals? . . . the situation in St. Lucia." *Caribbean Contact* (Port of Spain) 4, no. 1 (1976): 19, illus.
Rastas as craft workers and agriculturists, with effects seen in a fall in the crime rate but increased conflict with police over marijuana; no connection with the Ethiopian Orthodox Church.

1601 Bowen, W. Earl. "Rastafarianism and the New Society." *Savacou* (Mona; a journal of the Caribbean Artists' Movement), no. 5 (June 1971), pp. 41-50.
Surveys the background; includes attempts at explanation in terms of messianic movements, and discusses the future of the movements.

1602 Boyne, Ian. "Jamaica: Breaking barriers between churches and Rastafarians." *One World* (Geneva), no. 86 (May 1983), pp. 3-4, illus.

1603 Brake, Mike. *The sociology of youth culture and youth subcultures: Sex and drugs and rock 'n' roll.* London: Routledge & Kegan Paul, 1980, 204 pp.
Pp. 122-28, Rude Boys and Rastafarians in the United Kingdom.

Rastafari

1604 Brathwaite, Edward [Kamau]. *Rights of passage*. London: Oxford University Press, 1967. Reprint. 1971, 86 pp.
Pp. 41-44, poem, "Wings of a dove," on Rastafari.

1605 Breiner, Laurence A. "The English Bible in Jamaican Rastafarianism." *Journal of Religious Thought* 42, no. 2 (1985-86): 30-43.

1606 Brice-Laporte, Ray S. "The Rastas." *Caribbean Review*, Summer 1970, pp. 3-4.
Review of *The Rastafarians*, by L. E. Barrett (entry 1591).

1607 Brodber, Erna, and Greene, J. Edward. *Reggae and cultural identity in Jamaica*. Working Papers on Caribbean Society, Series C, no. 7. Mona, Kingston: Institute of Social and Economic Research, University of the West Indies, October 1981, 30 pp.
Analysis of "top hits" to reveal the dominant message of the lyrics, and their relation to the social context and the Rastafarian philosophy, and to development of a Jamaican cultural identity.

1608 Brooks, Cedric. [Interview with Cedric Brooks (by the editor, Shirley M. Burke).] *Jamaica Journal* (Kingston) 11, nos. 1-2 (1977): 14-15.
A noted Jamaican Rastafarian musician on Rastafari music's origins in the slave Burru music, and on Rastafarianism in general.

1609 Brown, John. *Shades of grey: A report on police-West Indian relations in Handsworth*. Cranfield: Cranfield Institute of Technology, 1977. Reprinted in *Policing by multi-racial consent: The Handsworth experience*. London: Bedford Square Press of the National Council for Voluntary Organisations, 1982.
Pp. 6-7, 8, 20, 22, 27, 33, 36, Rastafari and the problem of distinguishing them from the criminal subculture.

1610 Brown, [Ras] Sam[uel Elisha]. "Rastafari: Sam Brown interview." *Fuse* (Toronto) 6, no. 4 (1982): 177-80.
Interview by V. Harris with a Rastafari poet and philosopher, dealing mainly with the relationship of Rastafari to the outside world.

1611 Brown, [Ras] Samuel Elisha. "Treatise on the Rastafarian movement." *Caribbean Studies* (Río Piedras, University of Puerto Rico) 6, no. 1 (1966): 39-40.
A document; see D. W. Hogg (entry 1712).

1612   Brown, Ras Samuel Elisha. "The truth about Rastafarians." *Liberator* (Kingston) 3, no. 9 (1963).

1613   Burridge, Kenelm [Oswald Lancelot]. *Someone, no one: An essay on individuality*. Princeton, N.J.: Princeton University Press, 1979, 270 pp.
       Pp. 205-8, on Rastafari as a particular movement.

1614   Byfield, Bevis B. "Transformation and the Jamaican society." *Caribbean Journal of Religious Studies* (Kingston) 5, no. 1 (1983): 29-38.
       Pp. 32-34, Rastafarians as expressing the general plight of the masses; text of a Rastafari song recorded in 1971.

1615   Byfield, Hazel G. "Women in the struggle for true community–A Caribbean perspective." *Mid-Stream* 25, no. 1 (1986): 49-56.
       Pp. 52, 53, brief references to women and Rastafarianism.

1616   Callam, Neville G. "Invitation to docility: Defusing the Rastafarian challenge." *Caribbean Journal of Religious Studies* (Kingston) 3, no. 2 (1980): 28-48.
       Rastafarian withdrawal into "naturism" as a form of social protest; society's accommodation of Rastafarianism ensures its survival in some form.

1617   Calley, Malcolm J. C. *God's people: West Indian Pentecostal sects in England*. London: Oxford University Press, 1965, 182 pp.
       Pp. 8-9, on Rastafari not having migrated to England, and being opposed by Pentecostalists.

1618   *Calling Rastafari*.
       The newspaper of the Iyanola Rasta Improvement Association, set up by the Dreads in St. Lucia.

1619   Campbell, Gordon. "Rasta in Aotearoa." *New Zealand Listener* (Wellington), 17 January 1981, p. 18.
       The influence of Bob Marley and reggae music on Maori and Pacific-islander youth gangs in several areas of New Zealand.

1620   Campbell, Horace. *Rasta and resistance: From Marcus Garvey to Walter Rodney*. Dar es Salaam: Tanzanian Publishing House, 364 pp.; London: Hansib Publishing, 1985, 237 pp.
       By a Jamaican scholar. Pp. 1-67 (London ed.), historical background; pp. 69-92, origins of Rastafari; pp. 93-120, relations to

Rastafari

the state and ganja; pp. 121-52, reggae and cultural resistance; pp. 153-74, Rastas in the eastern Caribbean; pp. 175-209, Rastafari in the Metropole; pp. 211-31, relations to Ethiopia and the Sheshamane movement.

1621　Campbell, Horace. "The Rastafarians in the eastern Caribbean." *Caribbean Quarterly* (Kingston) 26, no. 4 (1980): 42-61. Reprinted in *Caribbean Quarterly Monograph*, 1985, pp. 42-61.

　　　　In St. Lucia, Dominica, Grenada, St. Vincent, and Trinidad (where Indian youths are included).

1622　Campbell, Horace. "Rastafari: Culture of resistance." *Race and Class* (London) 22, no. 1 (1980): 122.

　　　　Rastafari as a people's culture linked with international ideologies, Garveyism, and the struggle for independence, as well as Walter Rodney's materialistic analyses.

1623　Campbell, Horace. Review of *Rastaman*, by E. Cashmore (entry 1634). *Caribbean Quarterly* (Kingston) 26, no. 4 (1980): 86-91.

　　　　A highly critical review, from the standpoint of "a student of the fundamentals of Dr. Walter Rodney."

1624　*Caribbean Quarterly Monograph*. Mona: University of the West Indies, 1985, 6 pp. [unpaginated] + 121 pp.

　　　　Reprint of articles in special theme issue of the *Caribbean Quarterly* (Kingston) 26, no. 4 (December 1980), with two new articles and a foreword by R. [M.] Nettleford, 4 pp. (unpaginated).

1625　Carter, Adam, and Went, Earl. "Jamaicans live in fear of 'Rasta Men.'" *Sunday Guardian* (Kingston), 1 May 1960, p. 16.

　　　　With a probably exaggerated estimate of sixty thousand adherents in 1960.

1626　Case, Charles Gregory. "Ras Tafari and the religion of anthropology: An epistemological study." Ph.D. dissertation (cultural anthropology), McGill University, 1981.

　　　　Set in New York City, where eliciting Rastafarian beliefs proved impossible, so he changed to the researcher's beliefs in relation to anthropological theory.

1627　Cashmore, Ernest [Ellis H.]. "After the Rastas." *New Community* 9, no. 2 (1981): 173-81.

The nature of Rastafari in Britain: antiactivist and locked into stereotypes – their own of Babylon, and the police and the public's, of them as a criminal group.

1628   Cashmore, Ernest [Ellis H.]. "Black youths for whites." In *Black youth in crisis*, edited by E. E. Cashmore and B. Troyna. London: George Allen & Unwin, 1982, 176 pp.

Pp. 10-13, 19-20, 30-31; see also essays in same volume by J. Rex (entry 1837) and by Cashmore and Troyna (entry 1637).

1629   Cashmore, E[rnest] Ellis [H.]. "The decline of the Rastas." *Religion Today* 1, no. 1 (1984): 3-4.

1630   Cashmore, Ernest [Ellis H.]. "Jah people." *New Society*, no. 791 [42] (1 December 1977): 479-80.

Review of *The Rastafarians*, by L. E. Barrett (entry 1591).

1631   Cashmore, Ernest [Ellis H.]. "More than aversion: A study of reality creation." *British Journal of Sociology* 30, no. 3 (1979): 307-21.

1632   Cashmore, E[rnest] E[llis H.]. *The Rastafarians*. Minority Rights Group, Report no. 64. London: Minority Rights Group, 1984, 11 pp., with appendix by Jah Bones.

1633   Cashmore, Ernest [Ellis H.]. "The Rastaman cometh." *New Society*, no. 777 [41] (25 August 1977): 382-84, illus.

1634   Cashmore, Ernest E[llis H.]. *Rastaman: The Rastafarian movement in England*. London: George Allen & Unwin, 1979. 2d ed. London: Unwin Paperbacks, 1983, xiv + 263 pp., bib.

A study of Rastafari in their diaspora. Includes early Jamaican movements from G. Liele to Bedward and Garvey, pp. 14-27.

1635   Cashmore, Ernest [Ellis H.]. "Shades of black – shades of white." In *No future*. London: Heinemann, 1984, pp. 42-57.

1636   Cashmore, Ernest [Ellis H.], and Troyna, Barry. *Introduction to race relations*. London: Routledge & Kegan Paul, 1983, 272 pp.

Pp. 175-81, Rastafari; also pp. 164-69, religion and immigrants.

1637   Cashmore, Ernest [Ellis H.]., and Troyna, Barry, eds. "Growing up in Babylon." In *Black youth in crisis*. London: George Allen & Unwin, 1982, pp. 72-86.

Rastafari

1638   Catholic Commission for Racial Justice. *Rastafarians in Jamaica and Britain*. Notes and Reports, 10. London: CCRJ, January 1982, 12 pp.

    A most sympathetic survey, accepting the movement as deeply religious, examining its history and theology, and its course in Britain since the late 1950s, and offering a seven-point set of guidelines for Christians.

1639   Chevannes, Alston Barrington. "Lower-class religion in Jamaica: Struggle against oppression." M.Sc. thesis (sociology), University of the West Indies, 1970 [1971?], 155 pp.

    Especially on Claudius Henry and his followers, who separated from the Rastafarians. Pp. 34-43, Native Baptists; pp. 44-45, Myal; pp. 46-47, the Great Revival; pp. 47-53, Bedwardism; pp. 53-65, Rastafarians; chap. 4 (pp. 66-99), Revival and Revival Zion; chap. 5 (pp. 100-129), Claudius Henry and his followers; pp. 145-48, sermon on Psalm 68:30 by C. Henry.

1639a   Chevannes, [Alston] Barry [Barrington]. "The Rastafari and urban youth. In *Perspectives on Jamaica in the seventies*. Edited by C. Stone and A. Brown. Kingston: Jamaica Publishing House, 1981, pp. 392-422.

    Urban youth as more concerned with immediate physical survival than with Rastafarian beliefs and practices, which are vividly described.

1640   Chevannes, Alston Barrington. "The repairer of the breach: Reverend Claudius Henry and Jamaican society." In *Ethnicity in the Americas*, edited by F. Henry. World Anthropology Series. The Hague: Mouton Publishers, 1976, pp. 263-89.

1641   Chevannes, [Alston] Barry [Barrington]. Review of *Dread*, by J. V. Owens (entry 1799). *Caribbean Quarterly* (Kingston) 24, nos. 3-4 (1978): 61-69.

1642   Clarke, Colin G. *Kingston, Jamaica, urban development, and social change, 1692-1962*. Berkeley: University of California Press, 1975, 270 pp.

    Pp. 119-26, 130-31, 138, outline of Rastafari: the political significance, ideological divisions, and relation to black power.

1643   Clarke, Colin G. "An overcrowded metropolis: Kingston, Jamaica." In *Geography and a crowding world*, edited by W. Zelinsky, et al. New York and London: Oxford University Press, pp. 305-25, maps.

Pp. 318-19, Rastafarians (and Revival cults) in relation to population problems.

1644   Clarke, Peter B[ernard]. *Black paradise: The Rastafarian movement.* Wellingborough, Northamptonshire: Aquarian Press, 1986, 112 pp., illus. Reprint. San Bernardino, Calif.: Borgo Press, 1986.

A scholarly survey, with special reference to Britain; note especially pp. 88-94, lifestyles and ritual, and pp. 95-99, "From self-awareness to the brotherhood of men."

1645   Clarke, Sebastian. *Jah music: The evolution of the popular Jamaica song.* London: Heinemann Educational Books, 1980, 224 pp.

Studies the attempts of Rastafarians to reflect contemporary Jamaican society through their song and music.

1646   Clarke, Sebastian. "Reggae: A Jamaican musical phenomenon." *Unesco Courier* 34, no. 12 (1981): 43-46, illus.

1647   Cohen, Abner. "Drama and politics in the development of a London carnival." *Man,* n.s. 15 (March 1980): 65-87.

Pp. 75-79, 82, 85, the place of Rastafarians in the Notting Hill Carnival.

1648   Collum, Danny. "Jubilee, Rastafarian style: A vibrantly human film of reggae and justice." *Sojourners* (Washington, D.C.) 9 (November 1980): 35-36.

Rockers.

1649   Cronon, Edmund David. *Black Moses: The story of Marcus Garvey and the Universal Negro Improvement Association.* Madison: University of Wisconsin Press, 1955. Reprint. 1964, 278 pp.

Pp. 176-83, Garvey's ideas on religion and the African Orthodox Church.

1650   *Daily Gleaner* (Kingston). Many articles or reports, e.g.:

November 1930: death of Alexander Bedward;

14 and 15 March 1934: L. Howell jailed for sedition; 17 March 1934: relation to Bedwardism;

30 September 1955: Emperor Selassie's land grant;

17 October and 26 November 1958: clashes with police;

11 May 1959: police harrassment of Rastafarians; 6-8 October 1959: Claudius Henry bound over to good behavior;

7, 9, 10, 26, 30 April and 3, 4, 6, 12 May 1960: Henry's trial for treason; 22 June 1960: the Red Hills clash with police and soldiers;

Rastafari

25 August 1960, p. 10: Rastafarian response to the Smith, et al. report (entry 1871); 13, 20, 25 October 1960: C. Henry; 20 October 1960, p. 12, and 4 December 1960, p. 9: criticism of the Smith report;

11 and 13 January 1961: repatriation to Africa; 3 March 1961: letters criticizing the mission to Ethiopia;

25 January 1962, p. 2: Rastafarian repudiation of violence; 16 March 1962, p. 8: letter by "Peter the Great," et al.; 1 May 1962; 5 July 1962; 24 July 1962: editorial reminding Rastafarians of the liberties enjoyed in Jamaica;

11 February 1963: repatriation versus local integration; 12, 24 April 1963, and 25 May 1963, p. 1: ganja; 25 October 1963: demonstrations supporting repatriation to Africa;

16 March 1964, p. 16: letter from "Ras Peter de Rock"; 22 and 23 April 1966: Emperor Selassie's visit;

30 September and 12 October 1969: some twenty Rastafari settled in Ethiopia.

1651   Dalrymple, Henderson. *Bob Marley: Music, myth, and the Rastas.* Sudbury, Middlesex: Carib-Arawak Publishers, 1976, 77 pp., illus.

1652   D'Anna, A[ndrea]. "Peter Tosh 'il più forte': Musica reggae." *Nigrizia* 98, no. 18 (1980): 55-58, illus.

1653   Davis, Stephen. *Bob Marley: The biography.* London: Arthur Barker, 1983, 248 pp. Reprint. Panther Books (Grenada), 1984.
Pp. 41, 57-61, 66-67, 92, 114-15, 143-45, 150-52, more specifically on Rastafari.

1654   Davis, Stephen, and Simon, Peter. *Reggae bloodlines: In search of the music and culture of Jamaica.* Garden City, N.Y.: Doubleday, Anchor, 1977. Reprint. London: Heinemann Educational Books, 1978, 224 pp., illus.
Rastafari, passim, and more especially pp. 63-80, 141-46, 172-77, 179-83, 187-89; Maroons in relation to Rastafarians, 191-201.

1655   Davis, Stephen, and Simon, Peter. *Reggae International.* New York: Rogner & Bernhard; London: Thames & Hudson, 1983, 191 pp., illus., maps, music.
A substantial survey.

1655a   Dawey, Dawen. *We are fighting.* Roseau: Ites, Green, & Gold, 1983, 31 pp., illus.
Fifteen poems on Rastafarian beliefs and the black woman's responsibility for moral standards.

1655b De Albuquerque, Klaus. "Rastafarianism and cultural identity in the Caribbean." *Review Interamericana* (San Germain, P.R.) 10, no. 2 (Summer 1980): 230-47, bib.
The spread to the English-speaking Caribbean as a supranational movement.

1656 De Albuquerque, Klaus. "The future of the Rastafarian movement." *Caribbean Review* 8, no. 4 (Fall 1979): 22-25, 42-46, illus.

1657 De Albuquerque, Klaus. "Millenarian movements and the politics of liberation: The Rastafarians of Jamaica." Ph.D. dissertation (sociology), Virginia Polytechnic Institute and State University, 1976, 395 pp.
The transformation from a revolutionary religious to a revolutionary secular movement. Includes a case study of Rastafarians in Jamaica (pp. 133-306), and theoretical discussion of social movements; based on extensive use of Rastafarian publications and intimate association with the movement.

1658 Decraene, Philippe. *Le panafricanisme*. Paris: Presses Universitaires de France, 1970, 128 pp.
Pp. 18-20, "Marcus Garvey et le panafricanisme messianique."

1659 Dedi, Shakka Gyata. *Afrikan hartbeet 1: Songs of unity, love, and struggle*. London: Nubia Publications, 1982, 56 pp. + illus.
"Word-songs" showing the influence of Rastafarian language.

1660 Dix, Bob. *The Rastafarians*. Belfast: Breda Centre, 1985, 48 pp.
Useful summary treatment: outline history of early independent movements, and of Garveyism, in Jamaica (pp. 6-10), and of Rastafari (pp. 10-20); what Western Christians can learn from Rastafari (pp. 21-29); biblical and Christian critiques (pp. 30-43); Rastafari beliefs (pp. 44-46).

1661 Dodd, D. "Choke 'n' rob in Babylon (Georgetown, Guyana)." *New Society* 60 (10 June 1982): 418-20, illus.

1662 Dread, Selassie I. "Burning of the hair." *Rasta Voice* (Kingston), 28 February 1972, p. 3.

1663 Dreher, M[elanie] C[reagan]. "Marihuana and work: Cannabis smoking on a Jamaican sugar estate." *Human Organisation* 42, no. 1 (1983): 1-8.

Rastafari

1664 Edwards, Prince Emmanuel Charles. "Open letter to R. S. from Prince Emmanuel, JA." *Rastafari Speaks* (Trinidad), no. 10 (June-July 1983), pp. 26-27, 31.

Interpreting himself as a black Christ, criticizing some versions of Rastafarianism, and identifying with Nyabinghi.

1665 [Edwards, Prince Emmanuel Charles.] "RS reports from JA. Holy Emmanuel." *Rastafari Speaks* (Trinidad), no. 11 (October-December 1983), pp. 27, 35, photos.

1666 Edwards, William Arnold. "Garveyism: An ideology and a movement." Ph.D. dissertation (sociology), University of California (Berkeley), 1977, 229 pp.

Regarded as more complex than a back-to-Africa movement.

1667 Emtage, J[ames] B[ernard]. "The black man who was God." *Punch* (London), 13 November 1963, pp. 710-11.

On L. P. Howells, the Pinnacle community, and Rastafarians, especially the Nyabinghi section.

1668 Emtage, J[ames] B[ernard]. *Brown sugar: A vestigial tale.* London: Collins, 1966, 128 pp.

Fiction, based on fact: pp. 19-24, 64-65, 78-87, 93-98, 104-11, the Rastafarians.

1669 Eskelund, Karl. *Revolt in the tropics: Travels in the Caribbean.* London: A. Redman, 1963, 176 pp.

Chap. 6 (pp. 67-80), "The weed of wisdom" – a journalist's visit to the Rastafarians in Kingston.

1670 Ethiopian World Federation. *The Ethiopian Orthodox Church, St. Mary of Zion.* London: Ethiopian World Federation Local 33, January 1975.

1671 *Ethopian* [*sic*] *Heritage* (Kingston, Ethiopian Culture Committee) 1- (1962-).

A Rastafarian journal.

1671a Eyre, L. Alan. "Biblical imagery and the role of fantasy geography among the Rastafarians of Jamaica." *Journal of Geography* (Menasha) 84, no. 4 (July-August 1985): 144-48, photos.

Their worldview includes emotional attachment to specific places.

1672   Eyre, L. Alan. "Questions of fact and interpretation." *Journal of Geography* 83, no. 2 (1984): 51.

A letter in criticism of C. J. M. R. Gullick's article (entry 1698), asserting the peaceful nature of Rastafari and that reggae and Rastafari are less pervasive in Jamaica than an evangelical-Pentecostal Christianity.

1673   Faith, Karlene. "One love – one heart – one destiny: A report on the Rastafari movement in Jamaica." Senior thesis (anthropology), University of California at Santa Cruz, 1969, 54 pp. Rev. version. 1977, 78 pp. Also in *Cargo cults and millenarian movements*, edited by G. W. Trompf. Berlin and New York: Mouton de Gruyter, 1990, pp. 295-341.

By an anthropologist with considerable empathy with the movement – based on field work and Rastafari cooperation; four case studies of individuals, including Claudius Henry; present trends and relation to Black Power; epilogue (added to 1977 version) on Bob Marley and reggae music expressing Rastafari ideology.

1674   Farcia, (Sister). "Forward up daughters." *Grassroots* (Berkeley), October-November 1977, p. 10.

1675   Faristzaddi, Millard, et al. *Itations of Jamaica/art/iconographics*. New York: Rogner & Bernhard, 1982. Reprint. Miami: Judah Ambesas, 1987.

1676   Fineman, Mark. "On the Main Line, evil comes to 'Rastaman' gates." *Philadelphia Inquirer* 305, no. 89 (27 September 1981): 1, 24A-25A.

An investigative journalist's report on the shooting of a Rastafarian in the suburb of Main Line by the "Untouchables," a criminal group using the Rastafarian image and name.

1677   Finnegan, Tony. "It happened." *Rasta Voice*, 9 August 1974, p. 10.

A poem on police harrassment of Rastafarians reprinted in K. De Albuquerque (entry 1657), 244.

1678   Floyd, Barry. *Jamaica: An island microcosm*. London: Macmillan Education, 1979. Reprint. 1981, 164 pp., illus.

Pp. 140-42, the Rastafarian movement and its Back-to-Africa delegation.

1679   Ford, Arnold J. *The Ethiopian universal hymnal*. New York: Beth B'nai Abraham, n.d.

Rastafari

>By a Barbadian black Jew. Hymns with a redemption theme used in the Garvey movement.

1680 Ford, Barry. "A life in the day of Barry Ford." *Sunday Times* (London), 2 January 1983, p. 54, illus.
>Interview with a Jamaican Rastafarian "veteran of British reggae," singer and lead guitarist in the Steel and Skins group.

1681 Forsythe, Dennis. *Rastafari: For the healing of the nation.* Kingston: Zaika Publications, 1983, 236 pp.

1682 Forsythe, Dennis. "West Indian culture through the prism of Rastafarianism." *Caribbean Quarterly* (Kingston) 26, no. 4 (1980): 62-81. Reprinted in *Caribbean Quarterly Monograph*, 1985, pp. 62-81.

1683 Fox, James, and Jones, Colin (photographer). "The roots of the Rastas." *Observer Magazine* (London), 9 April 1978, pp. 26-31, 33-34, 36, 39, illus. (color).
>A vivid account of the most powerful cultural force among young Jamaicans, with descriptions of visits to a number of leaders such as Prince Edward Emmanuel (the "Black Christ"), Mortimer Planno, and Bongo Blackheart.

1684 Fraser, H. Aubrey. "The law and cannabis in the West Indies." *Social and Economic Studies* 23, no. 3 (1974): 361-85.
>Pp. 382-83, the distinctive features of use of cannabis in Jamaica, including brief summary of V. Rubin and L. Comitas (entry 1845), 15-19, on Rastafarian use.

1685 Fred, Dread. "Needle in groove–A reply to Linton Johnson." *Race Today* 7, no. 11 (1975): 262-63.
>On L. Johnson's review of Bob Marley's rise to success (entry 1735).

1686 Friday, Michael. "A comparison of 'Dharma' and 'Dread' as determinants of ethical standards." *Caribbean Journal of Religious Studies* 5, no. 2 (1983): 29-37.
>A point-by-point comparison, as Eastern and Western "determinants of deportment, duty and discipline."

1687 "Gangs a legacy." *Assembly News* (Presbyterian Church of New Zealand), November 1985, p. 6.
>On violent Maori youths adopting the name but not the philosophy of Rastafari.

1688   Gant, Liz. "Report from the Caribbean." *Black World* (Chicago) 22, no. 3 (1973): 74-78.
    Pp. 77-78, Rastafarians.

1689   Gardiner, Marilyn. "Rastafarian zealot has much to teach." *A.D. United Presbyterian [Life] Edition* (New York) 3, no. 3 (1974): p. 58.

1690   Garrison, Len [A.]. "Back to Africa. Rastafarians: Protest movement of Jamaica." *Afras Review* (University of Sussex) 1, no. 1 (1975): 10-12.

1691   Garrison, Len [A.]. *Black youth, Rastafarianism, and the identity crisis in Britain*. London: Afro-Caribbean Education Resource Project, 1979. 2d ed. 1983, illus.
    Pp. 010-013 [*sic*], 7-15, 18-25, 39-40, relevant to or on Rastafarians.

1692   Garrison, Len [A.]. "The Rastafarians: Journey out of exile." *Afras Review* (University of Sussex) 1, no. 2 (1976): 43-47.

1693   No entry.

1694   Gates, Skip. "Black music of sufferation." *Time*, 23 September 1974, pp. 9-10.

1695   Gerloff, Roswith I[ngebord] H[ildegard]. Review of *Rastaman*, by E. E. Cashmore (entry 1634). *Ethnic and Racial Studies* 4, no. 3 (1981): 357-59.

1696   "Get this man out of jail." *Caribbean Contact* (Port of Spain) 4, no. 2 (May 1976): 1 and back page, illus.
    Protest against wrongful life imprisonment of Desmond Trotter, Rastafari leader in Dominica, in 1974.

1697   Goffe, L. A. "Rastas in Ghana." *West Africa* (London), 19 November 1984, p. 2320.

1698   Gullick, C[harles] J[ohn] M[ontgomery] R[owley]. "Afro-American identity: The Jamaican nexus." *Journal Of Geography* (Macomb, Ill.) 82, no. 5 (1983): 205-11.
    Pp. 209, 210, origins and influence of Rastafari and relation to the ethnic situation.

Rastafari

1699   Gullick, C[harles] J[ohn] M[ontgomery] R[owley]. "Rastafarianism
        and Arawaks." *Journal of Geography* 83, no. 3 (1984): 98-99.
            A letter in reply to L. A. Eyre (entry 1672) describing Rastafari
        as moving from a pluralistic cultural position to that of being a third
        alternative in a tricultural Jamaica.

1700   Hanson, Avarita Laurel. "The Rastafarians of Kingston, Jamaica: A
        movement in search of a new social order." Honors thesis, Harvard
        University, 1975, vii + 125 pp. (bib., 119-25).

1701   Harris, Valerie. "Rastafari: Issues and aspirations of the Toronto
        community." *Fuse* (Toronto) 6, no. 4 (1982): 174-85, illus.
            Account of the first International Rastafarian Conference held
        in Toronto, July 1982.

1702   Hearne, John. *Land of the living*. London: Faber & Faber, 1961, 280
        pp.
            Fiction, by a West Indian novelist, including a sympathetic
        study of a messianic black leader; modeled on the Rastafarians. See
        especially pp. 46-56, 96-100, 106-21, 153-60, 202-7, 242-49, 262-67,
        272-78.

1703   Hearne, John, and Nettleford, Rex [M.]. *Our heritage*. Public Affairs
        in Jamaica, no. 1. Kingston: Department of Extra-Mural Studies,
        University of the West Indies, [1963], 56 pp.
            Nettleford's section: pp. 46-49, Garvey and his influence
        evaluated; pp. 50-52, Jamaican attitudes toward Africa, with
        Rastafari as unrealistic.

1704   Hebdige, Dick. "Reggae, Rastas, and Rudies: Style and the
        subversion of form." Stencilled Occasional Papers, 24. Birmingham:
        Centre for Contemporary Cultural Studies, University of
        Birmingham, [ca. 1975], 65 pp. Mimeo. Extract in *Resistance through
        rituals*, edited by S. Hall and T. Jefferson. London: Hutchinson, 1976,
        pp. 135-54. Both are included in his M.A. thesis, "Aspects of style in
        the deviant sub-cultures of the 1960's," University of Birmingham,
        1974-75.
            A cultural analysis of the development of the Rastafarians and
        their reggae music in relation to Jamaica and to other subcultures in
        Britain such as the "skinheads."

1705   Hebdige, Dick. *Subculture: The meaning of style*. London: Methuen
        & Co., 1979, 195 pp.

Pp. 30-45, 64-67 (and notes on pp. 143-46), on Rastafarians and their relations with other groups such as Punks.

1706   Hellstrom, Jan Arvid. "Jah live: Selassie-I live: En studie king reggae-musik och afrikansk messias kult pa Jamaica." *Svensk Teologisk Kvartalskrift* 53, no. 4 (1977): 145-55.
        A general survey of Rastafarianism and its reggae music, combining "African dreams and the Rasta way of reading the Bible."

1707   Hickling, Fred. "Herbs: In defence of ganja. Ganja in Jamaica." *Rastafari Speaks* (Trinidad), no. 10 (June-July 1983), pp. 6, 9.
        A Rastafarian medical doctor discusses ganja.

1708   Hill, Clifford. "Afro-Caribbean religion in Britain." In *Afro-Caribbean religions*, edited by B. Gates. London: Ward Lock Educational, 1980, pp. 67-86.
        Pp. 80-81, Rastafarians.

1709   Hill, Robert A. "Dread history: L. P. Howell and millenarian visions in early Rastafari religions in Jamaica." *Epoché* (Los Angeles, University of California) 9 (1981): 30-71, illus. Reprinted without footnotes in *Jamaica Journal* 16, no. 1 (1983): 23-40.
        Discusses the origins of Rastafarianism, its relation to Marcus Garvey, to *The Holy Piby* of R. A. Rogers (entry 1842), and to F. B. Pettersburgh's *The royal parchment scroll of black supremacy* (entry 1807) as sources for Howell; sets the movement in the wider social context of the 1930s.

1710   Historian, Ras. "Rastas discuss back-to-Africa plan." *Rasta Voice* (Kingston), 28 July 1973, p. 5.

1711   Hogg, Colin. "Real Rastaman fights back." *New Zealand Times*, 2 March 1986, p. 3, illus.
        Hensley Dyer, a Jamaican living in New Zealand, complaining that many troublemakers being labeled Rastafari are not true followers of the religion.

1712   Hogg, Donald W[illiam], ed. "Statement of a Rastafari leader." *Caribbean Studies* (Río Piedras, University of Puerto Rico) 6, no. 1 (1966): 37-38.
        "Treatise on the Rastafarian movement" by Samuel Elisha Brown, with an introduction by D. W. Hogg.

Rastafari

1713 Hoke, (Brother). "A wa-so." *Rasta Voice* (Kingston), 3 December 1972, p. 9.
      Police harrassment of Rastafarians; reprinted in K. De Albuquerque (entry 1657).

1714 Homiak, John P. "The mystic revelation of Rasta Far-Eye: Dreams as charismatic significance in a millenarian movement." Working Paper no. 3, at advanced seminar, "Dreams in cross-cultural perspective," School of American Research, Santa Fe, N.M., [probably 1983], 34 pp. + notes and bib.

1715 Howell, Leonard P. (G. G. Maragh; Gungunguru). *The promised key*. [Apparently printed in Accra]: African Morning Post, 1936, 14 pp.
      L. P. Howell created this mystical name from Hindi elements referring to "great king" (marragh) and "guru," and borrowed much material affirming black superiority from F. B. Pettersburgh (entry 1807).

1716 Humphrey, Derek, and Latibeaudiere, Grace. "Why black sect feels persecuted." *Sunday Times* (London), 3 October 1976, p. 6, illus.
      A report on genuine Rastafarians in Britain, and West Indian criminal elements assuming Rastafarian guise.

1717 "Hunting for the Rastas in Canada and the U.S.A.: But who are the racists?" *Caribbean Contact* 3, no. 4 (1975): 9, 12, illus.

1718 I, I Ras. "U blind you can't see." *Rasta Voice* (Kingston), 14 January 1972, pp. 4-5.
      Religious Rastafarians' contempt for those more politically inclined; reprinted in K. De Albuquerque (entry 1657).

1719 Ilaloo, (Sister). "Rastawoman as equal." *Yard Roots* 1, no. 1 (1981): 5-7.
      A Rasta sister in Jamaica on the emancipation of women in Rastafari, and on her conception of God as a human-generated ideal, of which Haile Selassie is one historical expression.

1720 International Rastafarian Conference. *Report on the First International Rastafarian Conference, held in Toronto, Ontario, Canada, July 23d-July 25th 1982*, 27 pp.

1721 Isaac, Les, and Forrest, Alistair. *Dreadlocks*. Basingstoke: Marshall, Morgan & Scott, 1984, 126 pp.

Pp. 28-33, the first author's experience as a Rastafari; pp. 86-87, conversation with a Rastafari after conversion to Christianity; pp. 116-21, outline of Rastafarianism; pp. 122-26, "reaching out to Rastas" as an evangelical Christian.

1722 Iwachiw, Adrian, and Krohn, M. Nico. "Rastafari voices." *Atkinsonian* (Toronto), October 1984, pp. 19, illus.
Report of conference at York University, involving Nyabinghi elders.

1723 "I was a Rastafarian." *Awake* (London, Watch Tower Bible and Tract Society) 66, no. 4 (1985): 14-17, photo.
Personal account of conversion to Rastafari, growing dissatisfactions, and later conversion to Jehovah's Witnesses.

1724 Jackson, Michael. "Rastafarianism." *Theology*, no. 691 [83] (1980): 26-34.
By an English Anglican vicar: a sympathetic survey from a Christian viewpoint.

1724a Jacobs, Virginia Lee. *Roots of Rastafari*. San Diego: Slawson Corp., 1985, 130 pp.
On history, and reggae music.

1725 Jah Bunny. "Ode." *Reggae and African Beat* (Los Angeles) 4, no. 2 (1985): 23.
Example of a Rastafarian poem.

1726 Jamaica Information Service. *Religion in Jamaica*. Rev. ed. Facts on Jamaica series, 3. Kingston: Jamaica Information Service, 1972, 22 pp.
Pp. 20-22, the establishment of the Ethiopian Orthodox Church in Kingston, 1970. No mention of Rastafarians.

1727 James, C[yril] L[ionel] R[obert]. "Rastafari at home and abroad." *New Left Review* (London), no. 25 [5] (May-June 1964): 74-76.
Review of *The children of Sisyphus*, by O. Patterson (entry 1803).

1728 Jenkins, David. *Black Zion: Africa, imagined and real, as seen by today's blacks*. New York: Harcourt, 1975, 284 pp. Also as *Black Zion: The return of Afro-Americans and West Indians to Africa*. London: Wildwood House, 1975, 285 pp.

Rastafari

> Pp. 111-21, M. Garvey; pp. 120-23, Rastafarians, including L. P. Howells's colony of "Dreadlocks"; p. 121, brief reference to Bedward – all in the context of the return to Africa.

1728a   Johnson, Howard, and Pines, Jim. *Reggae: Deep roots music*. London: Proteus – Channel Four Television, 1982, 127 pp., illus.
History and critique of this Rastafarian music.

1729   Johnson, Linton Kwesi. "Bob Marley and the Reggae International." *Race Today* 9, no. 4 (1977): 92-94, illus.
Review of Marley's LP *Exodus*.

1730   Johnson, Linton Kwesi. *Dread beat and blood*. London: Bogle-L'Ouverture Publications, 1975, 72 pp.
Poems in Jamaican Creole-English. Rastafarian themes in "Wi a warrijah" (p. 66), and "One love" (pp. 68-69).

1731   Johnson, Linton Kwesi. "Jamaican rebel music." *Race and Class* (London) 17, no. 4 (1976): 397-412, bib. and discography.
By a black poet; includes discussion of the religious elements in this music, and the contribution of Bob Marley, the Wailers, and the Rastafarians in focusing this aspect.

1732   Johnson, Linton Kwesi. "The Marley debate: Off the track." *Race Today* (London) 8, no. 1 (1976): 20-21.
Reply to Dread Fred (entry 1685). Fred was reacting to Johnson's original review (entry 1735). Includes a short letter by IMRUH (p. 21) on Fred's reply.

1733   Johnson, Linton Kwesi. "The politics of the lyrics of reggae music" (with introduction by Dick Hebdige). *Black Liberator* 2, no. 4 (1976): 363-73.

1734   Johnson, Linton Kwesi. "The reggae rebellion." *New Society*, no. 716 [36] (10 June 1976): 589.

1735   Johnson, Linton Kwesi. "Roots and rock: The Marley enigma." *Race Today* 7, no. 10 (1975): 237-38, illus.
See also reply by Dread Fred (entry 1685).

1736   Johnson, Linton Kwesi. "The struggle continues in Britain." *Reggae and African Beat* (Los Angeles) 4, no. 2 (1985): 25-27.

Interview with a Jamaican writer living in Britain – his religious position and views on Marley, Rastafari, and the back-to-Africa theme.

1737   Johnson-Hill, Jack Anthony. "Elements of an Afro-Caribbean social ethic: The world of Rastafari as liminal process." Ph.D. dissertation (sociology of religion), Vanderbilt University, 1988, 504 pp.
        Analysis of Rastafari literature as presenting a paradigm of a newly emerging social ethic.

1737a   Jones, Simon. *Black culture, white youth: The reggae tradition from Jamaica to U.K.* Basingstoke: Macmillan Education, 1988, xxviii + 251 pp.
        Published form of his doctoral thesis.

1738   Jones, Simon. "White youth in Jamaican popular culture." Ph.D. dissertation, University of Birmingham, Centre for Contemporay Cultural Studies, July 1986, 505 pp.
        Treats the impact of reggae music on white youth in Britain.

1739   Kallynder, Rolston, and Dalrymple, Henderson. *Reggae: A people's music*. London: Carib-Arawak, n.d.

1740   Kelly, Ras Carlisle A. *Revelation of God's throne: Dedicated to the King of Kings, Lord of Lords, conquering lion of the tribe of Judah who hath prevailed* (cover title: *Revelation of Jah throne*). Kingston: The Author, [1969?], 34 pp., illus.
        Comes nearest to a comprehensive survey by a Rastafarian; includes a "life of Jesus" and "signs heralding the second coming of Jesus" (both unusual for Rastafarians).

1741   Kewley, Vanya, et al. "God is black and is living in Ethiopia." *Listener* (London), no. 2515 [97] (30 June 1967): 841, illus.
        Edited version of a BBC TV program on the Rastafarians, with comments by Fr. Joseph Owens and Professor Rex Nettleford.

1741a   Kiev, Ari. "Ras tafari." In *Papers of the First Caribbean Psychiatric Association Meeting, Ocho Rios, Jamaica*. 1969, 11 pp.

1742   Kilgore, John Robert. "Rastafarian: A theology of the African American Church." D.Min. dissertation, School of Theology, Claremont, 1984, 138 pp.

Rastafari

1743   King, Audvil; Helps, Anthea; Wint, Pam; and Hasfal, Frank. *One love*. London: Bogle-L'Ouverture Publications, 1971, 82 pp.
        A symposium of articles and poems. King's letter-essay, "Letter to a friend," discusses Rastafarians, 15-41; pp. 75-81, his poem, "The awakening: A journey into Rastafarian experience." See also review article by S. Wynter (entry 1915).

1744   King, K. J. "Some notes on Arnold J. Ford and New World black attitudes to Ethiopia." *Journal of Ethiopian Studies* 10 (January 1972): 81-87.
        On a Barbadian black Jew, author of *The universal Ethiopian hymnal*, containing Garveyite redemption songs.

1745   King, Shirley. "The Rastafarian movement: Its influence belies its numbers." *Encore: American and Worldwide News* (New York) 2, no. 9 (1973): 58-59.

1746   Kitchin, Philip. "Life through Rasta eyes." *H.B. Herald-Tribune* (Hastings, N.Z.), 14 September 1985, illus.
        An extended interview; two young Maori men explain their beliefs and practices and correct the false image common among whites.

1747   Kitzinger, Sheila. "Protest and mysticism: The Rastafari cult of Jamaica." *Journal for the Scientific Study of Religion* 8, no. 2 (1969): 240-62.
        By an anthropologist, on the psychological aspects.

1748   Kitzinger, Sheila. "The Rastafarian brethren of Jamaica." *Comparative Studies in Society and History* 9, no. 1 (1966): 33-39. Reprinted in *Peoples and cultures of the Caribbean*, edited by M. Horowitz. New York: Natural History Press, 1971, pp. 580-88.
        Considerable evolution of religious doctrine since the 1960 Smith report (entry 1871) as less African, less millennial, and more mystical.

1749   Kuhl, Robin. "Marcus Garvey: Pride in black roots." *New Tomorrow* (London, Unification Church), no. 34 (August 1980), pp. 10-12, illus.

1750   Kuper, Adam. *Changing Jamaica*. London: Routledge & Kegan Paul, 1976, 163 pp.
        See pp. 58-59, 92-99 (and notes, p. 152), 103-7, 134-35.

1751 Kuper, Adam. "Looking to Ethiopia." *Times Literary Supplement*, 6 January 1978, p. 12.
      A review of *The Rastafarians*, by L. E. Barrett (entry 1591) as adding little to his previous work, except for reporting that Rastafarians are now "fashionable" among radical intellectuals.

1752 Laar, H. van. "Echo's uit Babylon: Theologie van een Rasta Kerk in Jamaica." Stichting Theol. Fac. (Tilburg), 1968, 167 + 25 pp.

1753 Lagerwerf, Leny, comp. "The Rastafarian movement." *Exchange* (Leiden) 16 (April 1977): 26-35.

1754 Lago, Colin. "Rastafarians researched." *UKCOSA News* 10, no. 1 (1978): 10-11.

1755 Landman-Bogues, Jacqueline. "Rastafarian food habits." *Cajanus* (Kingston, Caribbean Food and Nutrition Institute) 9, no. 4 (1976): 228-34.

1756 Lane, Winsome. "Diane Jobson – Militant woman crusader (Women in Law)." *Daily Gleaner* (Kingston), 31 March 1976, photo.
      A young lawyer who has become a Rastafarian in the course of her fight for social justice.

1757 Lee, Barbara M. *Rastafari: The new creation*. Kingston: Jamaica Media Production, 1981, 62 pp.

1758 Leevy, R. A. "The laird of the Pinnacle." *New Negro Voice* (Kingston), 10 and 17 April 1943.
      On L. P. Howell; Pinnacle became the main center of Rastafari after 1940.

1759 Legat, Nicola. "Rastaman vibration." *Metro* (Auckland), May 1985.
      On Bob Marley's visit to New Zealand in 1979, and the short-lived identification of young teenagers in the Auckland area with Rastafari, coupled with more permanent membership by Polynesian islanders in the Ponsonby city area.

1760 Leib, Elliott. *Churchical chants of the Nyabingi*. Heartbreak Records, LP HB 20, 1983, 6 pp.
      See liner/sleeve notes of the record.

Rastafari

1761   Leib, Elliott. "Film, ethnography, and the making of 'Rastafarian voices.'" In *Anthropological filmmaking*. New York: Harwood Academic, forthcoming 1989.
       The revised study guide to the film *Rastafarian voices*.

1762   Leigh-Fermor, Patrick M[ichael]. *The traveller's tale: A journey through the Caribbean islands*. New York: Harper, 1950, 403 pp., illus., maps. Reprint. London: Arrow Books, 1961, 286 pp., illus., maps.
       Pp. 348-52, a visit to Rastafari in the Dungle, Kingston.

1763   Levi, (Brother). *The special child: Interview with Levi, a Rastafarian photographer in Kingston*. Bayreuth: Iwalewa-Haus, 1984, 14 leaves.

1764   Lewis, Gordon [Kenneth]. "The apathy of the masses remains untouched." *Daily Gleaner* (Kingston), 15 March 1958.
       A university professor's article on the social grievances that gave rise to the Rastafarians, this serving as an apologia. Cited and quoted by L. E. Barrett in *Soul-force* (Garden City, N.Y.: Doubleday, Anchor, 1974), 167.

1765   Lomas, David. "Burning questions in a town of turmoil: The Rastas' rape of Ruatoria." Parts 1, 2. *New Zealand News, U.K.* (London), 8 April 1987, p. 13; 15 April 1987, p. 13.
       On violence among Maori youths operating under the name of Rastafari but repudiated by authentic members.

1765a Loth, Hans-Jürgen. *Rastafari: Bibel und afrikanische Spiritualität*. Cologne and Vienna: Böhlau Verlag, 1990, ca. 120 pp.

1766   McCarthy, Terry. "Completing the triangle: A brief study of the Rastafarian movement in Jamaica and England." Leicester: Leicester Council for Community Relations, [1977], 24 pp. Mimeo.
       Beliefs of the Ethiopian World Federation, and Orthodox Church; history and beliefs of Rastafarians, especially more recent developments in Jamaica and England (a staging post on the way back to Africa – hence the title); biographical outline of M. Garvey's history; glossary.

1767   McGlashen, Colin. "The sound system." *Sunday Times Colour Magazine* (London), 4 February 1973.
       Reporting a "Grand Rastafarian ball" in London.

1768   MacNeill, Anthony. "Saint Ras"; and "Ode to Brother Joe." *Savacou* (Mona; a journal of the Caribbean Artists' Movement) 1, no. 3 (1970): 155; 1, no. 4 (1971): 158-59.
        Two poems on Rastafarians.

1769   McPherson, E. S. P., and Semaj, Leahcim Tufani. "Rasta chronology." *Caribbean Quarterly* (Kingston) 26, no. 4 (1980): vii-viii, 97-98. Reprinted in *Caribbean Quarterly Monograph*, 1985, pp. 116-19.
        Commencing with Moses marrying an Ethiopian in the fourteenth century B.C., through the history of Ethiopia from the queen of Sheba to 1980 to show the historical roots and continuity of the movement.

1770   Mais, Roger. *Brother man*. London: J. Cape, [1954], 194 pp., illus. by the author. Reprinted with two other novels. 1966 and 1970, 191 pp. Reprint. London: Heinemann Educational Books, 1974, 208 pp.
        Fiction: focused on a saintly Rastafarian cobbler. Pp. 22-27, 29-33, 38-41, 63-66, 68-75, 107-13, 173-75, 185-91 (1954, 1970), are explicitly on this "Brother man" as an idealized individual.

1771   Malloch, Theodore R. "Rastafarianism: A radical Caribbean movement or religion." *Center Journal* (Notre Dame, Ind.) 4, no. 4 (1985): 67-87.

1772   Mandrefo, L. M. *The Ethiopian Orthodox Tewahedo Church and its activities in the West, Nation which has been the fountainhead of civilization*. New York, London, and Kingston: The Author, [1973?], 32 pp.
        By the Archimandrite who established the Church in Jamaica (1970) and in Britain, and who welcomed Rastafarians into it. "Tewahedo" refers to being theologically Monophysite.

1773   Mansingh, Ajai. "Rastafarianism: The Indian connection." *Daily Gleaner* (Kingston), 18 July 1982, pp. 12, 19.

1774   Mansingh, Ajai, and Mansingh, Laxmi. "Hindu influences on Rastafarianism." In *Caribbean Quarterly Monograph*, 1985, pp. 96-115.
        Asserts that the basic concepts, rituals, and codes derive from Hinduism, while claiming historical connections with Christianity and using the Bible to establish their African roots and lineage through Haile Selassie; Garvey's teachings are not the origin – refutes I. J. Tafari (entry 1880) in the same monograph.

Rastafari

1775   Marley, Bob, and the Wailers. *Burnin'*. London: Island Records, 1973, record sleeve of album.
        Texts of ten songs of a Rastafarian group. Examples of other titles of albums from same sources: *Natty Dread* (1974), *Exodus: Movement of the Jah people* (1977), and *Survival* (1979).

1776   Martin, Kingsley. "The Jamaican volcano." *New Statesman*, no. 1566 [61] (17 March 1961): 416, 418.
        Mostly on the Rastafarians, and with reference to the university team report of 1960; a sympathetic outline.

1777   Matura, Mustapha. *"Nice," "Rum an' Coca Cola," and "Welcome home Jacko": Three plays*. London: Eyre Methuen, 1980, 55 pp.
        Pp. 34-55, *Welcome home Jacko* – "in an inner-city youth club the Rastafarian beliefs of four black youths are shattered by the arrival of two outsiders from the real world."

1778   Mau, James A[nthony]. "Social change and belief in progress: A study of images of the future in Jamaica." Ph.D. dissertation (sociology), University of California, Los Angeles, 1964, 243 pp. Summarized as "Images of Jamaica's future." In *The democratic revolution in the West Indies*, edited by Wendell Bell. Cambridge, Mass.: Schenkman Publishing Co., 1967, pp. 197-223.
        P. 206, on Rastafarians, and Claudius Henry, as sources of anxiety among Jamaican leaders.

1779   May, Chris. "Living is hard in a Babylon yard: A party political broadcast on behalf of the Rastafarian party." *Black Music* (London), no. 48 (November 1977), pp. 12-13.

1780   May, Chris. "The state of British reggae: One – In the belly of the monster." *Black Music* (London), no. 44 (July 1977), pp. 14-18.

1781   Mieses, Stanley. "Rasta return." *Playboy* (Boulder, Colo.) 28 (January 1981): 36.

1781a   Miguel, Brother. *Rastaman chant*. Castries: African Children Unltd., 1983, 152 pp., illus.
        Poems and reflections on Rastafarian concerns in both English and Rastafarian language, by a lawyer.

1782   Miles, Robert. *Between two cultures? The case of Rastafarianism*. Working Papers on Ethnic Relations, 10. Bristol: Research Unit of Ethnic Relations, University of Bristol, 1978, 34 pp., bib.

Pp. 3-11, Rastafarian origins in Jamaica (largely based on L. E. Barrett); pp. 11-30, the changes found in Britain, and the wide spectrum of Rastafarianism from religious movement through symbolic protest movement to political protest movement.

1783   Montague, Charmaine. "Rastafari: Charmaine Montague interview (by V. Harris)." *Fuse* (Toronto) 6, no. 4 (1982): 186-89.
Interview with the coordinator at the first International Rastafarian Conference in Toronto, July 1982.

1784   Montague, Charmaine, and Yawney, Carole D. *Voice of thunder: Dialogue with Nyah Binghi elders*. Toronto: Masoni Productions, 1985, 32 pp., illus.
Report of month-long Rastafari Oral Culture Project, September-October 1984, held in Toronto and involving several Nyabinghi elders from Jamaica.

1785   Morrish, Ivor. *Obeah, Christ, and Rastaman*. Cambridge: James Clarke & Co., 1982, 122 pp.
Pp. 68-91, Rastafarians.

1786   Muscat, Frank. "West Indians in Britain." *Tablet*, 30 January 1982, pp. 102-4.
By a Catholic priest working among immigrants; their situation, especially that of young blacks, and the influence of Rastafari on them.

1787   Nagashima, Yosahiko S. *Rastafarian music in contemporary Jamaica: A study of socioreligious music in the Rastafarian movement in Jamaica*. Tokyo: Institute for the Study of Languages and Cultures of Asia and Africa, 1984, 227 pp, bib.
Focuses on Nyabingi music–its historical background, local development, and relation to reggae.

1788   Naipaul, V[idiadhar] S[urajprasad]. *The middle passage: Impressions of five societies. British, French, and Dutch in the West Indies and South America*. London: A. Deutsch, 1962, 232 pp. Reprint. Harmondsworth: Penguin Books, 1969, 256 pp.
Pp. 215-19 (1969 ed., pp. 236-44), Rastafari in Jamaica.

1789   Nettleford, Rex M. "Foreword." *Caribbean Quarterly* (Kingston) 26, no. 4 (1980): iii-vi. Reprinted in *Caribbean Quarterly Monograph*, 1985, unpaginated.

Rastafari

An editorial introduction to the articles on Rastafarianism in this whole issue.

1790   Nettleford, Rex M. *Mirror, mirror: Identity, race, and protest in Jamaica*. Kingston: William Collins & Sangster, 1970, 256 pp. Reprinted, with a new preface (pp. 8-16), as *Identity, race, and protest in Jamaica*. New York: William Morrow, 1972, 256 pp.
        Pp. 39-111, 218-21, 233, 253, Ras Tafari; p. 77, Zionism; pp. 77, 194, Pocomania; pp. 44, 75, 108-9, Ethiopian Orthodox Church; see index for M. Garvey.

1791   Nettleford, Rex M. "Rastafari in the sixties." In *Readings in government and politics of the West Indies*, edited by T. Munroe and R. Lewis. Mona, Jamaica: Department of Government, University of the West Indies, 1971, pp. 41-53.
        Excerpts from entry 1790.

1792   New York Times. *The New York Times index*. New York: the New York Times Co., annually.
        E.g., references under "Rastafarians": 1971, p. 1415 (killings, worship of Haile Selassie, marijuana); 1972, p. 1862 (music, mystic revelation); 1973, p. 2018 (murders); 1975, p. 2061 (bank robbery, killings); 1976, p. 1425 (New York kidnapping); 1977, p. 1127 (killings in Brooklyn; general articles; proliferation in New York; Bob Marley); 1978, p. 872 (two Brooklyn killings); 1979, p. 1105 (Bronx, Manhattan, and St. Vincent). These reports are obviously mainly on the activists or criminal elements who have adopted the Rastafari image.

1793   Nicholas, Tracy, and Sparrow, Bill. *Rastafari: A way of life*. Garden City, N.Y.: Doubleday, Anchor, 1979, text, pp. 1-90 + photography by Sparrow, 66 pp.
        Pp. 22-90, specifically on Rastafarians in Jamaica.

1794   Nowicka, Ewa. "The Ras Tafari movement: Its genesis and functions." *Estudios Latinoamericanos* (Warsaw, Polish Academy of Science), no. 2 (1974), pp. 61-89.
        Includes history, 1930-62; the movement as representative of many wider tendencies and not as an isolated phenomenon.

1794a   Obadiah. *I am a Rastafarian: Obadiah meets Petra Gayn*. London: F. Watts, 1986, 32 pp., illus.
        His own beliefs.

1795 O'Gorman, Pamela. "An approach to the study of Jamaican popular music." *Jamaican Journal* 6, no. 4 (1972): 50-54.
Pp. 53-54, Rastafarian influence running through ska, rock steady, and reggae; the group known as Mystic Revelations of Ras Tafari; "communal celebration of Rastafarian culture and ideology."

1796 Order of the Nyabinghi. "Youth black faith." Clarendon, Jamaica: Order of the Nyabinghi. Order of His Majesty. Circular no. 2, 21 September [19]84, 26 pp. Mimeo.
See especially pp. 7-26, "Rastafari, reggae, and the Bible, a taped reasoning held at the United Theological College, July 1981."

1797 Osula, Bramwell. "'Redemption song': Protest reggae and the Jamaican search for identity." Ph.D. dissertation (sociology, ethnic and racial studies), University of Waterloo, 1984.

1798 Owens, Joseph V. "Babylon, 'JAH,' and the holy herb." *New Internationalist*, no. 94 (December 1980), pp. 18-19, illus.

1799 Owens, Joseph V. *Dread: The Rastafarians of Jamaica*. Kingston: Sangster's Book Stores, 1976. Reprint. London: Heinemann Educational Books, 1979, xix + 282 pp.
An important, sympathetic study by a Jesuit.

1800 Owens, Joseph V. "Literature on the Rastafari: 1955-1974. A review." *Savacou* (Mona; a journal of the Caribbean Artists' Movement), nos. 11-12 (September 1975), pp. 86-105. Reprinted in *New Community* 6, nos. 1-2 (1977-78): 150-64.
Critical evaluations of the literature since 1955, with a very positive attitude toward the movement.

1801 Owens, Joseph V. "Prophets without honor." *Justice* (Kingston) 1 (May 1971): 5-8.
A popular article, sympathetic in attitude toward Rastafarians.

1802 Owens, Joseph V. "The Rastafarians of Jamaica." In *Troubling of the waters*, edited by I. Hamid. San Fernando, Trinidad: Rahaman Printery, 1973, pp. 164-70.

1803 Patterson, Horace Orlando. *The children of Sisyphus*. London: New Authors, 1964. Reprint. Boston: Houghton Mifflin Co., 1965, 206 pp.
A novel focused on the Rastafarians, Obeah practices, and the "Revivalist" church in West Kingston, Jamaica. A very sympathetic picture of the Rastafarians. For critical comment see "Some French

Rastafari

influences in the fiction of Orlando Patterson" by Bridget Jones, *Savacou* (Mona; a journal of the Caribbean Artists' Movement) 11-12 (September 1975), especially pp. 30-33; and review article by C. L. R. James (entry 1727).

1804   Patterson, Horace Orlando. "Ras Tafari – The cult of outcastes." *New Society*, no. 111 [4] (12 November 1964): 15-17. Reprinted in *Readings in government and politics of the West Indies*. Mona: University of the West Indies, 1968, pp. 266-71.
        Includes a definition of millennialism, and an interpretation as not really wanting the paradise but mainly to revolt against the status quo.

1805   "Pavement artist in London with portrait of Bob Marley." *Flying Springbok* (South African Airways) 3, no. 9 (1984): 107, color illus.
        In an article on the tourist "sights" of Britain.

1806   Peart, George S. "Rastafarianism." *Exodus* (London), December 1983-January 1984, pp. 9-11, 38, illus.
        A sympathetic account from a West Indian in Britain.

1807   Pettersburgh, Fitz Ballintine. *The royal parchment scroll of black supremacy*. Kingston: n.p., 1926, 14 pp.
        A proto-Rastafarian pamphlet designed as a kind of Bible and creed for affirmation of black superiority; influenced L. P. Howell (entry 1715).

1808   Philos, Frederico. "The black peril." *Magazine Digest* (Toronto) 5, no. 11 (1935): 80-83. Condensed from *Neues Wiener Tagblatt* (Vienna), 17 and 24 August 1935. Reprinted in *Jamaica Times*, 7 December 1935, pp. 1-6.
        A sensational, fantastic report of an alleged worldwide military alliance of blacks, inspired by an antiwhite secret society in the Congo, "Nya-Binghi," encouraged by Moscow, and led by the "Negus" or head of the race, Haile Selassie, in alliance with Japan, to expel whites from the colonial areas.

1809   Planno, Mortimo Togo Desta. "Maniaphobia of the invisible establishment (Lecture given to the Black Community movement, York University, Toronto, November 1973)." In "Head-decay-shun need an autopsy: Three lectures given on the Rastafarians of Jamaica 1973-74," by M. T. D. Planno and C. D. Yawney, pp. 13-36. Mimeo.

By a Rastafarian who was Bob Marley's spiritual and musical mentor in the 1960s. "Togo-Desta" is an Ethiopian name Planno added to his own.

1810   Planno, Mortimo Togo Desta. "Strangulation of I-generation." In "Head-decay-shun need an autopsy: Three lectures given on the Rastafarians of Jamaica 1973-74," by M. T. D. Planno and C. D. Yawney, pp. 38-49. Mimeo.

       Lecture given by a Rastafarian to Race and Racism class, Atkinson College, York University, Toronto, December 1973.

1811   Plummer, John. *Movement of Jah people: The growth of the Rastafarians*. Handsworth, Birmingham: Press Gang, 1978, 72 pp., illus. by Derek Bishton.

       The author lived in Handsworth for seven years and regards the Rastas as "the most persecuted minority in Britain today."

1812   Pobee, John [S.]. "Africa and the Rastas: Basic differences." *Jamaica Daily News*, 6 May 1975, pp. 8-9.

       A Ghanaian theologian on the problems of any Rastafarian return to Africa.

1813   "Policeman tells of gun ordeal"; and "Rastafarian tells court he felt invincible." *New Zealand Herald* (Auckland), 20 August and 27 August 1986.

       Reports of trial of young Maoris from Ruatoria claiming to be Rastafarians.

1814   Pollard, Velma. "Dread talk–The speech of the Rastafarians in Jamaica." *Caribbean Quarterly* (Kingston) 26, no. 4 (1980): 32-41. Reprinted in *Caribbean Quarterly Monograph*, 1985, pp. 32-41.

       New language as part of the defiance of society, but also as an enrichment of Jamaican English.

1815   Pollard, Velma. "The social history of Dread talk." *Caribbean Quarterly* (Kingston) 28, no. 4 (1982): 17-40.

       Rastafari speech has had much influence on Jamaican dance, drama, and Creole speech forms.

1816   Post, Ken[neth William John]. *Arise ye starvelings: The Jamaican labour rebellion of 1936 and its aftermath*. Development of Societies, 3. The Hague: M. Nijhoff, 1978, 502 pp., bib (pp. 475-85).

       Interprets the Rastafari as millennial, and traces the origins of the Nyabinghi doctrines.

Rastafari

1817   Post, Ken[neth William John]. "The Bible as ideology: Ethiopianism in Jamaica, 1930-38." In *African perspectives*, edited by C. Allen and R. W. Johnson. Cambridge: Cambridge University Press, 1970, pp. 185-207.

   The impact of Italy's invasion of Ethiopia on Garvey and Rastafari: a Marxist theory of their ideology.

1818   Post, Ken[neth] W[illiam] J[ohn]. "The politics of protest in Jamaica, 1938: Some problems of analysis and conceptualization." *Social and Economic Studies* 18, no. 4 (1969): 374-90.

   Pp. 387-88, 389, Garveyism and Rastafari (very brief mention).

1819   Prince, Raymond. "The Ras Tafari of Jamaica: A study of group beliefs and social stress." *Stethoscope* (New York) 4, no. 6 (1969): 4-8. Reprinted in *Newsletter-Review* (Montreal, R. M. Bucke Memorial Society) 4, nos. 1-2 (1971): 48-54.

   A paper presented at the conference of the Caribbean Psychiatric Association, Jamaica 1969.

1820   Pryce, Philip. "The origins and development of Rastafarian beliefs in Jamaica and Britain." Religious Studies dissertation for B.A. (Ord.), Liverpool College of Higher Education, 1981.

   From Garvey to respectability in Jamaica; the importance of Rastafari in Britain and Bob Marley's role in this.

1821   Ras Dizzy I. "The heat is on, but a poet was watching." *Abeng* (Rastafarian/Black Power newspaper), 5 July 1969, p. 2.

1822   Ras Dizzy I. *The human guide line*. Kingston: The Author, 1969, 53 pp.

   Includes poems and essays.

1823   Ras Dizzy I. *Rastafarians society watchman*. Kingston: The Author, [ca. 1971], 25 pp.

   Includes poems and essays. Rastafarians are religious, not political, and Haile Selassie is the returned Messiah.

1824   Ras Dizzy I. "The Rastas speak"; and "A poem by the poet: I wants no part with you." *Caribbean Quarterly* (Kingston) 13, no. 4 (1967): 41-42, 43.

1825   Ras Dizzy I. "Vision of black slaves." Kingston, 1971, 34 pp. Mimeo.
   Poetry.

1826 Ras Dizzy I. "Why rudies got to be ruder." *Abeng* (Rastafarian/Black Power newspaper), 2 August 1969, p. 2.
By a painter-poet who "set himself up as society's watchman."

1827 Ras Larry (Matthews). "Rastafarians." *Identity* (Woden, Australian Capital Territory) 4, no. 5 (1981): 18, 23.
An account presented to Australian Aborigines, implying common concerns. P. 18, Bob Marley songs in Australia.

1828 Ras Michael. "Reasoning with Ras Michael." *Reggae and African Beat* (Los Angeles) 4, no. 2 (1985): 11.
View of religion and the Bible.

1829 Rastafari Movement Association. *Rasta: A modern antique*. Kingston: Rastafari Movement Association, 1976.
Pamphlet from RMA at 53 Laws St., Kingston.

1830 Rastafari periodicals. There have been many periodicals from Rastafarian and kindred sources, often short-lived and from various sections of the movement. The following are examples only:
Abeng (Kingston newspaper, Black Power; title means "cowhorn");
Ethiopia Calls (76 King St., Kingston, weekly newsletter, e.g., vols. 1-5, 1966);
Ithiopian Defender (poems, essays, rights of women);
Our Own (Kingston; mostly poetry);
Rastafari Speaks (Rastafarian Brethren Organization, Trinidad), e.g., no. 8 (November-December 1983), 20 pp.; no. 10 (June-July 1983), 30 pp.; no. 11 (October-December 1983), 40 pp.;
Rasta Voice (Kingston; title varies: 1-, 1970-);
Rasta Voice Magazine (Kingston; e.g., no. 92 [1984], 14 pp.);
Voice of Rasta (London; eight-page tabloid of the Ethiopian World Federation Theocracy).

1831 "Rastas 'one-voice' C'bean movement: Two leading brethren banned from Trinidad." *Caribbean Contact* 8, no. 12 (1981): 1, 16, illus.
On Michael Lorne and Desmond Trotter.

1832 *Rasta Voice Magazine* (Kingston, Jamaica), no. 92 (1984), 14 pp.
Contains report, pp. 8-12, of Rastafari International Theocracy Assembly, 18-25 July 1983, Jamaica.

1833 Reckord, Verena. "Rastafarian music–An introductory study." *Jamaican Journal* (Kingston) 11, nos. 1-2 (1977): 2-13, illus.

Rastafari

An analysis of the music giving identity to Rastafarians, with drums at its center and origins in the popular Burru (African) music of the slave period, as against the European influence in Revivalism and Pocomania.

1833a   Reckord, Verena. "Reggae, Rastafarianism, and cultural identity." *Jamaica Journal* (Kingston) 26 (1982): 70-79, bib., illus.
The development and influence of Jamaican popular music.

1834   [Reggae music.] The Schomburg Center for Research in Black Culture, part of the New York Public Library research system, holds a constantly expanding select collection of reggae and other Caribbean black music. The Lambeth Public Library, London, claims to have the world's best collection of reggae music on tape.

1835   "Report on Rastas." *Newday* (Jamaica) 4, no. 2 (1960): 27-29, illus.
Not objective, but includes personal history of L. A. Aarons, an individual Rastafarian.

1836   "Rev. Claudius Henry lighting, whites must go, blood must flow." *Time*, 2 May 1960.
This issue of *Time* was seized by the police in Jamaica, as likely to injure the tourist trade.

1837   Rex, John. "West Indian and Asian youth." In *Black youth in crisis*, edited by E. E. Cashmore and B. Troyna. London: George Allen & Unwin, 1982, pp. 53-71.
Pp. 66-71, Rastafari.

1838   Rex, John, and Tomlinson, Sally. *Colonial immigrants in a British city: A class analysis*. London: Routledge, 1979, 357 pp.
Pp. 232-37, 251, 260, 264-67, Rastafari and other black religions in Handsworth.

1839   Robertson, Gladstone. "Unity or bust." *Ethiopia Calls* [A newsletter in Jamaica], n.d. ["recent" in 1973].
A play by a Rastafarian, showing new developments in the movement. Cited and quoted in *Soul-force*, by L. E. Barrett (entry 29), p. 189.

1840   Robinson, Lloyd [Obadiah]. *I am a Rastafarian: Obadiah meets Petra Gaynor*. London: Franklin Watts, 1986, 32 pp., color illus.
A former president, Birmingham branch, Ethiopian World Federation (converted in 1976), "meets" Petra Gaynor, eight-year-old

member of a Birmingham Rastafarian family. Lavishly produced, beautifully illustrated.

1841   Rogers, Claudia. "What's Rasta?" *Caribbean Review* (Tucson) 7, no. 1 (1975): 9-12, illus.

1842   Rogers, Robert Athlyi. *The Holy Piby*. Newark, N.J.: The Author, 1924.
Known as "the Black Man's Bible"; formed the doctrinal basis of the Afro-Athlican-Constructive Gaathly founded by Rogers.

1843   Root, John. "Ethiopia's Orthodox export." *Third Way* (Surrey) 1, no. 9 (1977): 10.

1844   Rowe, Maureen. "The woman in Rastafari." *Caribbean Quarterly* (Kingston) 26, no. 4 (1980): 13-21. Reprinted in *Caribbean Quarterly Monograph*, 1985, 13-21.
A Rastawoman discusses the patriarchal, male-dominated nature of the movement, from within.

1845   Rubin, Vera D., and Comitas, Lambros. *Effects of chronic smoking of cannabis in Jamaica*. A report by the Research Institute for the Study of Man, to the Center for Studies of Narcotics and Drug Abuse, National Institute of Mental Health [U.S.]. Contract no. HSM-42-70-97. N.d. [early 1970s?].
Pp. 15-19 et passim, ganja as used by Rastafarians. See digest in H. A. Fraser (entry 1684).

1846   Rubin, Vera D., and Comitas, Lambros. *Ganja in Jamaica: A medical anthropological study of chronic marihuana use*. New Babylon: Studies in the Social Sciences, 26. The Hague: Mouton, 1975, 205 pp. Reprint. New York: Anchor Press, 1976.
An authoritative statement, countering the negative image of marijuana as used by working-class Jamaicans. Not on Rastafari use, but important as background since it stresses the beneficial qualities of *cannabis sativa*.

1847   Ryan, Matthew. "Jamaica's Rastas." *Caribbean Contact* (Port of Spain) 3, no. 5 (1975): 17-18, illus.

1848   Ryle, John. "Bob Marley: Pop and the pursuit of the millennium." *Sunday Times* (London), 31 July 1983, p. 42.
Reviews of *Bob Marley: The biography*, by S. Davis (entry 1653) and *Catch a fire: The life of Bob Marley*, by T. White (entry 1908).

Rastafari

1849   Saakana, Amon Saba. *Blues dance*. London: Karnak House, 1985.
A novel about an unhappy young black in England in the 1970s who became a Rastafari.

1850   Saakana, Amon Saba. "Rastafari: History and philosophy." In *Shap handbook for world religions in education*. London: Commission on Racial Equality, 1987, pp. 160-61.
The author is from Caribbean Culture International.

1851   Sachs, Lloyd. "Reviving reggae." *Chicago* (Chicago) 27 (December 1978): 28f.
Reggae remains a "cult sound."

1852   Salewicz, Chris (text), and Boot, Adrian (photographs). "The chapel of love: Bob Marley's last resting place." *Face* (London), no. 37 (May 1983), pp. 52-54, 56-57, illus.
Bob Marley's funeral, burial place, and continuing influence.

1853   Salkey, Andrew. *The late emancipation of Jerry Stover*. London: Hutchinson & Co., 1968, 246 pp. Reprint. Drumbeat Series. Harlow, U.K.: Longman, 1982, 246 pp.
Fiction. A middle-class Jamaican identifies with the Rastafari at the Dungle, Kingston.

1854   Santos, Eduardo dos. "Sionismo negro." *Ultramar* (Lisbon), no. 21 [6, no. 3] (1965): 128-34.
On Marcus Garvey and the back-to-Africa movement.

1855   Scott, William R. "And Ethiopia shall stretch forth her hands: The origins of Ethiopianism in Afro-American thought, 1776-1896." *Umoja* (Boulder, Colo.), Spring 1978.
Cited by H. Campbell (entry 1620), p. 98, as background to Garveyism and Rastafari.

1856   Scott, William R. *Going to the promised land: Afro-American immigration in Ethiopia, 1930-1935*. Atlanta: Institute of the Black World, 1975, 16 pp.
Pre-Rastafarian immigrants, with similar motivations, including "Rabbi" Arnold Ford.

1857   Selassie, Wolde. *Ethiopian Orthodox Church, St. Mary's of Zion*. Leicester: Ethiopian World Federation, [1970s?], 1 p.
A Rastafarian interpretation of Christian history and of the church in Ethiopia.

1857a   Semaj, Leahcim T. "Inside Rasta." *Caribbean Review* (Miami) 14, no. 1 (Winter 1985): 8-11, 37-38, illus.

An overview of beliefs, social development, and significance in society.

1858   Semaj, Leahcim Tufani. "Race and identity and children of the African diaspora: Contributions of Rastafari." *Caribé* (Santiago de Cuba) 5 (1980): 14-18, illus., bib. Reprinted in *Studia Africana* (University of Cincinnati) 1, no. 4 (1981): 412-19.

1859   Semaj, Leahcim Tufani. "Rastafari: From religion to social theory." *Caribbean Quarterly* (Kingston) 26, no. 4 (1980): 22-31. Reprinted in *Caribbean Quarterly Monograph*, 1985, pp. 22-31.

A Rastafarian asserts the need and the ability to develop a coherent ideological and social theory or articulation of the movement.

1860   Sewell, Tony. "Rasta: The movement of Jah people." Parts 1-4. *The Voice*, 12 January 1985, p. 11; 19 January, pp. 14, 23; 26 January, pp. 14, 23; 3 February, pp. 14, 23, illus.

The history, development, and influence of Rastafarianism.

1861   Shapiro, Deanne. "Double damnation, double salvation: The sources and varieties of black Judaism in the United States." M.A. thesis (sociology of religion), Columbia University. Portion published as "Factors in the development of black Judaism." In *The black experience in religion*, edited by C. E. Lincoln. Garden City, N.Y.: Doubleday, Anchor, 1974, pp. 254-72 (introduction, pp. 253-54).

Makes frequent reference to Garvey, Garveyites, and the "Back to Africa" theme, as well as Rastafarians (p. 262); useful as background for the Caribbean.

1862   [Sheshamane Community.] *Rastafari Speaks* (Trinidad), no. 11 (October-December 1983), p. 37.

Letter from the Pioneer Settlers' Corporation, the Rastafarian community at Sheshamane, Ethiopia.

1863   [Sheshamane Community.] "The Shashamanne [*sic*] Declaration." *Rastafari Speaks* (Trinidad), no. 8 (November-December 1982), p. 15.

Outline history of the Rastafari in Ethiopia, and recent events regarding the more than sixty people living in the community.

Rastafari

1864   Shlachter, Barry. "Rastafarians worship Haile Selassie." *H.B. Herald-Tribune* (New Zealand), 18 February 1984.
         A report from Sheshamane, the Ethiopian town where the survivors of the original settlement sponsored by Haile Selassie eke out an existence, tolerated by the Marxist regime.

1865   Silvera, Makeda. "An open letter to Rastafarian sistrens." *Firewood* (Toronto) 16 (1983): 114-20.
         A Jamaican Rastafari woman in Canada, protesting against the inferior position of women in the movement.

1866   Simpson, George Eaton. *Black religions in the New World*. New York: Columbia University Press, 1978, 415 pp.
         Pp. 305-7 (and notes, p. 371), on Rastafarians in the Caribbean.

1867   Simpson, George Eaton. "Political cultism in West Kingston, Jamaica." *Social and Economic Studies* (Kingston) 4, no. 2 (1955): 133-49. Reprinted in *Caribbean papers*. Cuernavaca, Mexico: CIDOC, 1970.

1868   Simpson, George Eaton. "The Ras Tafari movement in Jamaica: A study of race and class conflict." *Social Forces* 34, no. 2 (1955): 167-71. Reprinted in *Religion, society, and the individual*, edited by J. M. Yinger. New York: Macmillan Co., 1957, pp. 507-14.

1869   Simpson, George E[aton]. "The Ras Tafari movement in Jamaica in its millennial aspects." In *Millennial dreams in action*, edited by S. L. Thrupp. The Hague: Mouton, 1962, pp. 160-65. Reprinted in *Cultural and social anthropology*, edited by P. B. Hammond. New York: Macmillan, 1964, pp. 334-38. Reprint. New York: Shocken Books, 1970. Reprinted in *Religious cults of the Caribbean*, by G. E. Simpson. Río Piedras: Institute of Caribbean Studies, University of Puerto Rico, 1970, pp. 224-28.

1870   Simpson, George Eaton. "Religion and justice: Some reflections on the Rastafari movement." *Phylon* 46, no. 4 (1985): 286-91. Reprinted in *Journal of Caribbean Studies* 5, no. 3 (Fall 1986): 145-53.
         Surveys his experience of the Rastafari over a period of nearly forty years, noting changed concepts of "Babylon" and "nature"; greater diversity through variations, divisions, and spread abroad; and more acceptance by society.

1871   Smith, M[ichael] G[arfield]; Augier, Roy; and Nettleford, Rex [M.]. *The Rastafari movement in Kingston, Jamaica*. London: Jamaican

High Commission, 1960, 39 pp. Reprint. Kingston: Institute of Social and Economic Research, 1960, 54 pp. Reprinted in *Caribbean Quarterly* (Kingston) 13, no. 3 (1967): 3-29; no. 4 (1967): 3-14. Also reprinted in *The black experience in religion*, edited by C. E. Lincoln. Garden City, N.Y.: Doubleday, Anchor, 1974, pp. 341-54.

The official report, commissioned by the government; now a classic source. It marks the turning point in public knowledge of and attitude toward the Rastafari. Note its primarily urban research base.

1871a Sotheby, Madeline. *The Bob Marley story*. London: Hutchinson Ace Series, 1985, 64 pp.

1872 Sparks, David. "The Rastafarian movement and black youth in Britain." In *From where I stand: Minority experiences of life in Britain*. London: Edward Arnold, 1986, pp. 32-39.

1873 Sparrow, Bill (photographs), and Nicholas, Tracy (text). *Rastafari: A way of life*. Garden City, N.Y.: Doubleday, Anchor, 1979.

1874 Spencer, Neil. "Third world superstar." *Observer Magazine* (London), 17 April 1977, pp. 34-35, photo.

On Bob Marley, the Jamaican reggae singer and Rastafarian, after the attempt to assassinate him on account of his political support for Michael Manley.

1875 Spencer, Neil (text), and Simon, Kate (photographs). "The Ja connection." *New Musical Express* (London), 16 October 1976, pp. 29-35, illus.

1876 *Spotlight Newsmagazine* (Kingston) 24, nos. 4-5 (1963): 17.
Report of the Rastafarian "uprising" of April 1963.

1877 Stickler, Michael. "Black diaspora: The Rasta chant: Out of many, one people." *New African* (London), no. 177 (June 1982), p. 60.

A general, sympathetic survey, predicting increasing importance in Jamaican society.

1878 Stone, Carl. *Class, race, and political behaviour in urban Jamaica*. Kingston: Institute of Social and Economic Research, University of the West Indies, 1973, 188 pp.

Pp. 153-57, the Rastafarian movement's changes since the 1940s and its new policies of coexistence and "Jamaicanization" rather than "Africanization"; pp. 13, 112, 121, 123, 128, 131, 133, 163-64, briefer references to Rastafarians, usually coupled with Black

Rastafari

Power; p. 159, note 21, the Claudius Henry movement. Rastafari interpreted as an embryonic political movement lacking coherent strategy or mass organization, hence depoliticized into a religio-cultural movement.

1879   Stone, Carl. *Electoral behaviour and public opinion in Jamaica*. Kingston: Institute of Social and Economic Research, University of the West Indies, 1974, 107 pp.
Pp. 18-19, 24-27, 31, 63, 65-66, Rastafarians as a political influence and Manley's symbolic "rod of correction" derived from Rastafarianism.

1880   Tafari, I. Jabulani [formerly Noel Carothers]. "The Rastafari–Successors to Marcus Garvey." *Caribbean Quarterly* (Kingston) 26, no. 4 (1980): 1-12. Reprinted in *Caribbean Quarterly Monograph*, 1985, pp. 1-12.
A Rastafarian asserts an unbroken succession and doctrinal coherence; for a denial of the succession see A. and L. Mansingh (entry 1774).

1881   Terry-Thompson, A. C. *The history of the African Orthodox Church*. New York: Beacon Press, 1956, 139 pp., illus.
Not directly on Jamaica, but historically intertwined with Marcus Garvey, and hence with Jamaica and the Rastafarians.

1882   "There is nowhere I would rather be than in Rasta country." *Black Music*, no. 38 (January 1977), pp. 16-23.

1883   Thomas, Michael. "The Rastas are coming, the Rastas are coming." *Rolling Stone* (Boulder, Colo.), 12 August 1976, pp. 32-37.

1884   Thomas, Michael, and Boot, Adrian. *Jah revenge – Babylon revisited*. London: Eel Pie Publishing Co., 1982, 96 pp., illus.
Revised edition of earlier title, *Babylon revisited*.

1885   Toch, Hans. *The social psychology of social movements*. Indianapolis: Bobbs-Merrill Co., 1965, 257 pp.
Pp. 30-33, Ras Tafari; pp. 33-38, A. C. Sam's back-to-Africa movement; pp. 28-44, theoretical discussion of illusions as solutions.

1886   Troyna, Barry. "Angry youngsters – A response to racism in Britain." *Youth in Society*, no. 26 (December 1977), pp. 13-15, illus.
Pp. 14-15, reggae music and Bob Marley as drawing youth toward Rastafari.

Rastafari

1887   Troyna, Barry. *Rastafarianism, reggae, and racism*. Derby: National Association for Multi-Racial Education, 1978, 22 pp.

   Based on research in 1975-77. Pp. 3-7, emergence and development of Rastafarianism; pp. 8-11, reggae and Rastafarianism; pp. 12-14, racism in Britain; pp. 15-18, "as they see it" – knowledge of Rastafarianism was through reggae; pp. 19-20, confusion – Rastafari as alienated from society and doomed to failure.

1888   Troyna, Barry. "The Rastafarians – The youth's response." *Journal of the Multi-Racial School* (Oxford, U.K.) 6, no. 1 (1977): 1-8.

1889   Troyna, Barry. "The reggae war." *New Society* (London), no. 753 [39] (10 March 1977): 491-92.

   Not on Rastafarians as such, but on the conflict between the police and black youths, which was being documented in reggae music.

1890   Troyna, Barry. "The significance of reggae music in the lives of black adolescent boys in Britain: An exploratory study." M.Phil. thesis, University of Leicester, 1978.

1891   Turner, H[arold] W[alter]. "Rastafari: A bibliographic paper." In *Shap handbook for world religions in education*. London: Commission on Racial Equality, 1987, p. 162.

1892   [Turner, Harold Walter.] "Rastafarians." *Encyclopaedia Britannica*, 1974. Micropaedia, vol. 8, p. 427a.

1893   University [of the West Indies] Radio Service. "The cult of Ras Tafari." Transcription of three half-hour programs. Mimeo.

   Interviews with Rastafarians; explanations of government policies, of the university report (entry 1871), and Rasta beliefs.

1894   Vieth, Udo. *Reggae musiker: Rastas in Jamaika*. Frankfurt: Fischer, 1981.

1895   Vincent, Theodore G. *Black power and the Garvey movement*. Berkeley, Calif.: Ramparts Press, [1971], 299 pp., illus.

   Pp. 133-37, et passim, African Orthodox Church; pp. 208, 227-28, Rastafarians.

1896   Walvin, James. *Passage to Britain: Immigration in British history and politics*. Harmondsworth: Penguin Books, 1984, 232 pp.

Rastafari

Pp. 86-87, influence of Bob Marley and Rastafari ideology; pp. 210, 212, attractions of Rastafari for young blacks in Britain.

1896a   Waters, Anita M. *Race, class, and political symbols: Rastafari and reggae in Jamaican politics*. New Brunswick, N.J.: Transaction Books, 1985, 343 pp.
Detailed analysis of these factors in every election since 1967.

1897   Watson, G. Llewellyn. "Patterns of black protest in Jamaica: The case of the Ras-Tafarians." *Journal of Black Studies* (Beverly Hills) 4, no. 3 (1974): 329-43.

1898   Watson, G. Llewellyn. "The Ras-Tafarian movement in Jamaica: An exploratory analysis." M.A. thesis, University of Guelph, 1970.

1899   Watson, G. Llewellyn. "Social structure and social movements: The Black Muslims in the U.S.A. and the Ras-Tafarians in Jamaica." *British Journal of Sociology* 24, no. 2 (1973): 188-204.
Suggests a theoretical similarity between the two, due to similar forces at work – class struggle, exploitation, and racism.

1900   Watts, Michael. "The Rasta connection." *Melody Maker* (London), 9 October 1976, p. 40, illus.
A good survey of Rastafarian history, connections with Ethiopia, interpretation of the Bible, relation to African "Ethiopianism" and to economic and political conditions in Jamaica; little reference to its music.

1901   Weisbord, Robert G. *Ebony kinship: Africa, Africans, and the Afro-American*. Westport, Conn.: Greenwood Press, 1973, 256 pp.
Pp. 123-27, 129, Rastafarians, including the Claudius Henry repatriation scheme of 1959; pp. 133-34, 151, "Black Israelites" in the U.S. and their immigration to Liberia and Israel between 1968 and 1971, resembling the Rastafarian schemes.

1902   *Westindian World* (London, weekly). Various relevant articles, e.g., in 1977: 4 March, "Jericho – A reggae opera"; 25 May, "The Mediations; a hot new trio in Jamaica"; 27 May, "Exodus, movement of Jah's people" (advertisement); 3 June, "L. K. Johnson 'Musical correction – Equal rights'"; "Birmingham, battle with police and youth" (reggae singer D. Wilson); 22 July, "Dread-A-than Dread" (concert); 14 October, "Lament for Rastafari" (theater report); 10 November, "'Burning spear, dry and heavy' – Children of Ethiopia present a night of Rasta harmony" (advertisement); 17 November,

"Oxford: Rastafarian members of the Order of African Descendant Youth and Roots"; 9 December, "Edgar White laments" (author of *Lament for Rastafari*); 18 December, review of L. E. Barrett's *The Rastafarians* (entry 1591); 30 December, "Doc. Alimantado, the mystical healer."

1903   West Midlands County Council. *Directory of workers cooperatives in the West Midlands*. Birmingham: West Midlands County Council, n.d., 65 pp., illus.
        P. 42 describes "Rastafari Progressive Arts," a cooperative specializing in the production of original paintings and drawings.

1904   White, Garth [Blacka Razac]. "Master drummer." *Jamaica Journal* (Kingston) 11, nos. 1-2 (1977): 16-17, illus.
        On Count Ossie, one of the earliest Rastafarian drummers.

1905   White, Garth. "Reggae: A musical weapon." *Caribe* (Santiago de Cuba), 1980, pp. 6-10, illus. Reprinted in *Caribe* (Honolulu) 6, no. 1 (1982): 21-25, illus.

1906   White, Gavin. "Patriarch McGuire and the Episcopal Church." *Historical Magazine of the Protestant Episcopal Church* (Church Historical Society) 38, no. 2 (1969): 109-41.
        A detailed study, including McGuire in relation to episcopal orders, and his influence in Africa; nothing on Rastafari but valuable as background.

1907   White, Timothy. "Bob Marley, 1945-1981: The King of Regae finds his Zion." *Rolling Stone* (Boulder, Colo.), 25 June 1981, pp. 25f.

1908   White, T[imothy]. *Catch a fire: The life of Bob Marley*. London: Hamish Hamilton, Elm Tree Books, 1983. Reprint. London: Corgi Books, 1984, 412 pp., illus.
        Including sections on Marcus Garvey and early history of Rastafari, 23-36, 50-70.

1909   Whitney, Malika Lee, and Hussey, Dermott. *Bob Marley, reggae king of the world*. London: Plexus; Kingston: Kingston Publishers, 1984, 200 pp., illus.

1910   Williams, Kathy. *The Rastafarians*. Living Religions Series. London: Ward Lock Educational, 1981. Reprint. 1985, 64 pp., illus.
        A useful survey.

Rastafari

1911   Williams, M. D. *Ikael Torass*. Havana: Casa de las Américas, 1976, 501 pp.
       Award-winning novel about a student at university in Jamaica, including contact with Rastafarians.

1912   Williams, Richard. "Marley mutes his anger." *Sunday Times* (London), 5 June 1977, p. 12, photo.
       On Bob Marley, "Jamaican star of Reggae music" and an exponent of Rastafarianism: his history since 1972, survival of an attempted assassination, new record *Exodus*, and plans to visit Ethiopia.

1913   Wilms, Anno, and Kliche, Lutz. *Rastafari*. Wuppertal: Jugenddienst-Verlag, 1982, 72 pp.
       Pp. 5-67, photographs (A. Wilms), text (L. Kliche); pp. 70-72, text based on R. M. Nettleford.

1913a Wilson, Bryan [Ronald]. "Lion of Judah." In *Man, myth, and magic*. Edited by R. Cavendish. Reference edition, vol. 7. New York and London: Marshall Cavendish, 1985, pp. 1832, 1834-35, illus.
       Popular outline of Rastafarianism.

1914   Witvliet, Theo. *A place in the sun: Liberation theology in the third world*. London: SCM Press, 1985, 182 pp.
       Pp. 110-17, includes an outline of Rastafari as an example of "underground survival" by Jamaican black culture; Marley, Garvey, and recent developments in relation to whites and to the churches.

1915   Wynter, Sylvia. "One love: Rhetoric or reality? – Aspects of Afro-Jamaicanism." *Caribbean Studies* (Río Piedras, University of Puerto Rico) 12, no. 3 (1972): 64-97.
       On the symposium by A. King, et al. (entry 1743). Pp. 88-92, 95-97, on Rastafarians.

1916   Yawney, Carole D. "The dialectics of black racism, the Rastafarians of Jamaica." In "Head-decay-shun need an autopsy: Three lectures given on the Rastafarians of Jamaica 1973-74," by M. T. D. Planno and C. D. Yawney, pp. 2-12. Mimeo.
       Lecture given at Race and Racism Conference, York University, Toronto, March 1974.

1917   Yawney, Carole D. "Dread wasteland: Rastafarian ritual in West Kingston, Jamaica." In *Ritual symbolism and ceremonialism in the*

Americas. University of Northern Colorado Occasional Publications in Anthropology, no. 33, 1979, pp. 154-78.

1918   Yawney, Carole D. "Moving with the dawtas of Rastafari: From myth to reality." In *El Caribe y América/The Caribbean and Latin America*, edited by U. Fleischmann and I. Phaf. Papers presented at the 3d interdisciplinary colloquium about the Caribbean, 9-10 November 1984. Berlin Institute of Latin American Studies, Free University of Berlin, 1987, pp. 193-99.

1919   Yawney, Carole D. "The Rastafarian community." In *Spirit of Toronto*. Toronto: Toronto Images Publishing, 1984, pp. 321-27.
        The Rastafari in Toronto.

1920   Yawney, Carole D. "Rastafarian sistren by the rivers of Babylon." *Canadian Woman Studies* (Toronto) 5, no. 2 (1983): 73-75.
        The place of women in the modern Rastafarian movement.

1921   Yawney, C[arole] D. "Remnants of all nations: Rastafarian attitudes to race and nationality." In *Ethnicity in the Americas*, edited by F. Henry. World Anthropology Series. The Hague: Mouton Publishers, 1976, pp. 231-62.
        Includes subjects of birth control and family planning, and Rastafarian images of Zion/Babylon, black/white, danger/purity. Appendix is a verbatim dialogue illustrating a Rastafarian "reasoning."

1922   Yawney, Carole D. "To grow a daughter: Cultural liberation and the dynamics of oppression in Jamaica." In *Feminism in Canada*, edited by A. R. Miles and G. Finn. Montreal: Black Rose Books, 1982, pp. 119-44.
        Outlines Rastafarianism; describes her field-work problems in the early 1970s; male-female roles in Jamaica, and in Rastafarianism (pp. 132-43).

1923   Yawney, Carole D. "Who killed Bob Marley?" *Canadian Forum* (Toronto), December 1984, pp. 29-31.
        Review of M. L. Whitney and D. Hussey (entry 1909).

1924   Yawney, Carole D., and Ananda, Clem. "Rastalogue." York University: Atkinson College, Downsview, Ontario, 1974, 46 pp. Mimeo.
        A dialogue between the two authors.

Rastafari

1925   A Young Jamaican Nationalist [pseud.]. "Two views on the problem
       of race and colour in Jamaica today: I. Realism and race." *West
       Indian Economist* (Kingston) 3, no. 10 (1961): 6-12. Reprinted in
       Consequences of class and culture, edited by D. Lowenthal and L.
       Comitas. Garden City, N.Y.: Doubleday, Anchor, 1973, 103-21.
           Pp. 6-7 (pp. 103-6), social unrest and Rastafari.

1926   Zeman, Brenda Maureen Alice. "Dread revitalization: The Rastafari
       of Jamaica." M.A. dissertation, California State University (Long
       Beach), 1974, 97 pp.

Index of Authors and Sources

Note: References are to entry numbers, not pages.

Index of Main Movements
and Individuals

The entry numbers of the main or more substantial or significant references are included here (i.e., those mentioned in the titles of the items or in the annotations). This list is therefore not exhaustive as to text references, but is fairly complete as to known named movements, apart from those that are designated only by general area or by dates. Founders, leaders, and other significant individuals appear under the most common form of their names, but alternative spellings and names also are given or cross-referenced.

The materials under Particular Movements placed in two separate sections at the end of the volume refer primarily to the movements concerned. Where these movements are treated along with others, they may be found through the various other entry numbers also given for them in this index.